THE SARACEN I: LAND OF THE INFIDEL

ROBERT SHEA, a former magazine editor, is the author of *Shiké*, the bestselling saga set in Japan in the days of the Shōgun, and *All Things are Lights*. He is also the co-author of the *Illuminatus!* trilogy. He lives in Glencoe, Illinois.

'As various guises and disguises are shattered by naked forces of greed, lust and ambition, the appropriately Byzantine plot, with its competing conspiracies, recalls more recent forms of lobbying, spying and dirty tricks.

This is a ripe, rich, devious novel.'

Publishers Weekly

ROBERT SHEA

The Saracen:
Land of the Infidel

FONTANA/Collins

First published in Great Britain by
William Collins Sons & Co. Ltd 1989

Copyright © Robert Shea 1989

Printed and bound in Great Britain by
William Collins Sons & Co. Ltd, Glasgow

TO MICHAEL ERIK SHEA

*who helped me learn many things
about the art of storytelling*

THE ASSASSIN
AND THE LOVE SLAVE

He is Daoud ibn Abdallah. A warrior who is not afraid to
go alone amid multitudes of enemies. The servant of a very
great ruler. Though young, a wealthy and powerful man
in his own land. A spy and a thief in the lands of others.

He is the man whom Sophia Karaiannides, accomplished
courtesan and mistress to a king, is to serve without
reservation.

The alliance has been struck. The adventure begins. . . .

BOOK ONE

LAND OF
THE INFIDEL

Anno Domini 1263–1264/Year of the Hegira 661–662

"Whoso fighteth in the way of God, be he slain or be he victorious, on him We shall bestow a vast reward."

—The Koran, Surah IV

"Nothing is true. Everything is permissible."

—Hasan ibn-al-Sabbah,
founder of the Hashishiyya

I

IN THE MIST-FILLED PLAINS AROUND LUCERA, COCKS CROWED.

Daoud ibn Abdallah pushed himself slowly to his feet. After days and nights of walking, his legs ached abominably.

Tired as he was, he looked around carefully, studying the other travelers who rested near him on the road, peering at the city wall a hundred paces away with its shut gate of iron-studded oak. In his stomach he felt the hollow ball of dread that had not left him since he landed in Italy.

I am alone in the land of the infidel.

Dawn gave a pink tint to the pale yellow stones of the wall, about twice the height of a man. Above it in the distance, covering the summit of the central hill, rose the citadel of Lucera, surrounded by its own huge wall set with more than a dozen many-sided towers.

Daoud's feet throbbed in his knee-high boots. For three days he had walked along the carter's track from the port of Manfredonia on the Adriatic coast into the hills around Lucera. Yesterday at daybreak he had been able to see, from a great distance, the outline of the fortress emerging from the center of a rolling plain. It had taken him another day and a night to reach its gate.

Around Daoud now were dozens of people who had gathered at the gate during the night, mostly merchants with packs on their backs. A few farmers, hitched to carts loaded with melons, peaches, and oranges, had dragged their burden over the plain. The more prosperous had donkeys to pull the wagons.

One man with a long stick drove six small sheep. And a cart near Daoud was piled high with wooden cages full of squawking chickens.

Walking in his direction was a tiny dwarf of a man who appeared permanently doubled over, as if his back had been broken. It seemed to Daoud that if the man were not holding his arms out from his sides for balance, his knuckles would almost have brushed the ground. His little cart was piled with broken tree limbs, firewood to sell in the city.

The dwarf lifted his head and grinned at Daoud through a bushy black mustache. Daoud smiled back, thinking, *God be kind to you, my friend.*

From within the city issued a familiar cry, in Arabic, that tore at Daoud's heart: "Come to prayer. Come to security. God is most great." It was the adhan, the cry of the muezzins in the minarets of Lucera's mosques. For, though he was in a Christian land, Lucera was a city mostly populated by Muslims.

Daoud wanted to fall to his knees, but he was pretending to be a Christian, and could only stand and ignore the call to prayer as the Christians around him did. He said the words of the salat, the required prayer, in his mind.

The people near Daoud spoke to one another sleepily, softly, in the tongue of southern Italy. Someone laughed. Someone sang a snatch of song. When the Muslim prayer ended, they expectantly looked up at the town wall.

Daoud saw two soldiers standing in the tower to the left of the gate. They were accoutred in the Muslim manner, with turbans wrapped around their helmets and scimitars at their belts. One lifted a long brass trumpet to his lips and blew a series of notes that sent shivers along Daoud's spine. With a few changes it could have been the call that had awakened him every morning in the Mameluke barracks on Raudha Island in the Nile.

Using ropes, the other soldier hoisted onto a tall pole a yellow banner bearing a black bird with spread wings and claws, and two heads facing in opposite directions. The double-headed eagle of King Manfred's family, the Hohenstaufen.

With a great squealing of cables and squeaking of hinges, the tall wooden door swung wide.

Daoud reached down and picked up the leather pack that had lain between his feet. Leaning forward, he pushed his arms through the shoulder straps.

He wore draped over his pack a long countryman's cloak of cheap brown wool. His tunic and hose were of lightweight undyed cotton. Only his high boots were expensive. He needed good ones for the long walk from the coast to Lucera. A sword swung at his belt, short and unadorned, the sort any man of small means might wear. He had chosen it in El Kahira out of a stack of swords taken from Christian men-at-arms during the last crusade.

He drew the hood of his cloak over his head. Later his blond hair and gray eyes would guarantee that no one would suspect what he was. But here in southern Italy, where most ordinary people were dark complexioned, his appearance might draw unwanted attention.

Even though the sun had just risen, he felt the heat on his back. But it was not the dry heat of Egypt that he had known most of his life. A heaviness in the air called forth a dampness from within his flesh. His tunic clung to him.

If a Christian asks me what month this is, I must remember to say July.

He brushed the dust from his clothing and fell into line behind the bent man with his cart of firewood.

Once inside Lucera, he would find his way to the inn of al-Kharim. And tonight the chancellor Aziz would come to him from King Manfred.

The line shuffled forward. Three guards were standing in the shadows just inside the gateway. They were big dark men wearing long green capes over red tunics. Red turbans were wrapped around their spike-topped helmets. Curving swords hung from their belts. A boy in a red tunic and turban held a sheaf of lightweight spears.

Their thick beards reminded Daoud how much he missed his own beard, shaved off in preparation for this mission.

My people. Daoud felt a sudden warmth at the familiar sight of warriors of Islam.

The feeling was nonsense, he told himself. These were not his people, but the Saracens of Manfred von Hohenstaufen. Their Arab ancestors had once ruled southern Italy, but the Christians had conquered them over a century before.

No, these Muslim warriors were not Daoud's people. In truth, on this whole earth there were no people Daoud ibn Abdallah could truly call his own.

Once he had been David Langmuir, living with his crusader father and mother, in a castle near Ascalon by the plain of Gaza. An English ancestor had been one of the first crusaders in the Holy Land.

Just after David's ninth birthday Geoffrey Langmuir, his father, had ridden out to war in gleaming mail with a cross of red silk sewn on his white surcoat. David never saw him again.

Some weeks later the Saracens appeared before the castle, and there were days of thirst and hunger and constant fear. He remembered the thunderous pounding at the walls and the dark men in their yellow robes and green turbans, their crescent-shaped swords coated with blood. He remembered his mother, Lady Evelyn, in her blue dress, running up the spiral stairs of a tower. He heard her distant scream. When the Saracens dragged him out of the castle, with men being cut down by swords all around him and women thrown to the ground by laughing Turks who fell upon them, he saw at the base of the tower a bundle of blue linen splashed with red that must have been his mother.

On their leisurely journey back to the Nile, the Turks forced him to lie on his belly, and they used him as men use women. He would never forget the needle-sharp tip of a curving dagger touched to his eyeball as a bashi with a flowing black beard demanded that Daoud use his mouth to give him pleasure. Whenever Daoud remembered that time, his insides knotted and his face burned with shame.

One day he stood naked on a platform in El Kahira, capital of the sultans—the city the Christians called Cairo. A fat, laughing slave dealer, who had raped him till he bled the night before, offered him for sale.

A tall man with one eye a glittering blue and the other a blank white, a scimitar in a jeweled scabbard thrust through the embroidered sash around his waist, came forward.

A silence fell over the crowd of slave buyers, followed by whispers. The one-eyed warrior paid the price asked in gold dinars and without haggling. And when the slaver fondled David's loins one last time as he covered him with a ragged tunic, the warrior seized the slaver by the throat with one hand, forcing him to his knees, and squeezed till he collapsed unconscious in the dust of the marketplace.

David was almost mad with terror as the one-eyed warrior took him to his mansion beside a lake in the center of El Kahira. But the tall man spoke kindly to him and treated him decently. Amazingly, he could speak French, David's language, though with a strange and heavy accent. He told David that he was called Baibars al-Bunduqdari, Baibars the Crossbowman. He was an emir of the Bhari Mamelukes, which meant, he said, "slaves of the river." But though the Mamelukes were slaves, they were also great and powerful warriors.

Baibars gave David a new name—Daoud—and told him that he had selected him to be a Mameluke. He explained in a firm but kindly way that Daoud did have a choice but that the alternative was a life of unrelieved wretchedness as a ghulman, a menial slave. As a Mameluke, Daoud would be set free when his training was complete, and he could win riches and glory and be a warrior for God and his emir.

"I have long watched for such a one as you," Baibars said, "who could look like a Christian but have the mind and heart of a Mameluke. One like you could be a great weapon against the enemies of the faith."

But your faith is not my faith, David, who was to be called Daoud, thought, not daring to speak, *and your enemies are not my enemies.*

His longing to please this man, the first Muslim to treat him with respect, struggled as the years passed with his memories of a Christian childhood. Daoud underwent the training of a Mameluke, and Baibars watched him closely. Daoud accepted Islam and took the common surname of a convert, ibn Abdallah. He took naturally to the life of a warrior and grew in strength and skill.

Year by year Baibars, too, became more powerful. At last he made himself sultan of El Kahira, ruler of an empire that stretched from North Africa to Syria. Daoud's hand had wielded the flame dagger of the Hashishiyya that ended the previous sultan's life.

Now, having raised Daoud, trained him as a Mameluke, and educated him in statecraft, having sent him to learn wisdom from the Sufi and terror from the Hashishiyya, having given him a new name and a new faith, Baibars had sent Daoud into the Christian country called Italy.

The stones of the gateway seemed to be marble, unusual for a fortification. Daoud noticed large iron rings set at intervals under the arch. His feet crunched on fresh straw.

The space under the arch was about ten paces from outer portal to inner. On one side a broad-shouldered official sat at a table. The man glanced up at Daoud, looked down at a leather-bound ledger in which he was writing, then raised his eyes again for a longer look. This time the brown eyes met Daoud's.

The official's grizzled hair formed a cap of curls around his head, hiding his ears. He had a thick mustache, black streaked with white. His shirt of violet silk looked costly. On the straw beside him lay a huge dog, doubtless bred for hunting, with short gray fur, forepaws stretched before it like a sphinx.

These people live with unclean animals, Daoud thought with distaste.

When the official leaned back in his chair, Daoud saw the long, straight dagger that hung from his belt in a scabbard decorated with crossed bands of gold ribbon.

Fear tightened Daoud's throat.

Will this man see through me? Will he guess what I am?

Come, come, he chided himself. *You have gone among Christians before. You have walked in the midst of crusaders in the streets of Acre and Antioch. You have landed on the island of Cyprus. You have even gone as Baibars's emissary to the Greeks of Constantinople. Commend yourself to God and cast fear aside.*

He visualized what the Hashishiyya called "the Face of Steel within the Mask of Clay." What he showed this official would be his Mask of Clay, the look and manner of the merchant he was pretending to be. Beneath it, unseen, was his true face, a Face of Steel forged over years of bodily and spiritual training.

The mustached man allowed most of the people in line to pass into the city after a few quick questions.

Daoud's heartbeat quickened and he tensed when his turn came to pass.

"Come here. Lower your hood," the man said.

Walking slowly toward him, Daoud reached up and pushed back his hood.

The official raised thick black brows and beckoned to a guard. "If he makes a move you do not like, skewer him."

"Yes, Messer Lorenzo."

Daoud felt a stiffness in his neck and a knot in his belly. King Manfred's chancellor, Aziz, had written that Daoud would be quietly admitted to the town.

The heavyset, black-bearded Muslim soldier took a spear from the boy standing near him and leveled it at Daoud, his face hard.

"Now then," said Lorenzo, "give us your sword."

This overzealous guard captain, or whatever he was, was paying too much attention to him. But to avoid more attention, he must readily cooperate. He unbuckled his sword belt and held it out. Another Muslim guard took it and stepped beyond Daoud's reach.

Messer Lorenzo said, "Open your pack and show me what is in it."

"Silk, Your Signory." Daoud shrugged the pack off his shoulders and laid it on the table. He unlaced its flap and drew out a folded length of deep blue silk and then a crimson one. The shiny cloth slid through his long fingers.

"I am not a lord," said Lorenzo softly, reaching out to caress the silk. "Do not insult me by addressing me incorrectly."

"Yes, Messere."

Lorenzo took the pack with both hands and shook it. A shiny circular object a little larger than a man's hand fell out. Lorenzo picked it up and frowned at it.

"What is this, a mirror?"

"Yes, Messere. Our Trebizond mirrors are famed in Byzantium, Persia, and the Holy Land. I brought this as another sample of what we can offer."

"It is a good mirror," Lorenzo agreed. "It shows me my ugly face all too well."

Daoud was relieved to see Lorenzo had not guessed the secret of the mirror, that it contained a deadly disk of Hindustan. Thrown properly, the sharp-edged disk would slice into an opponent like a knife.

At Lorenzo's command, two of the guards searched Daoud briskly and efficiently. They even made him take off his boots.

The fingers of one guard found the chain around Daoud's neck and pulled on it. The locket Daoud had hidden under his tunic came out.

"What is that?" Lorenzo growled.

A chill ran over Daoud's body. Could Lorenzo possibly guess what the locket was?

"A locket with a holy inscription in our Greek language, Messere."

"Open it up."

With a leaden feeling in his belly Daoud turned a small screw in the hammered silver case. Perhaps he should not have taken the locket with him. What would Lorenzo see when he looked at it? The cover fell open, and he glanced down at the intricate etched lines and curves on the rock-crystal inner face of the locket. When Daoud saw beginning to appear on the crystal the face of a dark-skinned woman with accents of blue-black paint around her eyes, he looked away.

He leaned forward to give Lorenzo a closer look at it without taking it from around his neck. The locket's magic should work only for the person to whom it was given.

Daoud heard a low growl. The great hound had risen to his feet and was staring at him with eyes as dark brown as his master's. His upper lip curled, revealing teeth like ivory scimitars.

"Silence, Scipio," Lorenzo said. His voice was soft, but iron with command. The dog sat down again, but kept his eyes fixed on Daoud.

Heart pounding, he waited for Lorenzo's reaction to the locket. The official grasped it, pulling Daoud's head closer still.

"Mh. This is Greek writing, you say? It looks more like Arabic to me."

"It is very ancient, Messere, and the two alphabets are similar. I cannot read it myself. But it has been blessed by our Christian priests."

Lorenzo let go of the locket and glowered at him.

"What Christian priests? Where did you say you are from? What is your name?"

With deep relief Daoud stepped back from Lorenzo, snapped the locket shut, and dropped it back inside the collar of his tunic.

"I am David Burian, from Trebizond, Messere."

"Trebizond? I never heard of it," said the mustached man.

"It is on the eastern shore of the Black Sea."

"You have come such a great distance with only a few yards of silk and a mirror in your pack? Would you have me believe this is how you expect to make your fortune?"

Daoud reached deep in his lungs for breath. Now he would see whether the Christians would believe the story he and Baibars had devised.

"Messere, my city, Trebizond, lies on the only road to the East not cut off by the Saracens. A few brave merchants come from the land called Cathay bearing silk and spices. The samples I have brought with me, doubtless you can see, are of the highest quality. We can send you many bales of such silk overland from Trebizond to Constantinople, then by ship to your port of Manfredonia. I am here to arrange this trade."

"Arrange it with whom?"

Daoud hesitated. He had come to Lucera to meet with King Manfred. If, through some mistake, he should fall into the wrong hands, he would try to get word to the king that he was there.

"Your local merchants, your royal officials," he said. "Even your King Manfred, if he wishes to talk to me."

"So, a dusty peddler comes to our city gate and wants to speak with the king." He turned to the guard with the spear. "Take him to the castello."

Daoud molded the Face of Clay into an expression of naive wonderment. "The castello? Where King Manfred is?"

Lorenzo grinned without mirth. "Where King Manfred's *prison* is, my man. Where we hang the people sent by the pope to murder King Manfred."

Lorenzo's eyes were hard as chips of obsidian, and when he said the word *hang*, Daoud could feel the rough rope tightening around his neck.

But he was more angry now than frightened. His jaw muscles clenched. Why had Aziz not made sure there would be no mistake like this?

"Why are you doing this to me, Messer Lorenzo? I mean no harm."

"And I intend to see to it that you *do* no harm in this place, Messere of Trebizond," Lorenzo shot back. He waved to the guard. "To the guardroom, Ahmad."

May a thousand afrits hound this infidel to his death, thought Daoud angrily. "And what will you do with me, Messer Lorenzo?"

"I will examine you further at my leisure, after I have passed all these good people into the city." One violet-sleeved arm made a flowing gesture toward the waiting throng.

Daoud noticed that the tiny firewood seller, who had already passed by the guards, had paused at the inner portal. He shook his head sadly and touched forehead, shoulders, and chest in that sign Christians made to recall the cross of Jesus, their Messiah.

Why, I believe he is praying for me. That is kindly done.

Ahmad, the guard, pointed his spear at Daoud and jerked his head. Daoud stood his ground.

"What of my silk? If you keep it, I will truly have no honest business in Lucera."

Lorenzo smiled. He stuffed the lengths of silk and the mirror back into the pack and held it out to Daoud.

"There is not enough here to be worth stealing. Take it, then."

"And my sword?"

Lorenzo laughed gruffly. "Forget your sword. Take him away, Ahmad."

They had missed the precious object hidden in a pouch tied in his groin. And they missed the Scorpion, the miniature crossbow devised by the Hashishiyya, its parts concealed in the hem of his cloak. Nor did they have any idea that the tie that held his cloak at the neck could be pulled loose to become a long strangling cord, flexible as silk and hard as steel.

Daoud pulled his hood back over his head, shrugged into the pack under his cloak, and began walking. Every step he took sent a jolt of anger through his body. He would like to use his strangling cord on the man responsible for this blunder.

The news might well travel northward that a blond merchant had been arrested trying to enter Lucera. And if that man should later appear at the court of the pope, there might be those who would remember hearing of him and wonder why he had gone first to the pope's enemy, Manfred von Hohenstaufen.

His first feelings of anger became a cold turmoil in his belly as he thought what could happen if his mission failed—El Kahira leveled, its people slaughtered, Islam crushed beneath the feet of barbarian conquerors.

He must not let that happen.

The narrow street he walked on was lined with circular houses, their brick walls a warm yellow color. The conical roofs were covered with thin slates.

A Muslim sword maker looked up from his forge to stare at Daoud and his guard as they passed. Veiled women with red pottery jars on their heads stopped and looked boldly into his eyes.

Daoud lifted his gaze to the octagonal central tower of the citadel, bright yellow-and-black flags flying from its battlements. Instead of being squared off, the battlements were topped by forked points, like the tails of swallows, proclaiming allegiance to the Ghibellini, partisans of the Hohenstaufen family, enemies of the pope.

Closer to the citadel, noises of men and animals came at Daoud from all directions. He saw many buildings, all connected with one another, their small windows protected by iron grillwork. To his right, in a large grassy open field, a hundred or more Muslim guards in red and green were swinging their scimitars as an officer on a stone platform called out the count in Arabic. Daoud and his guard passed by a second yard, where still more Muslim soldiers were grooming their slender Arab horses.

A pungent smell of many beasts and fowl pent up close hung in the warm, damp air. Another row of buildings echoed with the shrieks of birds. Falconers in yellow-and-black tunics walked up and down holding wicker cages. As he peered into a doorway,

Daoud saw the golden eyes of birds of prey gleaming at him out of the shadows.

The sun was high by the time they came to the gateway of the castello.

Well, so far they have taken me where I wanted to go, Daoud thought grimly.

The entry hall of the castello was a large, vaulted room, as Daoud had expected. He had studied the citadel of Lucera before leaving Egypt, as he had studied many other strongholds in Italy, memorizing building plans and talking at length with agents of the sultan who had been there.

A strange, almost dizzying sensation came over Daoud. He recognized the feeling. having had it several times before when, in disguise, he entered Christian fortresses. As he gazed around the shadowy stone hall, its gloom relieved by shafts of light streaming in through high, narrow windows, he seemed to be seeing everything through two pairs of eyes. One pair belonged to a Mameluke warrior, Daoud ibn Abdallah, scouting an enemy stronghold. The other eyes were those of a boy named David Langmuir, to whom a Christian castle had been home. And, as always on sensing that inner division, Daoud felt a crushing sadness.

Ahmad took Daoud through a series of small, low-ceilinged rooms in the base of the castle. He spoke briefly to an officer seated at a table, dressed like himself in red turban and green tunic. He gestured to a heavy-looking door reinforced with strips of iron.

"In there, Messer David."

Every muscle in Daoud's body screamed out in protest. As part of his initiation into the Hashishiyya, he had been locked in a tiny black chamber in the Great Pyramid for days, and, except for the deaths of his mother and father, it was the worst memory of his life. Now he ached to strike down Ahmad and the other Muslim soldier and flee.

Instead, he said quietly, "How long will I have to wait?"

Ahmad shrugged. "God alone knows." Ahmad's southern Italian dialect was as heavily accented as Daoud's own.

How surprised he would be if I were to address him in Arabic.

"Who is this man who orders me imprisoned?" Daoud demanded.

Ahmad and the other guard shrugged at the question. "He is Messer Lorenzo Celino of Sicily. He serves King Manfred."

"What does he do for King Manfred?"

"Whatever the king tells him to." Ahmad smiled at Daoud and gestured again at the iron-bound door. "Thank you for making the work of guarding you easy. May God be kind to you."

Daoud bowed in thanks. Remembering the proper Christian farewell, he said, "Addio."

The other soldier unlocked the door with a large iron key, and Daoud walked reluctantly into a shadowy room. The door slammed shut behind him, and again he went rigid with his hatred of confinement.

The walls had recently been whitewashed, but the little room stank abominably. The odor, Daoud saw, came from a privy hole in one corner, where large black flies circled in a humming swarm. Half-light came in through a window covered with a black iron grill whose openings were barely wide enough to push a finger through. Noticing what appeared to be a bundle of bedding against a wall, Daoud approached it and squatted down for a closer look. He prodded it, feeling straw under a stained cotton sheet. At his probing, black dots, almost too small to see, began moving about rapidly over the sheet.

Daoud crossed the room, unslung his pack from his back, and dropped it to the floor. He sat down on the flagstones, as far from the bedding and the privy opening as he could get, his back against the wall, his knees drawn up, like a Bedouin in his tent.

I am helpless, Daoud thought, and terror and rage rose up in him like two djinns released from their jars, threatening to overwhelm him. He sat perfectly still. To bring himself under control, he began the contemplative exercise his Sufi teacher, Sheikh Saadi, called the Presence of God.

"God is everywhere, and most of all in man's heart," Saadi had said, his old eyes twinkling. "He cannot be seen or heard or touched or smelled or tasted. Therefore, make your mind as empty as the Great Desert, and you may converse with God, Whose name be praised."

Daoud touched the farewell present Saadi had given him when he left El Kahira to begin the journey to Italy. It was a leather case tied around his neck, and it contained a piece of paper called a tawidh, an invocation whose words were represented by Arabic numerals.

Like the locket, it would arouse curiosity if someone searching him found it. But it could be simply explained as one of those curious objects a traveler from distant places might have about his person. And, like the locket, it was simply too precious *not* to be worn.

Saadi said the tawidh would help wounds heal faster. Daoud refused to let himself think about wounds. He tried to make his mind a blank, and in the effort he forgot for a time where he was.

II

MESSER LORENZO CELINO OF SICILY STRODE INTO THE CELL. HE held in his hands a large round slice of bread heaped with steaming slivers of meat that gave off an unfamiliar but succulent smell.

Daoud slowly climbed to his feet. The hound Scipio, trailing Celino, watched him, standing in the doorway, as if unwilling to enter the vile-smelling chamber.

Daoud measured Celino. The top of the Sicilian's head would come to Daoud's chin, but the shoulders under his violet tunic were broad and straight, and he moved with menacing grace. Daoud judged that, though Celino must be close to fifty, he would be quick and deadly with hands and feet, and a good swordsman as well.

"God's beard, man, I didn't mean to keep you sitting in this room all day without food or drink," Celino said. "The damned farmers and traders kept coming and coming. But you cannot eat in this stinking place. Come out."

Daoud emerged into the next room, and Lorenzo motioned him to sit at the guards' table. Even though Daoud felt deep relief at being out of the cell, he sensed he was in greater danger than before. His mouth went dry and the palms of his hands turned cold as his eyes scanned the room for weapons or an escape route.

Lorenzo set the trencher and its burden of meat down before Daoud.

"Just butchered. Here, eat in good health. And here is a beaker of our good red wine of Monte Vultura." Daoud heard a false note in Celino's present heartiness and liked it even less than his earlier gruff suspicion.

Wine. An abomination forbidden by the Prophet. As Celino set a pitcher and two cups down on the table, Daoud recalled the nights he had spent with Sheikh Saadi learning to master wine and other drugs.

God prohibits the drinking of wine and the eating of unclean foods, not for His good, for nothing can harm Him, but for our good. Therefore, when a man goes among the infidel as a spy, God permits him to eat and drink the forbidden things lest he be discovered and put to death. You must learn to separate your mind from your body so that what harms your body will not affect your mind.

Daoud raised the cup, wondering if he would have as much power over wine drunk in the land of the infidel as he did when he drank it with his teacher. He sipped. The red liquid was thick and bitter and burned his mouth, but he made himself smile, sigh appreciatively, and sip again. He kept God at the center of his thoughts.

Celino was watching him closely. Raising his cup in salute, he also drank.

"Good, good. Now eat. Fresh roasted. Pork."

Daoud's fingers, poised over the meat, stopped short. Already made ill by hunger, by the vile odor of the room in which he had been confined, and by the wine that made his stomach churn, he felt himself on the point of vomiting. For nearly twenty years the prohibition against eating the flesh of pigs had been impressed upon him until the very thought of pork made him sick. He knew he should have prepared himself by eating it before he left El Kahira, but he had never found time for that. So now, a prisoner of the enemy, he faced for the first time the test of pork.

Celino was watching him with a half smile.

He would not test me with wine and pig's meat unless he suspected I am a Muslim.

Daoud's fingers grasped a slice of the hot meat. He tore it in half, using both his clean right hand and his unclean left as a non-Muslim would.

He stuffed a slice of pork into his mouth. It had smelled good until he found out what it was. Now it seemed slimy and tasteless. His stomach clenched, but he held himself rigid, expressionless. He started to chew, and found that his mouth was dry. His life might depend on his giving a convincing imitation of pleasure. He chewed the meat to fragments and, as though savoring it, swallowed the abomination crumb by crumb.

He realized he was still holding the other scrap of pork in his left hand. To give himself a respite, he tossed it to the flagstone floor before Lorenzo's hound.

Unclean to the unclean, he thought.

Scipio looked at Daoud with an almost human look of surprise, then bent to devour the meat.

"Friday, Scipio," said Celino sharply. "You are forbidden meat."

The dog looked sadly up at Celino, licked its chops, and sat back on its haunches, leaving the meat untouched. In spite of his predicament, Daoud laughed.

"You see?" said Celino. "Even a dog can learn to obey the commandments."

Celino gestured to the dog. "All right, Scipio, the bishop of Palermo gives you a dispensation."

The dog stood and struck at the meat with his long muzzle. It vanished to the accompaniment of loud gulping sounds.

"He likes it better than you do," Celino said. "You do not act very hungry for a man who has not eaten all day. Come on, man, fill your belly."

Realizing that the pork would taste worse as it cooled, Daoud braced himself and stuffed piece after piece into his mouth, chewing and swallowing as rapidly as he could.

"And," said Celino, watching him with narrowed eyes, "a dog can be trained to break the commandments when permitted."

From time to time Daoud threw a scrap to Scipio, grateful for the hound's help. But as he ate, Daoud noticed that the meat began to taste better to him, and the juices of his mouth began to flow. The familiar feeling of sorrow came over him, and he looked around at the white walls and ceiling, the wooden beams overhead painted blue. In his mind's eye he saw in their place yellow stone walls and a vaulted ceiling, and remembered that he had last tasted the flesh of pig at table with his father and mother.

He wiped his mouth with his sleeve and sat back. "Thank you. I feel better now."

Celino stood up, took the stale disk of bread, and dropped it to the floor. Scipio picked it up in his mouth.

"Then have the goodness to accompany me to the Hall of Mars, Messer David," he said, and turned.

He shows me that he is not afraid to turn his back, Daoud thought, picking up his pack and following Celino. The Hall of Mars, he remembered, was an indoor exercise hall for Manfred's troops.

They climbed stairs and walked through rooms in which Muslim soldiers were cleaning and polishing helmets, coats of mail, and weapons. In one room, men were painting shields. All the shields were yellow and bore the black two-headed eagle of the Hohenstaufens.

Daoud followed Lorenzo into a very large, bare room with a floor of polished hardwood. Ropes and chains hung from the walls and the beamed ceiling. Tall windows cut high up in smooth walls—too high to jump to—let in afternoon sunlight and fresh air that did not quite dispel a heavy odor of sweat. Opposite the doorway through which they passed was another and larger entrance, with double doors. The room was not square; the walls were of differing lengths and set at angles. Daoud recalled the octagonal shape of Castello Lucera's central tower.

He reviewed the plan of the castle he had committed to memory in El Kahira. He was sure that behind the double doors was the great royal audience hall. The wide doorway would allow troops assembled in the Hall of Mars to march into the audience chamber for a review.

Daoud noticed a group of Muslim guards lounging in one corner. At Lorenzo's entrance they touched their hands to their turbans in salute. Lorenzo responded with the same gesture. Scipio carried the trencher in his mouth to a corner of the room, where he lay down and began pushing the hard bread around with his forepaws and, working at it with his formidable teeth, making loud crunching noises.

Celino led Daoud to the center of the room. He turned suddenly on Daoud.

"Now, spy, you will tell me exactly who you are and exactly where you come from," he said rapidly. "You will tell me the truth, or you will die here and now."

Daoud came within a breath of answering, then realized Lorenzo had spoken in Arabic. Relieved laughter bubbled up toward his throat—he had not been caught. He choked it down and assumed a puzzled expression.

"I do not understand," Daoud said in Italian. "What tongue are you speaking, Messer Lorenzo?"

"Liar," said Lorenzo, still in Arabic, his eyes narrowing.

"I understand Italian, Greek, and, of course, the speech of Scythia," said Daoud. "If you would question me, speak in one of those tongues." Daoud sensed that the Sicilian's sudden shifts of mood were calculated. While his mouth uttered accusations, Celino's eyes watched him with a calm intelligence that reminded Daoud of an emir examining a fine-looking horse for hidden flaws.

Daoud saw, at the edge of his vision, that the guards who had been lounging in the corner of the hall were now in motion. He glanced quickly left and right. Three men, about fifty paces away, were coming at him, curved swords drawn. The dog, Scipio, had abandoned the trencher and risen to his feet, and he, too, was advancing on Daoud, fangs bared.

Lorenzo stepped away from Daoud, still pointing at him.

"Spegni! Kill!"

Tension crackled across Daoud's stomach like a lash. Three swords, and a dog that looked capable of killing a man. None of the weapons he had hidden on him would do for this. He slung his pack toward the wall behind him, leaving both hands free.

He half turned, to keep Lorenzo in sight while watching the advancing men. The Sicilian had a long dagger in a scabbard hung by his right side, but he did not draw it.

Facing the three swords, Daoud had not yet raised his hands. But his legs tensed. He bent at the knees, shifted his weight to the balls of his feet.

He whirled and sprang at Lorenzo. The Sicilian jumped backward, and Daoud could hear behind him the pounding of booted feet on the wooden floor. The dog barked furiously.

Daoud grappled with Lorenzo. The Sicilian grabbed his forearms, trying to hold him at a distance, and his strength was almost a match for Daoud's. But Daoud twisted his arms free, drove in, and caught Celino's neck in the bend of his left arm. He swung him around so that the Sicilian's body was between himself and the three attacking soldiers. While Lorenzo stumbled, Daoud plucked the man's dagger out of its scabbard. It had two sharp edges and came to a diamond-bright point.

Scipio leapt at him, but Daoud shifted Lorenzo between himself and the hound, and Scipio fell back. His enraged barking was deafening, like the roar of a lion. His fangs were a row of bone spearpoints. He danced right and left, seeking a way to get past Lorenzo to Daoud.

The joy of battle, the weapon in his hand, made Daoud feel the power coursing through his arms. But that damned dog had to be stopped. His teeth were as dangerous to Daoud as the curving blades of the three Muslim soldiers. Those fangs could rip through his boots, tear the muscles of his legs, and cripple him. He would prefer death.

Releasing Lorenzo's neck, Daoud gripped Lorenzo's wrist and twisted, hard and fast. Biting his lip, Lorenzo resisted, but he had to turn and bend, or the pressure on his arm would break it. Daoud laid the edge of Lorenzo's dagger against his throat.

"Call off your dog or I cut your throat." Daoud glanced over his shoulder to make sure no one was behind him.

"By all means cut my throat," Lorenzo flung back at him. "And Scipio will tear *your* throat out."

"If the dog jumps at me, I will gut him."

"The devil roast your balls," Lorenzo growled. "Scipio, sit!"

The hound stopped barking and stared at Lorenzo.

"Down, Scipio!" Lorenzo said. "He will not hurt me." To Daoud he said, "If you do hurt me, you will suffer such things that you will beg us to kill you."

Scipio reluctantly crouched, murder in his brown eyes and a steady, low growling issuing from his throat. The three Muslim guards were still moving forward, far more warily.

Daoud felt strong and able now to deal with these four men, but he could almost feel the weight of the overwhelming trap he was in. The thick walls. The thousands of soldiers. It was hopeless. He could fight on only until he died. And that was not what he had come here for at all.

Daoud stepped back toward the farther doorway, pulling Lorenzo with him. He glanced over his shoulder to be sure no one was behind him.

"For my part," said Daoud, "I will hurt you till you beg *them* to put down their swords. I will start by breaking your arm." He gave the twisted arm a vicious upward push till he could almost feel the agony of the tendons. Lorenzo grunted, and Scipio barked angrily. Most men, Daoud thought, would have screamed aloud at that.

"No matter what you do to me, it will not help you," said Lorenzo.

Three more turbaned Muslim soldiers joined those coming at Daoud. They spread out in a wide circle, some of them trying to slip around to his rear.

"Stand where you are, or I'll kill him," Daoud shouted. To show he meant it, he pressed the knife edge hard against Celino's throat and sliced with it just enough to draw blood.

"I hope you will enjoy the taste of your own intestines," Lorenzo said. He dug his boot heels into the wooden floor, trying to slow down Daoud's effort to drag him to the door. Daoud pushed up harder on his arm to make him move faster.

Daoud felt no fear of death, and he would not let them take him prisoner to torture him. He would die fighting. And go straight to paradise.

But how foolish all this was. A waste of his own life and the lives he would take with him. And many of those he would kill were Muslims, like himself.

"You must know that you will be the first to die here," he said. "And believe me I will take many of your men with me. I may even manage to kill your precious dog. I did not come here to fight with King Manfred's men. Why are you doing this?"

Celino, who had been struggling against Daoud, now relaxed and turned his head. "You are too dangerous to live."

"Dangerous to whom?"

"To me," said a deep voice behind Daoud.

III

DAOUD TURNED, DRAGGING CELINO. A BLOND MAN STOOD, HANDS on hips, eyeing him with a faint smile. One of the big doors leading into the royal audience chamber was slightly ajar. Daoud was angry at himself for letting someone slip up behind him unnoticed.

"Sire, get back!" Lorenzo shouted.

Sire. Daoud knew at once who this was. The same height as Lorenzo, as Daoud now saw, the man had the very broad shoulders Christian knights developed from wielding their huge two-handed swords. Daoud guessed his age at a little over thirty. His hair, so blond it was almost silver, hung in soft waves below his ears, curling at the ends. His silver-blond mustache was carefully trimmed. His eyelids crinkled with amusement. He wore a tunic of lime-colored silk under a short forest-green cloak trimmed with white fur. His hose and boots were also shades of green. From a chain around his neck hung a five-pointed silver star with a spherical ruby in its center. In every point he fit the description Daoud had been given.

The despair Daoud had been feeling a moment before gave way to a profound relief. It had seemed that everything stood in the way of his meeting this man, and now at last they were face-to-face.

"Sire," Daoud said in Italian, "I know who you are, and you must know who I am."

"I do indeed," said Manfred von Hohenstaufen, still smiling. "Please release Messer Lorenzo."

Daoud hesitated only a moment. But if Manfred allowed Lorenzo to hurt him now, the mission was a failure anyway. Tensed for attack, he let go of Lorenzo, who sprang away.

In an instant the Sicilian had taken a curving Islamic sword from a soldier.

"Sire, at least move back from him," Lorenzo said. "You know what we are dealing with here."

"Quiet, Lorenzo," snapped Manfred. "What we are dealing with is a peddler from some misty land beyond the Black Sea who happens to be infernally nimble. That is all."

Daoud was pleased to hear Manfred go along with his disguise. He relaxed a bit and eyed the king of southern Italy and Sicily. A splendid-looking man with a charm that Daoud felt after only a moment's acquaintance.

"Will the peddler be so kind as to return my dagger?" Lorenzo asked with heavy irony. "This side of the Black Sea it is considered discourteous to stand in the king's presence holding a naked weapon."

"Of course," said Daoud, holding the dagger by its guard and handing it hilt-first to Lorenzo, who in turn gave the Saracen soldier back his sword.

Daoud was glad he had not had to kill Lorenzo. The Sicilian, like his master, Manfred, was clearly a man above the common run. His behavior toward Daoud so far had been a series of clever pretenses. Indeed, Daoud was sure he had not gotten to the bottom of Lorenzo yet.

"I thank you for entertaining us with this display of your fighting skills, Messer David," said King Manfred. "Now let us talk of the silk trade. Join us, Lorenzo."

Manfred led the way into the audience chamber beyond the Hall of Mars. Walking beside Daoud, Celino snapped his fingers at Scipio. The big gray hound rose and followed, casting a hostile look at Daoud.

Why did they try to kill me?

In the audience hall, marble pillars supported a vaulted ceiling pierced by circular glazed windows. A dozen or more men and women stood around, staring at Daoud. His glance quickly took in the feathered caps of the men, the pale rose and violet gowns of the women, and the gilded nets that held their hair.

He tried not to stare at the women, whose faces were bare in the manner of unbelievers. But they were all, he noted, beautiful in varying degrees. Several had striking blond hair and blue eyes. Though it was his own coloring, he was not used to seeing fair women, and his heartbeat quickened.

But the gaze of a darker woman met his. Her amber-colored eyes seemed to burn. Her nose was small, the nostrils flaring, her lips full and dark red. The face was carefully without expression, revealing as little as if it were indeed covered with a veil.

The dark woman's black hair was coiled on top of her head in braids intertwined with ropes of pearls. Her scarlet gown was decorated with long strips of satin embroidered in floral designs. Over her narrow shoulders she wore a shawl of flame-colored silk. Having been to Constantinople, Daoud recognized her style of dress as Byzantine. She made the other women of Manfred's court look like barbarians.

She held his gaze steadily. He bowed his head courteously, and she responded with a faint nod. Then he was past her.

Standing on a dais at the end of the hall was a large chair of black wood with painted panels; to the left of the dais sat a small group of purple-robed men holding string and wind instruments. On the right was a small doorway. A servant leapt to fling open the door for Manfred, who strode briskly toward it, tossing pleasantries to his courtiers.

The door led through a series of rooms where clerks wrote busily, and Daoud noticed with surprise that they went right on scribbling as their king walked through. Obviously Manfred preferred their work to their homage.

Daoud sensed that their path was taking them on a circuit of the great eight-sided structure. They passed through a small kitchen where bakers were preparing fruit pastries. Manfred plucked a

freshly baked cherry tart from a tray, bit into it, and nodded to the
bowing cook.

To his surprise, Daoud noticed a small figure in one corner, the
little bent man who had earlier looked on him with pity. The dwarf
lay curled up on his side with closed eyes on his empty firewood
cart. Not a bad occupation, Daoud thought, supplying firewood to
the king's pastry kitchen.

Beyond the kitchen the three men entered another great hall, so
brightly lit that Daoud's eyes hurt for a moment. The afternoon sun
streamed through arched windows of white glass set, as in the Hall
of Mars, high in the walls. The walls were lined with shelves loaded
with books and compartments filled with scrolls. Walkways at three
levels ran around the walls, and ladders were spaced along them.
Men in long gray tunics browsed at the shelves or sat at tables in
the center of the room reading books and scrolls and making notes
on parchment.

A servant opened a wrought-iron grill in the shortest wall of the
library, and the three men stepped out under the sky into an octagonal space filled with trees and plants, enclosed on all sides by a
colonnaded gallery. In the center of the garden a small fountain
played, topped by a small bronze statue of a naked woman strad-
dling a dolphin, the water spurting from the dolphin's mouth. Daoud
was momentarily shocked. The most powerful and corrupt emir in
Egypt would not dare to have such a statue where strangers might
see it.

Manfred beckoned, and Daoud followed him down a pebble path
to the basin of the fountain. Small dark green fish flickered through
the water. The king seated himself on a marble bench, and the two
men stood before him. At a gesture from Lorenzo, Scipio lay down
in the sun beside a bush bearing dozens of dark-red roses.

The sun gleamed on Manfred's pale hair. "What does your sultan
want of me?" he asked.

"I am ordered to speak openly only to you and your secretary
Aziz," said Daoud, his glance shifting to Lorenzo.

"Ah, you did not know, then, that Aziz is the name Lorenzo
Celino uses when he writes to the Sultan of Cairo for me?"

Lorenzo Celino—Aziz? Daoud turned to Celino and laughed with
delighted surprise.

"You write excellent Arabic. I would never have guessed that
you were not one of us."

Lorenzo accepted Daoud's compliment with a small bow.

"One of *us*?" said Manfred. "And what are you, then, Messere? I see before me a strapping man, blond enough to be one of my Swabian knights, yet who claims to come from the Sultan of Cairo. You are no Arab or Turk."

"Indeed not, Sire," said Daoud. "I am a Mameluke."

"A blond Mameluke." Manfred nodded. "Where are you from, then, Russia or Circassia?"

Without emotion Daoud told the king of his descent from crusaders and his capture by the Muslims.

"What a strange world this is," said Manfred. "And when did this happen to you?"

"Twenty years ago, Sire. For most of those years I have served my lord Baibars al-Bunduqdari, who is now Sultan of Cairo."

"And you are a Muslim?"

"Of course, Sire."

Manfred stood up and came close to him. "Of course? You say that so firmly. Do you not remember the Christian teachings of your childhood?"

The question made Daoud angry. *My soul is undivided. King or not, how dare this infidel question that!*

"God willed that I find the truth, Sire," he said simply.

Manfred shrugged. "It is all the same to me. I have lived among Muslims all my life."

"May I know, Sire, why your secretary, to whom my master sent me in good faith, tried to kill me?" Daoud asked.

Manfred turned his back on Daoud and strolled a short distance down the pebble path. "Lorenzo is neither my secretary nor does he normally command my gate guards. He performs for me *unusual* tasks that require a man of uncommon courage, loyalty, and wit. Such as testing you—first, by taking you prisoner, then by giving you pork and wine and speaking to you in Arabic, finally by trying to kill you."

"But I might have killed him."

"I did not realize how much of a risk I was taking," said Lorenzo.

"We did not think Baibars could find anywhere in his empire a man who could go to the papal court undetected. We hoped to show him his error and send you back. But you are quite a remarkable man, David."

Show Baibars his error! Manfred might be a brilliant man, but he evidently underestimated Baibars. Daoud sensed himself feeling a bit superior and warned himself not to make the same mistake and underestimate Manfred.

"Perhaps now that you have tested my ability, Sire, you might be more inclined to help me."

"Help you to do what?" There was a note of irritation in Manfred's voice. "Your Sultan Baibars has asked me only to help you carry out a mission in the Papal States. What is your mission?"

Daoud said, "Sire, my master chose not to entrust his plan to writing, but sent me to tell it to you instead. I am here for one purpose, to prevent the forming of an alliance between Christians and Tartars."

Manfred looked surprised, and stared intently at Daoud. "Tartars? Those barbarians who invaded Europe—how long ago, Lorenzo?"

Lorenzo frowned. "Over twenty years, Sire."

Daoud said, "Fifty years ago they were nothing. A scattering of herdsmen, like the Bedouin. Now they are the most powerful people on earth."

Manfred nodded. "Yes, I remember now. When they rode into Poland and Hungary I was just a boy. Everyone was in terror of them. Their emperor sent letters to all the monarchs of Europe demanding that they surrender. He contemptuously offered them positions in his court." He grinned at Daoud. "My father showed me the letter he was sending back. If Tartar emperor succeeded in conquering Europe, my father said, he would be well qualified to serve as his falconer."

Daoud inclined his head. "Your family's love of falconry is well known to your admirers in the lands of Islam. My lord the sultan considers you an old friend and hopes that you will see fit to help him in his time of need."

Manfred held out his hands, palms up. "If I can."

"Now the Tartars have fallen upon the lands of Islam," Daoud said. "They have conquered Persia. They have a hundred thousand mounted warriors in the field, and allies and auxiliaries. They have leveled our holy city of Baghdad, destroyed it utterly, and killed every man, woman, and child who lived there, even the Commander of the Faithful, our caliph himself. These are no fanciful tales, Sire. I have fought against the Tartars. I have seen with my own eyes the ashes of Baghdad and the heaps of its dead."

The scene of desolation arose in his mind as it had so many times before, the gray plain where a city had been, the unbelievable sight of a landscape strewn with rotting, headless corpses as far as the eye could see. To put it out of his mind, he hurried on with what he had to say.

"Now their armies advance through Syria, threatening the realm of my lord, the Sultan of Cairo. We have had word that Hulagu Khan, commander of the Tartar armies in Persia, has sent two high-ranking emissaries to the pope. They are sailing across the Middle Sea now, from the island of Cyprus to Venice. Hulagu Khan wants to form an alliance with the Christian rulers of Europe to attack us from both directions at once, east and west. Our whole people, our whole Muslim faith, could be utterly wiped out."

Manfred nodded grimly. "And all of Christian Europe would rejoice at your destruction. Not I, certainly, but the rest of them. What do you propose to do about these Tartar emissaries to the pope?"

"For that I will need your help, Sire. I, too, will go to the pope's court. I understand that he resides at Orvieto, a small town north of Rome."

"Yes," Lorenzo put in, "and there he will stay. He has not set foot in Rome since he galloped in to be crowned at Saint Peter's and galloped out again. He is terrified of the Roman mob. As well he should be, since most of their leaders are in our pay."

"Trade secrets, Celino," said Manfred, raising a cautioning finger. "So, you will go to Orvieto. And then?"

"I will present myself at the pope's court as I have here, as David, a merchant of Trebizond. I will take up residence with—friends—who can help me reach the ears of men of influence. I will spread stories throughout Orvieto—true stories—of the horrors the Tartars have perpetrated everywhere they have gone, of their determination to conquer the entire world."

Manfred shook his head. "What you plan to do is very dangerous. You've proven to us that you are a skilled and resourceful man, but still, what if you are discovered?" He shook his head. "Have you any idea of how your people are *hated* in Europe, David? If it were known that I helped a Muslim spy to steal into the court of the pope, all the kingdoms of Christendom would turn against me. The pope need but snap his fingers and I and my little realm would be swept away. No, David. You ask me to risk too much."

Daoud was momentarily surprised, then angry. He had expected that Manfred would cooperate with him. If the young king vacillated, Daoud might have journeyed from Egypt to Italy for nothing.

And then a ripple of fear crept up his spine. If he failed to persuade Manfred, the Tartars might destroy the world he had come to love and believe in.

God, help me to stop them. I must not go back to El Kahira a failure.

He must choose his words with care. He was dealing here with a king, and one did not argue with kings. Better to ask questions than offer arguments.

"Does not the pope wish even now to take your throne from you, Sire?" he said. "How can matters between you and him be any worse?"

Manfred nodded. "True, Pope Urban keeps offering my crown to this prince and that, claiming that I had no right to inherit it from my father. And that he had no right to have it in the first place." Manfred bit his lip, and the light pink of his cheeks reddened. "But only the French are powerful enough to take it from me. And King Louis of France is kindly disposed to me and will not permit any of his great barons to make war on me. I rely on Louis's continued goodwill."

"But the man who wants to join with the Tartars to annihilate Islam is that same King Louis of France," Daoud said. "France, as you said, is the only kingdom with the power to help the pope dethrone you. Should the pope decide against allying with the Tartars, King Louis will continue to prohibit his subjects from joining the pope's war against you. Help me, and you come between King Louis and the pope."

"Intrigue requires gold," said Manfred. "Does your master expect me to pay for your activities?"

"What I have brought with me will pay for all," Daoud replied. He unbuckled his belt and undid the laces that held his hose tight around his waist. Celino moved closer, tense, ready in case Daoud should reach for a weapon. Daoud slipped his fingers into the breeches he wore under his hose and found the bag tied to the drawstring.

"What is the man doing?" said Manfred with a wondering smile. Celino shook his head.

Daoud pulled out a bag of heavy red silk, full and round with what it held. He felt a childlike delight in mystifying the two men.

"Pay me from your royal treasury what this is worth," said Daoud, "and I shall have gold enough for all I need to do." He pulled apart the mouth of the silk bag and drew out of it a globe of green fire. He held it out to Manfred. Celino gasped.

Daoud was gratified at their wonderment.

"Are you not afraid I will steal this from you and dump you in an unmarked grave?" said Manfred with a bright grin.

"The Hohenstaufen family have been friends of the sultans of Egypt since your father's day," said Daoud. "We have learned to trust you."

"Just listen to that, Lorenzo," said Manfred. "The Saracens think better of me than the pope does."

Besides, Daoud thought, Manfred knew that Baibars's arm was long. Manfred, Daoud was sure, knew that Baibars would not permit anyone, even a distant head of state, to betray him so flagrantly.

His eyes wide, Manfred extended his palm, and Daoud unhesitatingly placed the emerald in it. Manfred raised it close to his face, peering through the dark depths into its glowing heart. The jewel, irregular in shape but nearly spherical, reflected little spots of pale green light on his cheeks. He shook his head.

"Green, the color I love best in all the world. The color of hope." He encircled it with thumb and forefinger. "Look, Lorenzo, I cannot get my fingers around it. I am amazed that your master is willing to part with such a wonder. How did he come by it?"

"It has been through many hands, Sire," said Daoud. "It once belonged to Emir Fakr ad-Din, who commanded the army of Egypt when King Louis invaded our land."

"To think Baibars let you take this emerald from him, and you came all this way from Alexandria with it and delivered it to me. And Baibars trusted you."

"As he trusts you, Sire," Daoud put in quickly.

"*You* are like a falcon, are you not?" said Manfred, smiling into Daoud's eyes. "Released to fly far afield for your sultan."

Manfred strode to Daoud suddenly and clapped him on the shoulder. "Let it be done as your master wishes, then. The trader from Trebizond will go to Orvieto with my help."

A surge of joy sprang up within Daoud and almost burst past his lips. He bowed, his heart pounding.

God be thanked!

Manfred said, "We must see about turning this jewel of yours into gold coins. Or smaller jewels. They would be easier to carry than gold." Manfred looked lovingly at the emerald again, then carefully dropped it into his belt pouch and smiled at Daoud.

"You should not go alone into the Papal States, David. You may have studied Europe from afar, but you do not know Italy firsthand. Lorenzo here shall go with you. I trust Lorenzo to travel far and secretly in my service, even as your master trusts you."

Celino sighed. Daoud and Celino eyed each other.

Daoud began searching for ways to dissuade Manfred. A short while earlier he and Celino had been trying to kill each other. And Celino would be putting Manfred's interests first, not those of Islam.

Obviously aware of his hesitation, Manfred took his arm. "Listen to me, Mameluke. You will be wise to accept every bit of help that is offered to you. I have powerful allies in northern Italy, in Florence, Pisa, Siena, and other cities. But you do not know them and they do not know you. Lorenzo speaks for me. He knows who the key Ghibellini are in the north, and they know him. Do not object to taking him with you."

Manfred would not let him go, Daoud realized, unless Celino went with him. And the argument that Celino could put him in touch with the Ghibellini of the north was a strong one.

Lorenzo is perhaps twenty years older than I, but he is quick-witted and quick on his feet. And, yes, I would rather not go alone. I could easily make a mistake from ignorance. I am better off with a man like this to guide me.

A tentative smile played under Celino's grizzled mustache. "My royal master is determined in this. What do you say?"

Daoud bowed. "I accept. With gratitude. We shall travel this road together."

"Whatever happens to the two of you," Manfred said, "no one must ever know that I am involved."

"I guarantee that, Sire," said Celino.

Manfred rubbed the palms of his hands together. "There is one other person I propose to send with you. She can be a great help to you."

Celino turned quickly to Manfred. "I do not advise it, Sire."

"Why not?" said Manfred. "She will be perfect."

"Because she will not want to go." There was censure in Celino's dark stare—and a boyish defiance in Manfred's answering look.

"Do not question me," said Manfred. "I have no choice. For her good and for my own, she must leave here. And she *will* be useful to you."

Instead of replying, Celino only sighed again.

"A woman?" Daoud was thunderstruck. In El Kahira women left their homes only to visit other women. He felt anxiety claw at his belly. Any mistake in planning might wreck the mission and doom him, and Celino, to a horrible death. And to send a woman to the court of the pope on such a venture seemed not just a mistake, but utter madness.

"A very beautiful woman," said Manfred, a grin stretching his blond mustache. "One who has had a lifetime's schooling in intrigue. She is from Constantinople, and her name is Sophia, which means wisdom in Greek."

There are no more treacherous people on this earth than the Byzantines, Daoud thought, *and they have ever been enemies of Islam.*

Argument surged up in him, but he saw a hardness in Manfred's eyes that told him nothing he might say would sway the king. He looked at Celino, and saw in the dark, mustached face the same reluctant acceptance he had heard in the sigh.

Whoever this Sophia might be, he would have to take her with him.

IV

SOPHIA PRESSED HER HEAD BACK AGAINST THE PILLOW AND screamed with pleasure. Her loins dissolved into rippling liquid gold. Her fingers dug into the man's back and her legs clenched around his hips, trying to crush him against her.

"Oh—oh—oh—" she moaned. The warmth spread to her toes, her fingertips, her scalp, filling her with joy. She was so happy that she wanted to cry.

As the blaze of ekstasia died down, she felt Manfred driving deep inside her. She felt his hardness, his separateness, as she could not feel it a moment ago when she was at her peak and they seemed to melt together, one being.

His rhythm was insistent, inexorable, like a heartbeat. His hands under her back were tense. He was fighting for his climax.

She delighted in the sight of his massive shoulders overshadowing her. It was almost like being loved by a god.

Manfred's face was pressed against her shoulder, his open mouth on her collarbone. She turned toward him and saw the light in his white-gold hair. She slid one hand up to his hair and stroked it, while with the other she rubbed his back in a circular motion.

She felt the muscles in his body tighten against her. He drew in a shuddering breath.

"Yes—yes—good," she whispered, still stroking his hair, still caressing his back.

He relaxed, panting heavily.

He never makes much noise. Nothing like my outcries.

They lay without moving, she pleased by the warm weight of him lying upon her, as if it protected her from floating away. The feel of him still inside her sent wavelets of pleasure through her.

Still adrift on sensations of delight, she opened her eyes to stare up into the shadows of the canopy overhead. On the heavy bed curtains to her left, the late afternoon sun cast an oblong of yellow light with a pointed arch at the top, the shape of an open window nearby. She knew well the play of light in this unoccupied bedchamber in an upper part of the castle. Manfred and she had met here many times.

They rolled together so that they lay side by side in a nest of red and purple cushions. The down-filled silk bolster under them whispered as they shifted their weight, and the rope netting that held it creaked. Manfred propped his head up with one arm. His free hand toyed with the ringlets of her unbound hair. She slid her palm over his chest.

She remembered an ancient sculpture she had seen in a home outside Athens. The torso of a man, head missing, arms broken off at the shoulders, legs gone below the knees, the magnificent body had survived barbarian invasions, the coming of Christianity, the iconoclasts, the Frankish conquest, to stand now on a plain pedestal in a room with purple walls, the yellowish marble gleaming in the light of many candles. Her host showed it only to his most trusted guests.

"Which god is this?" she had asked.

"I think it is just an athlete," said her host. "The old Greeks made gods of their athletes."

Manfred's naked torso, pale as marble, seemed as beautiful. And was alive.

She sighed happily. "How lucky I am that there was time for love in my king's life this afternoon." She spoke in the Sicilian dialect, Manfred's favorite of all his languages.

How lucky, she thought, that after all her years of wandering she had at last found a place in the world where she was loved and needed.

His lips stretched in a smile, but his blue eyes were empty. Uneasiness took hold of her. She sensed from the look on his face that he was about to tell her something she did not want to hear.

In memory she heard a voice say, *Italy was ours not so long ago and might be ours again.* So Michael Paleologos, the Basileus, Emperor of Constantinople, had introduced the suggestion that she go to Italy, and at just such a moment as this, when they were in bed together in his hunting lodge outside Nicaea.

She had felt no distress at the idea of being parted from Michael. He was a scrawny man with a long gray beard, and though she counted herself enormously lucky to have attracted his attention, she felt no love for him.

She had come to Lucera acting as Michael's agent and personal emissary to Manfred—and resenting Michael's use of her but feeling she had no choice. She was a present from one monarch to another. She ought to be flattered, she supposed.

She had walked into Manfred's court in the embroidered jeweled mantle Michael had given her, her hair bound up in silver netting. Lorenzo Celino had conducted her to the throne, and she bowed and looked up. And it was like gazing upon the sun.

Manfred von Hohenstaufen's smile was brilliant, his hair white-gold, his eyes sapphires.

He stepped down from his throne, took her hand, and led her to his eight-sided garden. First she gave him Michael's messages— news that a Tartar army had stormed the crusader city of Sidon, leveled it, and ridden off again—a warning that Pope Urban had secretly offered the crown of Naples and Sicily, Manfred's crown, to Prince Edward, heir apparent to the throne of England.

"Your royal master is kind, but the pope's secret is no secret," Manfred had said, laughing and unconcerned. "The nobility of England have flatly told Prince Edward that they will supply neither money nor men for an adventure in Italy. The pope must find another robber baron to steal my crown." And then he asked her about herself, and they talked about her and about him.

She had thought all westerners were savages, but Manfred amazed her with his cultivation. He knew more than many Byzantines, for whom Constantinople—which they always called "the Polis," the City, as if it were the only one—was the whole world. In the short time she and Manfred strolled together that day, he spoke to her in Greek, Latin, and Italian, and she later found out that he knew French, German, and Arabic as well.

He sang a song to her in a tongue she did not recognize, and he told her it was Provençal, the language of the troubadours.

He undid the clasp of her mantle and let it fall to the gravel. He kissed her in the bright sunlight, and she forgot Michael Paleologos. She belonged altogether to Manfred von Hohenstaufen.

Now, with a chill, she remembered that she did indeed *belong* to Manfred. She was not his mate but his servant.

His fingertips stroked her nipple lightly, but she ignored the tingle of pleasure. She waited for him to say what he had to say.

He said, "Remember the fair-haired Muslim who came to the court today?"

"The man from Egypt? You had him killed?"

"I changed my mind," Manfred said.

She felt relief. She was surprised at herself. She had wanted the man to live. She remembered her astonishment when, with a gesture like a performing magician's, Manfred threw open the doors of his audience hall and the entire court saw the blond man with his dagger at Celino's throat.

She had been surprised when Manfred told her that this man, dressed in a drab tunic and hose like a less-than-prosperous Italian merchant, was the awaited Saracen from the Sultan of Egypt.

The sight of him as he passed through the audience hall had left her momentarily breathless. He looked like one of those blond men of western Europe the people of Constantinople called Franks and had learned to hate at sight. His hair was not as light as Manfred's; it was darker, more the color of brass than of gold. Manfred's lips were full and red, but this man's mouth was a down-curving line, the mouth of a man who had endured cruelty without complaint and could himself be cruel. She wondered what he had seen and done.

As he had passed her, his eyes caught hers. Strange eyes, she could not tell what color they were. There was a fixity in them akin to madness. The face was expressionless, rocklike. This, she was sure, was no ordinary man, to be disposed of as an inconvenience. She was not surprised Manfred had decided to let him live.

"Why did you change your mind?"

"I think this Mameluke can help me," Manfred said. "Therefore I am going to help him. He is going to Orvieto on a mission for his sultan. I am sending Lorenzo with him."

"What did you call him?"

"A Mameluke. A slave warrior. The Turks who rule in Muslim lands take very young boys as slaves and raise them in barracks to be soldiers. They forget their parents and are trained with the utmost rigor. They are said to be the finest warriors in the world."

What does a life like that do to a man? It must either destroy him or make him invincible.

"The man looks like a Frank," she said.

"He comes of English stock," said Manfred. "You Byzantines lump all of us together, English and French and Germans, as Franks, do you not? So you can call him a Frank if you like. But whatever he looks like, he is a Turk at heart. I've learned that from talking to him. It's really quite amazing."

They were plunged into deep shadow as the arched golden shape on the bed curtain disappeared, a cloud having passed over the sun. Despite the summer's heat she felt cold, and even though she did not trust Manfred she reached for him, wanting him close.

But Manfred drew away from her, preoccupied. She pulled a crimson cushion from behind him and hugged it against her breasts.

How alone the Mameluke must feel. Even here, where Muslims are tolerated, they have tried to kill him. And when he is in the pope's territory, every man will be his enemy.

She remembered the harsh face with its prominent cheekbones and gray eyes and thought, Perhaps being alone holds no terror for him.

After all, I am alone, and I have made the best of it.

"What is his mission in Orvieto?" she asked.

She listened intently as Manfred told her a tale of trying to prevent the great powers of East and West from joining together to crush Islam between them.

Manfred continued, "David hopes to influence the pope's counselors to turn against the Tartars, that they may sway the pope himself."

"How can one man attempt such a huge undertaking?"

"He brought me an exceedingly valuable stone, an emerald, which I will trade for jewels he can carry to Orvieto and exchange for coins. It pleases me greatly that the sultan would entrust me with such a gem. That helped to change my mind about this David. The Saracens are men of honor in their way." He smiled at her, looking pleased with the situation and pleased with himself. But she was quiet, unmoving, waiting for him to say the thing she feared to hear.

"But you are right," Manfred went on. "He cannot do it alone."

Warm yellow light once more filled their curtained cubicle. The cloud had passed away from the sun. But her heart froze.

"I have decided I must entrust my own most precious jewel to David." He put his hand on hers.

Oh, no! she thought, anguish tearing at her heart as his words confirmed her guess. She felt a terrible pain, as if he had run her through with a spear. She wanted to clutch at him, hold him in spite of himself. She had not felt so lost since her mother and father and the boy she loved were killed by the Franks.

She studied his face to memorize it, because soon she would leave him and probably never see him again. It would do her no good to let him see how she felt. She must decide what face to show him.

I am a woman of Constantinople, alone in a country of strangers. And we are an ancient people, wise and subtle, and we bide our time.

She sat up in the bed, hugging her knees, thinking.

"How will my going with him help you?"

He grunted softly, and she looked at him. He appeared relieved. She was making it easy for him. She felt the beginning of dislike for him stirring within her.

"I thought you would be perfect for this. And you are."

His words puzzled her, and she almost let her growing anger show. "I do not see what you see, Sire."

"We are in bed. You may call me Manfred."

But I do not want to call you Manfred.

"What is it you think I would be so good at?"

"You can mask your feelings," he said with a smile. "You are doing it now. You are very good at it."

"Thank you, Sire."

He shook his head, sat up beside her, and put an arm around her shoulders. "I meant it when I said you are precious to me. But you must go with this man. I cannot tell you all my reasons, but it is for your own safety as well.''

No doubt he was being honest with her, though he was not telling her everything. Just the other day one of Manfred's servants, whom she had cultivated with gifts, warned her that Manfred's queen, Helene of Cyprus, was demanding that Manfred break with Sophia. Of course, Manfred would never be willing to admit that his wife could force him to do such a thing.

She wanted to get off by herself and think this out, and cry, let tears release some of the pain she felt. This curtained bed confined her like a dungeon cell. She found her white shift amid the rumpled bedclothes. Getting up on her knees, she raised the shift over her head and struggled into it.

''Where are you going?'' Manfred asked.

She crawled around the bed to look for her gown and her belt. ''I have arrangements to make. Packing to do.''

''I have not dismissed you,'' he said a bit sullenly.

''Yes, you have,'' she said, deliberately making her voice so low that it would be hard for him to hear.

''You have not heard everything.'' He took her arm. She wanted to pull away, but she let him hold her.

''I need your help,'' he went on. ''You see, if David fails, in a year or two I may be dead.''

He let go of her. She picked up the blue gown she had so eagerly thrown off an hour ago. Her fingers crushed the silk. She wanted to be alone, but she needed to learn more. She paused, kneeling beside him.

''God forbid, Sire! Why should you be dead?''

''This time the pope is offering my crown to the French.''

Sitting down, laying the gown in her lap, she sighed and turned all her attention to him.

''Why can you not make peace with the pope? Why is he so determined to dethrone you?''

''Like all storied feuds, it goes back so far that no one can remember what started it,'' said Manfred, smiling with his lips but not his eyes. ''At present the pope refuses to recognize me because my father promised to give up the crown of Sicily.''

He paused a moment, and fixed her with a strangely intent stare. ''And because my father did not marry my mother. Even though he loved her only, and never loved any of his three empresses.''

He is trying to tell me something, Sophia thought.

But before she could reply, he went on with his tale of the Hohenstaufens and the popes. "As the popes see it, to have a Hohenstaufen ruling southern Italy and Sicily is like having a knife at their throats. This pope, Urban, is a Frenchman, and he is trying to get the French to help him drive us out."

The French. It was the French who, over fifty years ago, had stormed Constantinople, looted it, and ruled over it until driven out by Michael Paleologos.

And now the French threatened Manfred.

From his island of Sicily, how easy to launch another invasion of Constantinople.

In memory she saw Alexis, the boy she loved, fall as the French crossbow bolt hit him. She heard him cry out to her.

Go, Sophia, go!

Why was I saved that night if not that I might help to stop the French from conquering Constantinople again?

"I cannot send an army to Orvieto to stop the pope's intrigues against me," Manfred said. "That would turn all Christendom against me. But I can send my two best people, my brave and clever Lorenzo and my beautiful and clever Sophia. Together with David, you two perhaps can turn my enemies against each other. You may be gone six months or a year. And afterward you can come back."

He did not take his eyes from hers as he said it, but there was a flickering in their depths that told her he was not being honest with her.

"When will I meet this—Mameluke?"

"Tomorrow we go falconing. The forest is a good place to talk freely." He paused and grinned at her. "But do not dress just yet. This may be my last chance to enjoy your lovely body."

She looked away. She felt no desire for him. She was sick of being enjoyed.

"Forgive me, Sire, I have much to do," she said. Before he could object, she had slipped through the curtains around the bed and was pulling her blue gown over her head. She had left half her clothes behind with Manfred, but that did not matter. Her own quarters were near, and later she could send a servant for her things.

As she hurried out the door, she pretended not to hear Manfred's angry cry, muffled by the bed's thick curtains.

Sophia wrapped in white linen the satin mantle in which she had been presented at Manfred's court. She laid it in her traveling chest, then brought her jewel box from the table on which it had stood since she'd arrived here, and laid it on the mantle.

Manfred would gladly have ordered servants to do this packing for her, but it was easier to preserve her privacy when she did for herself.

She looked down at the polished ebony box with the double-headed eagle of Constantinople in mother-of-pearl inlay. A gift from the Basileus when he sent her to Sicily. The eagle of Constantinople, tradition said, was the inspiration for the two-headed Hohenstaufen eagle.

She folded a green woolen tunic and laid it over the jewel box. As she stood with her hands pressed on the tunic, sorrow welled up within her.

Was there ever a woman more alone in the world than I am?

In one night made hideous by the flames of the burning city and the screams of the dying, she had lost her father, Demetrios Karaiannides, the silversmith, and her mother, Danuta, and her two sisters, Euphemia and Eirene. The people of the Polis had risen against the Franks, and the Franks had retaliated by killing everyone they could lay hands upon.

The boy she was going to marry, the boy she loved, had fled with her to the Marmara waterfront. There they found a small boat, and then the crossbow bolt had torn through his back. Dying, he cast her adrift.

Go, Sophia, go!

From then on she was alone.

What am I? What is a woman alone?

Not a queen or an empress, not a wife or a mother, not a daughter, not a nun. Not mistress, now that Michael and Manfred had each sent her away. Not courtesan or even harlot.

Crossing the Bosporus to Asia Minor, she had survived. She did not care to remember the means by which she survived. Of all of them, the least dishonorable was theft.

She let herself be used, and she could be very useful. She found her way to the Byzantine general Michael Paleologos, who wanted to take Constantinople back from the Franks.

Her help had been important to Michael, and he had rewarded her after he reconquered the Polis and made himself its Basileus by keeping her as his favorite for a time. And she had rejoiced to see Constantinople liberated from the barbarians, even though no one she loved was left alive in it.

Then Michael had made her leave the one place she loved, sending her to Manfred in Italy.

And now, just when she had begun to lose the feeling of not belonging anywhere, just when she felt she had found safe harbor with Manfred, she was cut loose again.

She felt the tears coming, and fought them. She turned her mind away from the questions that plagued her and thought about her packing.

Saint Simon should go into the chest next.

In the center, where clothing above and below would protect him.

She went to the table by the window, where the small icon stood between two candles in tall brass candlesticks. She picked up the saint and reverently kissed his forehead, then held the icon out at arm's length to look at it. The eyes dominated the portrait, transfixing her with a blue stare.

She had painted it herself a few years before, copying another, larger icon that belonged to the Basileus Michael. Simon's cheeks were hollow, his mouth a tight line, his chin sharp. His hair hung brown and lank to his shoulders, framing his face.

She had used real gold dust in the paint for the halo. Michael was generous to her, and he laughed when she told him that she spent some of the money he gave her on expensive paint for an icon. The idea of a woman who painted amused him, like the bear that danced in the Hippodrome.

Beyond the gold of the halo was the ocher of the desert and, standing lonely over the saint's right shoulder, the pillar on which he had lived in penance for fifteen years, the pillar that had given him his name—Simon Stylites.

Why do I reverence this saint? Because he knew how to endure alone, and that is what is most important.

Rest well, dear saint, she prayed as she lowered the icon into the cedar chest. She closed the gilded wooden doors that protected the painting, breaking the grip of Simon's staring blue eyes.

She next opened a small box of dark, polished wood, its lid inlaid with bits of mother-of-pearl forming a bird with swirling wings. A dozen small porcelain jars lay in velvet-lined recesses shaped to hold them. Each jar was ornamented with the same floral pattern in a different color, each color that of the powdered pigment the tightly corked jar contained. Take a pinch of the powder, add water and the clear liquid from a raw egg, and you had a jewel-bright paint. Wrapped in linen at one end of the box were her quill pens, brushes, and charcoal sticks.

As always, the sight of her materials made her want to stop what she was doing and paint. She closed the lid gently, stroking its cover, remembering the merchant from Soldaia in the Crimea who had sold her the box outside the Church of Saint John in Stoudion, telling her it came from a land far to the east called Cathay.

The Cathayans must be as civilized as we are to make such a thing, she thought as she put the box in her chest.

This blond Saracen—this Mameluke—whom she had seen briefly and would meet again tomorrow, would not be a civilized man. He was both Turk and Frank—barbarity coupled with barbarity.

"Kriste eleison!" she whispered. "Christ have mercy." Until this moment she had been able to stave off her fear of the danger she was going into. Now it struck her full force, leaving her paralyzed over her traveling chest, her trembling hand still resting on her box of paints as if it were a talisman that could protect her.

She was going among the worst enemies her people had on earth, more to be feared than the Saracens—the Latin Christians of the West. The floor seemed to shake under her, and her body went cold and then hot as she thought of what she must face. If they found out that she was a woman of Constantinople, they would tear the flesh from her bones.

A woman of Constantinople helping a Saracen to plot against the pope!

Fear was like a cold, black ocean, and she was drowning in it. She dared not even let herself imagine the horrors, the torments that would end her life if those people in Orvieto found her out.

She did not have to go through with it. Once she and Lorenzo and this David—this Mameluke—were on the road, she could slip away. Manfred had said they would be carrying jewels. Perhaps she could take some, use them to buy passage for herself.

Passage to where?

There was no place in the world she belonged but Constantinople. And her place in the Polis was dependent on the basileus, Michael. If she angered Manfred, she could not dare go back to Michael.

To be forever exiled from Constantinople would be a living death.

In her mind she saw the Polis, glowing golden at the edge of the sea. She saw the great gray walls that had protected Constantinople against barbarian invaders from East and West for a thousand years.

She saw the gorgeous pink marble of the Blachernae Palace of the Basileus, the statue of Justinian astride his horse, his hand raised toward the East, the great dome of Hagia Sophia, her namesake saint, that seemed to float over the city, held in place by an army of angels. She heard the roar of the crowd watching chariots race in the Hippodrome and the cries of the merchants from their shops along the arcaded Mese. The Polis was the hub of the world, the fulfillment of all desires.

The vision sent strength and purpose surging through her body, and she straightened up, took her hand from the paint box, and began moving around the room again, collecting her possessions.

She would go with Lorenzo and the Mameluke and do, as she had always done, whatever was necessary. She would see this thing through. With the help of God, she might prevail.

And after that?

What future for a woman as alone as Sophia Karaiannides?

She shrugged. Time enough to think about the future after she had been to Orvieto and lived through it.

Of one thing she was already sure. She would not come back to Manfred.

She went back to her table. From a reading stand at its side she picked up her leather-bound book of parchment sheets and opened it to a page marked by a ribbon. She studied the portrait of Manfred she had begun only two days before. Most of it was still rough charcoal strokes, but she had colored his beard in a mixture of yellow and white paints, because it was the most important color and she wanted to get it down first so it could control her choice of the other colors. The eyes would be last, because when she painted in the eyes the picture would, in a sense, come to life.

Even with the eyes blank the portrait seemed to smile at her, and she felt a ripple of remembered pleasure. Grief followed almost at once.

Shall I try to finish this tonight and give it to him as a parting gift?

After a moment's thought her fingers clawed at the parchment and tore it free of the stitches that held it in the book. She rolled it up and held an end to a candle flame.

V

KEEPING HIS FACE SEVERE, SIMON DE GOBIGNON WALKED SLOWLY past the six knights lined up on the wharf. The men's faces were scarlet and glistening with sweat under their conical steel helmets. Simon felt rivulets running down his own back, under his padded cotton undershirt, mail hauberk, and surcoat.

Gulls screamed overhead, and the smell of the salt sea and of rotting fish hung heavy in the warm air.

Venice in July, Simon thought, was no place to be dressed in full battle gear.

The two banners held by men-at-arms at the end of the line hung limply: the royal standard of France, gold fleurs-de-lis on an azure ground, and that of Gobignon, gold crowns on purple.

Simon reproached himself. He had brought his company down to the waterfront too early, as soon as he had word that the galley bearing the Tartar ambassadors from Cyprus was in the harbor. It was there, sure enough; he could see it, a long, dark shape a few hundred feet from shore. But it rode at anchor while officials of the Most Serene Republic inspected it for diseases and registered its cargo, a task that had already taken hours while Simon and his men sweltered onshore.

Behind the knights stood a lance of archers, forty men in four rows. They were talking and laughing among themselves in the Venetian dialect, which Simon could barely understand. While growing up he had learned the speech of Sicily, but that was nearly a different language.

The crossbowmen should not be chattering, Simon thought. It was unmilitary. Besides, it irritated him and added to the tension of this endless waiting.

He took a step back and shouted, "Silencio!" The archers looked up, and he saw more surprise and annoyance than respect in their faces. Some eyed him expectantly, as if they thought him about to make a speech. He glared at the archers for what he felt was a suitable interval, then turned away and walked out to the edge of the jetty, his thumbs hooked in his sword belt. He ignored the muttering that arose the moment he turned his back.

"Scusi, Your Signory," said a rasping voice at his elbow. Simon turned.

Andrea Sordello, capitano of the archers, smiled broadly at him, revealing a gap where one of his eye teeth should have been. The bridge of his nose was smashed flat.

"What is it, Sordello?" The capitano had met him in Venice with a letter of recommendation from Count Charles d'Anjou, brother of King Louis of France, but a not-quite-hidden insolence in the manner of this bravo made Simon uneasy.

"If Your Signory wishes to command the crossbowmen, perhaps it would be better to transmit your orders through me. The men do not understand why you silenced them just now. They are not used to being told to stand like statues for no reason."

And you would like to make yourself popular with them by disputing my order, would you not?

"Tell them they have entered the service of the kingdom of France," he told Sordello. "It is customary for French soldiers to maintain a military bearing and discipline."

"Forgive me, Your Signory, but that may offend them."

"It is not my duty to tell them what they want to hear but what they *must* hear," said Simon. *Rather well put,* he thought to himself.

"Sì, Your Signory." Sordello walked away. He had a slight limp, Simon noticed. The man had certainly been battered. Even so, Uncle Charles's letter said he was a fine troubadour. Or trovatore, as they called them in Italy.

"Monseigneur!" A shout broke in on his thoughts. Alain de Pirenne, his closest friend among the six Gobignon knights he had brought with him, was pointing out at the harbor. The two rows of oars on either side of the long-delayed galley were in motion. Even at this distance Simon could hear the drumbeat and the overseer calling count. Simon had heard songs comparing the oars of galleys to the wings of birds, and he could see the resemblance as the rows of oars, looking delicate as feathers from this distance, rose and fell over the water in unison.

"Thank heaven," said Simon.

"Indeed," said Alain. "I am starting to feel more like a baked pigeon than a man."

As the galley swung in to the wharf, ropes flying through the air to make her fast to shore, Simon heard a sudden outcry behind him and jerked his head around.

"Make way for the most serene! Make way for the doge!" runners shouted. Musicians blowing oliphants, cranking hurdy-gurdies, and pounding on drums led a bright procession along the wharves. Two men in knee-length scarlet tunics stiff with gold braid held poles between which swung a huge banner. On the banner a winged lion in gold strode across a green background. Simon saw rows of gleaming helmets and naked swords held upright, followed by ranks of men in glittering brocaded robes, emerald and silver, maroon and gold. Towering over all was a huge sedan chair with a gilded roof and cloth of gold curtains, followed by a troop of men with tall spears. A crowd of men and women in bright silk tunics and satin gowns, laughing and chattering, brought up the rear.

A man in an ankle-length gown, his cap heavy with gold thread, confronted Simon. He was, Simon recalled, a camerlengo who had been present two weeks before when he had his brief audience with the doge and presented his charter from King Louis.

"Count, your troops are occupying the place needed by the doge, that he may properly greet our guests. Move them, if you please." The "if you please" was uttered in a tone so perfunctory as to be almost insulting. Simon's face burned and his muscles tensed, but when the ruler of Venice demanded that he give way, he was in no position to quarrel. He bowed curtly and turned to order his men to vacate the wharf.

And so, after waiting for hours, Simon suddenly found himself watching the arrival of the ambassadors from behind ranks of Venetian archers far more smartly turned out than his own mercenaries.

Why, Simon wondered, had the doge not made a place for him in this welcoming ceremony? The slight made him feel angry at himself as much as at the doge.

It is me. Uncle Charles should have sent an older man, more able to command respect.

First to come down the boarding ramp of the galley from Cyprus was a friar in a brown robe with a white cord wrapped around his waist. The crown of his scalp was shaved, and his beard was long and white. He threw himself on the ground and kissed it with a loud smacking sound. He rose and bowed to the doge's sedan chair.

The doge of Venice, Rainerio Zeno, emerged through curtains held for him by two equerries in purple. Zeno was a very old, toothless man whose black eyes glittered like a raven's. His bald head was covered by a white cap bordered with pearls. His gold-embroidered mantle looked stiff and hard as the shell of a beetle. Pages stood on either side of him, and he leaned heavily on their shoulders, using them as crutches. The friar bent and kissed Zeno's ring.

Simon could not hear what the doge and the friar said to each other. The friar gestured toward the ship. Armed men—Simon counted ten of them—tramped down the boarding ramp and formed two lines leading to the doge. They were short and swarthy, wearing red and black breastplates of lacquered leather and round steel helmets polished to a dazzling finish, topped with spikes. Bows were slung crosswise over their shoulders, and long, curved swords hung from their belts. Were these Tartars, he wondered.

Their swords looked very much like the one Simon wore. Simon's was an Egyptian scimitar, one of his most precious possessions, not because of its jeweled hilt—a pearl set just behind the guard, a ruby at the end of the hilt, and a row of smaller precious stones all along the grip—but because of the one who had given it to him. And yet, much as he prized it, the scimitar hurt him each time he looked at it, reminding him of his darkest secret, a secret known to only three living people. Simon's whole life, the scimitar reminded him, was built on a lie.

And he had accepted this mission, in part, to expiate the shame he felt when he remembered that.

Now Simon, feeling very much out of his depth, touched the hilt of his scimitar for reassurance. But as he recalled that the sword had once belonged to a Saracen ruler, his heart leapt in fear.

One never knows when or how the Saracens may strike, Count Charles d'Anjou—Uncle Charles—had warned him. *The arrow from ambush . . . the dagger that cuts the throat of a sleeping victim . . . poison. When they cannot kill they try to corrupt, with gold and lies. And they have allies in Italy—the Pope's enemy, Manfred von Hohenstaufen, and his supporters, the Ghibellini. You must be on guard every moment.*

Simon's eyes swept the row of stone palaces that overlooked this part of the waterfront, their battlements offering hundreds of fine hiding places for killers. An enemy had only to gain surreptitious entrance to one of those great houses—not hard to do when everyone's attention was turned toward the galley bringing the Tartars.

What should I do? The doge's men-at-arms outnumber mine, and look to be better soldiers. And it seems the Tartars have brought their own warriors. Perhaps I am not needed now.

The thought brought him momentary relief. But then Simon realized that he was yielding to the temptation that had assailed him throughout his life, the urge to conceal himself.

But did I not undertake this task to uphold my family's good name and my right to bear it? And besides, it is not only my dignity that must be upheld here, but the honor of King Louis. If anything happens to the Tartars now that they are on Christian soil, I will have failed my king.

Simon was about to push forward to demand room for his men when the friar who had just disembarked raised his arm. Simon's gaze followed the direction of the gesture, and came to rest at the head of the boarding ramp.

There stood two of the strangest-looking men Simon had ever seen. Their faces were the deep brown of well-tanned leather. The eyebrows were little black banners flying above black, slitted eyes that peered out over the battlements of jutting cheekbones. Their mustaches were thin and hung down in long strands below small chins adorned with sparse beards. One man's beard was white, the other's black. But even the black-bearded man was not young; there were deep creases in his face. Both men wore cylindrical caps, each topped with a polished, spherical red stone. Their ankle-length robes were of maroon silk, brocaded with gold thread, and they wore short jackets with flowing sleeves. From the neck of each man hung a rectangular tablet on a gold chain.

Simon's wonder turned to fear as he realized what perfect targets the Tartar ambassadors were making of themselves.

He threw his weight against the men and women in front of him, forcing his way through the crowd—and found himself facing one of the doge's archers. The man raised his crossbow threateningly, but Simon saw immediately that it was not loaded. Fine protection for the emissaries.

"De Pirenne! De Puys!" Simon called to the two French knights nearest him. "Follow me." He turned back to the Venetian crossbowman and shouted, "Stand aside!" in his loudest voice. "I am the Count de Gobignon."

As he had hoped, the sound of his command carried to Doge
Zeno, whose face, wrinkled as a yellow raisin, turned in Simon's
direction.

"Serenity!" Simon called, using the customary form of address
for the doge. "It is my duty to guard these ambassadors."

Sordello, at Simon's elbow, said in a low voice, "You are a great
lord in your own land, Your Signory, but it would be best if you
did not arouse the wrath of the doge of Venice."

"Be still," Simon snapped.

Helmeted archers moved in on Simon from all sides, but Simon
saw the doge give an abrupt hand signal to their capitano. At a
shouted order from the capitano, the men-at-arms fell back, letting
Simon through.

"Why do you disturb our ceremonies, young count?" The doge's
voice was a hoarse whisper. He smiled faintly, but his eyes were
cold as winter. Simon felt painfully embarrassed. The ruler of the
mightiest city on the Middle Sea was, after all, as puissant as any
king on earth.

Simon fell to one knee before the doge. "Forgive me, Serenity.
I only wish to aid you in protecting the emissaries from Tartary, as
my king has commanded me." His knees trembled, and he felt as
if his heart were hammering hard enough to break his ribs.

The smile faded and the aged eyes grew icier. "Does the Frankish count think Venice too feeble to protect her distinguished visitors?"

"Not at all, Serenity," said Simon hastily. "Only let me add my
strength to yours."

"Say no more," said the doge in a voice as sharp as a dagger.

By now the two Tartars had descended the ramp and were standing before the doge. For a moment Simon's eyes met those of the
white-bearded Tartar, and he felt a new, inexplicable, and powerful
fear. He took a step backward, almost as if he had been struck a
physical blow, and he gripped his sword hilt for reassurance.

The Tartar turned his gaze to the doge, and Simon's fear faded,
leaving him to wonder what there was in this little brown-skinned
man to inspire it. What he had seen in those eyes? A hardness, a
gaze as empty of concern for Simon de Gobignon as the cloudless
blue sky overhead.

The friar said, "Serenity, this is John Chagan Noyon," indicat-
ing the older Tartar. "A noyon among the Tartars is equal in rank
to a prince in our lands. The Khan Hulagu sends you a prince to

show how earnestly he wishes to ally himself with Christendom to destroy our mutual enemies, the Muslims. This other gentleman is Philip Uzbek Baghadur. 'Baghadur' means valiant, and he is a tuman-bashi, a commander of ten thousand. He holds high place in the councils of Hulagu Khan.'' Each Tartar clasped his hands before him and bowed low to the doge as his name was spoken.

''How is it that they have Christian names?'' asked the doge.

The Franciscan friar smiled. ''John Chagan comes of an old Christian family, formerly subject to the great Christian King of Asia, Prester John. And Philip Uzbek was baptized in his youth by the Bishop of Karakorum.''

The doge waved his bony hands, making his heavy garments rustle. ''Christian Tartars! Prester John! The Bishop of *Karakorum*? This is too much for an old man to grasp all at once. But surely I can learn much from you and these noble gentlemen that will be good for Venice. Tell them that I invite them to bear me company to my palace, where we will dine together tonight and I will learn more of the marvels of the empire of Tartary.''

Simon knew that the doge's palace was more than half a mile down the avenue along this bank of the Grand Canal, and the prospect of the ambassadors parading that distance alarmed him again. His fear of disaster came back full force, driving him once again, against all courtesy, to speak out.

''Serenity! I beg the privilege of joining forces with you to escort the ambassadors to your palace.''

Anger blazed in the gaze the doge turned upon him this time. ''Young man, if you speak out of turn once more, I will have you thrown into the canal.''

Simon had no doubt that the doge would enjoy making good on his threat. But would the ruler of Venice allow an undignified scuffle on the waterfront in the presence of two ambassadors? Simon doubted it, and decided to stand his ground.

''Forgive me, Serenity,'' he said, inclining his head. ''It is my concern for these precious lives that urges me to speak out.''

The doge took a deep breath. Then his small mouth twitched in a smile.

''Very well, Count. You may follow after us.''

While the doge presented the assembled Venetian dignitaries to the Tartars, Simon ordered Henri de Puys and Alain de Pirenne to draw up the knights and Sordello to form up the archers and be ready to follow the ambassadors' train.

Bearers brought a sedan chair for the Tartars, who climbed into it with bows and smiles. To Simon's distress, the conveyance was open, naturally enough, since the Tartars would want to see Venice and the Venetians would want to see them. But it meant still more danger.

The Franciscan friar came over and put his hand on Simon's arm. "You are very brave, young man, to speak up to the ruler of Venice as you did. And who might you be?"

Simon introduced himself, and the friar bowed and addressed him in French. "How good to speak the language of my homeland again. I am Mathieu d'Alcon of the Little Brothers of San Francesco, and I was born near Limoges, which is not far from your estate, Count. Of course, no place in France is far from Gobignon lands." His broad smile told Simon the remark was meant in friendly jest. "It was our good King Louis who sent me to the Tartars years ago. I am glad we will be in French hands after we leave Venice." He gave Simon's arm a squeeze and returned to the doge's procession.

Simon had begun to think the whole world had turned against him, and Friar Mathieu's friendly words cheered him immensely. He watched the white-bearded friar with a warm feeling as he shook his head at the attendants who held a sedan chair for him. As befitted a good Franciscan, sworn to poverty and dedicated to simplicity, the friar would allow no one to carry him but insisted on walking on his own sandaled feet behind the Tartars' chair.

Simon and his men followed the last contingent of the doge's foot soldiers along the waterfront. Ahead, a stone bridge arched over one of the many Venetian canals.

The procession was moving slowly now. After crossing the bridge, Simon saw the ambassadors' sedan chair swing around a corner, and his pulse quickened because those he was to protect were out of his sight.

He wanted to hurry to the corner, but the street narrowed here, with the windowless white ground floor of a palazzo on one side and an iron railing on the other. There was no room to bypass those ahead. Simon hurried his pace until he was all but treading on the leather-shod heels of the spearman in front of him.

He turned the corner into the small square in front of the doge's palace. He saw the doge's sedan chair and that of the Tartars pass through the gateway between the palace and the great basilica of San Marco.

Then he stopped short, feeling as if he had crashed headfirst into a wall. The tall gates leading into the palace swung shut, and facing him was a triple line of men-at-arms of the Most Serene Republic, in green and gold tunics and armed with long spears.

"Mère de Dieu!" he whispered.

He could not force his way into the palace. If he even tried, he would only look ridiculous. Indeed, he doubted that his men would fight. The ill-disciplined mercenaries were Venetians, too, and why would they obey the command of a French seigneur, who had hired them only yesterday, to fight their own countrymen?

"It appears we are not welcome at the palace, Your Signory," said a voice at his side. Simon turned and glared at Sordello, whose weatherbeaten face seemed to mask amusement.

Simon tried to think of a way to rescue his dignity. "Find the leader of the palace guards and tell him I want to speak to him."

Sordello shrugged. "As you wish, Your Signory."

Alain de Pirenne, his gauntleted fist clenched on the hilt of his sword, blustered out, "Damned Italian discourtesy! It would serve them right if somebody did slip a dagger into those Tartars while we stand out here."

God forbid! thought Simon.

Sordello came back with a Venetian man-at-arms, who touched the brim of his polished kettle-helmet respectfully.

"This sergente has a message for you from His Serenity, the doge, Your Signory."

"Let him tell it."

Simon's command of the Venetian dialect was not good enough to follow what the man in the kettle-helmet said, and to make it harder, he spoke in what appeared to be an embarrassed mumble.

"What did he say, Sordello?"

"Forgive me, Your Signory," said Sordello. "The message may offend you. I will repeat it only if you wish it."

"What did he say?" said Simon again in a tight voice.

"The doge says you are to wait in quarters of your own choosing until the ambassadors from Tartary are ready to travel. At that time he will place them in your keeping. Until then you are to trouble him no more, unless you are a very good swimmer."

Simon felt rage boil up within him. He clenched his fists and fought it down.

"Tell him I thank His Serenity for his courtesy and will forever honor him for it."

Sordello nodded, and there was a look of respect in his craggy face.

As Sordello repeated Simon's words to the sergente of the doge's guards, Simon wheeled and strode back the way he had come, to stare out to sea. Tears of frustrated fury burned his eyes. He could feel hot blood beating in his temples. The doge had treated him like a small boy. That old gargoyle had insulted him, had insulted the house of Gobignon, had insulted King Louis.

And there was nothing Simon could do about it. He felt furious and miserable. A failure, at the very start of his task.

VI

CRUSHED, SIMON DECIDED THAT AT LEAST HE WOULD QUARTER his French knights and the Venetian archers as near to the doge's palace as possible. The doge alone would be protecting the Tartars for the time being, and Simon had no choice about it.

With Sordello's help he found lodgings for his men at the outrageous price of two deniers a night per man—not all the thieves were on the highways—at the nearest inn to the Piazza San Marco, just a short distance down a side street. How much of what he paid the innkeeper, he wondered, would end up in Sordello's purse?

Then, accompanied by Alain de Pirenne, he walked back to the entrance gate to the doge's palace, a long three-story building that stretched from the waterfront to the basilica. He sent a message in by way of a guard, asking Friar Mathieu to meet him in the piazza. The kindly Franciscan was, he suspected, the most important person in the Tartars' entourage.

Simon and Alain had taken off their mail and were more comfortably dressed in silk tunics, short capes, and velvet caps. Each still wore his weapons belt, with longsword hung on the left and dagger on the right. The leather heels of their point-toed boots rang on the stones of the piazza as they paced, waiting to see if Friar Mathieu would come out.

Alain was still indignant.

"They have no idea who you are, Simon. Why, you could take this whole city and set it in one corner of the Gobignon domain and it would never be noticed." Normally ruddy, Alain was even redder with anger. His blond mustache bristled.

As much as Paris goes unnoticed in the midst of the Île de France, Simon thought with a smile.

Now that his armor was off and an hour or more had passed, Simon felt more at ease and was inclined to accept the situation. After all, if he could not get into the doge's palace, he might reasonably hope that neither could anyone who would want to harm the Tartars.

"It is wealth and ships that make this city great, Alain, not its size."

"That is all these Venetians care about—money." Like any proper knight, Alain despised money and those who loved it. In the course of learning to manage his estate, Simon had acquired more respect for money.

"Even Paris has no beauty to rival this," said Simon, feeling a shade disloyal even as he said so. "Look at those horses." He pointed to the façade above the central doorway of the cathedral of San Marco, where four gilded bronze horses pranced, so proud and energetic as to seem almost in motion.

Alain whistled in appreciation. "What wizard wrought them, I wonder."

Simon, who had been asking questions in the week they had been there, said, "They come from Constantinople. About sixty years ago the Venetians paid an army of French crusaders—our forefathers—to turn aside from the Holy Land and conquer Constantinople instead. The Venetians took those horses and set them here to proclaim their triumph."

"Diverting a crusade is surely a great sin," said Alain. "And theft is theft. But none of my forefathers had anything to do with the foul deed you tell of."

"No, nor mine," said Simon. "The French knights who conquered Constantinople were our forefathers only in a manner of speaking."

But my predecessor, Count Amalric de Gobignon, did fouler things by far. As Alain well knows, though he is too good a friend to mention it.

"Still, the good taste of the Venetians is admirable," Simon said aloud, still gazing at the horses.

"For all I know, this could be the richest city in the world," said Alain, missing the point. "But what matter, Simon, if its riches are stolen goods?"

"Venice is by no means the richest city in the world, Messire," someone beside them said.

Startled, Simon turned to see Friar Mathieu, who had fallen into step with them, his eyes warm and friendly. Simon wanted to throw his arms around the old man and hug him.

"There are cities in the Far East so big and so rich they make Venice look like a fishing village," Friar Mathieu went on, his long white beard blowing gently in the breeze from the waterfront.

"People love to tell wild stories about the East," said Alain skeptically. "I've heard of cities of solid gold, birds as big as an elephant, and so on and on."

But this man has been there! Simon wanted to shout. Much though he liked Alain, Simon was discovering in his friend a narrowness that made him a frustrating traveling companion. With Alain here, the conversation with Friar Mathieu would plod, and Simon wanted it to gallop.

"Sire Alain," he said, "I fear our hired men-at-arms may get into trouble drinking, fighting, and wenching unless someone keeps a sharp eye on them. Will you see to them, please?"

De Pirenne held up a broad hand. "I will slap them down for you, if need be, Monseigneur." Now that a third party was present, he addressed Simon formally.

"Travel is said to open a man's mind," said Friar Mathieu when de Pirenne was gone. "But some minds are like country châteaus. Let anything strange approach, and the doors and windows slam shut."

He took Simon's arm and steered him over the flagstones of the piazza toward the cathedral. The many-columned façade of pink, white, and green marble, sculptures, and mosaics filling the spaces between them took Simon's breath away. There was an opulence to the five great domes that seemed to Simon to speak of the storied wealth of the East. They were so different from the pointed spires of the cathedrals newly built in France.

"I am very grateful to you, Simon, for trying so hard to protect us today," Friar Mathieu said. "The doge's discourtesy to you was the worst kind of rudeness, the rudeness of one who thinks himself more refined than all others.''

Simon felt better, but he wondered if the friar was speaking so only out of kindness to him.

''It is good of you to reassure me,'' he said, ''but the doge seems to be guarding the ambassadors well enough.''

''All show,'' said Friar Mathieu. ''The Venetians are not alert enough. The doge has no idea that we are in any danger. Nor does he seem to care. I believe he has not decided whether he has anything to gain from an alliance between Christians and Tartars. After all, the Venetians trade quite happily with the Muslims these days.''

Simon was shocked. ''Is that not a sin?''

''Against God, perhaps, but not against profit. And the common heading on your Venetian merchant's account book is 'For God and Profit.' Young Seigneur de Gobignon, you do not know how happy I am to talk to a Frenchman again after so many years.''

''How long have you been among the Tartars, Friar Mathieu?''

The old Franciscan sighed. ''Long enough to learn the Eastern peoples' way of counting the years in twelve-year cycles. They give each year the name of a certain animal.''

''A strange system.''

''A sensible system. It is easier to remember beasts than numbers. Let me see, this year, Anno Domini 1263, they call the Year of the Sheep, and when I first entered the camp of Hulagu Khan the Tartars told me it was the Year of the Dragon. From Dragon to Sheep there are''—he counted on his fingers while muttering the names of beasts under his breath—''seven animals. So, seven years since our good King Louis sent me to bear his messages to the Tartars.''

''Then you went in 1256?''

''Anno Domini 1256. That is right.''

Simon wanted very much to know more about life among the Tartars. But he and the old friar could have long talks on the road to Orvieto. For now there were more pressing questions.

Just as he was about to speak, the friar pointed to the gateway between the basilica and the doge's palace. ''There go the Armenians.''

Simon saw six of the swarthy men crossing the piazza in a line. Short-statured though they were, there was a swagger in the way they walked. They had doffed their leather armor and wore tunics of white silk with billowing red trousers over short black boots.

Their tunics were cinched at the waist with black leather belts, and in each belt was thrust a curving saber in a jeweled scabbard. Their bows were slung across their backs, along with black leather quivers.

"Four of them stayed behind to guard the Tartars," Friar Mathieu said.

Simon had been wondering just how his knights and archers would share with the Armenian guards the responsibility of protecting the Tartars.

"Why did the ambassadors bring Armenians, and not their own Tartar warriors?" he asked Friar Mathieu.

"Because the Armenians are Christians and are more like Europeans than themselves. The Armenians are allies, not subjects of the Tartars. These ten who travel with us are great men among the Armenian people. One of them, Hethum, is in line to be King of Armenia some day. One feels safer, traveling with such men."

Simon watched the half-dozen Armenians disappear down a narrow side street leading off the piazza. He felt a twinge of worry, seeing that they were heading toward the street in which his own men were quartered. He wanted to follow after the men from the East, but he did not want to interrupt his conversation with Friar Mathieu. Feeling pulled in two directions, he held himself to the friar's slow, thoughtful pace as they approached the cathedral.

"Even some Tartars are Christians, I have heard," Simon said.

"There are many religions among the Tartars." They had reached the front of San Marco, and Friar Mathieu, still holding Simon's arm, wheeled them around and started them walking back toward the doge's palace. "Hulagu Khan's wife, the Khatun, is a Christian, although he is a pagan. But what all Tartars really worship is strength. In their own language they call themselves 'Mongols,' which means strong." Simon looked at the friar and saw a faraway, awe-struck look in those old eyes. "One wonders why God created them. To punish us for our sins? Or to rule the world and to bring order to all mankind?"

"Rule the world?" said Simon. He thought about the two slit-eyed men in silk robes he had seen disembarking from the galley a few hours before. He remembered the look the older Tartar had given him, so unfeeling, as if looking down upon him from a vast distance.

"They think it is their destiny to rule the world," said Friar Mathieu. "And it is not a foolish dream. They have already conquered much of it. You might sneer at me as your skeptical knight did, Monseigneur, if I told you how vast the Tartar empire is. Take France, England, and the Holy Roman Empire together, and they would be swallowed up in the lands ruled by the Tartars.''

''Please call me Simon, Father, if you will. It embarrasses me to be addressed as monseigneur by one such as you.''

Friar Mathieu patted Simon's hand. ''Very well, Simon. That is kindly spoken. It will be good for us to be friends, because we have a very difficult and doubtful mission.''

''Why doubtful?''

''We cannot be sure we are doing the right thing. These two men, John and Philip, command great armies in the Tartar empire. Watch them, Simon. Notice how they observe fortifications and weapons. The same monks who made Christians of them also taught them how to write. Many times at day's end in Syria and on Cyprus I have seen them talking together, making notes, drawing maps. Whether they form this alliance or not, they will have much useful knowledge to bring back to their khan.''

Then might it not be better for all of us if I fail to protect the Tartars, and some enemy of Christendom succeeds in killing them?

Simon felt an aching tightness in his forehead. He desperately wanted the alliance to succeed, and thereby show the nobility of France that neither he nor his family any longer deserved their scorn. If the alliance failed, he failed, and the house of Gobignon would sink deeper into dishonor.

Let others worry, he decided, about whether it was right or wrong to protect the Tartars.

''Monseigneur!''

There was urgency in the voice that hailed Simon from across the square, and a feeling of dread came over him. He turned to see his equerry, Thierry d'Hauteville, his wavy black hair uncovered, running across the piazza.

''They are fighting, Monseigneur!'' Thierry panted. ''Our Venetian archers and those men from Tartary. You'd best come at once.''

''Jesus, save us!'' Simon heard Friar Mathieu whisper beside him.

Staring into Thierry's anxious eyes, Simon felt himself getting angry. Six knights he had brought with him. Any knight worthy of his spurs should be able to stop any pack of commoners from fighting. And if they could not, he thought with a sudden shift from anger to anxiety, what more could he do?

There was no time to think. "Father, will you come, please?" he said to Mathieu, and without waiting for a reply struck Thierry on the shoulder and began to run with him.

"I follow, as quickly as I can, my son," he heard from behind him.

"Could you not stop them?" he demanded of Thierry as they headed down a narrow cobblestoned street at a dead run.

Dread made his legs heavy. De Puys, a veteran of the last crusade, de Pirenne, a strong and well-trained knight—*they* had sent for *him*. For Simon de Gobignon, twenty years of age, who had never in his life been in a battle.

Breath of God, what did they expect of him?

"There was nothing we could do without killing the Tartars' bodyguard," said Thierry. "You will see how it is when you get there."

The inn was a stone building with houses on either side. The lower half of the divided door was shut, but the upper half was open, and Simon heard shouts from within. Thierry, ahead of him, yanked the door open for him.

It took his eyes a moment to adjust to the darkness of the large room. Shadowy figures jostled him as he pushed his way through. A little light came from the grilled windows and from a single huge yellow candle burning in a candlestick on a table. The room reeked of sweaty bodies and old wine.

"Make way for Monseigneur le Comte!" Thierry called uselessly as the Venetian mercenaries jabbered angrily in Italian.

Simon pushed his way into the corner of the room lit by the candle and found himself facing a scowling, dark-skinned man pointing a gleaming sword at him. Five of the Armenians, sabers out, had formed a protective ring.

Within the ring, the sixth Armenian had a man bent forward over a table. The man's arms flailed feebly and his eyes bulged. Even in the poor light Simon could see that his face, turned on its side toward him, was purple. The Armenian was holding his bow behind the man's neck and was turning it slowly. Now Simon saw the string cutting into the neck.

It hurt Simon to look at what was happening. He felt his own breath cut off, his heart pounding as if he were laboring for air. He wanted to turn away and knew he could not. He must somehow stop this before that Venetian died.

"Blood of God!" he whispered. He recognized the darkened, distorted face.

Sordello.

All around Simon the Venetians were edging closer to the Armenians, their daggers gleaming in the candlelight. But none of the foot soldiers wanted to be the first to brave those sabers.

That meant, Simon thought, heart pounding, that he would have to face them.

Where the devil are my knights?

Looking to the right and left Simon saw Alain, Henri de Puys, and the four others, swords out but—like himself—unarmored, standing irresolutely between the Venetians and the Armenians. Against one wall he saw a huddle of women, their bare bosoms gleaming in the dim light. Standing protectively in front of the women was a man Simon recognized as the innkeeper. For the price Simon was paying, why could not this man keep order in his own house?

"Aha, now we have the stinking figlii di cagne!" a man behind Simon cried. Simon turned and saw a crossbow leveled at shoulder height. He had ordered that the Venetians' weapons be kept under lock and key. Evidently someone had broken them out. Once the rest of the Venetians armed themselves with their bows, the Armenians would be slaughtered.

Simon's body grew hot with anger. He would like to kill the fool who helped the Venetians to their arms.

But the Armenians had their bows, too, and one by one they started to unsling them. Simon heard the ominous squeaking as the Venetians wound back their crossbow strings. The Armenians would never be able to get their arrows nocked and their bows drawn before the crossbow bolts began to fly.

Simon's actions followed instantly on his thoughts. "Cessi!" he shouted, hoping the Venetians would understand him.

Now all eyes were turned toward him. The muscles of his belly tightened as he cast about in his mind for the right thing to do.

The hands of the Venetians hesitated on their crossbows as they recognized their master.

"De Pirenne, de Puys, the rest of you. Make our men put down their crossbows."

But just as Simon spoke, the Armenian strangling Sordello gave another turn to his bow, and the old bravo gagged and gasped.

Simon realized that if he drew his scimitar, the room would be a charnel house in moments. He approached the Armenian nearest him, spreading his hands to show their emptiness. He prayed that the man, whose bow and arrow was aimed at his chest, would not see how those outstretched hands were trembling.

In his strongest voice he said, "Hold your arrow!" hoping the man would understand his tone. As he spoke, he firmly grasped the arrow near its head and pushed it aside. His heart thudded, and he could almost feel that steel tip stabbing into his chest. And how bare was his back to the crossbow quarrels!

The Armenian took a step to the side and let Simon pass. Simon let out a deep breath of relief. As he stepped forward, the soles of his boots slid a little. The floor, he realized, must be slippery with spilled wine.

Now he was facing the man who was murdering Sordello. A vagrant thought struck Simon: *I do not like Sordello. I would not mind if the Armenian killed him. Why risk my life for him?*

Because a good seigneur is loyal to his men, the answer came at once.

He spoke commandingly but softly. "Stop. This is my man and you must not kill him. Let him go." He put his hand firmly on the forearm of the Armenian, who was a good deal shorter than he was. The man's dark brows drew together in a puzzled frown. He was studying Simon's face. Simon could feel a faint tremor in the muscles under his hand.

Any man would be frightened at a moment like this, no matter how brave, how hardened, Simon thought. But he saw that the Armenian's face was unlined, his eyes clear. His black mustache was small and fine.

He must be about my age. Maybe even younger.

Simon felt a warmth toward the young Armenian, and hoped he could win him over. But how could such a pleasant-looking fellow bring himself to strangle a man with a bowstring? Perhaps Sordello had done something truly evil.

"Come now," Simon said, giving the young man's arm a gentle shake. "Do let him go." He essayed a smile, hoping it would look friendly.

The Armenian let out a deep sigh and closed his eyes. Then he released his grip on the bow. He slapped it with one hand to make it twirl. Simon heard a faint choking sound from Sordello, and then the Italian slid to the stone floor.

A woman, her henna-dyed hair gleaming red-gold in the candle-light, rushed to the young Armenian and held his arm, talking soothingly in Italian. He stiffened at first, then smiled at her.

"Thank you," said Simon to the Armenian, shaky with relief.

He smiled and patted the dark man's free arm, feeling foolish about his simple words of gratitude. If only Friar Mathieu would get here so that he could talk to these men from the East.

A cool feeling of relief bathed Simon. So far all had gone amazingly well. But, he reminded himself, this was not over yet. He must continue to think quickly.

"De Puys, clear the Venetians out of here. Assemble them outside. Then march them away from this street altogether. And collect their crossbows and get them locked up again. You should never have let them get at those weapons. De Pirenne, you stay here and tell me what happened."

"Well, this is how it was, Monseigneur," said Alain, looking abashed. "Our men were drinking quietly, and this redheaded woman was sitting with Sordello. Then these men from Tartary came in. They made no trouble, just sat down in their own corner. But the woman, she took a fancy to that man you saw trying to kill Sordello. She served him wine and sat down with him. Sordello went over and tried to get her back. There were words. They didn't understand each other, but the meaning was clear. Sordello went for the other with a knife. And then the other man *kicked* it out of his hand—rather a surprise, that was—to Sordello, too, I think. And the next thing I know he was strangling Sordello and his companions would not let anyone stop it. Sordello had the key to the storeroom where the crossbows were kept. After the Armenian seized him, he threw it to one of the Venetians."

A typical muddle, Simon thought, like most of the cases brought to him for justice since he had become Seigneur of Gobignon. He felt disgusted with all these fools. No saying who was at fault. Most likely the damned woman. Thank the Virgin he did not have to fix blame, just put a stop to the fighting.

Sordello, who had been lying curled up on the floor, suddenly lashed out with a booted foot.

The woman screamed. As Simon stared, the young Armenian fell heavily to the wine-wet floor. Sordello sprang upon him, and a dagger flashed. He was striking at the Armenian's chest.

Simon had no time to feel the panic that flooded through him. He grabbed for Sordello's arm, too late to stop the dagger but pulling it back so that it drove upward through the muscles of the chest instead of plunging deep. The Armenian bellowed in pain. With all his strength, Simon yanked Sordello off the Armenian and threw him backward. De Pirenne caught him and held him.

Shouting in their own language and brandishing their swords, the other Armenians rushed at Sordello.

A familiar voice cried out a sentence in a strange tongue. Friar Mathieu rushed into the circle of candlelight, his white beard flying, his arms upraised. At his sudden appearance the Armenians, who were ready to make mincemeat of Sordello—and perhaps de Pirenne with him—hesitated.

Oh, thank God! The weight of struggling to control this dreadful situation was no longer Simon's alone to bear.

Friar Mathieu spoke several sentences to the Armenians. Simon could not tell from his tone whether he was scolding them or trying to placate them. There were in the room five angry men who looked to be formidable fighters, armed with swords and bows and arrows. And, Simon realized, he had just sent away all but one of his knights and all of his crossbowmen.

Simon cursed himself for letting Sordello wound the young man. *Alain said Sordello dropped a dagger. Why did I not think to look for it?*

He felt himself growing hot and cold as he realized this incident might wreck everything—for Christendom, for Louis, and for the honor of the House of Gobignon.

Now Friar Mathieu fell to his knees beside the young Armenian, whose white tunic was splashed deep scarlet with blood. He spoke comforting words to him and then turned an agonized face to Simon.

"This is Prince Hethum," said the friar. "The Tartars will be furious when they learn what has happened. This may destroy any chance of an alliance. At the very least, they will demand satisfaction."

I am to protect these emissaries, and one of my own men has stabbed a prince of Armenia.

Despair was an ache in Simon's chest.

"What sort of satisfaction?"

"I fear they will require that man's life," said Friar Mathieu sadly.

"By God's beard, I have done no wrong!" Sordello rasped. His voice was a croak.

"Be silent!" Simon snapped, his rage against himself turning to fury at Sordello. "You are a fool, but being a fool will not save you."

"Your Signory!" Sordello cried. "How could I let him take the woman from me? My honor—"

"*Your* honor!" Simon raged. "What is your wandering black-guard's honor compared to the honor of France? The woman chose him over you. Look at her."

Sordello glared at Simon, but was silent. The red-haired woman crouched over the fallen Prince Hethum, crooning softly in Italian.

And yet, Uncle Charles would not want me to sacrifice Sordello. And the Armenian did try to kill him. My knights and men-at-arms will lose all respect for me if I let the Tartars have their way with Sordello.

But if he goes unpunished, if the Armenian prince goes unrevenged, there will be no alliance at all.

And it would be his fault. The little honor that was left to the House of Gobignon would be lost.

A wave of anger at himself swept over him. Had he dedicated himself to the alliance only so that he might free himself from the agony of his guilty secret and his house from dishonor? He thought of King Louis and how pure was his desire to win back for Christendom the places where Christ had lived. How impure were Simon's own motives!

As long as he put his own needs first, he would continue to deserve the burdens of guilt and shame.

VII

In the Name of God, the Beneficent, the Merciful.
All praise be to God, Lord of the Worlds.
Master of the Day of Judgment.

Daoud stood perfectly still, looking into the violet sky, reciting in his mind the salat, the prayer required of a Muslim five times daily. This was Mughrab, the moment when the last light of sunset had drained away. An evening breeze cooled his face, welcome after a day of traveling under the summer sky of Italy. Oriented by a bright crescent moon just rising, he faced southeast, toward Mecca. His back was to the stone wall of the inn called the Capo di Bue, the Ox's Head, where he and Sophia and Celino had decided to spend the night. On the other side of the wall, loud voices contended for attention, the sound of travelers in the common room settling down to supper.

Praying in the dusk reminded Daoud that he was alone. What would it be like now in El Kahira, the Guarded One? He would be praying with hundreds of fellow Muslimin, standing shoulder to shoulder, all equal before God, in the Gray Mosque, all listening to the call of the blind muezzins from the minarets—"Come to the house of praise. God is Almighty. There is no god but God."—all facing the Prophet's birthplace together in holy submission. Daoud's prayer might be the only one going up to God tonight from anywhere near Rome.

All around him towered ruins. The silhouettes of broken columns rose against the darkening sky, and across the Appian Way the ragged shape of what had once been a wall. Pines stood tall and black where, according to Lorenzo, some wealthy woman of ancient Rome had her tomb.

He tried to forget his surroundings and to think only of the salat. It was hard to concentrate when he could not assume the proper positions for prayer—raise his hands, kneel, strike his forehead on the ground. He fixed his mind on the infinity of God.

"Do not try to see Him," Abu Hamid al-Din Saadi had told him. "If you see Him in your mind, you are looking at an idol."

Daoud did not try to see God, but as he prayed, a Muslim all alone in the heart of Christendom, he could not help but see Sheikh Saadi, the Sufi master who had brought him to Islam.

The face was very dark, the rich black of a cup of kaviyeh. Out of the blackness peered eyes that *saw*—saw into the very souls of his students.

Often as he sat listening to Sheikh Saadi read from the Koran, the Book to be Read, and explain its meaning, voices from the past reproached him. The voice of Father Adrian, the chaplain of their castle, rang in his mind. The quiet voice of his mother, teaching him the Lord's Prayer and the Hail Mary, whispered to him. Like thunder his father spoke of war and of what it was to be a knight.

He could escape the torment of these voices only by listening closely to the Sufi sheikh. Saadi was trying to teach him how to be good, and that was the same thing his mother and father had wanted for him. So they would not mind if he learned from Saadi.

Sheikh Saadi, wearing the white woolen robe of a Sufi, sat on a many-colored carpet of Mosul, an open copy of the Koran resting on an ornately carved lectern before him. His hand, as dark as the mahogany of the stand, caressed the page as he read aloud.

" 'Such as persevere in seeking their Lord's countenance and are regular in prayer and spend of that which We bestow upon them secretly and openly, and overcome evil with good: Theirs will be the Heavenly Home.' "

Mohammedan dogs! Daoud remembered Father Adrian in his black and white robes shouting in the chapel at Château Langmuir. *Satan is the author of that vile book they call the Koran.*

By the age of eleven Daoud had already known cruelty and evil at the hands of the Turks who had captured him, kindness with Baibars, and goodness with Sheikh Saadi. The Sufi sheikh had never made any claim, but Daoud had no doubt that he often walked and talked with God.

"Secretly and openly are we to give," the old man was saying. "God has been generous to us, and we must be generous in turn. When you are kind to a bird or a donkey, or even to an unclean animal like a pig or a dog, He loves you for it. He loves you more when you are kind to a slave or to a woman or to one of the unfortunate, like a cripple or an unbeliever."

"Daoud is both a slave and unbeliever," said Gamal ibn Nasir with a faint sneer. "Must I be kind to him?" Daoud stared at Gamal, burning with hatred, all the more because what he said was true.

Gamal was a slender, olive-skinned boy whom no one dared cross, because he was a grandson of the reigning Sultan of Egypt, Al Salih Ayub. Most of Saadi's students were boys of noble family, and Daoud knew that he was permitted to enter this circle only because all men feared and respected Baibars. And even though he studied Islam with them because it was Baibars's wish, Daoud remained fil-kharij, an outsider, because he was an unbeliever.

The boys sat in a semicircle, their rectangles of carpet spread over the blue and white tiles of the inner courtyard of the Gray Mosque, where Saadi had been teaching since long before these students were born. The old black man sat with his back to the gray stones of the western wall, the stones that gave the mosque its name. He taught in the late afternoon, when he and the boys could sit in the shade.

"God is compassion itself, Gamal," Sheikh Saadi said with a smile, "but even He may find it hard to love a mean spirit." The sultan's grandson blushed angrily, and his eyes fell.

Thinking about the compassion of God, Daoud opened his eyes wide as a startling idea occurred to him. But after the insult from Gamal his tongue felt thick in his throat and the palms of his hands went cold at the thought of speaking. He still stumbled over the Arabic tongue in which Sheikh Saadi conducted his lessons.

Saadi looked warmly upon him. "Daoud has a question?"

Daoud stared down at his hands, which seemed very large as they lay in his lap. "Yes, master." Those kindly velvet-black eyes seemed to draw speech out of him. "If God loves the compassionate, how can he look with favor upon the warrior, who wounds and kills?"

Saadi's turbaned head lifted. His grizzled beard thrust forward, and his eyes grew round and serious. He looked, Daoud thought, like a thoroughbred steed pricking up his ears to a trumpet call.

"I say to you, Daoud, and to Gamal and to all of you—the work of a warrior is a holy calling. When the Prophet Muhammad, may God bless and salute him, began to teach, he did not want the believers to be men of the sword. But the pagans beat those who went to hear him, and they would not let him teach. And so he learned that a true man of God must go forth with the Book in one hand and the sword in the other."

Daoud felt a warm pride in his chest. He was not a despicable slave. He would one day be a warrior, in a way a holy man, like Saadi, who helped spread the teachings of God.

But I am an unbeliever.

He listened for the Frankish voices in his mind crying out against the Saracens, against the devilish religion of the one they called Mahound. But the voices were silent.

A pale boy with a grave face asked, "If God made man, how can He love one who butchers His creatures?"

Sheikh Saadi raised an admonishing finger. "The Warrior of God is no butcher. He strikes with sorrow and compassion. He hates evil, but he loves his fellow men, even the one he fights against. The Warrior of God is known, not by his willingness to kill, but by his willingness to die. He is a man who would give his life for his friends."

Saadi went on to speak of other things, but Daoud's mind remained fixed on the words "Warrior of God."

Ever since the day the Saracens carried him off, he had lived without a home. He had drunk from gold cups in the palace of Baibars, had seen that a Mameluke might rise to earthly glory. But such rewards fell to only one in a thousand. For the rank and file, the life of a Mameluke was a hard one, often ending in early death.

Lately Baibars had sent him to live with the other Mameluke boys in training on the island of Raudha in the Bhar al-Nil, the river Nile. Every morning, when he woke to the rapping of the drill master's stick on the wooden wall of his sleeping shed, his first feeling was anguish. Sometimes he prayed before sleeping that he might not wake up again. Only when he journeyed twice a week, by boat and on foot, to sit at the feet of Saadi, did he feel any peace.

But what if God had chosen him to be a Mameluke? Then it was a blessed life, a holy calling, as Saadi had said. There was a world beyond this one, a place the Koran called a "Heavenly Home." All men, Christian and Muslim, believed that. As a warrior he could hope that his hardship would be turned to joy in that Heavenly Home. In that world, not one in ten thousand, but every good man, would dwell in a palace.

Absorbed in his own thoughts, he heard the soft, deep voice of Saadi as one hears the constant murmur of the windblown sand in the desert. The boys around him and the men who came and went in the Gray Mosque—all were believers. As a warrior of God he could be part of that, and not the least part. He would no longer be fil-kharij, a stranger in this world. He would be fil-dakhil, at home.

The lesson was over. The boys stood with Saadi and bowed their heads in prayer. After the prayers they bowed again to their teacher and, alone or in pairs, pattered out of the courtyard of the Gray Mosque.

When they were all gone, Daoud stood alone facing Saadi.

"What does Daoud have to say to me?"

In a rush of love for his master, Daoud threw himself to his knees and struck his forehead on Saadi's red carpet, bumping his head hard enough to be slightly stunned.

"What is it, Daoud?" Saadi's voice was a comforting rumble.

Daoud sat back and looked up. The figure of the Sufi towered over him. But Saadi bent his head, and looking into the dark face, Daoud felt as if someone huge and powerful had taken him into his arms.

"Master, I want to embrace Islam."

Daoud was mentally repeating the salat for the third time when he heard footsteps and the click of hooves coming up the road. He shut his eyes to resist the distraction.

A voice interrupted the fourth repetition. "Peace be unto you, Signore. Can you tell me if there is room at the sign of the Capo di Bue for my son and me and our donkey?"

Daoud was annoyed at having to stop his prayers, but he had to reply or call unwanted attention to himself. He opened his eyes and saw in the shadows before him a short man with a full white beard holding the reins of a donkey that breathed heavily and shifted its feet nervously on the great black paving stones of the Appian Way. A second figure, obscure in the darkness, sat on the donkey. The two seemed heavily dressed for summer. The bearded man wore a round black hat with a narrow brim, of a type Daoud had never seen before.

"It is not overly full," he said impatiently.

But the man with the black hat still stood before him. "Are you sure that we will be welcome, Signore?"

"You can pay for a place in the common bed, can you not?" said Daoud, eager to finish the prayer.

"Oh, we do not require a bed, Signore," said the old man. "We will sleep in the stable, or sit up"—he chuckled—"or even sleep standing up, as our donkey does. It is just that we cannot go farther tonight. Rome has more robbers than a dog has fleas."

Why in the name of God was the man so hesitant? Daoud, seeing no need to continue the conversation, remained silent.

The old man sighed. "Peace be to you, Signore," he said again. "Come, my son."

The man's son climbed down, and the two travelers pulled the donkey through the inn's gate. Leather packs hung from either side of the donkey, and Daoud wondered what was in them. Probably nothing of value, but robbers would attack anyone who looked vulnerable, and the old man's fear was doubtless justified.

Daoud thought of the precious stones he and Celino carried between them. He felt the cold breath of danger on the back of his neck.

Here in this inn they may all be honest men, but if they knew what wealth we had, even honest men would try to cut our throats.

He turned his mind again to his prayers. By the time he finished and turned to go through the gate leading to the courtyard, he sensed a change in the noises from within. Shrill, angry voices had replaced the cheerful murmur of general conversation.

The donkey and the boy who had ridden it huddled in the corner where the stables met the main building.

Daoud stood listening in the center of the inn yard, his hand resting lightly on the dagger at his belt. He faced the two-story main building, the dining hall at ground level, the beds that slept six or more upstairs. Access to the sleeping room was by way of a flight of outside wooden stairs leading to a platform and an upper door. The doors and the window shutters on both levels were open to let in the cool night air. Stables secured with half doors on his left, a storage shed on his right.

As Daoud strode past the old man's son, he caught a glimpse of bright black eyes reflecting the light from oil lanterns hung on wooden pegs set high on either side of the inn door.

Daoud moved to the doorway, and as he looked into the smoky, candlelit hall, his heart sank.

The crowd of men and women in the room were turned toward Lorenzo Celino. He stood against the far wall, the long blade of his sword gleaming in the candlelight, facing six naked daggers.

Beside Celino, the hound Scipio stood stiff-legged, tail whipping from side to side, fangs bared, growling softly. Fear of that dog was keeping Celino's opponents back as much as fear of his sword, thought Daoud.

The bearded old man who had spoken to Daoud was standing to Celino's left and a little behind him. Celino's eyes flicked toward Daoud for an instant, and then quickly away before anyone might notice that he had looked toward the doorway.

Daoud scanned the room for Sophia. She was standing in the shadows, almost invisible in a long, hooded cloak. No one was threatening her.

One of the men facing Celino, Daoud recognized, was the innkeeper himself. He was a huge man with broad, rounded shoulders and a shock of thick black hair cut off at the same length all the way around, so it looked like a bowl. The dagger he held was a long, murderous blade, but his big hand made it look like a toy.

"Give us the Jew," the innkeeper said to Celino. "We have no quarrel with you."

The old man was a Jew? How was it, Daoud demanded of himself, that these people had known that and he had not?

"You do have a quarrel with me," said Celino, "because I do not care to see you torment and rob this old man."

Daoud swore to himself. Was this the kind of madman Manfred had yoked him with? Sworn to the utmost secrecy, carrying a fortune in jewels, and now he brings a whole inn down around his ears by defending some dusty old man?

But does not God love the compassionate?

Give us the Jew, the innkeeper had said. Daoud knew that Christians took delight in mistreating Jews.

And I told the old man to go in there. But I did not know he was a Jew. Or that these people would harm him.

Whether Celino was a madman or not, Daoud would have to get him out of this, because he was carrying half of their supply of precious stones. When they left Lucera, Daoud and Celino had divided the twenty-four jewels Manfred had traded for the great emerald. Each carried half of the precious stones in a pouch hidden under his tunic.

Daoud studied the room. There must be a good thirty people there, most of them men. Aside from the six surrounding Celino, few of them seemed menacing. But if someone jumped in to help Celino, more might join the other side.

What do I have to help me? That boy who came with the old man. Sophia. And Celino and the dog.

If only, he thought, he had the Scorpion. But that was in the dining hall there, with all their other baggage, which Celino—the fool!—was supposed to be guarding.

He backed out into the small courtyard and bumped into the boy, who had followed him to the door. "You. Your father is in danger in there. And my friend has gotten into trouble trying to help him. We must get them out, you and I."

"Why should Christians help us?" The bitter voice was high. The boy must be very young. He was wrapped up like a Bedouin. His head and face were swathed in a dark cloth, his body cloaked. Only those sparkling eyes showed.

"I must help my friend," Daoud said. "If he lives, you can ask him why he chose to defend your father. Are you just going to cower here?''

''What should I do?''

What would make those men leave Celino alone long enough to give him a chance to escape? Standing outside the doorway with the boy, Daoud's eyes searched the courtyard again as his mind tried to fit what he saw into a plan.

Daoud looked up at the lanterns again. Fire was sure to take men's minds off a fight.

''Take the lanterns and run up those stairs. Throw them into the bedding and get a good fire going. Make sure the floor is burning. Then come back down to me.''

Daoud took the two lanterns down from their pegs and handed them to the boy, who raced up the stairs that clung to the outer wall of the inn. Daoud went to the stable and opened the doors of the stalls that held their four horses. He dragged out the saddles and bridles and threw them over the horses' backs. Trained with horses since boyhood, he worked with practiced speed. By the time the boy was beside him again, he had two of the horses saddled.

He looked up and saw bright yellow flames flickering in the upper windows.

''You did that well,'' he said. ''You know how to saddle horses?''

''Yes, Messere.''

''Get these two ready, then. Do it right; you will be riding one. And hold them here with your donkey.''

Daoud turned and shouted, ''Fire!''

He ran to the doorway, looked in long enough to see the darkened spot with its glowing center in the wooden ceiling of the dining hall, and gestured toward it as he again shouted, ''Fire!'' Then he stepped back to let the crowd tumble out past him.

The burly innkeeper was among the first to exit, jamming his dagger back into its scabbard and shouting for help. ''Take water from the horse trough. Get buckets, pots, anything!'' Waving his long arms, he towered over the men milling around him like a giant commanding an army of dwarves.

When the first rush had pushed through the doorway, Daoud ran into the dining hall. He could see the blackening circle spreading in the ceiling and flames licking around its edges.

Celino and the old Jew were still standing together by the far wall. Only three men faced them now.

"Come on!" Daoud shouted. He strode to the table where they had been sitting and grabbed up their packs.

"Stay where you are!" a woman's voice cried. It was the inn-keeper's wife, a gaunt woman nearly as tall as her husband, with bulging eyes and a face as sharp as the carving knife she brandished.

An earthenware jug crashed down on her head. Her eyes rolled up till only the whites showed. As she slumped to the floor, Daoud saw Sophia behind her.

Well done, Byzantine woman.

"Scipio! Spegni!" Celino shouted. With a roar like a lion's, Scipio leapt at the central figure among the three men confronting his master. Scipio's prey screamed, then stumbled over a bench and fell to the floor on his back. The hound sprang onto his chest, snarls of rage all but drowning out his victim's shrieks. The other two men, their mouths gaping, their eyes fixed on nothing, ran past Daoud without seeing him.

"Stop your dog," Daoud called to Celino. "I want no killing." Smoke spreading from above was searing his nostrils.

Daoud, Celino, and Sophia, followed by the old man and the dog, made their way to the door.

Daoud threw saddlebags to Celino and Sophia. Men were dragging their panic-stricken, rearing horses out of the stables and through the gate. The giant innkeeper and other men were racing up and down the outside stairs, which had also begun to burn, dumping buckets of water on the fire. Men were fighting their way through smoke and flame into the bedroom, trying to rescue belongings they had left there.

The boy stood by their horses, exactly where Daoud had left him. Bravely done, Daoud thought. Hastily tying his packs down, Daoud unlaced one. There were two weapons inside—a Scorpion, the miniature crossbow of the Hashishiyya, and a full-size crossbow. Daoud chose the bigger one, a Genoese arbalest drawn by crank, a present from King Manfred. The quarrels were loaded by spring from a chamber within the stock that could hold six at a time, so that the bowman could fire it as quickly as he could draw it.

Holding the arbalest with one hand, Daoud vaulted into the saddle. Celino and Sophia were already up. The old man had clambered onto their spare horse, and his son was on the donkey.

I should leave that old man behind, Daoud thought angrily. *Were it not for him, I would be sleeping comfortably right now.*

"*They* started the fire!" It was the innkeeper's wife in the doorway, her tall body and long arms silhouetted by leaping flames. She pointed an accusing hand at Daoud's party. "Stop them!"

The men who had been trying to put out the fire were giving up, and they turned and started for Daoud and his companions.

"Throw them into the fire!" shrieked the woman in the doorway.

Motioning the others toward the gate, Daoud turned his horse sideways and swung the crossbow in an arc to cover the attackers. The men stopped their rush, but the tall woman pushed her way through them, screaming curses.

Her hulking husband joined her, his long arms reaching for Daoud. He looked able to knock a horse to the ground.

Daoud used both hands to aim the crossbow at him, gripping the horse with his knees. He hoped the threat would be enough to stop the man. He did not want to shoot the innkeeper. If anyone were killed, the deed could follow them to Orvieto.

As he hesitated, the huge man drew back his arm and threw the dagger with the force of a catapult. Daoud heard a thump and a groan behind him. Daoud's thumb pressed the crossbow's release, and the string snapped forward with a reverberating bang. The innkeeper bellowed with pain, the cry dying away as he collapsed. The bolt probably went right through him, thought Daoud.

As the man's dying groan faded, his wife's scream rose. She fell on her knees beside him, and the other men crowded around them.

"Blood of Jesus! Pandolfo!" the innkeeper's wife wailed.

Jerking the reins with his left hand, Daoud wheeled the horse out the gate.

God help us, now they will be after us.

Which one of his people had been hurt?

He found himself, in his anger, hoping it was Celino.

The three other horses and the donkey were bunched together outside the gate, on the dirt path that led through trees to the Appian Way. Some of the men from the inn were out there, too, but when Daoud swung the crossbow in their direction, they backed into the inn yard.

"Leave me here," the old man gasped. "I am dying." So it was he the dagger had hit. They would have to leave him, Daoud thought, and his son would insist on staying with him. And the vengeful crowd from the inn would tear the two of them to pieces. All this fighting would have been for nothing.

Celino spurred his horse over to where the old man swayed in the saddle clutching his stomach. "Sorry to hurt you, but we are not leaving you," he said. He pulled the groaning wounded man across to his own horse and swung one of his legs over so that he was riding astride.

Daoud saw blood, black in the faint light of the crescent moon, running out of the old man's mouth, staining his white beard.

"Can you ride a horse?" Celino barked at the son.

"Yes," the boy sobbed.

"Get up on this one." Celino indicated the horse from which he had just dragged the old man. "Take your packs off the donkey and put them on this horse if you want them. Quickly, quickly. Leave the donkey."

Daoud fingered the crossbow as the boy hastily transferred himself and his goods to the horse.

Still Celino risks our lives with his care for these strangers. Damned infidel. I am the leader of this party.

"Here they come!" cried Sophia. Waving swords and long-handled halberds—God knew where they had gotten them—and sticks and pitchforks, the crowd from the inn tumbled through the gate. Some of them were on horses.

"Ride!" shouted Daoud in the voice he used to command his Mameluke troop.

He kicked his spurs into his horse's side and sent it galloping down the road.

He and Celino had not talked about which way to flee, but there was really only one direction they could go—north, toward their destination. That, he knew, would take them straight into the heart of Rome.

There would be a price to pay for the blood they had shed this night.

The great Salah al-Din had said it:

Blood never sleeps.

VIII

THE CLATTER OF FOUR HORSES' HOOVES OVER THE BROKEN PAVING
stones of the Appian Way rang in Daoud's ears. He heard shouts
behind him as the men from the Ox's Head organized a pursuit.
And beside him the old man, held erect by Celino's powerful arm,
groaned again and again as the wild ride jolted his stomach wound.
His legs dangled lifelessly on either side of the horse.

Daoud looked over his shoulder and saw that the boy was keeping
up, riding next to Celino. His robes were hiked up and his skinny,
bare legs gleamed in the faint moonlight. Daoud could hear him
sobbing loudly, in time with his father's groans, as the horses
pounded onward.

Glancing over at Sophia, on his right, he saw that she was stiff
in the saddle, like one not used to riding, and the moonlight showed
her lips tight and her jaw clenched. But she rode hard and made no
complaint. She sat astride, wearing trousers under a divided skirt.
Daoud felt himself admiring her. So far the woman had proved no
burden. Celino had caused trouble, but not she.

Glancing quickly again at her profile, outlined by moonlight, he
realized with a start that she reminded him of a face he had not
seen in many years. Nicetas. She had the same high forehead and
long, straight nose. Her mouth was fuller, but her lips had the
chiseled shape of Nicetas's lips. Nicetas. Even amid this moment's
perils sorrow gripped his heart for the one who was lost and could
never be recovered.

As if she sensed him looking at her, Sophia turned her face
toward him, but this put her face in shadow, and he could not
make out her expression. He shrugged and looked away.

He rode with one hand holding the arbalest across the saddle in
front of him, the other on the reins, guiding his mount. The horses
Manfred had given them ran well, aided a little by the high crescent
moon. Daoud tried to maneuver his small party to skirt dark patches

in the road where there might be holes in the pavement that could trip them.

The cries of the pursuers were louder, and Daoud heard hoofbeats behind them. He looked back and saw a dark cluster of horsemen rushing down the road. Five or six men, he guessed. There could not have been many more horses than that stabled at the inn.

He felt no fear for himself. The country might be strange to him, but riding and fighting in darkness were not. But his stomach tensed with worry about the four people with him. One of them was already badly hurt. Could he get them away safely? They were in his care now, and it was a duty.

Celino was the only one of his charges who could look out for himself. And he, thought Daoud angrily, was the one who had least deserved to survive.

But he is carrying half the accursed jewels.

If we survive this, it might be best for me to kill Celino.

As they rode on, Daoud kept glancing over his shoulder. Their pursuers were gaining on them. Celino's horse, carrying two riders, was holding Daoud's party back. But that meant the men from the inn would soon be within the arbalest's short range. He had only three bolts left in the box under the stock. He wished he had a heavy Turkish bow, the kind he had used at the battle of the Well of Goliath. Almost as powerful as a crossbow, it was easier to handle on horseback and would shoot much farther.

Now they will see how Mamelukes fight.

His eyes were now completely adjusted to the faint moonlight. The road took them into a deep pine wood. They splashed through a puddle in a low place, then clambered up a slope.

Down the other side. At the bottom of the next slope, Daoud twisted around in the saddle. Letting go of the reins and guiding the horse with his knees, he aimed the crossbow at the top of the hill. When the first rider came over the crest, clearly visible in the moonlight, Daoud pressed the catch with his thumb and released the bolt. An instant later the man fell without a sound.

He told himself a warrior of God should not rejoice at the death of an enemy, but he could not help a small surge of satisfaction at his good shooting.

Daoud cranked the string back and another bolt snapped into place. He hit the next man on the downslope. It was a harder shot, and this man did not die instantly but toppled screaming out of the saddle.

After glancing forward to make sure of the road ahead, Daoud turned again and saw that the three remaining men had stopped, their horses milling around the fallen men. They would give up pursuit now, Daoud was sure of it. Doubtless none of them had any real weapons, and they could not contend with a crossbow.

He felt his lips stretch in a grin, and he sighed deeply with relief. He had been more worried than he realized.

He and his companions topped another hill, and when he looked back again their pursuers had disappeared below its crest.

Daoud raised his hand and called out, "Slow down to a trot. No one seems to be following us. We can be easier on the old man and the horses."

"And on Scipio," Celino said, pointing down to a great shadow racing with them along the side of the road. Daoud could hear the hound panting and his claws drumming on the paving stones. He wondered how long Scipio could keep up with galloping horses, then reminded himself that this was a hunting dog. Scipio could probably outrun horses.

"Soon the Appian Way will take us to the old walls of Rome," said Celino. "The watchmen there would question us. But we can go off to the left toward the Tiber and skirt the city."

And because Celino knows such things, I cannot kill him. But I must see to it that he never again does anything like this to endanger us.

As they rode on, Daoud realized that the old man had stopped moaning. He heard Celino whispering something that sounded like a prayer.

"How fares the old man?"

Celino sounded angry. "He's dead."

On the other side of Celino the boy let out a wail of anguish, and then sobbed bitterly. Daoud felt a surge of grief. He was not sure whether it was for the boy or for himself.

"We should leave his body behind," he said to Celino. "Going this fast, that horse cannot carry both of you much farther." Anger at all this useless trouble constricted his throat and made his voice husky.

The boy cried, "No!" It was almost a scream.

"I can manage," said Celino.

"I will not leave him!" the boy shouted.

Sophia whispered, "I wish we had never seen them—without our help, they might only have been robbed. That poor boy!"

Celino clenched his fist and muttered to himself. Then he looked up and motioned to Daoud, pointing out a road diverging westward from the Appian Way. Daoud jerked the reins of his horse, and the hooves no longer rang on old Roman paving stones but thudded on hard-packed dirt. The trees closed together overhead, and they rode for a time in almost total darkness.

Celino dropped back now, and Daoud, glancing over his shoulder a little later, saw the boy and Celino in conversation as they rode side by side. After they had gone a mile or so, Celino rode back to join Daoud and Sophia. The old man's body was draped over his horse's back in front of him.

"You have much to answer to me for," Daoud said.

"I know that," said Celino. "But as long as we are out of Rome by morning, we are safe. The Giudecca, the Jewish quarter, is along the Tiber on the south side of the city. We can leave the boy with them and they will help him bury his father and take him in. It is not far from here." Daoud could not see his face clearly in the dark, but there was a note of pleading in his tone.

"How far?" Daoud demanded.

"We will be there long before dawn."

"But then we will have to go into the city," Daoud said. "How do we explain to the Roman watchmen why we are carrying an old man, dead of a knife wound? Surely they will be at least as thorough in inspecting baggage as you were at Lucera."

Celino was silent a moment. "You two can cross a bridge that will take you west of the city. I will take the old man's body and the boy to the Giudecca, and I will be the only one who will have to deal with the watch."

Sophia spoke up. "As you dealt with those ruffians at the inn? Then we will have all of Rome hunting us."

"All of Rome?" Celino chuckled. "The Romans can agree on only one thing—fighting among themselves. There are powerful Ghibellino families here who will protect us if need be."

He needed this damned Lorenzo, Daoud thought, because of his connections with the Ghibellini.

"How did the men at the inn know the old man was a Jew?" Daoud asked Celino.

"The hat he was wearing," Celino said. "All Jews are required to wear those round black hats in the Papal States. To make it easier for good Christians to persecute them." Daoud shook his head. Even Christians were treated better than that in al-Islam.

I did not know. Somehow, out of all that I learned about the Christian world, that detail about hats for Jews was left out. A little thing, too trivial to be mentioned. What other deadly little omissions lie in wait for me?

He felt like a man in chains. He would have to keep Celino with him, and the prospect infuriated him.

As they continued riding westward, Daoud heard the boy weeping. It made him think of nights in the Mameluke barracks on Raudha Island when he lay on his pallet, biting his knuckles so no one would hear him sob as he cried for his mother and father and for himself so lost and lonely.

I will help the boy bury his father. If it does not endanger us.

This boy, too, was lost and lonely. As Daoud had been while training to be a Mameluke.

As Nicetas had been.

It had been a chilly day, the day that Daoud and Nicetas became friends.

Huge gray clouds billowed in the east, over the Sinai desert. In the lee of a cliff formed of giant blocks of red sandstone, a dozen small tents clustered.

On a restless brown pony with a barrel-shaped body, Daoud waited in a line of nearly thirty julbans, Mamelukes in training, similarly mounted. Soon it would be his turn to ride past the wooden ring that a pair of slaves was swinging from side to side between the legs of a scaffold. In his hand Daoud grasped a rumh, a lightweight lance longer than a man's body, with a tip of sharpened bone.

On a low rise of brown gravel, Mahmoud, the Circassian naqeeb in charge of their training troop, sat astride a sleek brown Arab half blood. He looked almost regal in his long scarlet kaftan and reddish-brown fur cap. His beard was full and gray, and a necklace of gold coins hung down to his waist. The boys wore round caps of undyed cotton cloth and striped robes, and they rode scrubby ponies.

From atop a galloping horse, each boy was expected to hurl his rumh unerringly through the ring, whose diameter was two handspans. The ring was attached to three strong, slender ropes. One rope suspended it from the scaffold; the other two went out to either side, where the slaves held them. Pulling in turn on the ropes, the two slaves swung the ring from side to side.

The boy just ahead of Daoud in line was a new member of the troop of young Mamelukes. His face was smooth and his skin pale, his hair and eyes very black.

He turned to Daoud and said, "What if we hit one of those slaves by mistake?"

Daoud had once seen a slave transfixed by a wild cast of the rumh. It hurt to remember his screams and thrashings.

"Wound a slave and you will be beaten," he said. "Kill a slave, and you go without water for three days. In this desert that is a death sentence."

The boy whistled and shrugged. "Hard punishments for us, but not much comfort to the slaves, I'd say."

"It comforts them to know we have reason to be careful," Daoud answered.

After a moment, the boy smiled hesitantly and said, "I am Nicetas. From Trebizond. Where are you from?"

Daoud rubbed his pony's neck to settle it down. "Ascalon, not far from here. I am called Daoud." He saw the puzzlement in Nicetas's face and added, "My parents were Franks."

"Oh," said Nicetas, and looked sympathetic, as if he had instantly grasped what had happened to Daoud's mother and father and how he came to be a Mameluke.

"My mother was a whore," Nicetas said without any sign of embarrassment. "She sold me to the Turks when I was eight, and I was glad to go. She had sold me for other things before that. This is a good life. You learn to ride and shoot. Mamelukes wear gold, and they lord it over everybody else."

Daoud felt a slight easing of the tension of waiting to cast the rumh. He enjoyed talking to this new boy. There was a warmth and liveliness in him that Daoud liked. And even though their lives had been different, Daoud felt more of a kinship with this boy than he ever had with any of the others in his training group.

"Mamelukes have a good life if they live," said Daoud. "Where is Trebizond?"

Nicetas waved his left hand. "North of here. It is a Greek city on the Black Sea. But I suppose you have never heard of the Black Sea."

"I know where the Black Sea is," said Daoud, somewhat annoyed that Nicetas should think him totally ignorant. "How did you come to join our orta?"

"I was enrolled in the Fakri, the Mamelukes of Emir Fakr

a-Din. The emir was killed by the Frankish invaders last year. The older Fakri are staying together, but the young ones have been transferred out to the other ortas.''

Daoud found himself feeling somewhat sorry for Nicetas. He knew how lonely the Greek boy must be. His khushdashiya, his barracks comrades, were the nearest he had to a family. And even at that he was not really close to the other boys. He was the only Frank among them, and to talk to them at all he had to learn their various languages—Turkish, Kurd, Farsi, Circassian, Tartar. They would not bother to learn the Norman French, which was still the language he heard in his dreams. Most of the boys slept two by two in the field, but Daoud had no close friend to share a tent with.

"Go!" shouted Mahmoud the Circassian to Nicetas.

The Greek boy stood up in the saddle, and rode down the field with a warbling scream that was a perfect imitation of a Bedouin war cry. His trousers billowed against his long legs. Daoud watched his handsome, straight-nosed profile as he turned to fix his eyes on the swinging target. The lean-muscled bare arm drew back and snapped forward. The long black pole of the rumh whistled through the air, shot smoothly through the ring and landed upright, quivering, in the dune beyond it.

Daoud heard murmurs of appreciation around him. At the naqeeb's next cry of, "Go!" Daoud kicked his pony in the ribs and plunged forward to try his own cast.

He tried to ignore the fear of missing that knotted his belly muscles, tried not to think at all about his desperate need to make a good cast.

He guided his mount with the pressure of his knees. He squinted his eyes against the wind of his rush and fixed them on the ring. His body moved up and down with the action of the horse, and the ring swung back and forth. He twisted sideways in the saddle, steadying himself with one hand on the pony's back. Grasping the rumh at the middle so that it balanced, he lifted it high over his head. The little horse's muscles rippled under his palm. If he fixed his gaze and his aim on the point in space that the ring occupied at the lowest point of its arc, and released his rumh just as the ring reached the extremity of its swing, the target and rumh should arrive together.

The pony had carried him opposite the ring now, and he took a deep breath and whipped his arm forward.

His lance reached the right spot—an instant too late. He wanted to throw himself down from his horse and weep with frustration.

He heard groans and curses from behind him. Not once this morning had the troop had a perfect round. He rode around to the back of the scaffold, where the two slaves were sitting until the next boy should take his turn. The ghulmans kept their eyes down, their black faces expressionless. Angrily he yanked his rumh out of the sand and rode back to the end of the line.

Nicetas patted his arm reassuringly. Two more boys missed after Daoud, and that also made him feel a bit better. It occurred to Daoud that Nicetas was one of the few who had not once missed the ring that morning. He was a good horseman and seemed to have a remarkably keen eye with the rumh.

The only other boy in the troop who was that good, Daoud thought, was Kassar, the Kipchaq Tartar. Daoud looked around for Kassar and saw him sitting on his pony partway out of line, eyeing Nicetas sourly. Kassar's head was round, his face flat, and he was already old enough to have grown a small black mustache.

"From now on," the naqeeb bellowed from his hilltop, "anyone who misses once will not eat today. Anyone who misses twice will sleep in the desert tonight without tent or blankets."

Nicetas, who was wearing a long, sleeveless robe, grinned and shook himself. "It will be cold out there tonight."

"What if someone misses a third time, naqeeb?" someone called out.

"He is no longer Mameluke," said Mahmoud in a soft voice that carried. "He goes back to El Kahira. To be a ghulman for the rest of his life."

He would kill himself first, Daoud thought. He would plunge his dagger into his own heart before he would let that happen to him.

A frozen silence fell over the troop. The only sound Daoud could hear was the desert wind hissing past his ears. But he felt the fear all around him just as he felt the wind.

Mahmoud's threat seemed to help the troop's marksmanship. Only one boy missed in the next round. In that round and the one that followed, Daoud's rumh flew true both times. The second time, he felt dizzy with relief, and he leaned forward and hugged his horse's neck as he rode back to his place.

One more round and they could rest. Daoud's body ached, especially his back and his arms. He felt a clenching in his stomach, knowing that he had to get his lance through the ring this time. His khushdashiya would hate him, and he would hate himself, if he missed. And the more he feared missing, the more he would be likely to miss.

"Never mind hitting a slave," said Nicetas just before his turn. "Do us all a favor, hit the naqeeb."

Daoud laughed. Nicetas rode out and hit the target as usual. Feeling less tense, Daoud rode out to make his third cast. He held his breath until he saw his long lance sail smoothly through the dark-rimmed circle.

He shouted with joy and turned his mount back toward the troop. He did not hug his horse this time. Laughing, he rode up beside Nicetas, threw his arms around him, and pulled the skinny body against his larger frame. Nicetas's eyes seemed to sparkle as they looked into his when Daoud let him go.

It turned out to be another perfect round, and Mahmoud declared they could stop to pray and eat.

Thank God! Daoud said fervently to himself.

The sun had crossed from the zenith to the western part of the sky. Mahmoud led them in reciting the prayers, facing south toward Mecca. Then each julban took a portion of stale bread and dry goat cheese from a pouch hanging from his saddle, and a single draft from his water skin. The swallow of warm water Daoud took tasted foul, but he had to fight down the impulse to drink more. He sat down before his small tent to eat.

"May I sit with you?" Daoud squinted up into the sun to see the Greek boy standing over him.

"Please," said Daoud, gesturing to the sand beside him.

They ate in silence for a time. Daoud looked up from the hard bread he was relentlessly chewing and saw Nicetas smiling at him. He smiled back.

"You were eating by yourself," Nicetas said. "Do you sleep alone, too?" Daoud nodded.

"Would you like to have a tent mate?"

Before Daoud could answer, a shadow fell over them. Daoud looked up. Kassar stood between them and the sun, half a dozen of his friends around him. He glowered down at Nicetas.

"You think you are good?"

Nicetas's smile was friendly. "It is in the blood. Greeks are good at games."

"You throw like a girl," Kassar said to Nicetas. The Kipchaq's followers laughed dutifully.

Daoud felt his face burn with anger. He wanted to say something on Nicetas's behalf, even though it was the rule that each boy must defend himself.

Nicetas, still smiling pleasantly and looking quite unafraid, stood up with lithe grace to face Kassar.

"My rumh pierces the target," he said, making a circle with thumb and forefinger and pushing his other forefinger into it. "You have to be a man to do that."

This time the laughter was spontaneous, but Kassar did not smile.

"I will bet with you that I can throw the rumh better than you can," said Kassar grimly. "I will make you a handsome bet. I will put up the mail shirt that I took from a Frankish knight at Mansura."

Daoud felt the sting of envy. If he had only been a year or two older, he, too, might have souvenirs of that battle.

"I possess nothing of value," said Nicetas. "What can I put up against your mail shirt?"

Grinning, Kassar stepped closer to the Greek, bringing his face down till Nicetas's sharp-pointed nose almost touched his flat one. "You will spend the night in my tent whenever I want you." His thick fingers gripped Nicetas's chin, kneading the flesh of his face.

Nicetas blushed and pulled away, rubbing his chin, but still he smiled. "If your hand is that rough, I do not wonder you need a new tent mate."

This time the boys all roared with laughter, and Kassar's eyes narrowed to angry slits.

Daoud had never before heard anyone speak openly of what all the boys were aware of but only whispered about. For more than a year Daoud had seen and felt his body changing and had been tormented by steadily growing needs within himself. He sensed that others of his khushdashiya were tormented by the same nearly unbearable hungers. He knew, from listening to the talk of older men, that the answer to all these yearnings lay in women. But julbans were forbidden the company of women. He quickly learned how to relieve himself in solitude, and suspected many of the others did the same. But some, he was sure, made use of each other's bodies.

"I accept the contest," said Nicetas, staring fearlessly into Kassar's eyes.

"We must go to the naqeeb for permission," said Kassar. "But we will not tell him the stakes. He might get ideas about you." He

grinned at Nicetas with such frank lasciviousness that Daoud, remembering how his captors had raped him years ago, wanted to
smash his fist into the Tartar's big white teeth.

He followed Nicetas and Kassar as they went to Mahmoud's large
silk tent and explained the contest.

"Yes," said Mahmoud, leading the way back to the practice
field. "Put the one-handspan ring on, and you will ride fifty paces
from the target. You will cast until one of you misses and the other
follows with a hit. If both of you miss, you will be beaten for
disturbing my rest."

The slaves changed the two-handspan target ring for the smaller
one and began pulling on the guide ropes that swung the ring from
side to side. The naqeeb paced off the distance for Kassar and
Nicetas.

At Mahmoud's command, Kassar rode down the field. He made
a perfect cast, and his friends cheered. It was Nicetas's turn, and
he flew past the target with his warbling scream, standing in the
stirrups. There was something dance-like in the way he stood swaying with the jolting movement of his pony, left arm outstretched to
balance himself, rumh poised to throw.

He is beautiful, Daoud thought.

Nicetas's rumh went perfectly through the ring. The cheer for
him was lower; after all, nobody knew him.

Daoud called out, "God guides your arm, Nicetas!" Some of
the other boys stared at him, and his face grew hot.

Both contestants made successful second casts. But when Kassar
made his third throw, Daoud saw the ring wobble slightly. The
rumh must have brushed its inner edge. Nicetas's third try, once
again, was flawless.

"We cannot be at this till sunset," Mahmoud grumbled. "Move
out to seventy paces." He paced off the new distance, and Kassar
and Nicetas, stone-faced, not looking at each other, rode to the
spot he pointed out.

To throw the rumh accurately from that distance would take great
strength as well as a keen eye, Daoud thought. Looking at Nicetas's
slender arms and narrow shoulders, he wondered if the Greek boy
could manage it.

A wind rose, stinging Daoud's face with tiny sand particles. It
was blowing from the east, across the field where the boys rode.
Nicetas would be lucky to get his lance anywhere near the scaffold.

At Mahmoud's barking command, Kassar galloped out across

the field. He half rose as he came abreast of the target, and Daoud saw his powerful shoulder muscles bunch under his thin robe.

There was a loud crack as Kassar's rumh hit the ring. Daoud saw black fragments fly though the air. He gasped in surprise.

Kassar's lance had hit the side of the target ring, and the desert-dried wood had shattered under the impact.

"Well." Mahmoud turned to Nicetas with a laugh. "The target is destroyed."

"Let us put another ring on," said Nicetas promptly, just as Kassar rode up.

Kassar's face was tight with fury. "The rings are different sizes. It will not be fair if you have a bigger ring to hit."

"I want a smaller ring," said Nicetas with a faint smile.

Mahmoud sent a boy galloping to the target pullers with the order to attach a new ring to the ropes. From where he stood, Daoud could not even see daylight through the new ring. In the distance he saw a whirlwind raising a cone of sand, a sand devil, spinning near the red cliff.

"Think that there is a crusader charging at you, and you have to hit him in the eye to stop him," Mahmoud suggested to Nicetas.

"If it were, I would not let him get close enough for me to *see* his eye," said Nicetas dryly.

"Go!" Mahmoud roared.

Nicetas screamed across the field. The rumh flew.

Daoud cried out in amazement as the lance, no bigger than a splinter at this distance, shot perfectly through the ring.

Joy was a white light momentarily blinding Daoud. His heart was beating as hard and fast as if it had been he who had made the cast.

"Nicetas! Yah, Nicetas!" he cheered.

Loud cries of admiration went up. Nicetas retrieved his rumh and waved it over his head, standing in the stirrups as he rode back to the troop.

He jumped down from his horse, and Kassar, already dismounted, went to meet him. Kassar's heavy walk, his clenched fists, the rage in his face, told Daoud there was going to be trouble.

He felt hot anger surging up inside him, but he reminded himself again that Nicetas must fight his own battles.

The boys surrounded Kassar and Nicetas, the naqeeb with his green turban in their midst. Daoud pushed himself into the innermost circle.

"Bring me the mail shirt," said Nicetas.

"*I* won," Kassar declared, glowering down at him. "I smashed the ring, a thing you are too weak to do." He looked away from Nicetas and moved his head from side to side, glaring around the circle of boys, challenging any of them to contradict him. No one spoke. No one wanted to quarrel with Kassar, especially on behalf of a boy no one knew.

Daoud felt angry words rushing up inside him, but he kept himself in check. To take up Nicetas's quarrel unasked would insult Nicetas. If things got too far out of hand, the naqeeb would intervene.

Daoud felt himself abruptly pushed to one side. He turned to protest, and then checked himself. It was Mahmoud, leaving the circle that surrounded Nicetas and Kassar. As Daoud watched in amazement, the gray-bearded naqeeb walked to his red-and-white-striped tent and sat down cross-legged on the carpet in front of it, calmly gazing at the sandstone cliffs as if what was going on did not concern him at all.

He should be the one to declare Nicetas the winner, Daoud thought, as angry now as he was astonished. *Is he, too, afraid of Kassar?*

"When you broke the ring, that was a miss," said Nicetas. "You lost. The shirt is mine."

"You will have to take it from me," said Kassar with a grin. "Come to my tent and you can wrestle me for it." Now he made the gesture encircling his forefinger that Nicetas had made before.

What would Nicetas do, Daoud wondered. He was not big enough to hurt Kassar—but if he yielded, Kassar would make a slave of him and subject him to abominations.

"I had heard that a Tartar never goes back on his word," said Nicetas. "I see now that at least one Tartar is a lying jackal."

Good! Daoud thought fiercely. In a battle of insults, he felt sure, the talkative Greek would have the upper hand over the dour Tartar.

Kassar reddened, and he smashed his fist into Nicetas's jaw. The Greek boy fell to the ground, and Daoud saw that his eyes were blank, dazed. But Nicetas shook his head and forced himself to his feet.

"Your fist can't restore your honor, Kassar. You have fucked it too many times."

Loud laughter burst out from the watching boys, choked off as again the Tartar swung, hitting Nicetas in the mouth. The boy was thrown back against the onlookers, and blood ran from his nose and mouth.

Daoud felt the blood pounding his temples as his anger grew. As long as it was just Kassar against Nicetas, he could not get into the fight. But if Kassar's friends joined in, he promised himself he would help Nicetas.

"Take back what you said," Kassar growled, advancing on him.

Daoud could not see Nicetas behind Kassar's bulky form. But suddenly Kassar's head snapped back and his white cap fell off into the sand. The Kipchaq fell back, and Daoud saw that Nicetas was on his feet, grinning through the blood and rubbing his knuckles.

"Yah, Nicetas!" he shouted, but he was alone in cheering. He sensed others looking at him. May they burn in the flames if they did not see that Nicetas was the better man.

Kassar plowed into Nicetas, pummeling him with both fists. When Nicetas collapsed under the punishment, Kassar kicked him in the head, sending him flying backward. Kassar's friends shouted encouragement. Daoud felt his whole body growing hot with anger.

Nicetas rolled over on his stomach, raised himself on hands and knees, and spat blood. His eyes searched the crowd of boys watching him and Kassar, and Daoud knew that he was looking for a friend.

"Nicetas!" Daoud cried, and the Greek boy's dazed eyes found him and his bloody mouth stretched in a grin.

But if Nicetas did not give up, Kassar would kill him.

Suddenly Daoud turned and pushed his way through the crowd and hurried to where Mahmoud was still sitting.

"Why do you not stop this?" he demanded. "It is your duty to keep order among us."

"Do not tell me my duty," said Mahmoud. "Have you forgotten what my cane feels like?"

"You would use the cane on *me*?" Daoud exclaimed, outraged. "When Kassar is cheating?"

There were a thousand tiny wrinkles around Mahmoud's blue Circassian eyes, from a lifetime of squinting into the sun.

"Daoud, I will tell you what my duty is. My duty is to take miserable julbans and make Mamelukes of you. When you are a full-fledged Mameluke, there will be no naqeeb over you to right your wrongs. Among Mamelukes, he who is strongest rules. If Kassar is the strongest among you, you must be ruled by him."

Daoud growled with disgust and ran back to the fight.

Nicetas had somehow gotten back on his feet, though his face was a mass of blood and dirt and his breath was coming in gasps. His eyes were glazed, but he managed to stagger forward and hit Kassar in the nose with his fist. Blood began to flow from the young Tartar's wide nostrils into his mustache.

Kassar put his fingers to his upper lip, took them away and stared at the blood. His eyes widened in fury. His head swung right and left; then he sidestepped to a boy in front of the circle. From the boy's sash he pulled a dabbus, a fluted iron cylinder mounted on a wooden staff.

Swinging the dabbus so it whistled through the air, Kassar charged at Nicetas. The boys fell back, opening the circle wider.

For the first time, Daoud saw fear in Nicetas's eyes. He ducked as Kassar swung the mace at his head, but his movements were slow and awkward. He had been hit too many times. He fell, stood up, and staggered backward.

The naqeeb would not interfere. This could end only one way.

And Daoud knew that he did not want to see Nicetas die before his eyes.

He would not allow it.

Only moments ago rage had raised a great storm within him, but now his mind was like the desert after the storm has passed, still and empty. Like the desert, he felt himself full of a terrible power.

Without any more thought he stepped out into the ring behind Kassar and shouted, "Kassar! Enough!"

The Tartar whirled, holding the dabbus at shoulder height.

"Stay out of this, pigshit Frank."

"Let him be, Kassar." Almost all Daoud's attention was on Kassar, but a part of his mind was free to wonder why he felt no fear at all. Somehow, he was not sure how, the hours with Saadi had something to do with it.

"Put that down," Daoud said, pointing at the dabbus.

"In your head!" Kassar shouted, and charged at him.

Daoud kept his eyes on Kassar's, but in the edge of his vision he saw the ridged mass of iron, heavy enough to crack a steel helmet, rushing toward his head—his head protected only by a cloth cap.

At the last possible moment he threw up his hand and caught Kassar's wrist. He stepped back out of the path of the dabbus and jerked downward on Kassar's arm. The weight of the mace helped throw Kassar off balance, and he landed on his chest with a grunt, the air driven out of him.

Daoud stamped on Kassar's forearm and yanked the dabbus out of his grasp. He flung himself down on Kassar and pinned him to the sand.

Though all his attention was on Kassar, there was room in his mind for a triumphant surprise.

Allahu akbar! God is great! I never thought I had the strength to throw the Kipchaq.

"Nicetas won the contest. Admit it, or I'll break your skull," he growled, holding the dabbus over Kassar's head.

Kassar remained silent. Daoud lowered the dabbus and tapped the Tartar's round skull through his mop of straight black hair. He hit Kassar just hard enough to let him feel the weight of the dabbus.

"Admit that Nicetas won."

"All right," Kassar grunted, his face in the sand. "He won."

"Swear by the Prophet you will leave him alone from now on."

"I swear," came the muffled voice.

"By the Prophet."

"By the Prophet."

Daoud stood up warily and handed the dabbus back to the boy Kassar had taken it from.

Kassar rose slowly, wiping sand from his face. His eyes seemed to spark with hatred.

This is not finished yet, Daoud thought.

He looked for Nicetas. The Greek boy was on his feet. He was wiping the dirt and blood from his face with the hem of his robe. He looked at Daoud, and there was something bright and solemn in his eyes. No one had ever looked at Daoud like that before.

Daoud felt a great rush of gratitude to God for giving him the strength to save Nicetas's life.

If I had not fought Kassar, Nicetas would be dead.

That clean-lined face so full of warmth and wit would be so much lifeless clay. Daoud felt a lightness in his heart and a smile bubbling to his lips. He was proud of his strength. He had used it to save a precious life. He was a warrior of God.

Smiling, he went to Nicetas and threw his arm around his shoulders.

He should force Kassar to give Nicetas the mail shirt. But he had done enough fighting for one day. Nicetas did not need the damned shirt. Let the Tartar keep it.

"Now then, you wretched sons of desert rats!" came Mahmoud's voice. He pushed his way into the middle of the ring, coin necklace glittering, eyes flashing in anger.

"Fighting, eh? Trying to kill each other? Save your fighting for the emir's enemies. You are khushdashiya, brother Mamelukes of Emir Baibars. If again I see one of you raise a hand against his brother, I swear I will stake him out on the sand." He raised his right hand to heaven. "Hear me, God!"

The naqeeb had a strange way of making Mamelukes out of them, Daoud thought. But perhaps he knew what he was doing.

That night, without anyone's saying any more, Nicetas brought his tent and his bedding to Daoud. They compared tents and decided that Daoud's was the larger. They would sleep in it.

After they had tended their ponies and joined with the rest of the troop in the final prayer of the night, they crawled into the tent and spread their bedding side by side. Daoud felt Nicetas moving in his half of the tent and heard a rustling, as if his new tent mate were shedding his clothes. Why would he do that on such a cold night?

Nicetas pulled his blankets over both of them and rolled toward Daoud. The Greek boy's skin felt warm and silk-smooth. Nicetas wriggled even closer and stroked Daoud's chest, arousing pleasant tingles. Daoud felt, keener than ever, the powerful longings that had been troubling him. But then he remembered cruel Turkish laughter and rough hands, the unbearable pain and shame of his first nights of captivity. He struggled to free himself from Nicetas's arms.

All at once Nicetas let go of him and turned over, leaving a small space in the tent between them.

"Sleep well, Daoud." There was hurt in the soft voice.

Remorseful, Daoud reached for his friend. When his hand grasped the bare shoulder, his fingers tightened of their own volition. Nicetas drew closer again, until their bodies were pressed together.

"Ah, Daoud!" Nicetas whispered.

After they had made love, Daoud thought, *Perhaps God sent Nicetas to me.*

Fearing that the thought might be blasphemous, he put it out of his mind and fell into a sated sleep.

Daoud, Sophia, Celino, and the boy came to a riverbank. They had ridden in silence for so long that the moon's crescent hung low in the western sky, casting a glow on rippling water. Daoud called a halt and sat gazing at the Tiber. *Next to the Bhar al-Nil, the river Nile, this is the most famous river in the world.*

It was wide and flowed fast, judging by the ripples, and looked deep. Looking upriver, he saw that it followed a winding course leading toward black bulks, lit with yellow lights here and there, that must be great buildings. Rome.

They laid the old man's body down on a cracked marble platform beside the river. Celino had long since pulled the dagger out of the old man's flesh, and now he handed it to Daoud. The dagger was a well-balanced throwing knife of good steel, stained with a film of dried blood. Daoud knelt, washed it in the Tiber, and wiped it with the hem of his cloak. He held it out to the boy.

"I do not want it." The boy's face was still wrapped in a blue scarf, but Daoud could see tears glittering on his cheek.

"It is a good knife. You may have need of it now that you have no father."

"It is the knife that killed him." The boy hesitated. "All right, give it to me."

Daoud handed it to him, and the boy turned and hurled the knife out over the river. It flew a short distance, and the splash threw off light like a handful of pearls.

"Well," Daoud said, "no one had a better right to do that than you." He smiled to himself. He could understand quite well the lad's feelings.

But there was something odd about the way the boy's arm had moved when he threw the knife. Daoud recalled a phrase that he had heard in memory while they were riding toward the river.

You throw like a girl.

That had not been true of Nicetas, but it was true of this boy.

And his voice, though high, was not as light and clear as the voice of a child. Moved by a sudden suspicion, Daoud reached out too quickly for the boy to draw away and pulled loose the scarf.

He leaned closer for a good look. He heard Celino, standing behind him, grunt with surprise. Revealed in the moonlight was, not a lad whose voice had not yet changed, but a girl. Her eyelids were puffy from her weeping, but the eyelashes were long and thick, her nose delicate, her lips full. The eyes that looked back at him with a mixture of fear and defiance were, in this light, black as obsidian. Her hair was coiled in a thick braid at the back of her head, where the scarf had hidden it.

He did not have to ask the reason for the pretense. Traveling with only an aged father to protect her, she was far safer as a boy.

Sophia pushed past Daoud and put her arms around the girl, who began to cry again. "You poor child, are you all alone now? There, it's all right. We will help you."

"Who was your father?" said Celino in an equally kindly voice.

"He was not my father," the girl whispered. "He was Angelo Ben Ezra of Florence, a seller of books, and he was my husband."

Sophia drew back in surprise, then hugged the girl tighter. "Oh, poor little one. So young, and wed to such an old man. How could your parents do that to you?"

The girl angrily drew back from Sophia. "Do not speak so! My parents were good to me—and my husband was. He never touched me. When my mother and father died of tertian fever, he took me in, and he married me so as not to give scandal. He taught me to read."

"What is your name, girl?" Celino asked.

"Rachel." She dropped to her knees beside the body stretched out on the marble, and her tears splashed on the white face. She bent over and kissed him.

"He is so cold."

"We must wrap him quickly and be on our way," said Daoud. "We have killed three people and burned down an inn. I assure you, they have stopped chasing us only for the moment. Celino, I want a word with you. Sophia, help the girl wrap her husband's body so we can travel on."

"I do not need to be commanded," said Sophia sharply as Daoud turned his back on her, motioning Celino to follow him.

What in the name of God am I to do with these people?

Daoud strode across the marble platform and picked his way down a flight of cracked stairs to the edge of the Tiber. He followed a line of tumbled stones, once part of an embankment, until he felt sure Sophia and the girl could not hear them.

Then he whirled, bringing his face inches from Celino's.

"You fool! I ought to kill you for what you have done."

He heard a soft growl to his right.

"Send your damned dog away," he said, without taking his eyes off Celino.

"Of course," said Celino calmly. "Scipio!" He snapped his fingers. "To the horses. Go!"

The hound turned, head and tail lowered, and walked away. But he swung his long muzzle around to glance back at Daoud as he moved off. His pupils reflected the moonlight like two silver coins.

"Give me the jewels you're carrying," said Daoud.

"Of course," said Celino again, promptly unbuckling his belt. Daoud tensed himself in case the Sicilian should go for his dagger. But Celino held the belt up so that the twelve unset stones—rubies, pearls and amethysts—could roll out of the hidden pocket into Daoud's palm. Daoud added them to the twelve already in his pouch.

"There, now you have the stones back. And now are you going to try to kill me?"

There was a hint of challenge in that word *try*.

"If I had had all these jewels at the inn, I would have left you for that crowd to kill. How could you be so stupid as to involve us in a tavern quarrel?"

"I am no man's slave," Celino growled. "Not Manfred's, and surely not yours."

But I am a slave. That is what the very word Mameluke means, and I am proud to be a Mameluke.

"Do you think, Celino," Daoud said softly, "that you are a better man than I?"

"I think myself better than no man, and no man better than me."

Daoud looked away. *Madman's talk.*

Gazing up the river, he noticed a huge round shape bulking against the horizon, a fortress of some kind. There might be danger from that direction.

"Celino, you and Sophia and I are a little army in the land of our enemies. An army can have only one leader."

Celino nodded. "I know that. But you must understand that if I accept you as our leader, it is of my own free will. I am still my own master."

Daoud felt a strange mixture of admiration and uneasiness at this. He was painfully aware that among Mamelukes a warrior of Celino's age would be treated with great respect. Indeed, King Manfred clearly held Lorenzo in high esteem. His effort to save the old man had been noble in its way. But an impulse at the wrong time, even a noble impulse, could mean death for all of them.

"Does that mean you feel free to disobey me?"

"I have done whatever you wanted up to now. Except for what happened at the inn. That was different."

"Why different?" Daoud demanded. "You are not a stupid man, Celino. Why did you do such a stupid thing?"

Celino shook his head and turned away. "Angry as you are at me, Daoud, you cannot be angrier than I am at myself. If I had not intervened, that man Angelo Ben Ezra might yet be alive and his child-wife not widowed. They might have been hurt, and they surely would have been robbed. But I do not think those tavern louts would have gone so far as to kill them."

Daoud was astonished that Celino did not even defend his actions.

"Any more than we meant to kill any of those men," Daoud agreed. "But a man of your experience knows that once the sword is drawn, only God knows who will live or die. Yet you drew your sword against them."

"The old man wandered in out of the night seeking hospitality. Instead, they were beating him, and they were going to take his donkey and everything he owned and cast him out. Because he was a Jew."

"Yes, you Christians are very cruel to Jews. It is not so in the lands of Islam. But you should be used to seeing such things."

"I am not a Christian, Daoud. I am a Jew myself. And that is why I went to that old man's aid."

Daoud blinked in surprise, then began to laugh.

"You find that funny?"

"I am just as surprised to find out that you are a Jew as others would be to find out that I am a Muslim." Daoud stopped laughing. "I have known many Jews in Egypt. Abd ibn Adam, Sultan Baibars's personal physician, is a Jew. But why do you not wear the required hat?"

"It is not required in Manfred's kingdom. And I would not wear it on this mission any more than you would wear a Muslim's turban." Then Celino laughed. "But if I were to drop my breeches, you would see the mark of Abraham."

"I have that as well," said Daoud with a smile. "Muslims are also circumcised. I was eleven." He remembered with a twinge the old mullah chanting prayers in Arabic, the knife whose steel looked sharper and colder than any he had seen before or since.

"Now that mark is all I have left of the religion I was born into," Celino said.

"What do you mean? Did you convert to Christianity?"

"I told you I am not a Christian. I profess no faith."

Daoud drew back. A man who had no faith at all was somehow less than human.

"You believe in nothing?"

"One of Manfred's Saracen scholars gave me a book by your Arab philosopher Averroës. In it he taught that there are no spirits, no gods, no angels, no human souls. All things are matter only. That is what I believe."

Daoud made a casting-away motion. "I have been taught that Averroës is a great heretic. Now I see how wise we are not to read him."

"It was life that made me a nonbeliever. Averroës only showed me that there are learned men who think likewise."

Daoud shook his head. Baibars would never allow such a man near him.

"Why does your king permit you to have no religion?"

"The truth of it is, he thinks as I do. As his father, Emperor Frederic, did before him. In the kingdom of Sicily under the Hohenstaufens, people may believe as they please, as long as they are discreet about it. Of course, King Manfred must pretend to be a Catholic, or all the hosts of Christendom would fall upon his kingdom and destroy him. As for me, Manfred trusts me because he knows I do not stand in awe of the pope. The same reason he relies on his Saracen warriors."

Yes, Daoud thought, having no religion might make Celino a more useful companion for a mission like this. But how could Daoud trust a man who had no faith in a higher power?

"But why did you try to fight for that old man? Look what you have done to us."

Celino sighed and shook his head. "He was so much like my own father. I could not help myself."

"That is a poor excuse."

Celino looked steadily into Daoud's eyes. "It may seem so to you. It is said that Mamelukes scarcely remember their mothers and fathers."

Daoud's body stiffened with rage. Celino's words were a blow that tore open an old wound.

"You know nothing of that, and for your own safety you had best not speak of it to me," Daoud said in a choked whisper.

Celino inclined his head. "I ask your forgiveness."

"Remember that if we fail in this mission, it will mean great harm to your King Manfred, who has been so good to you and raised you so high," Daoud said.

Celino's head was still lowered in submission. "You are right to remind me of that. I have been foolish."

Daoud gripped Celino's wrist. The Sicilian raised his head and stared into Daoud's eyes.

Daoud said, "I must have your oath that this will never happen again. Should you see a hundred Jews having their throats cut, you will smile like a good Christian and declare the sight pleasing to God."

"I will do my best, Daoud. That is all I can honestly promise you, but I think it will be good enough."

By being honest, as he puts it, he still leaves himself room to defy me.

"And you will obey my commands from now on, as if they came from your king?"

"You have my word of honor."

Whatever the honor of an unbeliever is worth. Manfred, what kind of a crazed camel have you foisted off on me?

Here he was, far across the sea from the only home he had ever known, in the midst of people who would kill him in an instant if they knew who he was. And now he felt he could not trust one of the few men he must depend upon. He felt a coldness beginning in his palms and spreading through his body as he wondered what further calamities like tonight's might lie before them.

IX

THE CITY THAT FOUNDED MY CITY, Sophia thought.

Sophia and David rode along the Tiber as it wound its way through Rome like a brown serpent. Looking up from the riverbank, Sophia saw the peaked roofs and domes of churches, and the battlements of fortified palaces. The houses of the common folk huddled at the feet of the hills, and here and there remnants of old Rome rose like yellowed tombstones. Today's Romans, Sophia thought, built their hovels in the shadows of marble ruins.

Sophia was impressed only by the age of the place. Her own city, the Polis, was everything now that this place had been centuries ago. Rome had possessed civilization and had lost it. Constantinople had it still, on a grander scale.

At dawn David's party had reached the place where the Tiber passed through crumbling city walls. Lorenzo and Rachel crossed the river into the Trastevere quarter, where the Jews lived. Sophia wondered how they would get past the watchmen at the city gate with the old man's body. Would Lorenzo tell a clever story, try bribery, or use his Ghibellino connections? Or would he fail, and he and Rachel be arrested?

David did not seem worried. She had seen his anger at Lorenzo. Perhaps he hoped to be rid of him. For her part, she felt Lorenzo was far more her friend than David. She had known Lorenzo longer, and he had always been kind to her. She prayed he would return safely to them after finding a haven for Rachel among the Jews of Rome.

She and David had entered the city through a gate on the east side of the Tiber without difficulty. Evidently news of the incident at the inn had not reached the Roman watch. In the city she rode beside David along the river's east bank.

She touched David's shoulder and pointed to a hilltop.

"That hill is called the Capitoline," she said. "At one time the whole world was ruled from there."

She supposed David would find that hard to believe, though the hill was still impressive, with a cluster of marble palaces at its top.

They were passing through one of the most crowded parts of Rome. On their left, fishermen hauled their nets out of the river, throwing flopping fish into baskets. On their right, shops in the ground floors of overhanging houses offered fruits and flowers and vegetables, fish, shoes, straw, rosaries, icons, relics, candles. Even at this early hour the street was crowded. Romans jostled the horses David and Sophia rode, but they gave Scipio plenty of room. Lorenzo had given the great boarhound a stern lecture, after which Scipio docilely allowed David to lead him on a leash.

"I have seen two other great imperial cities," said David. "One was Baghdad, before the Tartars destroyed it. It was then much like this city is now—its glory shrunken and faded, but still the center of our faith, as Rome is the center of Christendom."

Sophia was taken aback at his casual error.

"Rome is the center of *Latin* Christendom," she said sharply.

"Ah, how could I have neglected Constantinople and the Greek church?" He smiled. The smile lit his deeply tanned face in a way that surprised her, held her gaze. She felt a warmth.

How smooth and brown his skin is.

"You must never forget Constantinople," she admonished him with a small smile.

"I spent a month in Constantinople some years ago—that was the other imperial city—and I shall not forget it." This made her feel warmer still toward him.

Then his smile faded. "Your city, too, has suffered at the hands of barbarians—the Franks, who would destroy us."

Destroy us? she repeated in her mind. *Is he not a child of those Frankish barbarians?*

On the road from Lucera to Rome, he had told her—in a brusque fashion, as if he were speaking of someone other than himself— the story of his childhood and how he came to be a Mameluke. She found it hard to believe that he spoke of the killing of his parents and his enslavement by the Saracens as if it were some kind of blessing—but she had no doubt that he was a believing Muslim through and through.

"Do you never think of yourself as a Frank, David?"

He smiled again. "Never. And I hope you will not think of me as one either. Because I know you must hate Franks."

Hate Franks? Dread them was closer to the truth. Last night, when they fought their way free of those people from the inn, she had remembered the terror she had known as a girl in Constantinople. It was the return of that terror that had given her the strength to smash a jug over that horrid woman's head.

She was about to reply to David when Scipio broke into loud barking. David frowned at the sight of something ahead. The Tiber made a sharp bend, and beyond that, on the opposite bank, towered a huge fortress, a great cylinder of age-browned marble—Castel Sant' Angelo.

At the base of the citadel was a bridge, and Lorenzo was crossing it. She knew him even from this distance by his purple cap and brown cloak.

Sophia had expected to see Lorenzo return alone. It gave her a little start of surprise to see that Rachel was still with him, still riding their spare horse.

David angrily muttered something that Sophia guessed must be an Arabic curse. He checked his horse. Sophia reined up her gray mare, and they sat waiting for Rachel and Lorenzo to come up to them.

"They want me as far away from them as possible," Rachel said. She climbed down from her mount at once, as if acknowledging that she had no right to be riding it. She looked at David with an expression of appeal.

This was the first time Sophia had gotten a good look at Rachel. The girl had removed the scarf that hid her hair, which was midnight-black and hung in a single braid down below her shoulders. A dusty purple traveling cloak enveloped her slight body. Her skin was white as fine porcelain. The eyes under her straight black brows were bright, but Sophia could see fear in them. She remembered herself ten years earlier, a bewildered, terrified, orphaned girl in Constantinople.

I must help this child.

"Why will your people not take you?" David said gruffly.

"They are afraid," said Rachel. "When we told them what happened at the inn last night, they said we had put them all in deadly danger."

Lorenzo looked up from where he crouched scratching Scipio's long jaw. "And we had better get out of the city quickly, before the rulers of Rome start hunting for us."

Rachel went on. "One of the rabbis took Angelo's body, and promised to bury him at once. That much they are willing to do. But they said they could not protect me if I were discovered. Not only that, but it would bring persecution down on them."

David said, "But did you not appear to be a boy at the inn?"

"The people at the inn saw a young person who could be boy or girl," said Lorenzo. "The Jews here are constantly spied upon. There are malshins, paid informers, among them. Their leaders think keeping Rachel too much of a risk, and knowing how many lives they have in their care, I cannot blame them."

David glared at Lorenzo. "Could you not do more to persuade them?"

Lorenzo spread his hands. "At first they did not trust me because they thought I was a Christian. When I told them I am a Jew, they still distrusted me because I admitted being from Sicily. That must have made them suspect that I am connected with King Manfred. The Jews of Rome live as clients of the pope. They cannot afford to get involved with Ghibellini."

Rachel pressed her hands on David's knee as he sat on his horse looking grimly down at her. "I beg you, let me come with you. There is no place for me here in Rome."

"There is no place for you where we are going," he said gruffly.

Sophia felt herself melting within as she saw the misery on Rachel's face. Swinging her leg over her mare's back, she slid down, rushed over to the girl, and put her arms around her. She looked up at David.

"David, please."

David looked down at her, his face hard, as if carved from dark wood, the eyes glittering like shards of glass. She could not read his expression.

How can I know what is in the mind of a Frank turned Turk?

David got down from his horse and beckoned to Sophia and Lorenzo. They followed him a short way along the street. When he turned to face them, Sophia saw fury in his eyes, and her heart fluttered like a trapped bird.

He spoke softly, through tight lips, and his voice was as frightening as the hiss of a viper. "I begin to think King Manfred is my enemy, and the enemy of my people, sending the two of you with me on this journey. From now on both of you will do as I command, and you will not question me."

Desperately Sophia turned to Lorenzo. "Can you not speak to him?"

Looking down at the cobblestones, Lorenzo shook his head. "I made a terrible blunder, trying to help Rachel and her husband. From now on things must go as David commands."

If Sophia had been arguing for herself, she could have said no more in the face of David's fury. But she looked away from him to the small figure standing by the horses, and her anguish for the child forced her to speak.

"But, David, what harm can Rachel do?"

Now the burning gaze was bent on her alone. "We will be saying things about ourselves in Orvieto that she already knows are not true." He turned to Lorenzo. "You talk of the lives the Jewish leaders have in their care. You do not understand—you cannot understand—what will happen to my people if I fail. What is it to you if the Tartars kill every man, woman, and child in Cairo?"

His voice was trembling, and Sophia realized he must have seen sights in the East that made the terror of the Tartars real to him, as it could not be to her.

"I owe the girl nothing," David went on vehemently. "Nothing. It was not I who caused this."

But a little girl with her whole life before her, hanged or torn to pieces by a mob— The thought of it made Sophia want to scream at David. She remembered the awful, mindless terror when she and Alexis ran through the streets of Constantinople with a roaring pack of Frankish men-at-arms hunting them. Last night she had relived that terror when they fled from the inn. She thought she would rather die herself than let Rachel be taken by a mob.

I cannot abandon Rachel. I must try to sway him. Is there any way I can touch David's heart?

Of course. The same thing that moves me.

"David," she said, "years ago, when you were a little boy— when the Turks killed your parents. Do you remember how you felt?"

David stared at her. So fixed were his eyes that for a moment she thought he might draw his sword and strike her down. She waited, trembling.

"You have no right to speak of that to me," he said. His voice was tight with pain.

"I know I have no right," she said. "Can't you see how desperate I am?" Hope dawned faintly within her. She had touched him.

His silence stretched on while the turmoil of the city eddied about them. She waited, trembling.

He spoke. "He who taught me Islam said to me, 'To lift up a fallen swallow is to raise up your heart to God.' "

Relief flooded Sophia's body. She wanted to weep. Instead, she felt herself smiling. But David did not return her smile.

"Swear that this girl will learn nothing of our mission from you," he said. "And you also, Celino. Swear it by all that you hold most holy."

"I swear it by Constantinople," said Sophia fervently and gladly.

"I will swear it on the lives of my wife and my children," said Lorenzo.

"I accept that," said David. "And when we reach Orvieto, the girl leaves us, even if she starves in the streets."

"I will accept *that*," said Lorenzo.

"Lest you later forswear yourselves, there is one more thing that will assure your compliance," said David. "Know that if this girl learns a word of what we are doing, she will die by my hand." He dropped his hand to the unadorned hilt of his sword.

Sophia felt cold inside. He cared about one thing only, after all.

They turned back. Sophia saw Rachel standing by a straw-seller's shop, looking anxiously at them, holding the gathered reins of their horses in both hands. Sophia realized that the girl might be thinking that they were going to drive her off, and she hurried to Rachel with a smile, holding out her arms. She hugged Rachel, and tentatively, fearfully, Rachel smiled back at her.

"You will come with us," she said. "As far as we are going, to Orvieto. You will have to leave us there, but we will help you find a home."

"Oh, thank you, thank you," Rachel cried, and she burst into tears.

Lorenzo grinned reassuringly at Rachel. "I told you it would be all right." When he grinned like that, his teeth white under his thick black mustache, he reminded Sophia of a large and satisfied cat.

Rachel looked up at David. "I thank *you*, Signore. I know this is your decision. May I know the name of my benefactor?"

David smiled bitterly. "Benefactor? Rachel, if you had not met us, your protector would still be alive. I am David Burian, a silk merchant of Trebizond. I go to Orvieto hoping to open trade between Trebizond and the Papal States, and I have hired these people to help me."

"May I also help you, Signore?" Rachel said. "I learned something of commerce from my husband."

"I think," David said, looking at Sophia and Lorenzo with sour humor, "I already have all the help I need."

At least the man is human, thought Sophia. *He can joke a bit.*

She felt encouraged. She had actually been able to touch the heart of this man whose life and world were utterly strange to her.

X

THERE IS SO MUCH WATER IN THIS COUNTRY, THOUGHT DAOUD. Raindrops sparkled on every branch and leaf of the trees around him. The sky, once more a bright blue after the thunderstorm that had passed over them, was reflected in water that still streamed through the ditches beside the roadway.

Fortunate that Rachel's husband, a man who had spent many months of the year on the roads of Italy buying and selling books in the Jewish communities, had carried a tent with him. Daoud, Sophia, Rachel, and even Scipio had all crowded into it when they saw the storm coming. The tent had leaked, but the heat of the August afternoon would soon dry them.

Daoud hoped none of the others had noticed his fear during the storm. He had been in the desert when lightning crackled in black clouds and the wind blew smothering waves of sand. But the thunderstorms they had been through had seemed to be just overhead, and so much water had fallen from the sky, Daoud was sure they would soon be drowned. It seemed almost miraculous to him that he could emerge from Rachel's tent alive and find the world outside as intact as he had left it. Better than he left it, because it was now washed clean of dust.

He walked to the edge of the road to see if Lorenzo was returning from Orvieto.

Orvieto.

Across the valley, out of a deep-green forest rose a gigantic yellow rock shaped like a camel's hump. Crowning the hump, a wall of gray stone encircled the peaked roofs and bell towers of churches, the battlements of palaces and the red-tiled roofs of houses. One narrow road zigzagged up the steep side of the great rock, sometimes disappearing into clumps of trees, a white streak against the ocher cliffs. A city built on an almost inaccessible mountaintop, like the strongholds of the Hashishiyya.

He spied a horseman in purple cap and brown cloak descending the road from the city. Celino. Following him was a glittering gilt sedan chair carried by four bearers.

The breeze that had brought the storm had died away, and Daoud was beginning to feel the heat of the sun on the back of his neck. A mild sun compared to that of Egypt, even though this was the middle of the Italian summer, but he drew up his cotton hood to shade his head. He glanced over his shoulder. Rachel and Sophia were in the clearing on the other side of the road, watering the horses in a stream that ran down the hillside. Rachel was nodding eagerly as Sophia talked. He hoped she was not telling Rachel too much. Just as he himself might have told Sophia too much, he thought ruefully.

Celino arrived at Daoud's camp well ahead of the sedan chair. Scipio had bounded up the road to meet his master, and now licked the hand that Celino held out as he dismounted.

Celino said, "Cardinal Ugolini sends this messenger, who may surprise you."

When the sedan chair came to rest on the side of the road, Daoud saw that the four bearers were black men of Africa. They wore scarlet vests, and sweat glistened on their bare arms and chests. Sheikh Saadi had been such a man, and there were many such men in the Egyptian army. Daoud wondered if these, too, were Muslims. In the city of the pope? Not likely.

Two of the bearers drew back the curtains of the chair and reached within. Bejeweled white fingers grasped the bearers' muscular arms, and a turban brocaded with gold pushed out past the curtains, followed by a round body swathed in lime-green silk.

Daoud was not surprised. This must be the one who called herself Morgiana in the letters to Baibars that came regularly from Italy by carrier pigeon and ship, thought Daoud. Still clinging to the bearers, the stout woman pulled herself erect. Then she waved her servants away with a flapping of sleeves and a jangling of bracelets and squinted at Daoud.

"Is it time?" said Daoud. He spoke in Arabic.

"Not yet," she answered in the same language. "But presently." That completed their prearranged words of recognition.

"Salaam aleikum, Morgiana," he said, smiling. "Peace be to you." He pushed back his hood and bowed to her. He had a warm sense of meeting an old friend. He had read many of her reports on matters of state in Italy.

"Wa aleikum es-salaam, Daoud," she replied. "And peace also to you. You will have to know my real name now. Tilia Caballo, at your service."

He had pictured Morgiana as a tall, slender woman of mature years, darkly attractive. The real Morgiana was quite different. Her eyebrows were thick and black, her nose a tiny button between round red cheeks. Her face was shiny with sweat even though she had been doing nothing but sitting in a sedan chair. Looking at her spherical body, Daoud felt great respect for the strength of the men who carried her. The silk clinging to her body outlined breasts like divan cushions, and her belly protruded in a parody of pregnancy. Could she truly be a cardinal's mistress? Just as sultans and emirs had chief wives who were old and honored and younger wives for play, perhaps Cardinal Ugolini kept Tilia Caballo only as his official mistress.

The clasp on her turban was studded with diamonds. A heavy gold necklace spilled down the broad, bare slope of her chest. From the necklace dangled a cross set with blue and red jewels.

The gold Baibars has sent her helped buy the fortune she wears. He wondered, how much did Baibars really know about this woman?

"I saw Cardinal Ugolini for a moment only, Messer David," said Celino. "As soon as he found out I was from you, he insisted that I go to this lady's establishment." Celino, speaking the dialect of Sicily, uttered the word stabilimento with a curious intonation. Scipio stood with his forepaws on Celino's chest, and Celino scratched the hound behind the ears.

"He means the finest house of pleasure in all the Papal States," said Tilia Caballo, smoothing the front of her gown with a self-satisfied look. "Naturally his eminence Cardinal Ugolini cannot risk meeting openly with you until I have seen you on his behalf." She had switched from Arabic to an Italian dialect that was new to Daoud. He had trouble understanding her.

He did not think it had been mentioned, in her letters or by Baibars, that she was a brothel keeper. He felt slightly repelled. He wondered if Baibars knew. He must. Baibars knew everything.

"Take yourself away, Celino," Daoud ordered. "And tell those two to come no closer." He pointed to the forest clearing where Sophia and Rachel were already starting toward him. "I must be alone with Madonna Tilia."

"Yes, Messere," said Celino with a bow. Scipio paced ahead of him like a tame lion as he walked off.

"We expected you to enter Orvieto alone," said Tilia, looking at Sophia and Rachel, who were staring back at her from across the road. "Why this entourage?"

And I expected to meet with Cardinal Ugolini at once, thought Daoud with growing irritation. *Has he set this woman up as a barrier between himself and me?*

He explained briefly how Celino, Sophia, and Rachel came to be traveling with him. Tilia gazed at him with a falcon's piercing stare. Daoud was not used to being stared at by a woman, and she made him uneasy. But he met her eyes in silence until she turned to her slaves and made a dropping gesture with her hand. The Africans immediately squatted in the grassy clearing where they had set Tilia's chair. Daoud realized that he had not heard a sound from them, and suspected they must have been made dumb.

"Come." Tilia took his arm, again surprising him. In Egypt women did not touch men they had just met. But she owned a house of pleasure. She was not a respectable woman.

Why should that bother him, he asked himself. He had spent his share of time in houses of pleasure along the Bhar al-Nil. What he felt toward their owners was mostly gratitude.

Tilia drew Daoud with her into the thicket along the hillside, stepping gracefully, despite her bulk, around shrubs and over rocks and fallen branches. She led him away from the road and into a grove of pine trees a little way up the slope. Daoud felt his muscles tightening. He was going to have to undergo more testing before she would let him meet Ugolini. Did they really think that Baibars would send a fool to Orvieto?

"Spread your cloak for me." She pointed to a spot under an old pine whose trunk rose straight and bare twice the height of a man before the first branch sprouted. Daoud unclasped his brown cloak and laid it on the thick bed of brown pine needles. Tilia sat down, smiled, and patted the place beside her.

"A messenger brought the news to the pope yesterday that the Tartar ambassadors have landed at Venice," she said. "They are on their way to Orvieto and should be here in a week or so. They are well protected. They brought their own bodyguard, which is now reinforced by a company of French knights and Venetian men-at-arms under a certain Count de Gobignon."

Daoud felt a tingle of anticipation, as he did when he was about to close with the enemy in a battle.

"So I will be in Orvieto before them. That is good."

"Yes, but Cardinal Paulus de Verceuil has arrived here before *you*. He speaks for the King of France, and he has already begun to press the case for a Tartar alliance before Pope Urban. He has arranged for the Tartars and their guards to live at the palace of the Monaldeschi family."

Daoud caught an intonation in Tilia's voice that suggested it was a great accomplishment for the Tartars to live at the Monaldeschi palace. Was she trying to discourage him?

"What is this Monaldeschi family?" he asked.

"The oldest and richest family in Orvieto," she said. "Right now the capo della famiglia, the head of the family, is the Contessa Elvira di Monaldeschi, who is over eighty years old. But she is more ruthless and savage than many a younger man. Almost all her menfolk have been killed off by their blood enemies, the Filippeschi, and she has had many Filippeschi killed."

"What do they fight about?" said Daoud.

"Who knows? A Monaldeschi kills a Filippeschi, so a Filippeschi kills a Monaldeschi. It has been going on forever." Tilia went on. "What you must realize is that the Tartars will be well guarded because the contessa has more men-at-arms than the pope and a very strong palace."

He turned away from Tilia. Daoud stared out through the screen of pine branches at Orvieto's sunlit rock platform. A wagon inched its way up the narrow road.

"Who is this French count who guards the Tartars?" he asked.

"Count Simon de Gobignon. He is very young and very rich. He holds huge estates in France and numbers his vassals in the thousands. He is close to the French royal family, even King Louis himself and the king's brother, Charles d'Anjou."

Charles d'Anjou. Daoud remembered Lorenzo saying that Charles d'Anjou coveted the throne of Sicily.

A flash of light caught Daoud's eye. A party of helmeted men in yellow and white surcoats had come out of the main gate of Orvieto, formed a ragged column and were patrolling along the base of the city wall, led by a man with a white plume on his helmet.

"Who are those soldiers?" he asked.

Tilia leaned forward to peer through the trees and across the valley, then resettled herself against the tree trunk.

"Pope Urban has two hundred Guelfo fighting men quartered in Orvieto. In all honesty, Daoud—"

"Call me David," he interrupted. "Here I must be known by a Christian name."

"Well, David, I think you had best go quickly back to Egypt. What can one man do against the French royal family, half the cardinals, the pope, the Monaldeschi, and the Tartars themselves?"

He felt a quick spurt of anger. He knew as well as she did the odds he faced. Why was she trying to weaken him by making him afraid?

Ugolini sent her to discourage me. It is he who is afraid.

He felt more respect for her, coming out and meeting him and trying to influence him, than he did for this Cardinal Ugolini, who was trying to protect himself. He knew from having read her letters that she was a shrewd and brave woman. He had to win her cooperation. There was only one way he might hope to do that.

Daoud smiled at her. "Does not great wealth give one great power?"

She smiled back. He noticed that she had rubbed some kind of red coloring on her cheeks to make herself look healthier. And she had painted blue-black shadows around her eyes, as Egyptian women did. But here and there her sweat had made the paint run in rivulets.

She said, "Only faith is more powerful than money."

"Then here is power." Daoud unbuckled his belt and let the jewels spill out of its hollow interior into his hand. He heard Tilia gasp. When the glittering stones filled his hand, he dropped them gently to the thin woolen cloak he had spread on the ground and shook the rest out of the belt. In the shadow of the pines the jewels seemed to give off their own light from their polished, rounded surfaces, red and blue, green and yellow. A sapphire, a topaz, and a pearl were each set in heavy gold rings. The others were loose. Some were so small that three or four of them would fit on the tip of Daoud's finger. One, a ruby, was the size of a whole fingertip. There were too many of them to count quickly, but Daoud knew that Manfred had given him twenty-five, and one had gone to equip them for the journey.

"Sanctissima Maria! May I touch them?"

"You are welcome to," he said, smiling, "but make sure none of them sticks to your fingers."

She plucked some of the jewels from the cloak and let them

trickle through her fingers, catching the light as they tumbled to the cloak. She held the big ruby up between thumb and forefinger and studied it, turning it this way and that.

"A drop of God's blood."

"You should have seen the single emerald I traded to King Manfred for these smaller stones. There was beauty. A few at a time, these can be turned into gold."

She looked into his eyes. She took him more seriously now, he thought. He was not just some strange Muslim whose rashness might get her killed. He was a source of wealth.

"They must be sold carefully, or their sudden appearance will be noticed," she said. "After all, even the princes of the church would have to stretch their purses for these."

"I have it in mind to buy princes of the church, not to sell jewelry to them."

"We can sell some of these gems to the Templars. They have enormous wealth and they are very discreet."

Noting that she had said "we," Daoud smiled at the thought of those ferocious enemies of the Mamelukes, the Knights Templar, helping to provide the financing that would weaken their foothold in Islamic lands.

"Now," he said, "do you think we can accomplish something to keep Tartars and Christians apart?"

"Yes—something. Used wisely, these jewels—or their worth in gold—will gain you influence among the men around the pope. You might even pry a few of the French cardinals loose from their loyalty to King Louis."

Daoud began scooping up the stones and funneling them into the hidden pocket of his belt. "You must help me to use them wisely."

"Exactly what do you have in mind?" she asked, her eyes fixed on the jewels as they disappeared.

"I expect Cardinal Ugolini to take some of the gold and use it to build a strong party in Orvieto that will oppose the alliance." He eyed her, trying to see into her heart. "Can he manage such a thing?"

"Oh, Adelberto is an old hand at intrigue. How else do you suppose he got to be a cardinal? Indeed, he is the camerlengo for the College of Cardinals."

"What does that mean?" Daoud asked as he buckled his belt.

"He acts as a kind of chancellor to the pope, making announcements, calling the College together, conducting ceremonies—that sort of thing."

Daoud nodded. "Good. It is my hope that he can use this money to draw cardinals and church officials to him, one way or another. And they will join together to turn the pope against the Tartars."

"With all the money those jewels will bring, you can indeed create such a faction, but I don't know what effect it will have on the pope. The Tartars offer the pope a chance to wipe out Islam once and for all."

"Yes, and then after that the Tartars will wipe out Christianity," Daoud said. "I can tell those who will work with us what the Tartars are truly like. I have seen them, fought against them. I have seen what they have done to those they conquered." Like a cloud passing over the sun, a memory of ruined Baghdad darkened his mind.

Tilia's eyes opened wide. "You intend to meet and talk—to bishops, to cardinals?"

He touched his face with his fingertips. "This is why Baibars sent me—because I can go among Christians as a Christian. I will be David of Trebizond, a silk merchant who has traveled in the lands ravaged by the Tartars."

"Trebizond?"

He could see the doubt in her face. He must seem confident to her. He must not let her know that he himself wondered how he, a warrior from a land utterly strange to these people, could make the great ones of Christendom listen to him and believe in him. He could do it only with the help of Tilia and Cardinal Ugolini—and they would not help him unless they believed he could do it.

"Trebizond is on the eastern shore of the Black Sea. Far enough away that I am not likely to meet anyone in Orvieto who knows anything about it."

"Do not be too sure. The pope makes a point of seeing people from everywhere."

"Then he will probably want to meet me, since I am from a strange and faraway place."

Her eyes widened and her full lips parted. Her teeth were small, bright, and widely spaced.

"You even want to meet with the *pope*?"

He knew the enormity of what he was proposing. But he fought down the doubt that her evident horror had aroused in him. He made himself sound absolutely sure when he answered.

"Certainly. Cardinal Ugolini will arrange an audience for me. If the pope has not yet made a decision, he will want to listen to one who has seen with his own eyes what these Tartars are. I will tell him that an agreement with them would be like a lamb allying itself with a panther.''

"Talk to the pope! How would you know how to behave before the pope?''

"Among my people, Madonna, I am not just a warrior. I stand high in the highest councils. I have met with kings and great men of religion. As for the details of etiquette of an audience with the pope, as a traveler from Trebizond I might be expected to make mistakes.''

Daoud saw that her olive skin had turned a yellowish-white. "Do you want to be torn to pieces by teams of horses?'' she whispered. "I do not, and neither does Cardinal Ugolini. We cannot risk your being found out.''

He must overcome her doubt of him by seeming supremely confident.

He said, "Then, for your own protection, you will teach me everything I need to know.''

And if Christians moved closer to Tartars despite intrigue and persuasion, he and Baibars had already considered more desperate measures. The risk of failure would be greater and the consequences more dire. He would not tell Tilia about these more drastic steps. If his presence and intentions already frightened her and Ugolini, it was best they not know the lengths he was prepared to go to.

He hoped he would not have to attempt such things. The complexities and difficulties of making them happen, the likelihood of things going disastrously wrong, all made these courses too daunting.

Inshallah, if it be God's will, he would manage, with the help of such allies as he found in Orvieto, to oppose and obstruct and delay the alliance until the project died of old age, or the Tartar ambassadors themselves died.

Time fights for Islam, Baibars had told him. *The Tartar empire is beginning to break apart, and the Christians are losing their eagerness for crusading. Only delay this alliance long enough, and their opportunity to destroy us will be lost.*

Tilia broke in on his thoughts, holding out her hands to him. "Help me up. My legs are getting cramped. I feel hungry. Do you have anything to eat?''

He was not surprised that she asked for food. Mustapha al-Zaid, the chief eunuch of Baibars's harem, was monstrously fat, and was always eating.

He sprang to his feet and pulled her up. The cross on her bosom swung and flashed. The top of her head came only to the middle of his chest, but he suspected that she weighed as much or more than he did.

She smiled at him. "You are strong, and you move like a warrior."

Ignoring the flattery, he said, "Sophia has bread and cheese that we bought at a village called Bagnioregio. And some red wine to wash it down."

Tilia laughed. "Bagnioregio? Then you must have passed near the ruins of Ferento—the town that was destroyed for the heresy of displaying a statue of Christ on the cross with open eyes."

"What? I saw no ruins. Open eyes?"

"The ruins are off the road. But that will give you an idea of how careful one must be where religion is concerned. I cannot imagine that anyone makes decent wine in Bagnioregio. There is another town near here, Montefiascone, where they make the best wine in the world. Wait until you taste that."

"I drink wine only to deceive Christians," he said gruffly. "I do not like it. Let us finish this conversation before you refresh yourself. I do not want those two to know any more than I tell them."

Annoyance flickered in her face. She was not used to being denied, Daoud thought. But she shrugged. "I presume you plan to use that beautiful woman who travels with you as bait to win over some of the high-ranking churchmen."

To Daoud's surprise, the thought pained him.

"She is a skilled courtesan and was Manfred's mistress," he said. "And before that, King Manfred told me, she was a favorite of the Emperor of Constantinople. We will want to keep her in reserve. I have in mind that she could live with the cardinal, pose as his niece."

"Hm. And the other girl? She is very pretty and very young. The older and more powerful churchmen are, the more they are drawn to youth."

"We owe Rachel a debt. We have promised to find a home for her among the Jews of Orvieto."

"Oh, is she a Jew? But there are no Jews in Orvieto."

"Somewhere nearby, then."

"The nearest Jews live in Rome."

Rome—where the Jews had already turned Rachel away. "She cannot go to Rome."

"Well, the girl would find working for me far more rewarding than living on charity."

"I am sure of it," said Daoud. But a dark memory from long ago rose to trouble him.

He fixed his eyes on hers. "You would not force her into whoring, would you?"

Tilia pressed her hand to her bosom in mock horror. "Force! Women *beg* to be accepted into the family of Tilia Caballo."

A terrible thing to do to the child, but it would solve my problem, thought David. *Rachel already must be aware that Sophia and Lorenzo and I are involved together in some secret enterprise. It would be best to keep her where we can watch her.*

"For the time being, Rachel will stay with us at the cardinal's mansion, serving Sophia as her maid," he said.

Tilia looked up at him, startled. "You *all* intend to live with the cardinal?"

Her surprise, in turn, startled Daoud. But then he saw that her eyes were too firmly fixed upon him, and knew that she was dissembling.

"As Morgiana, did you not approve this arrangement with my lord the sultan?"

She shrugged. "That was when we thought you were coming alone."

"Sophia and Lorenzo will be of great help to us. We will give it out that I am the cardinal's guest. Lorenzo will be my servant, Giancarlo. And Sophia will be the cardinal's niece."

"Hm." Tilia frowned. "I am *very* hungry. Let me sample the delicacies your Greek woman bought in Bagnioregio. Then I will go back to the city and send word to the cardinal of what you have told me."

Daoud heard the false note in her voice and bristled with suspicion.

And you would keep me waiting out here while you warn him of what a danger I am to him.

"I will tell him everything myself."

Her eyes clouded over. "The cardinal will send for you when he has heard my report."

"Great God, woman!" Daoud's voice rasped in his anger. "Do

you expect me to wait out here until the Tartars come to Orvieto? I am sent by the sultan, I bring great wealth to you and your master, I am fighting for my faith, *and I will not wait!*"

Tilia patted his arm placatingly. "Look here, Daoud, in all honesty, Cardinal Ugolini is terrified. When he first got Baibars's message about you, he wept for hours, cursing himself over and over for a fool. Imagine the outrage if the Christians were to discover that a Muslim agent has come so close to their pope. The cardinal would never have taken the first denaro picciolo from your sultan if he had ever known that it would lead to this—a Turk at his door demanding his help in a plot against the pope."

"I am not at his door," said Daoud pointedly.

"No, and before you arrive there, you must give me time to assure him that you know what you are doing, that you do not look anything like a Turk, and above all that you bring him such great wealth as to make the risk worthwhile. If you just appear at his palace when he has insisted that you wait here, it might throw him into a panic. He might do something very foolish."

Anger flared up in him. She was obstructing him and threatening him, and he had had enough.

She means he might expose me. Or order his men-at-arms to kill me. This is Manfred's indecision all over again.

He seized Tilia's arm, his fingers sinking into soft flesh under her silk sleeve. "I am going to the cardinal, with my party. And you will equip me with a message for him, telling him you feel assured it is safe for him to admit us."

She stared up at him, expressionless, for a long time. He sensed that she was trying to see into his heart, to weigh his will.

"No," she said. "You are not going now. First—"

His grip on her arm tightened, and in his anger he was about to shake her, when her hand darted to lift the pectoral cross from her breast. Her thumb pressed a dark red carbuncle between the arms, and a thin blade sprang out of the shaft.

"Please notice that the cross is attached to my neck by a chain, David. I cannot hurt you unless you come too close to me. I have no wish to attack you. There is asp venom on the blade, by the way."

His anger turned against himself. It was foolish to try violence on a woman like this. Had he not told himself he could not force Tilia and Ugolini to do anything, that he must persuade them?

This woman herself is as dangerous as an asp. But I need her.

He let go of her arm. "Pardon my crudity, Madama."

Tilia pointed her blade straight up and pressed another jewel in the cross. The blade dropped back into the shaft.

"I do not mind crudity," she said, "but I do not like to be manhandled." She smiled slyly. "Unless I've invited it. I had already made my mind up, before you laid violent hands on me, that I would agree to your going at once to the cardinal. I have decided that you may be able to accomplish what you set out to do without getting us all killed. You are brave and intelligent, but you know how to bargain, too. You know when to yield and you know when to stand your ground."

Daoud felt pleasure at her compliments, but even more pleasure that she was going to cooperate with him.

"Then why did you just say we would not be going to the cardinal?"

"I was about to add that first you *will* feed me bread and cheese and the execrable wine of Bagnioregio. *Then* I *will* give you a message that will get you into Cardinal Ugolini's mansion."

Daoud laughed. That Tilia had yielded was a great relief. And she was both witty and dangerous, a combination he admired.

XI

Simon was surprised at how young Cardinal Paulus de Verceuil looked. The man who stood with him in a vineyard on the road to Orvieto had a long, fine-skinned face and glossy black hair that fell in waves to his shoulders. If his scalp was shaved in a clerical tonsure, his red velvet cap covered it. His handsome violet silk tunic reminded Simon that his own surcoat was travel-stained and that Thierry had not polished his mail in days.

De Verceuil tossed away the cluster of pale green grapes he had been nibbling and spoke suddenly.

"Count, a report has reached me that you spoke rudely to the doge of Venice." His booming bass voice sounded as if it were emerging from the depths of a tomb. "You do realize that your actions reflect on the crown of France?"

He thrust his face into Simon's as he spoke, which made Simon involuntarily draw back. De Verceuil was one of the few men Simon had ever met who matched his own unusual height.

Simon felt his face grow hot. "Yes, Your Eminence."

"And how could you dismiss the trovatore Sordello from the post to which Count Charles himself appointed him?"

"If Sordello had stayed with us, the Tartars might have taken such offense as to go back to Outremer."

"Do not be absurd. Would they abandon a mission of such importance because of a tavern brawl?"

Simon felt shame, but, deeper than that, resentment. He was the Count de Gobignon, and not since he was a child had anyone chastised him like this.

He heard a rustling as someone came down the row of vines where they were standing. He turned to see Friar Mathieu, and hoped he was about to be rescued.

After the Franciscan had humbly greeted the cardinal and kissed his sapphire ring, he said, "I must tell Your Eminence that what happened was not a mere tavern brawl. Sordello stabbed and nearly killed the heir to the throne of Armenia, an important ally of the Tartars."

De Verceuil stared at Friar Mathieu. The cardinal had a mouth so small it looked quite out of place below his large nose and above his large chin. A mean mouth, Simon thought.

"Your opinion does not interest me," de Verceuil said. "I cannot imagine why King Louis trusted a beggar-priest to conduct diplomacy with the empire of Tartary."

The resentment Simon had felt at the cardinal's harsh speech at his expense now flared up in anger.

I am young and I do make mistakes, Simon thought. *But, cardinal or not, this man has no right to stand there in his velvet and satin and jewels and sneer at this fine old man. No right at all.*

But the old friar merely stroked his white beard with a wry smile and said, "I said that very thing to him myself, when he ordered me to go."

Still angry, Simon took a deep breath and said, "Since Your Eminence feels I have embarrassed the king and displeased the Count of Anjou, there is only one course open to me. I will resign my command of the ambassadors' guards."

Simon stared into de Verceuil's eyes, and the cardinal's eyelids fluttered. In the silence Simon heard a blackbird calling in nearby olive trees.

I never wanted to come here. I let Uncle Charles talk me into it. I do not mind the danger. And it would be exciting to outguess a hidden enemy who is trying to murder the Tartars. But I cannot endure the way this man humiliates me and my friends. I will go back to Gobignon now.

"You must not let a bit of fatherly correction wound you so deeply, Count," said the cardinal, his voice still deep and dirgelike but no longer full of scorn. "I would never suggest the Count of Anjou had made a mistake in choosing you for this post."

Fatherly! What a disgusting thought!

But Simon could see that his resigning worried de Verceuil. Uncle Charles wanted Simon to guard the ambassadors, just as he had wanted Sordello to head the archers. He had his reasons. And de Verceuil did not want to cross Charles d'Anjou.

Friar Mathieu laughed gently, and patted Simon on the shoulder. "If you please, be kind enough to change your mind about resigning. All of us are aware that you have carried out the task with intelligence and zeal. Is that not right, Your Eminence?"

"Of course," said de Verceuil, his mouth puckered and sour. "Count, I would have you present these Tartar dignitaries to me."

"I will be happy to interpret for you, Your Eminence," said Friar Mathieu. De Verceuil did not answer him.

As they crossed the vineyard, the cardinal stretched out his long arm and said, "I have brought musicians, jongleurs, senators of Orvieto, men-at-arms, two archbishops, six bishops, an abbot, and many monsignors and priests." A long line of men stretched down the road into the nearby woods. Most of them wore various shades of red; a few were in cloth-of-gold or blue. The points of long spears flashed in the sunlight. Banners with fringes of gold and silver swung at the tops of poles. Seeking protection from the mid-August heat, men walked horses in the shade of the woods.

Beyond the treetops rose a distant pedestal of grayish-yellow rock crowned by a city. An astonishing sight, Orvieto.

"The Holy Father will be meeting us at the cathedral and will say a special mass of thanksgiving for the safe arrival of the ambassadors," said de Verceuil. "I want the entry of the Tartars into Orvieto to impress both the Tartars themselves and the pope and his courtiers."

* * *

"Monsters!"

"Cannibals!"

Rotten apples, pears and onions, chunks of moldy bread, flew through the air. Small stones that did not injure, but stung. And worse.

The shouts and missiles came from both sides of the street, but always when Simon was looking the other way, so he could not see his assailants. The people crowded in front of the shops were mostly young men, but women and children were scattered among them. They wore the dull grayish and brownish garments of workers and peasants. The street-level windows behind them were shuttered, and the doors were closed tight. That was a sure sign, Simon knew from his Paris student days, that the shopkeepers expected trouble.

From the Porta Maggiore, the main gate where they had entered, the street curved toward the south side of the town. Though the upper stories of many houses overshadowed the street, there was room enough for the procession to move along, four horses abreast, and for the unruly people to gather on either side. Approaching the south wall of the city, the street made a sharp bend to the left, and Simon had lost sight of the Tartar emissaries behind, who were— *What a mistake!*—being carried in an open sedan chair. Were they being pelted with garbage?

Why were the people of Orvieto doing this? True, everyone in Christendom had heard wild tales of the Tartars. That they were monsters with dogs' heads. That they bit off the breasts of women. That they stank so abominably they overcame whole armies just with their smell. That they were determined to kill or enslave everyone on earth. There were churches where people prayed every Sunday to be delivered "from the fury of the Tartars."

But it had been over twenty years since the Tartars had invaded Europe, and even then they had come no farther than Poland and Hungary. Why should these people of Orvieto turn so violently against them now, when they came in peace?

Undoubtedly someone was stirring them up.

Hang de Verceuil and his orders, Simon thought. *I should be with the ambassadors. If someone wants to kill them, this would be a perfect chance.*

He tugged on the reins of his palfrey, pulling her head around. "Make way!" he shouted, spurring his horse back the way he had come. Men-at-arms with spears and crossbows cursed at him in various Italian dialects, but they opened a path, pushing back the people. Thierry rode a small horse in Simon's wake.

"Imps of Satan!" came a shout from the crowd. "The Tartars are devils!"

Simon scanned the faces below him. Some looked angry, some frightened, many bewildered. No one looked happy. The cardinal's hope for an impressive entry into Orvieto had been quite dashed, and Simon felt a sneaking pleasure at that.

Passing the corner where the procession had turned, he saw again a building he had passed earlier, a formidable three-story cube of yellow stone with slotted windows on the ground floor and iron bars over the wider upper windows.

And there is a man who looks happy.

He was standing in sunlight, leaning out from the square Guelfo battlements on the roof of the big building. His hair was the color of brass, his skin a smooth brown, such as Simon had seen on pilgrims newly returned from the crusader strongholds in Outremer. The blond man gazed down on the jostling, shouting crowd, smiling faintly.

As Simon rode past him, their eyes met. Simon was startled by the intensity of the other's gaze. It was as if a wordless message had crossed the space between them. A challenge. But then the blond man looked away.

The Tartar ambassadors, seated side by side in a large sedan chair, were farther up the street. Here, Simon noticed with relief, the crowd had fallen quiet. Perhaps curiosity about the Tartars, with their round brown faces and many-colored robes, had overcome whatever had roused these people against them. Then, too, the Tartars were surrounded by their Armenians marching on foot, curved swords drawn, as well as by Simon's knights on horseback, and Venetian crossbowmen. The archers' bows, Simon noticed, were loaded and drawn. Who had ordered that?

De Verceuil on a huge black horse—no palfrey this, but a powerful charger—rode up to Simon. "Why did you not remain in the forefront? What is going on up ahead?"

Without trying to defend himself, Simon described the disturbance.

"Could you not control the rabble?" de Verceuil growled, and turned to take a position beside the Tartars' sedan chair.

Simon's face burned, and his hands trembled as he stared after de Verceuil.

When they passed the yellow stone building, Simon looked up and saw the blond man still there on the roof. The man was staring down at the Tartars with that same burning look he had thrown at Simon, but there were no weapons in the hands that gripped the battlements.

Simon heard a slapping sound and an angry cry. He turned to see de Verceuil, his right cheek smeared brown.

God's death! Someone threw shit at him! And hit him right in the face.

The cardinal, his face distorted as if he were about to vomit, was staring at the stained hand with which he had just wiped his cheek.

There was laughter from the crowd, mixed with angry cries of, "Bestioni! Creatures from hell!"

For an instant Simon felt laughter bubbling up to his lips, but cold horror swept all amusement away as he sensed what was about to happen.

De Verceuil turned to the nearest crossbowmen, who had not suppressed their own smiles.

"Shoot!" he shouted. "Shoot whoever did that!"

The smiles remained fixed on the faces of the Venetians as three of them aimed their already-loaded crossbows at the crowd. They did not hesitate. This was not their city; these were not their people. They were fighting men who did as they were ordered.

People screamed and shrank back against the shuttered doors and windows.

Three loud snaps of the bowstrings came at the same moment as Simon's cry of "No!"

He shouted without thinking, and was surprised to hear his own voice. His cry echoed in a sudden and terrible quiet.

Screams of agony immediately followed. People darted away from the place where the crossbowmen had aimed, leaving that part of the street empty.

Empty save for three people. Two of them screamed. One was silent—a young man who half sat, half lay against the stone wall of a house. Blood was pouring out of his mouth and more blood was running from a hole in his chest. Simon saw that the blood was coming in a steady stream, not in rhythmic spurts, which meant the fellow's heart had stopped. A glance at the white face told Simon the dead youth could be no more than sixteen.

Beside the boy, a woman knelt and wept. She was plump and

middle-aged, perhaps his mother. Her white linen tunic was bloodied.

"He did nothing!" she cried. "Oh, Jesus! Mary! He did nothing!" There was a plea in her voice, as if she might bring the boy back to life if only she could persuade people of his innocence.

The other cries came from a man who stood about a yard from the dead boy. The bolt had gone through his left shoulder just above the armpit and pinned him to the oaken post of a doorway. He wanted to fall, but he had to stand or suffer unbearable pain.

"Help me!" he begged, casting pain-blinded eyes right and left. "Help me!"

Simon jumped down from his horse, throwing the reins to Thierry, and ran to the man. He put his left hand on the chest and pulled at the flaring end of the quarrel with his right. He could not move it. The bolt was buried too deeply in the wood. The man's forehead fell against Simon's shoulder, and he was silent. Simon hoped he had fainted.

Now Simon saw where the third bolt had gone. Six inches of it, half its length, was buried in a wall a few feet to Simon's right. The wall was made of the same grayish-yellow stone Orvieto was built on.

The crossbow bolt in the man's shoulder was thick and made of hard wood. Simon had nothing that would cut the man loose without hurting him even more. He looked up and down the street. It was quite empty now, except for a few people watching from a distance. The procession had gone on. He glanced up and saw that the blond man had left his place on the roof.

Friar Mathieu knelt beside the dead young man, one hand moving in blessing, the other resting on the shoulder of the weeping woman.

De Pirenne and Thierry, both mounted, the equerry holding Simon's horse, looked at him uncertainly.

"Go, Alain!" said Simon impatiently. "Stay with the Tartars."

He himself was neglecting his duty, he thought, as de Pirenne galloped off. But now that he was trying to help this poor devil, he could not abandon him.

"Can I do anything, Monseigneur?" Thierry asked.

As Simon was about to answer, he saw a middle-aged man wearing a carpenter's apron.

"Messere, can you bring a saw?" he called. "Hurry!"

It seemed hours before the man returned with a small saw with a pointed end and widely spaced teeth. He held it out to Simon.

Simon wanted to shout at the carpenter, but he took a grip on himself and said patiently, "You are bound to be better at sawing than I. Per favore, cut away the end of the crossbow bolt so we can free this man."

Gingerly at first, then working with a will, the carpenter sawed off the flaring end of the bolt with its thin wooden vanes. The pinned man awoke and was sobbing and groaning.

Once the protruding part of the bolt was sawed away, Simon took a deep breath, wrapped his arms around the sobbing man, and pulled him away from the wall. The man screamed so loudly that Simon's ears rang; then the man sagged to the ground. Blood flowed from the wound in his shoulder, soaking his tunic. Blood coated the stump of the bolt, still stuck in the door post. Simon dropped to his knees beside the wounded man. A pool of bright red widened rapidly on the flat paving stones.

Now what do I do with him? I must get back to my duty.

He spoke with the carpenter. "Press your hand on the wound, hard. That will slow the bleeding." Simon took the man's hand and put it on the hole the crossbow bolt had made.

"Here, let me do that." Friar Mathieu was on his knees beside the hurt man, his hand covering the wound. "Messere," he said to the carpenter, "ride my donkey to the hospital of the Franciscans. Tell them there is a man badly hurt here and Friar Mathieu d'Alcon says they are to send brothers to take him for treatment."

Simon stood up slowly as the carpenter climbed on Mathieu's donkey.

"It is not safe for you to stay here," he said to Friar Mathieu. "The people know you were part of the procession and may blame you for what happened."

Mathieu shook his head. "No one will hurt me. Go along now."

Simon jumped into the saddle and spurred his palfrey to a trot. Thierry rode beside him.

"Those two didn't throw anything," Thierry said.

"Of course not." Simon wondered if de Verceuil cared that the Venetians had shot two innocent men.

When Simon caught up with the procession, de Verceuil was still furiously scrubbing his face with his pale violet cloak.

"If you had done something sooner about the rioting, this outrage would not have happened to me," he said, a quaver of anger in his deep voice.

God help me, thought Simon. *I could easily grow to hate him. Cardinal or not.*

Word of the shootings must have spread through the city, Simon thought, because the twisting street leading to the cathedral was nearly empty.

But the piazza in front of Orvieto's cathedral of San Giovenale was packed with people. Simon's eye was immediately drawn to the top of the cathedral steps. There stood a white-bearded man wearing a red mantle over white robes glittering with gold ornament. On his head a tall white lozenge-shaped miter embroidered with a red and gold cross. In his hand, a great golden shepherd's crook at least seven feet tall. Simon's mouth fell open and he held his breath.

The ruler of the whole Catholic Church the world over, the chosen of God, the anointed of Christ, the heir of Saint Peter. His Holiness, Urban IV, the pope himself. Simon felt almost as much awe as he had that day in Paris when King Louis had let him kiss the Crown of Thorns.

How lucky I am to be here and see this man whom most Christians never see. It is close as one can come to seeing Jesus Christ Himself.

It looked to Simon as if the Holy Father were glowing with a supernatural light. To his left and his right stood a dozen or more men in bright red robes and wide-brimmed red hats with long red tassels dangling down to their shoulders. The cardinals, the princes of the Church. Simon wondered if the Tartars realized what honor this did them.

As soon as their sedan chair was set before the pope, the two short brown men stepped out of it, knelt, and pressed their foreheads to the cobblestones. They stayed that way until the pope gestured to de Verceuil, who bent and touched them on the shoulder and raised them up.

The pope turned and, followed by the Tartars and then the cardinals, proceeded into the cathedral. For this meeting to succeed, a papal mass was the best possible beginning.

So many people were ahead of Simon that Friar Mathieu caught up with him before he was able to enter the door of the cathedral.

"What do you think stirred up the crowd like that?" Simon asked as they pushed through the people standing in the nave of the church.

"In the cities of Italy the mob is always either furious or ecstatic," said Friar Mathieu.

"But to defile a cardinal!" Simon said. "That would never happen in France."

"Italians do not reverence the clergy as much as Frenchmen do," the Franciscan said with a little smile. "They have had to put up with the princes of the Church for so long that they are a good deal less awed by them."

The interior of the cathedral was ablaze with the light of a thousand candles, but Simon was not impressed by the windows, which were small and narrow and filled with dull-colored glass. This was an old church, he thought, remembering the huge windows of many-colored glass in the newer cathedrals of France.

The crowd was so tightly packed that Simon and Friar Mathieu could not get to the front of the nave, where chairs had been set before the altar for dignitaries. They had to be content with standing halfway down the length of the church. Simon thought wryly that he was getting used to being pushed into the background. Perhaps he was accepting it too easily.

Pope Urban, his white hair uncovered, had raised high the round wafer of bread for the Consecration of the Mass, when an angry shout echoed through the cathedral.

A chill went through Simon's body, cold as a knife blade. Using his shoulder as a wedge, he forced his way through the crowd toward the source of the sound, near the front of the church.

"Ex Tartari furiosi!" the man was shouting in Latin. "Libera nos, Domine!" *From the fury of the Tartars, Lord deliver us!* Cries of dismay rang out near the disturbance, and people began shouting in Italian.

"Stand aside! Let me through!" Simon shouted. If this were an assassin, reverence for the mass, even for the pope, must be set aside. Again and again the shout rose, "Ex Tartari furiosi!" It was harder to move through the crowd. People were struggling to get away from the man making the uproar.

Simon stopped, shoved men right and left to make room, and pulled his scimitar from his scabbard.

People around him turned at the unmistakable rasp of steel on leather, a sound that so often preceded sudden death. They saw the Saracen sword in Simon's hands and drew back. As Simon hoped, more people noticed and fell over one another trying to get out of his way.

Like Moses' rod parting the Red Sea, Simon's scimitar opened a path for him.

Simon saw a young man with a tangled mass of brown hair whipping about his face and a brown beard that spread over his chest. He was big and broad-shouldered, and he wore a plain white robe, ragged and gray with dirt, and sandals. In one hand he held a dagger.

Blood of Jesus! He must have come here to kill the Tartars.

Terrified people had opened a circle around the white-robed man, and as he moved toward the front of the cathedral the open space moved with him.

"Stop!" Simon cried.

Baring greenish-looking teeth in a snarl, the man swiveled his shaggy head toward Simon, then immediately rushed at him.

He's crazy, Simon thought, a hollow feeling in the pit of his stomach. He crouched, holding his sword out before him, diagonally across his chest.

"Do not kill him!" boomed a deep voice that Simon recognized as de Verceuil's.

The man with the dagger hesitated now, just out of reach of Simon's sword.

Am I to risk my life to keep this madman alive?

But de Verceuil's demand made sense. They must try to find out who sent the man.

Simon took a deep breath. He had practiced sword fighting innumerable times, but only twice in his life had he come up against an armed man with a look in his eyes that said he was willing to kill.

But this is no different from practice, he told himself.

He feinted to the white-robed man's left, then jumped forward, lifting his sword high and bringing the flat of it down with all his strength on the hand that held the dagger. The dagger tumbled through the air. Simon saw at once that the man had no martial skill.

The madman darted forward in a crouch to retrieve his dagger, and as he did so Simon kicked him in the chin. The thick beard protected the man's chin from the full force of Simon's pointed leather boot, but he staggered. Before the bearded man recovered himself, Alain de Pirenne charged out of the crowd, seized him in a bear hug, and wrestled him to the ground.

"Ex Tartari furiosi!" The shouts rang out again and again as the pope's guards dragged the would-be assassin out of the church.

Simon saw Pope Urban shake his bare white head slowly, then turn back to the high marble altar and raise the Host overhead once more.

De Verceuil and Friar Mathieu reached Simon at the same time. The cardinal held out his hand for the dagger, which Simon had retrieved, and studied it. "One could buy a hundred like it in any marketplace," he said, keeping his voice low now that the mass had resumed. He thrust the dagger into his black leather belt with a shrug.

"The white robe and sandals are the mark of the Apostolic Brethren," said Friar Mathieu. "Heretics who preach the doctrine of Joachim of Floris about a coming new age of enlightenment and equality."

"When it comes to heresy," said de Verceuil with an unfriendly grin, "there is little to choose between the Apostolic Brethren and the Franciscans. Many of your brethren are secret Joachimites."

"Of course, he might have been dressed that way only to deceive us," Friar Mathieu went on, ignoring the insult.

"We will find out who he is and whence he comes," said de Verceuil. "When we are through with him he will tell us everything. I have ordered him handed over to the podesta of Orvieto, who will subject him to questioning in his chamber of torment." He turned on the ball of his foot, his violet cloak swinging out behind him, and headed back toward the altar.

And not a word about my disarming the assassin, Simon thought angrily.

Friar Mathieu winced and shook his head sadly. "Then again, that man may not be able to say anything. And the less he can tell us, the more he will suffer. I pity him."

Simon cringed inwardly at the thought that by capturing the mad heretic he was the cause of the man's being subjected to horrible tortures. But greater fears preoccupied him. The Tartars had been in Orvieto only a few hours, and already the people had been stirred up against them and they had nearly been assassinated. Somewhere in this town an enemy lurked, and Simon's body turned cold as he wondered what that enemy would do next.

XII

A letter from Emir Daoud ibn Abdallah to El Malik Baibars al-Bunduqdari, from Orvieto, 21st day of Rajab, 662 A.H.:

Although the central part of Italy, the Papal States, is said to be under the control of the pope, I have learned that his army is barely large enough to protect his person and nowhere near enough to enforce his authority. Manfred could attack the pope whenever he wished, but he does not do so because he fears that the other princes of Europe would then attack him.

The northern part of Italy is divided among a number of cities, each of which is a small independent nation. These cities are often at war with one another. The most important are Venice, Genoa, Florence, Milan, Siena, Pisa, and Lucca.

Within each city there is also constant warfare among various factions. The palaces of the great families are all heavily fortified.

Italy is also divided between two parties, the Ghibellini and the Guelfi. These parties are to be found everywhere, constantly at each other's throats. They arose long ago in the northern part of the Holy Roman Empire, where the German language is spoken. The Hohenstaufen emperors came from the town of Waiblingen. And in the early days of the Hohenstaufens their enemies were a family named Welf. In Italy Welfs and Waiblings have become Guelfi and Ghibellini.

Each day I come to realize more and more how complicated the history of Europe is. It seems that most of Italy has been claimed by the Holy Roman Empire—but Rome itself is not part of that empire. Members of the Hohenstaufen family have been Holy Roman Emperors for over two hundred years, and they have always been at war with the popes. Why the emperor should be called "holy" when he is traditionally the enemy of the pope I do not understand.

Furthermore, at this time there is no Holy Roman Emperor. The last one was Conrad, son of Frederic and half brother of Manfred. He died ten years ago, and then Manfred proclaimed himself king of southern Italy and Sicily. The German part of the Holy Roman Empire is in a more chaotic state than Italy, if my lord can imagine such a thing.

Here in Orvieto, where the pope has settled for his safety, there are no Ghibellini. The townsmen have managed to find other reasons to fight among themselves. The chief rivalry is between two great families, the Monaldeschi and the Filippeschi. Since the Tartar emissaries are guests of the Monaldeschi, I hope to make friends with the Filippeschi.

Seated at a table in his little room at Cardinal Ugolini's, Daoud made two copies of his letter to Baibars on small sheets of parchment scraped so thin as to be almost transparent. He had written the letters in a code using the Arabian system of numbers. Even if the message suffered the unlikely fate of being intercepted and finding its way to one of the few Arabic-reading Christians, it would remain an enigma.

Daoud rolled up the two letters tightly and put them in the leather scrip at his belt. He stepped out of his room into a narrow corridor. Doors on his right opened into rooms for Ugolini's guests and high-ranking members of his staff. On his left, oiled-parchment windows let light into the corridor from the atrium of the mansion.

Ugolini's cabinet, his private workroom, was at the end of the corridor, where it turned a corner. Daoud walked up to the heavy oaken door and raised his fist to knock.

He felt light-headed, as he did when going into combat. This was combat of a kind. He had been a guest in Ugolini's mansion for over two weeks now, and he had already, he thought, hurt the Tartars' prospects for an alliance with the Christians. But he needed to do much more, with help from Ugolini. The cardinal, Daoud knew, would be absolutely terrified at the thought of his Muslim guest appearing before the pope.

And to appear before the pope, with the cardinal presenting him, was precisely what Daoud wanted to do.

He knocked on the cabinet door.

To the muffled query from within he answered, "It is David."

He heard a bolt slide back, and he entered the cabinet. Cardinal Ugolini returned to the high-backed chair at his worktable, which was strewn with leather-bound books and parchment scrolls. In the middle of the table lay a large, circular brass instrument Daoud recognized as an astrolabe. On shelves behind the cardinal, besides many more books and papers, were a stuffed falcon, a stuffed owl, and a human skull with a strange diagram painted on the cranium. Windows of translucent white glass in two walls let in an abundance of light. A good place to work, thought Daoud.

"I hope I do not disturb you, Your Eminence," said Daoud.

"Not at all, David," said the cardinal. "It is very necessary that we talk."

Cardinal Adelberto Ugolini was a short, stout man with long gray whiskers that swept out like wings from his full cheeks. His receding chin was as bare as the bald top of his head, partly covered now by a red skullcap. He wore a plain black robe, like a priest's, but from a chain around his neck hung a gold cross set with five matching blue jewels. Daoud wondered if the cross concealed a poisoned stiletto like Tilia's. Besides books and scrolls, Daoud noticed, there were rows of porcelain jars on the shelves against the wall. Each had a Latin word painted on it. Ugolini might well dabble in poison.

"The man they seized in the cathedral is to be publicly torn to pieces," Ugolini said. "They have been torturing him in the Palazzo del Podesta for three days and two nights, but they have learned nothing from him, except that he is a member of the Apostolic Brethren, a follower of the heretic Joachim of Floris."

If I am to go before the pope, I must learn about the disputes among Christians. It would not do to offend the Christian leaders by accidentally uttering heresy.

"What does this Joachim teach?"

Ugolini waved his hands dismissively. "Joachim died long ago, but his rubbish and madness still stir up the simple folk. The Church is too wealthy. The clergy are corrupt. The Age of the Holy Spirit is coming, in which there will be peace, justice, and freedom and all property will be owned in common."

The doctrines of the Apostolic Brethren sounded to Daoud like the teachings of the Hashishiyya, as told to him by Imam Fayum al-Burz.

Ugolini shook himself like a wet dog. "It is dangerous for you to involve yourself with such people as the Brethren."

It is dangerous for me to be here at all, Daoud thought, irritated at Ugolini's timidity.

"This heretic does not know me, so there is nothing he can tell them that will point to us. You need not fear."

"I feel no fear," Ugolini said grandly. "How did you get that man to draw a dagger in the cathedral?" Ugolini asked. "And the crowd, how did you stir them up?"

Daoud saw the tiny quiverings of Ugolini's pupils, the tightness of his lips, the clenching of his jaws, the signs of a man in a permanent state of terror.

Daoud shrugged and smiled. "Celino found the madman preaching against the Tartars at a crossroads and had men in his pay bring him to Orvieto. We did not tell him what to do. He did what he was moved to do. As for the crowd, all that was needed was for Celino to drop a word here and a coin there. Many people believe the Tartars are demons from hell. Perhaps they are. Anyway, I think we have turned the people of Orvieto against the Tartars.''

"You are like a child playing with flint and tinder in a barn full of straw," said Ugolini, blinking his eyes rapidly.

He must be prodded into action, Daoud thought. *Tilia said the idea of my appearing before the pope would terrify him. We must settle that today.*

Daoud walked to one of the four mullioned windows. The casements swung inward for air. Looking down through the iron bars on the outside of the window, Daoud regarded the street where the Tartars had passed. The pottery maker across the road had washed away the bloodstains and was sitting in front of his shop displaying his brightly colored wares.

What would move this man Ugolini—money, threats, the promise of personal power?

He turned back and made himself smile.

"You do not want me here, Your Eminence."

Ugolini looked at him for a long moment, and finally said, "For over a dozen years Baibars has been a far-off figure who sends me small rewards in return for scraps of harmless information. Now, suddenly, his agent is in my home, demanding that I, the cardinal camerlengo of the Sacred College, risk death by torture to deceive the pope and betray the Church. In a week or two in the cathedral piazza, they will do horrible things to that poor mad heretic. But his sufferings will not be the tenth part of what they will do to me—and to you—if we are found out.''

Daoud bowed his head. "The sooner I complete my work, the sooner I am gone."

While he let that sink in, he decided that with his next words he would pit his boldness against Ugolini's timidity.

"So, you must present me to the pope as soon as possible."

Ugolini's eyes grew wide and his mouth trembled. His stare, with his sharp nose, tiny chin, and trembling whiskers, gave him the look of a jerboa, one of those desert rats that Daoud had hunted with hawks in Palestine.

"Tilia told me you had some such mad notion," said the cardinal. "If you speak to the pope and his court, every important man in Orvieto will see you. If you make the slightest slip that could reveal what you really are, they will be on you like hounds on a fox.'' He laughed nervously. ''No, no, no, no. I might as well take you to de Verceuil and say, 'Here is the enemy you are looking for. Behold, a Muslim, even a Mameluke! And, by the way, it was *I* who brought him into Orvieto.' ''

Ugolini covered his eyes with his hand. He did look as if he had been losing sleep, Daoud thought, remembering what Tilia had told him.

Daoud felt his teeth grinding together in frustration. It would be easier to fight a band of Tartars than to try to put courage into this one little man. And he needed more from the cardinal than compliance.

I must make him want, not just to help me, but to lead the opposition to the Tartars. Otherwise this will be like trying to move the arms and legs of a dead man.

''The cardinals speak Latin to one another, do they not?'' Daoud asked. ''I will say my piece in Greek and you will translate it into Latin for me. So you will have a chance to cover any errors I make.''

''Why must you go before the pope?'' Ugolini demanded. ''It is foolish bravado. Remain in seclusion and tell me what you want done and I will have it done for you.''

The thought of keeping himself in hiding while trying to act through others made Daoud's flesh crawl. But there was a bit of hope here. At least Ugolini was offering to do *something*.

''This is a thing only I can do,'' Daoud said. ''Only I have seen the Tartars, met them in battle. Only I have seen what they do to a conquered city.'' The sight and smell of those heaps of rotting corpses arose in his mind, and he shut his eyes momentarily. ''What I can say is too important a weapon to be left unwielded. I know the Tartars better than any man in Orvieto, except for that priest in the brown robe who came with them. And he is on the other side.''

''How will you tell what you know without admitting that you are a Muslim warrior?''

''Many Christian traders now visit the lands occupied by the Tartars. David of Trebizond has been one of them.'' He spread his arms. ''As you see, I now dress like a wealthy merchant.''

Celino had gone out with a bag of florins from Ugolini's first sale of jewels, and he had come back with a chest full of new clothes for Daoud. Today Daoud wore a silk cape as red as a cardinal's robe. It was light in weight and came down to his knees, more for display than for covering. Under the cloak he wore a tunic of deep purple embroidered with gold thread.

Ugolini shook his head. "Clothing will not deceive the pope and those around him. You are asking too much of me."

Daoud wished he could give this up. Ugolini was nothing but a sodden lump of fear. But he had no choice but to keep trying. The cardinal was his gateway to the papal court.

"Think of the reward," Daoud urged. "Part of the wealth I have brought with me is already yours. If the pope sends the Tartars away without an agreement, my sultan will give to you with both hands."

Ugolini looked tormented. "But the peril—"

Daoud had been certain that money would not be enough to enlist Ugolini's cooperation. Baibars already had been generous with him. *Bribes alone will not move this man.*

As he searched his brain for another approach, his eyes explored the room. The skull, the powders, the brass instruments. Ugolini was a student of many strange things, things verging on magic. Were these not odd interests for a Christian prelate? He knew Greek, which was rare for a Latin Christian. He had spoken of heresy before. Was he not, in his willingness to correspond with Baibars, a heretic of a kind? And perhaps in these studies of his as well.

I must remind him that he sympathizes with us.

"My master sent me to you because he knows you are a friend to Islam."

Ugolini raised a cautioning hand. "Mind you, I am a Christian."

"I do not doubt it," said Daoud.

"Not a very good Christian," Ugolini went on, sighing and looking off into space. "God grant that I make a good confession before I breathe my last. But I am also of the south of Italy, and in my youth I lived side by side with Muslims. I had Muslim teachers, wise men. From them I learned about philosophy, medicine, astrology, alchemy. I learned how much there is to know that I may never know."

Daoud felt his eager heart beat more rapidly. Ugolini was speaking just as he wanted.

"God help me, I yearn so for more worldly knowledge," Ugolini went on. "That was why I studied for the priesthood, so I could go to the University of Napoli. But what one can learn at a Christian university is not enough. I want to know what you Saracens know. And so I long for peace between Christendom and Islam.''

Daoud felt excitement surge through his arms and legs. He was exhilarated, as when in battle he sensed his opponent was weakening.

He pressed his point. "You will never possess the knowledge you long for if the Tartars destroy it. Think what was lost when they leveled Baghdad. Think what will be lost if they destroy Cairo, Thebes, Alexandria.''

"Oh, God!" Ugolini cried, waving hands bent like claws. "There is so much I could learn in Egypt. If only this stupid enmity between Muslim and Christian did not hold me back. I am tortured like Tantalus.''

"As cardinal camerlengo, the pope's chamberlain, you could bring before the pope a traveler from far away whose testimony might influence his decisions about the Tartars. Because of you, all that would be lost might be saved.''

Daoud held his breath, waiting for Ugolini's reply.

Ugolini smiled resignedly. "To work for what I believe in, to help my friends. And to be rewarded with riches. How can I refuse?" His expression changed again as he looked earnestly at Daoud. "I do not know as much as your great Islamic astronomers, but I have plotted the courses of some stars, and I know how they rule our destinies. And my recent readings have told me that I will take a risk that will yield me rewards beyond my hopes.''

"Then you will present me to the pope as a witness?"

Ugolini first shook his head, but then sighed and nodded. "I can propose a meeting. And may the stars watch over us," he added as his right hand traced the Christian sign of the cross on his forehead, shoulders, and breast.

The stars, your Messiah, and the One God I worship, thought Daoud. He allowed himself momentarily to feel the thrill of triumph. Ugolini had begun to move as he wanted him to. But now he must prepare himself for a much greater trial, his meeting with the pope.

A little while later, walking through a ground-floor doorway into the sunlit atrium of Ugolini's mansion, Daoud saw Sophia and Rachel standing by the fish pond, under orange and lemon trees. The polished dark-green leaves reflected the mid-morning sun upward and cast shade downward on the stone paths and the pool.

Reflected sunlight rippled over Sophia's peach-colored gown. A narrow gold bracelet on her wrist flashed as she raised her hand to make a point. The answering smile that lit Rachel's face foretold that she would be a beautiful woman in a few years. She was dressed better than she had been when they first met her, Daoud noticed. That ankle-length blue silk gown must belong to Sophia.

"The cardinal has just had an immense turbot delivered all the way from Livorno, Messer David," said Rachel, her black eyes bright with wonder. "Alive, in a barrel of water. Look, you can see it down there at the bottom."

Daoud looked down into the clear water, saw a tapering dark shape moving gently just above the yellow pebbles lining the bottom of the pool. Smaller brown carp darted this way and that above it.

"The cardinal's gold makes great things possible," he said. "Will you leave us for a while, Rachel?"

Sophia handed a small leather-bound book to Rachel. "You may read these poems of Ovid if you like."

Rachel clasped the book to her narrow chest. "I do not read Latin, Signora, but I will look at the pictures."

"Have a care," said Sophia with a light laugh. "Some of them may shock you."

"Then I will try to enjoy being shocked." Rachel bowed and hurried away.

Daoud listened to the banter between the woman and the girl with mixed feelings. He liked both of them, and he enjoyed hearing them joke with each other. He imagined women must talk that way among themselves back in El Kahira, but if they did, men never had a chance to hear.

He also felt deeply uneasy at the growing closeness between Rachel and Sophia. The two of them shared a room on the top floor of Ugolini's mansion, next to Daoud's and Lorenzo's. His stomach tightened as he thought of the long talks they might have. What if Rachel learned that Sophia was actually a Byzantine woman, when she was supposed to be the cardinal's niece from Sicily? And what if Rachel then let that slip to a servant? Byzantines, Greek Catholics, were hated almost as much as Muslims here in the lands of the Latin Church. One small, seemingly harmless revelation like that could destroy them utterly.

I must get them separated.

Turning to Sophia, Daoud was struck once again that so much

beauty should openly display itself outside a harem. A narrow cloth-of-gold ribbon wound around her neck, crossed between her breasts and tied her pale peach gown tightly at the waist. Her lustrous black hair was bound in a net of gold thread.

She looked at him quizzically. Daoud studied her face. Her long, straight nose, dark red lips and delicate chin made him glad that Christian women went unveiled. He could well believe this woman had enjoyed the attentions of an emperor and a king. He himself could not look at her without wishing he might take her in his arms.

"Well, my Frankish-Turkish master-slave, what has your busy mind found for me to do? Do you wish me to get myself shot in the street by Venetians? Or create a disturbance in church and be tortured to death?"

Her thrusts caught Daoud off balance. Feeling a surge of anger, he was silent for a moment.

Then he jabbed a finger at her. "Do you understand what is at stake here?"

Her full lower lip pushed out. "I do not understand why you had to send a pious simpleton to a horrible death."

Guilt twisted in Daoud's guts like a Hashishiyya dagger. Yet he could not admit to Sophia that he regretted what happened to the heretic. She might approve his feeling, but she would also lose confidence in him.

"I will use any weapon I can find," he said. "Even if it breaks in my hand."

Sophia sat down on the marble lip of the fish pond. After a moment's hesitation Daoud sat beside her, smoothing his red cloak under him.

"Where is Lorenzo?" she asked. "I have not seen him since the day the Tartars arrived."

"He visits Spoleto, to find a few bold men for me." Lorenzo would bring back two or three men from Spoleto. Later he would gather more men in Viterbo, Chiusi, and other nearby cities. Imperceptibly over the coming months, bands of armed men—the Italians called them "bravos"—would gather in Orvieto to do Daoud's bidding.

Acting as a go-between for Daoud and the bravos was a mission at which Lorenzo should do well.

"The men Lorenzo brings here will not know my name or my face," he went on. "In a few days Cardinal Ugolini will take me before the pope, and I will warn him against the Tartars from my own true experience of them. I must not be connected with other things done against the Tartars, disturbances among the people, armed attacks. That is why Rachel is such a danger."

She had been looking thoughtfully at the pebbled path. When he spoke Rachel's name, she lifted her head to stare at him.

"Are you going to make me give up Rachel?"

That annoyed him. "You agreed. Have you forgotten?"

"No, but I thought now that she has been with us awhile and there has been no trouble, you might change your mind."

"I do not change my mind so easily." By God, working with this woman was an ordeal. She argued and complained far too much. He wondered whether showing their faces in public made Christian women overbold.

"But where can she go? You would not really cast her out to starve."

"Tilia Caballo will take her in."

"You will force her into that horrible fat woman's brothel? And she only a child?"

"She is nearly thirteen. Many women are married by then."

"She has not even started bleeding yet."

"How do you know that?" Daoud felt somewhat embarrassed.

"She told me, of course."

"She need only be a serving girl at Tilia's."

"No doubt Tilia would find her too precious a commodity *not* to be sold. There are old men who would give that woman her own weight in gold to get their hands on an intact virgin child. And these high churchmen can afford it."

Daoud remembered the rough hands of the first Turks who captured him and shuddered inside himself. "She does not have to lie with men unless she chooses that life."

"Do you really think you and Tilia would be giving her a choice?" said Sophia angrily.

Again Daoud's feelings struggled against each other. He liked the way she spoke up fiercely for the child. Yet it angered him that she was making it harder for him to deal with the painful problem of Rachel.

"How much choice is anyone in this world given?" he demanded.

"Are you not here by choice, David?"

"I am the slave of my sultan," he said. "That is what the word

Mameluke means—slave. He sent me here. But I am also here by choice.''

"To save Islam from the Tartars." She reached her fingertips into the water and dabbed the droplets on her forehead.

He caught the note of skepticism in her voice. "Yes. Do you not believe that?"

"Can you see yourself through my eyes?" There was an earnestness in her face, as if she badly wanted not to doubt him.

"No, how do you see me?" he asked gently.

"I see a Frankish warrior, fair of hair and face." She turned and looked directly at him, then quickly cast her eyes down. "Good looking enough, for a Frank." She gestured toward his knee, encased in scarlet silk. "You show a handsome leg in your new hose."

Why, she cares for me! He felt a little leap of delight, and reminded himself that he must not let himself be drawn to Sophia.

"You and the Turks call all men from western Europe Franks," he said. "But my parents were not from France, but of English descent."

"You could go back to France or England with your jewels and buy a castle and lands and an army of retainers and live like a little king. And forget all about Islam and the Tartars."

He did not want to argue with her. He wanted to reach out and touch her lips with his fingertips.

"I consider myself blessed by God to have been raised amid the glories of Egypt rather than in ignorance and dirt among those you call Franks."

She nodded. "We Greeks think the people of Arabia and Egypt are the only other civilized people in the world. Almost as civilized as we Greeks." She said the last with a smile, and he noticed that her cheeks dimpled.

He laughed. "What makes you so civilized?"

She clasped her hands between her knees and cast her eyes upward as if in deep thought. "Ah, well, our churches are huge and magnificent."

"So are our mosques."

"Our paintings and mosaics and statues of saints and angels and emperors are the most beautiful in the world."

"Idols," he interrupted, but he turned to her and smiled as she had. "The Prophet ordered idols destroyed."

"And therefore the art of painting languishes among you," she said, poking her forefinger into his shoulder. "Someday I will show you my paintings if you promise not to destroy them."

His shoulder tingled where she had touched him. She must have been carried away by her feelings about the arts of her homeland to make such a gesture. Surely it could not have been deliberate. His hand rested between them on the edge of the fountain. He moved a bit closer to her so that the edge of his hand nearly touched her thigh.

He nodded. "I will teach you the art of calligraphy as my Sufi master practiced it, and save your soul."

I would really like to do that. Ah, but I cannot teach her to write Arabic. What if someone were to see her practice work?

He sighed inwardly.

"Hm," she grunted. "I doubt that *you* can save *my* soul. But as for writing, we are familiar with dramatists like Sophocles, philosophers like Aristotle. We read Latin poets like Ovid, whose book I just gave to Rachel. Here in his native Italy his work is thought licentious."

"I have read Aristotle and Plato in Arabic," he said. "And I have no doubt our Persian poets sing as gloriously as your Greeks and Latins. And for licentious tales, those told in our bazaars would turn your cheeks bright red."

Those cheeks were a smooth cream color, he observed. He looked about him. There was no one but himself and Sophia in the atrium. A multistoried gallery lined with columns and arches ran around all four sides of the central courtyard. There might be servants, spies for the cardinal, watching them, but he could see no one on any of the levels.

To the devil with them all.

For weeks he had been wanting to reach out and touch that unveiled beauty, that ivory skin. Now he did it. Very lightly his fingers traveled from her cheekbone to her jaw.

She reached up and took his hand—not to remove it, as he had momentarily thought she might, but to hold it briefly against her cheek, then let it go.

They sat silently looking at each other. She was so still that she seemed not even to breathe, while he discovered that his heart was beating fast and hard. He wanted to kiss her, but not here, where hidden eyes might be watching.

But kissing her at all would be a mistake.

The thought shook him—the realization that he must not get any closer to her. He felt as if a rope were tied around his neck and a cruel slave master had jerked on it.

She is not for me. She is for my mission.

He turned away from her.

"It is better if we do not grow too close," he said, fixing his eyes on a nearby orange tree. "I must use you. I will send you as my sultan has sent me, and you will lie with the man I choose as my quarry."

He looked back and saw that she was smiling sadly, her eyes clouded with disappointment. It pleased him in a bittersweet way to see that she shared his unhappiness.

"I am *your* slave, then?"

He shook his head. "I do not know whose you are—King Manfred's, I suppose. Or perhaps Emperor Michael's? You have been given to me in trust, like that emerald I brought here from El Kahira—from Cairo. What you will have to do here will be no worse, I am sure, than what you must have had to do before this."

"I am sure." There was a dark note in her voice now. He wished he could take back what he said and ease her bitterness, but he had spoken truly, and it was needful that she realize it.

"If you serve me well, I will reward you," he promised. "You will be able to do anything in the world you want."

"Of that I cannot be sure," she said.

This time it was he who took her hand and held it tightly for a moment. Her hand felt cool and lifeless in his grasp.

"We may not be lovers," he said, "but perhaps we can be friends."

"Perhaps," she said distantly.

Nettled, he rose and left her. If she would not accept him on those terms, could he trust her? He turned his back on her and left the garden.

He longed to know her thoughts. Could she love him? He knew he should not hope for that, because it would have to come to nothing, but he hoped she loved him at least a little.

It was not until he was back in his apartment, about to begin his noon prayer, facing the charcoal mark he had made on the wall to point out the direction of Mecca, that he realized what she had done to him.

Rachel! We settled nothing about Rachel.

He struck his fist on the wall. He would have to be more careful with Sophia. She could be very difficult. Even dangerous.

It is time I had a woman.

When a man went without the delights of the bedchamber for too long, he became too susceptible to the cleverness of beautiful women.

It had been four months since that last night in El Kahira when his wife, Baibars's favorite daughter, Blossoming Reed, had kept him awake all night with her devouring love, not caring that he must begin a great journey the following day—yes, *because* he was leaving her.

He remembered the words she had said to him when she gave him the locket just before the battle of the Well of Goliath. *Take for your pleasure as many women as you like. But love always and only me. For if you do love another, I promise you that your love will destroy both her and you.*

It would be best if he went to Tilia Caballo's brothel and enjoyed a woman he was not so likely to fall in love with.

Daoud strode through the crowded streets at dusk, enjoying the golden light that fell on the upper stories of the yellow houses of Orvieto. His scarlet cape blew out behind him, and out of the corner of his eye he saw heads turn to follow his passage. He walked close to the houses on his right, keeping away from the ruts and the rivulets of sewage in the center of the street. Men stepped into the filth, making way for him. He was bigger and better dressed than anyone he met, and a new sword with a jeweled hilt swung at his belt. The glances he caught from the short, dark men of Orvieto were not friendly.

They think I am a Frank, and like Sophia they hate Franks.

Pigs rooted in garbage in the quintane, the narrow spaces between the houses. Small dogs ran under his feet. What backward, unsanitary people these Europeans were! The sights and smells of Orvieto made him wish for the paved streets of El Kahira, where every day an army of slaves swept and cleared away refuse.

The cardinal had drawn a map of Orvieto for him, showing the principal streets and the way to Tilia's house. Daoud had committed the map to memory, using the concentration technique Saadi had taught him. Most of the streets had no names. He would have to find his way by landmarks. In the days to come, he planned, he would explore and add to the map in his mind until he knew every street in Orvieto.

The house of Tilia Caballo stood on a street that was wider than most at the east end of town. Even though Ugolini had described it as ordinary-looking, Daoud was surprised to see how much it resembled the shabby buildings on either side of it. He had expected some sign of luxury, some flamboyance. He had thought to hear music as he approached, as he would have outside one of the brothels of El Kahira—before Baibars closed them. The house was quiet, unadorned save for a third-floor balcony above the entryway. It gave no sign of who its occupants were. He knew it only by counting—fifth house from the corner, Ugolini had said. Unlike the roof of the cardinal's palace, which was flat, the roof of Tilia's house was sharply peaked.

It looked like anything but a brothel. And though there were enough small houses near it to hold two or three hundred people, the street was not crowded, as were streets everywhere else in Orvieto. He saw a few men lounging in doorways, a pair of men walking arm in arm past Tilia's front door, but that was all. Distinguished churchmen and men of wealth and good family could come here without attracting notice.

Even so, I seem to be the only visitor who comes before dusk. Well, if people see me and think I am a well-to-do merchant who frequents Orvieto's finest brothel, that is exactly what I want them to think.

He felt the heaviness in his groin and the lightness in his stomach that always accompanied his visits to women when he had done without pleasure for a long time. He wondered if the Christian courtesan he picked tonight would be able to match the accomplishments of the women who served the Mamelukes in El Kahira. She would surely not be able to equal the incredible pleasures he had enjoyed with Blossoming Reed.

He knocked at the plain dark-brown door, and it swung open immediately, as if the one behind it had watched him approach. There stood one of Tilia's black men, wearing a turban, robes, and pantaloons that for all the world made him look like a harem guard in El Kahira. The costume made Daoud uneasy. The slave bowed in silence, and with a sweep of his arm bade Daoud enter.

The entrance hall was a surprise. It seemed much too large for the building he had just entered. He stood on a Persian carpet in a wide, high-ceilinged room filled with light. Candles burned in sconces around the walls and in two chandeliers hanging from the ceiling. Two tall, thick candles stood in twisting brass stands the height of a man on either side of a marble staircase. A pungent fragrance filled the air, and Daoud realized that the candles were scented. If Tilia could afford to burn this many candles every night, her trade must be profitable indeed.

He understood now why the interior of Tilia's establishment was so different from the exterior. She must have acquired all the buildings side by side along this street and then hollowed them out. He noticed that where the walls of the building through which he had entered should have been, there stood marble Roman columns two stories high. Counting the rows of columns stretching right and left, he estimated that this great hall must be as wide as five of the original houses that had been absorbed into Tilia's mansion.

The black man struck a large gong beside the door, giving off a low, mellow note. Almost immediately Tilia appeared at the top of the staircase. Smiling broadly, she flounced down the steps, the gold and jewels scattered over her person throwing off sparks in every direction.

"I knew you would be coming soon, David," she said in a low voice. "I am glad you came early in the evening. We can talk freely now. If more of my clients were here, we would have to seclude ourselves."

Daoud jerked his head at the black servant. "Why in God's name do you dress your men as Muslims here, where there is so much fear and hatred of 'Saracens,' as they call us?"

Tilia laughed, the pillow of flesh under her chin quivering. "Do you not know that it has long been fashionable among Christians to borrow from the world of Islam? They copy everything from ways of dressing to words and ideas. Most people think the Hohenstaufens have gone too far with their Saracen army, but among the great houses of Italy each must have its Moorish servants with great turbans and sashes and pantaloons. And here in Orvieto, the pope's city, it makes my clients feel especially wicked to enter a house staffed with slaves so dressed."

"I would not enjoy going into a brothel where the servants were dressed like Christian monks," Daoud said scornfully.

Tilia sighed. "I will tell you what seeing these men in Saracen garb does for me. It reminds me of when I was a young woman in Cairo." She looked around at her hall and sighed again. "Young and beautiful and unhappy. Now I am rich and content, but I tell you in all honesty I would give all this up to be young and beautiful."

Daoud was surprised. He had not known that Tilia had once lived in El Kahira. Was that, he wondered, how Baibars came to know her? Was that why, even though Daoud did not fully trust her, he felt oddly comfortable with her?

"And where are the young and beautiful and unhappy women in this house, then?"

She smiled and laid a hand on his arm. "Are you here to avail yourself?"

"First, I want to send a message to my master. Then that."

"Of course. Come with me."

He followed her up the marble steps, idly wondering if her rump looked as huge with her gown off, and whether Cardinal Ugolini actually did go to bed with her, and if so how he could be aroused by such a grossly fat woman. Not that Ugolini, with his rodent's face, was any more attractive than his mistress.

The stairs to the third floor were narrower and darker and more winding, and after that there was a maze of corridors to negotiate. Even with the help of the Sufi mental training for warriors, Daoud knew he would never be able to find his way here again.

Tilia gestured to a trapdoor. "Push that back for me."

Daoud climbed a ladder, raised the heavy door, and found himself on a walkway built over the centerline of a roof. It was wide enough for two men to stand side by side, but there was no railing, and on either side the red-tiled roof sloped down sharply. The walkway led to a small structure made of wooden slats, from which Daoud heard fluttering and cooing. The sight of the dovecote and the sound of the warbling pigeons reminded Daoud of the rooftops of El Kahira, and for a moment he yearned for a sight of the Bhar al-Nil flowing swiftly past the city or the sound of the muezzin's call to prayer.

He stopped to look around. This was an excellent vantage point. From here he could see that Tilia's mansion was actually shaped like Ugolini's, a hollow square around an atrium. The difference was that her establishment was made from the joining of many houses that had once been separate. From here he could also see most of Orvieto. Rows and rows of peaked roofs glowed warm red and orange in the sunset. Off in the northwest corner of the city bulked the great roof of the cathedral, like a galley among rowboats. To the south, the six square turrets of the pope's palace. And on all sides of the city, the rounded green hills of this part of Italy called Umbria.

"The piccioni fly to Napoli," said Tilia breathlessly behind him.

Daoud was amazed at how she had managed to climb so many steps and finally a ladder. There must be muscle under all that fat.

He pulled open the whitewashed wooden door of the dovecote. His entry set off a furious flapping of wings, unleashing a storm of feathers in the dark enclosure. The smell of pigeon droppings was heavy in the warm air. He began breathing through his mouth to keep the odor out of his nose. Tilia pushed past him, whistling and clucking to the pigeons and calming them down.

"Who gets the messages in Napoli?" he asked.

She turned to him with a smile. "Another brothel keeper. A man. I will not tell you his name. The wives of my piccioni live in his dovecote. When I release a piccione here, he flies to Napoli and visits with his wife until one of my servants rides there and brings him back. Piccioni are much more faithful to their mates than men and women."

Daoud laughed. He enjoyed Tilia's cynicism. The strong light of the setting sun fell in bars through the slats across her face and body.

"How long does it take for the messages to reach El Kahira?"

She looked at him as if he were a simpleton. "Who can say? From Napoli someone must take the message capsules aboard a ship to a port in Outremer. So, how long it takes depends on whether the sea is angry or calm. Once in Outremer they might go on by piccioni again or by camel caravan. Once I had a reply within two months. The longest I had to wait was a year and three months." She had, Daoud noted, the brothel keeper's good memory for numbers.

"May this arrive sooner than that." Daoud reached into a leather scrip at his belt and drew out the two rolled slips of parchment, each crowded with tiny Arabic characters.

"Two letters? Where is the other one going?"

"Both to Baibars. They are duplicates. We do that in the field whenever possible. Twice as much chance that the message will get through."

"I will send one tonight and the other tomorrow morning. What are you telling him?"

Daoud was not sure Tilia should be asking him that. But as "Morgiana" she had sent Baibars dozens of long letters from Orvieto. Surely no one had a better right to know about this correspondence.

Daoud shrugged. "That I have arrived here safely with two companions sent with me by King Manfred, and that we have been welcomed by the one who was awaiting me. Even though this is written in a cipher, your name and the cardinal's name are not mentioned. I go on to say that we have stirred up the people of Orvieto against the Tartars and that I will soon speak against them before the pope. And I tell him something of what I have learned about Italy. He is very curious about the lands of the infidel.''

"The cardinal has agreed to present you to Pope Urban, then?'' Her eyebrows twitched and her mouth tightened.

Her look of displeasure irritated him. For all he knew, it was her influence that made Ugolini so difficult. But, he thought with grudging admiration, she herself seemed more resolute than the cardinal.

"He came to see that it was the only course open to us.''

"You are persuasive. I see better why your master sent you.'' She took the parchments from him, rolled them even tighter, and tied each one into a tiny leather capsule. One capsule disappeared into a jeweled purse that hung on her hip. The other she put aside while she reached into a cage, whistling and twittering. Her hand came out again grasping a pigeon.

"This is Tonio. He is ten years old. He always gets through.'' Daoud was amazed at how calmly the pigeon reposed in Tilia's hand. He was even more surprised when she handed the bird to him, but he quickly took him, holding him around the back with thumb and forefinger behind his head, leaving his chest free so he could breathe easily.

"You've handled birds before,'' she said, deftly fastening a capsule under Tonio's wing. She took the bird back from Daoud. Outside the coop, she opened her hands and the bird took off with a fanning of wings.

"There now,'' said Tilia. "With that out of the way, perhaps you would like a piccione of another sort for your pleasure.''

"I would indeed,'' said Daoud, feeling a warmth spread through his body.

"I have just the one for you,'' Tilia said, patting him on the arm as they returned to the trap door. "Her name is Francesca. She is beautiful, warm-hearted, and very discreet. She will serve you supper, and if you like her, you may spend the night with her. And you need pay me nothing.''

"You are too generous, Madama,'' said Daoud, recovering from a small surprise. He had assumed that Tilia would give him access to her women out of simple hospitality, and it had never occurred to him that he would have to pay.

XIII

SIMON STOOD SHIFTING FROM FOOT TO FOOT IN THE GRAVELED yard before the palace of Pope Urban. An Italian cardinal had just arrived with his retinue of bishops, monsignori, priests, and monks, and Simon knew it would be some time before the procession passed all the guards and the majordomo at the main door.

Alain de Pirenne, beside him, said in a low voice, "I still can't believe it. We are about to attend a council called by the pope himself." His blue eyes were huge, and his fair skin was flushed with excitement. He was dressed in his best, an azure tunic with silver embroidery at the sleeves and collar, and on his feet poulaines, black deerskin shoes whose elongated toes came to points. The hilt of the longsword hanging at his waist was plain, but Simon knew it had been in the Pirenne family for generations.

"Do not believe it yet, Alain," Simon said wryly. "We were not invited, and we have not yet been let in."

"Surely they would not keep out so great a seigneur as you," said Alain. "Especially when you have been faithfully protecting the Tartars for a month."

"Well, that is what I am counting on," Simon said.

They stood inside a high wall of cream-colored tufa, the same rock on which Orvieto stood. The wall, topped with square battlements, surrounded the papal palace. Simon's gaze swept beyond the wall toward the bluish tops of nearby hills, wreathed in morning mist, then back to the row of pine trees that stood between the wall and the palace, the massed green of the needles almost so dark as to appear black. The palace itself, fortified by six square turrets, was of white limestone. It must have cost the papal treasury a fortune, Simon thought, to haul all those big blocks up here. Within this solid edifice, surrounded by this high wall, atop the impregnable mesa of Orvieto, the Holy Father was certainly well protected.

The last monk in his gray gown had passed the guards at the door, and Simon saw more clergymen massing at the outer gate. He took a deep breath and started up the stairs, de Pirenne hurrying behind him. He reminded himself, *I am the Count de Gobignon.*

He said as much to the majordomo, who stood before him in white silk tunic with the keys of Peter embroidered in black on the left breast.

"Ah, Your Signory, I saw your brave battle in the cathedral with that heretic assassin." The majordomo had a prominent upper lip that made him look like a horse. "A thousand welcomes to the palace of His Holiness. I will be happy to tell him that you are attending the council." He showed big yellow teeth in an unctuous grin.

Then his face fell as he looked down at Simon's belt. "I regret, Your Signory, but you may not wear your sword in the palace of the pope. Even though you wielded it most gloriously in His Holiness's service. Only the papal guards may bear arms within. A thousand pardons, but you must take it off. You may leave it with the capitano of the guard if you wish."

Simon's face burned with embarrassment as he realized he was going to have to disappoint Alain. The scimitar was one of his most precious possessions, and he would not entrust it to a stranger, even a stranger in the service of the pope. With a sigh he unbuckled his belt and handed it, with his dagger and the jewel-handled scimitar, to de Pirenne.

"If only I had thought to bring Thierry with us," he said. "Forgive me, Alain, but would you be good enough to take these back to the Palazzo Monaldeschi? Then you can meet me back here."

"Forgive *me*, Your Signory!" the majordomo interjected. "I am desolate, but His Holiness himself has commanded that no one is to enter after the council begins."

Simon felt angry words forcing their way to his lips. But he clamped his mouth shut. This was, after all, the court of the Vicar of Christ on earth, and he did not dare protest against its customs. He had the reputation of France to think of. These Italians already thought the French were all barbarians.

"I knew it was too good to be true," de Pirenne said with a rueful smile as he turned away. "I will be waiting for you in the yard outside, Monseigneur."

Simon shared his friend's unhappiness. This would have been something for Alain to remember for the rest of his life.

"Bring our horses," Simon said. "We can go riding in the country after the council is over." Alain's downcast face brightened at that. Simon knew that Alain, born and reared in a country castle, hated being cooped up in town.

Simon turned away, feeling dread at having to go into the papal court alone.

The great hall of the pope's palace was long, high, narrow, and shadowy. Even though it was a sunny day outside, the small windows of white glass on both sides of the room admitted insufficient light, and had to be supplemented by a double row of three-tiered chandeliers, each bearing dozens of candles. The pope could have saved himself the cost of a great many candles, Simon thought, if he had built his great hall in the new style, like the king's palace in Paris, with buttresses that allowed for much larger windows.

But this was Italy, he reminded himself, where there was war in the city streets, even war against the pope. Large glass windows would offer poor protection. The King of France did not have such worries.

At the far end of the room a long flight of marble steps swept up to an enormous gilded throne, empty at present. Down the center of the steps ran a purple carpet, and over the carpet lay a wide strip of white linen.

Two rows of high-backed pews faced each other on either side of the throne. Between them was a table laid with rolls of parchment, an inkstand, and a sheaf of quills. The pews were as yet empty, but around them stood cardinals in bright red robes with flat, broad-brimmed red hats—some of them Simon remembered seeing at the cathedral two weeks before. Farther removed from the throne and more numerous were the purple-robed archbishops and bishops. Scattered around the hall were priests, monks, and friars in black, white, brown, and gray. There must be nearly a hundred men in the room, Simon guessed. The air was filled with a buzz of conversation.

He felt the hollow in his stomach and the trembling in his knees that disturbed him whenever he entered a roomful of strangers. And these strangers were, most of them, the spiritual lords of the Church. He looked for a place where he could stand inconspicuously. He dared not speak to anyone. He felt as if a frown from one of these men would be enough to send him into disordered retreat.

And suddenly before him there was the frowning face of Cardinal Paulus de Verceuil. The wide red hat with its heavy tassels seemed precariously balanced on his head. His gold pectoral cross was set with emeralds and rubies. The buttons that ran down the front of his scarlet cassock, Simon noticed, were embroidered with gold thread.

"What the devil are you doing here?"

Simon cast about wildly in his mind for a sensible answer. Nothing he could say, he was sure, would win this cardinal's approval.

"I—I feel it is important that I know what is decided here, Your Eminence."

"These deliberations are no business of yours. Your duty is to protect the ambassadors. You have deserted your post."

Stung, Simon wished de Verceuil were not an ordained priest and a prince of the Church, so that he could challenge him. That he could do nothing about de Verceuil's accusation infuriated him.

"The Tartars are safely at the Monaldeschi palace guarded by all of our knights and men-at-arms. When Count Charles d'Anjou laid this task upon me, I understood that I was to help advance the alliance with the Tartars. I cannot do that if I am kept in ignorance." After a pause he added, "Your Eminence."

That was almost as good as a challenge. Simon felt light-headed, and his limbs tingled. He wanted to raise his arms and shake his fists.

De Verceuil's face turned a deep maroon, but before he could speak, a figure also in cardinal's red appeared beside them.

"Paulus de Verceuil! Is this not the young Count de Gobignon, Peer of the Realm? You are remiss, mon ami. You should have realized that the French cardinals here in Orvieto would wish to meet one of France's greatest barons."

This cardinal had a long black beard, and eyes set in deep hollows. He could easily have presented a dour figure, but stood smiling with his hands clasped over a broad stomach.

De Verceuil took several deep breaths, and his cheeks returned to their normal color. "Monseigneur the Cardinal Guy le Gros, I present the Count Simon de Gobignon," he said in a sour monotone.

Simon immediately dropped to one knee and bent his head toward the ring the cardinal held out to him. The stone, as big as

Cardinal le Gros's knuckle, was a spherical, polished sapphire with a cross-shaped four-pointed star glowing in its center. Holding the cardinal's cold, soft hand, Simon touched the gem lightly with his lips.

I believe I am supposed to gain an indulgence from kissing this ring, he thought. He rose to his feet. He tried to remember what he knew about Guy le Gros. He had heard a bit about each of the fourteen French cardinals. Le Gros, he recalled, had been a knight and a prominent lawyer, ultimately a member of the king's cabinet. Then he had joined the clergy. He had been the first cardinal elevated by Pope Urban.

"Doubtless you knew Count Simon's late father," said de Verceuil to le Gros. "Since you served as a counselor to the king."

Simon wanted to shrink out of sight at the reminder of Amalric de Gobignon. De Verceuil had mentioned him out of deliberate cruelty, Simon was certain. He felt even more crushed when he saw the pained look that passed briefly over Cardinal le Gros's features.

"Oh, yes, I met your father many years ago," said le Gros, his light tone reassuring Simon a bit. "He was a tall man like you, but blond, as I recall."

The suggestion that he did not resemble Amalric de Gobignon chilled Simon.

"As a father of unmarried daughters, Cardinal le Gros," de Verceuil said, "you might be interested to know that the count has no wife."

Le Gros shrugged and smiled at Simon. "His Eminence never misses an opportunity to remind me that I was once a family man. Perhaps Paulus envies my wider experience of life."

"Not at all!" de Verceuil protested.

"Or perhaps he thinks it a scandal that a cardinal should have daughters," said le Gros, still addressing Simon. "At least mine are legitimate, unlike the offspring of certain other princes of the Church. As for the high office, it was not my choice. His Holiness commanded me." He leaned confidentially toward Simon. "He needed more French cardinals. He cannot trust the Italians to support him against the accursed Manfred von Hohenstaufen."

"Even more than that, he was hoping you could persuade King Louis to give his brother Charles permission to fight Manfred," said de Verceuil. "You failed him in that."

"That case is not closed," said le Gros. "Indeed, what we do here today may lead directly to the overthrow of the odious Manfred, as I am sure you both understand." He smiled, first at Simon, then at de Verceuil. "But should we not be speaking Latin, the mother tongue of the Church? Some lupus might be spying on us."

In Latin de Verceuil answered, "I fear Count Simon would be unable to follow us."

"Not at all, domini mei," Simon cut in quickly, also in Latin. "I have had some instruction in that language." His many and often quarreling guardians had agreed at least that he should have an education far superior to that of most other great barons. Having studied for two years at the University of Paris, Simon had once been the victim of a lupus, a wolf, an informer who reported students for breaking the university rule that Latin must be spoken at all times. The fine he paid was negligible, but his embarrassment was keen.

"Good for you, my boy," said le Gros, patting him lightly on the shoulder. De Verceuil's lips puckered as if he had been sucking on a lemon.

A sudden blast of trumpets silenced the conversation in the hall. Servants swung open double doors near the papal throne, and two men entered. One was Pope Urban, whom Simon had not seen since the day of that ill-omened papal mass for the Tartar ambassadors. His white beard fanned in wispy locks over his chest. The mouth framed by his beard was compressed, and his eyes were hard. Simon knew that he had been born Jacques Pantaleone at Troyes in France, not far from Gobignon, and was a shoemaker's son. Only in the Church could a man from such a humble beginning rise to such high position. Urban had the face of a man who could cut the toughest leather to his pattern.

Age had bent the pope somewhat, and he leaned on the shoulder of a man who walked beside him. This man was so unusual a figure that he drew Simon's attention away from Pope Urban. Like the Holy Father, he was wearing white, but it was the white robe of a Dominican friar, and it curved out around his belly like the sail of a galley with the wind behind it. He was partially bald, his face round as a full moon, and his eyes, nose, and mouth were half buried in flesh the sallow color of new wheat. He nodded repeatedly in response to something the pope was earnestly saying to him.

"Who is *that*?" Simon whispered, earning himself a black look from de Verceuil.

"Fra Tomasso d'Aquino," said Cardinal le Gros. "I am told he is the wisest man alive. Papa Pantaleone has appointed him to conduct this inquiry, unfortunately.''

''Why unfortunately, dominus meus?''

''Bad enough for us that d'Aquino is Italian, he is also a relative of the Hohenstaufens. His older brothers have served both Frederic and Manfred.''

''A relative of the Hohenstaufens!'' de Verceuil exclaimed loud enough for two nearby bishops to turn and stare at him. ''How can His Holiness trust such a man?''

''Fra Tomasso is not *that* close a relative,'' said le Gros. ''Papa Pantaleone hates the Hohenstaufens more than anyone. Have they not forced him to immure himself here in the hills, when he should by rights be reigning in Rome? And yet he favors Aquino because Aquino is loyal to the Church and well informed. Come, let us find our seats.'' They walked together toward the pews near the papal throne.

And Simon was suddenly standing alone at the back of the congregation.

Standing at the foot of the steps leading up to his throne, Pope Urban turned, smiled, and spread his hands in benediction. He intoned a prayer beginning, ''Dominus Deus,'' very rapidly in Latin and followed with greetings to all present. He mentioned each cardinal, archbishop, and bishop by name, then several distinguished abbots and monsignori. His white beard fluttered as he spoke.

Then Simon heard, ''And we greet with joy our countryman, Simon, Count de Gobignon, who bears one of France's most ancient and honored names.''

A stunning brightness blinded Simon, as if lightning had struck right in front of him. *Ancient and honored!* In front of so many leaders of the Church. If at this moment some hidden enemy were to shoot an arrow at the pope, Simon would have leapt to take it in his own breast with joy.

What magnanimity! Simon thought. He remembered the major-domo saying he would tell the pope Simon was there. He looked to see how de Verceuil had reacted to the pope's singling him out, but the cardinal was hidden somewhere in the rows of red-hatted figures lined up in their pews on either side of the pope. Simon noticed other prelates staring at him, then turning away as he looked at them, and his face went hot.

Meanwhile the pope was talking about the Tartars. ''We must soon decide whether it be God's will that Christian princes join with the Tartars and aid them in their war against the Saracens, or whether we should forbid this alliance with pagans. We shall have a private audience later this week with the two ambassadors from Tartary. But today we ask your counsel. So that all may speak freely, we have expressly not invited the Tartar emissaries. We ask God to help us make a wise decision." He introduced Fra Tomasso d'Aquino.

To Simon's surprise, Pope Urban did not then ascend to his throne but instead came down, disappearing into the midst of his counselors. The cardinals sat in their pews. The lesser dignitaries sat on smaller chairs in rows facing the throne. When everyone was in place, Simon could see Pope Urban in a tall oaken chair at the foot of the steps.

There was no chair for Simon, even though the pope had greeted him by name. No matter, many of the lesser clergy also remained standing. He pressed forward through the crowd until he was just behind the seated men so that he could see and hear better.

The corpulent Fra Tomasso took his place behind the table in a heavy chair wider than the pope's, though its back was not as high. He called for Cardinal Adelberto Ugolini. The cardinal, a tiny man with flowing side whiskers and a receding chin, stood up at his place in the pews. He in turn summoned from the audience a knight called Sire Cosmas.

Sire Cosmas, an elderly man, walked stiffly to the pope and knelt before him. Ugolini told the assembly that Cosmas had seen and fought the Tartar invaders in his native Hungary and was driven from his home by them.

The Tartars have long since withdrawn from Hungary, Simon thought. *Why did Sire Cosmas never go back there?*

Sire Cosmas was lean and dark, with gray hair that fell to his shoulders. Over scarlet gloves he wore many rings that flashed as he gestured.

"They came without warning and all at once, like a summer cloudburst," the Hungarian said. "One moment we were at peace, the next the lines of Tartar horsemen darkened the eastern horizon from the Baltic to the Adriatic."

Sire Cosmas's Latin was very good, fast and fluent.

Simon stood transfixed as Cosmas described the fall of one Russian city after another, how the Tartars leveled Riazan, Moscow, and Kiev and butchered all their people. They would gather all the women, rape them, and cut their throats. The men they cut in two, impaled on stakes, roasted, flayed alive, used as archery targets, or suffocated by pounding dirt down their throats. The details of the atrocities sickened Simon. On into Poland the Tartars came.

Cosmas's tale of the trumpeter of Krakow, who kept sounding the alarm from the cathedral tower until Tartar arrows struck him down, brought tears to Simon's eyes.

Simon found the Hungarian's recital spellbinding. Cosmas had undoubtedly repeated his account many times, polishing his storytelling skills a little more with each occasion. It was probably easy and perhaps profitable for him to remain in western Europe telling and retelling, in great halls and at dinner tables, his adventures with the Tartars.

How much is Cardinal Ugolini paying him for this performance?

The flower of European chivalry engaged the Tartars at Liegnitz in Poland, Sire Cosmas said, and when the battle was over, thousands of knights from Hungary, Poland, Germany, Italy, France, England, and as far away as Spain lay dead and dying on the field and the Tartars were triumphant. They turned then to meet another mighty Christian army, that of King Bela of Hungary, at Mohi.

"I fought in that battle," Cosmas declared. "The dog-faced Tartars bombarded us with terrible weapons that burst into flame and gave off poisonous smoke, so that men died of breathing it. We advanced against them and discovered that we were surrounded. Their pitiless volleys of arrows slowly reduced our numbers all that long day. In the late afternoon we saw their columns gathering for a charge, but we also saw a gap in their line. Many of us, myself among them, rushed for that gap, throwing down our arms and armor so we could escape more quickly. It was a devilish trick. The Tartar heavy cavalry fell upon those who remained behind, now few in number, and slaughtered all. The light cavalry rode along the flanks of those who retreated, shooting them down till bodies in their thousands littered the road. I was one of the few who, by God's grace and by feigning death, lived."

The Tartars advanced to the Danube, he went on, burning everything, killing all the people in towns and villages. They burned Pest to the ground. On Christmas Day in the year 1241 the Danube froze hard. The Tartars crossed and destroyed Buda. They advanced into Austria. Tartar columns were sighted from the walls of Vienna. Europe lay helpless before them.

"Only the hand of God saved us. He willed that at that very moment the emperor of the Tartars in their far-off homeland should die,'' Sire Cosmas concluded. "All the kings and generals of the Tartars had to depart from Europe, with their armies, to choose their next emperor. Those parts of Poland and Hungary they had occupied, they left a dead, silent desert.

"Since then the Tartars have made war on the Saracens, which pleases us, of course. But is the enemy of our enemy truly our friend? Permit me to doubt it, good Fathers. We are no better able to fight the Tartars now than we were after Mohi. I urge you to let the Tartars and Saracens wear themselves out fighting each other. Let us not help the Tartars with their distant wars, losing knights and men we might later need to defend Europe against those devils themselves.''

Sire Cosmas's words chilled Simon. He felt himself almost persuaded that the Tartars were a menace to the world. It might be a grave error to work for an alliance with them. And yet, for the sake of his family he had accepted this mission. He could not back down now. Uneasily he rubbed his damp palms on his tunic.

There was a murmur of conversation as Sire Cosmas finished and bowed.

Fra Tomasso, scribbling notes on a parchment, looked up and asked, "Did you say that the Tartar soldiers have the faces of dogs, Sire Cosmas?''

Cosmas shook his head, looking himself somewhat sheepish, Simon thought. "We spoke of them so because their pointed fur caps made them look like dogs.''

"I wondered, because Aristotle writes of men with animals' heads living in remote regions," said the stout Dominican. He made a note.

Cosmas brightened. "They do eat the flesh of living prisoners. And I hope I may not offend your chastity by telling you this, but they slice off the breasts of the women they rape and serve them as delicacies to their princes. Raw.''

Simon thought of John and Philip and wondered whether they had ever done such horrible things. He wished he had learned more about the Tartars before agreeing to pursue this cause.

"To hear of such deeds is not likely to cause concupiscent movements in normal men," said Fra Tomasso dryly. "Have you seen such abominations with your own eyes?''

"No," said Cosmas, "but I heard it from many people when the Tartars were invading us.''

"Thank you," said d'Aquino, making another note. He put his

quill down and started to heave his bulk up from his chair. Cardinal Ugolini darted past him, resting his hand momentarily on d'Aquino's shoulder, and the Dominican settled back down again.

That cardinal looks just like a fat little mouse, Simon thought. One of the Italians. And it was he who had brought this Sire Cosmas to speak against the Tartars. He might well be a key opponent of the alliance. What would it take to change his mind?

Ugolini beckoned toward the audience, and a tall blond man came forward now to stand beside him.

I have seen him before, Simon thought. *Where?*

"Holy Fathers," said Ugolini, "Providence sends us this man, David of Trebizond, a trader in Cathayan silks. He has traveled in recent years among the Tartars. David speaks Greek but not Latin. I will translate what he says."

Simon remembered at last where he had seen David of Trebizond. Standing on a balcony and looking pleased as the people rioted against the Tartar ambassadors. And now here to speak against the alliance.

The back of his neck tingling, Simon thought, *This man is an enemy.*

XIV

UGOLINI SPOKE IN A LOW VOICE TO THE BLOND MAN IN A LANguage Simon guessed was Greek, and David answered at some length.

"You must suppose now that I am David speaking directly to you," said Ugolini in Latin to the assembly, patting the front of his red satin robe. "I come from an old merchant family of Trebizond. Caravans from across Turkestan bring us silks from Cathay. We are Christians according to the Greek rite."

This provoked a hostile murmur from the audience.

Ugolini hesitated, then said, "I speak in my own person for a moment—I, too, am inclined to treat as suspect what a so-called

Catholic of the schismatic Greek Church tells me. But I have talked long with David, and I am convinced he is a virtuous man. After all, the Greeks, like us, are believers in Christ. And Trebizond is at war with Constantinople, so we can trust this man the more for that.''

Again David spoke in Greek to Ugolini. Unable to understand David's words, Simon listened to his voice. It was rich and resonant. A virtuous man? A traveling mountebank, more likely. He felt a deep distrust of both David and Ugolini.

''From time to time the Saracens tried to conquer us, but with the grace of God we fought them off,'' said David through Ugolini. ''And when we were not at war with them we traded with them, for Trebizond lives by trade. And now that the Tartars have conquered all of Persia, we trade with them.''

Fra Tomasso raised a broad hand and asked, ''Do you find the Tartars honest traders?''

''They would rather take what they want by looting or tribute or taxation. Eventually they think they will not have to trade. They believe the blue sky, which they worship, will permit them to conquer the whole world, and then all peoples will slave for them. Just as they use subject people, so, if you ally yourselves with them, they will use you. You will help them destroy the Moslems, and then they will turn on you.''

He hates the Tartars. I can hear it in his voice, see it in the glow in his eyes. He is sincere enough about that.

A cardinal shouted out something in Latin too rapid for Simon to understand. An archbishop bellowed an answer. Two cardinals were arguing loudly in the pews on the other side of the room. Suddenly all the church leaders seemed to be talking at once. Fra Tomasso picked up a little bell from his desk and rang it vigorously. Simon could barely hear it, and everyone ignored it.

The princes of the church quarrel among themselves like ordinary men.

Pope Urban stood up and lifted his arms. ''Silence!'' he cried. His voice was shrill and louder than Fra Tomasso's bell. The argument died down.

''Have you seen the Tartar army in action, Messer David?'' d'Aquino asked.

David was silent a long time before answering. His face took on a haunted look. His eyes seemed to gaze at something far away.

''I was at Baghdad a week after they took it. I came to trade with the Tartars. There were no other people left in that country to trade with. The Tartar camp was many leagues away from the ruins of Baghdad. They had to move away from the city to escape the smell of the dead. I went to Baghdad because I wanted to see. I saw nothing but ashes and corpses for miles and miles. The stink of rotting flesh nearly killed me.

"I found people who had survived. Those who had not gone mad told me what had happened. The Tartars commanded the caliph to surrender. He said he would pay tribute, but he could not surrender his authority to them because he was the spiritual head of Islam."

Simon heard murmurs of derision at this, but David ignored them and, speaking through Ugolini, went on.

"Over a hundred thousand Tartars surrounded Baghdad, and their siege machines began smashing its walls with great rocks brought down from the mountains by slave caravans. Soon their standards, which are made of the horns and hides and tails of beasts, were raised over the southeastern wall from the Racecourse Gate to the Persian Tower. The city was lost. The Tartars promised to spare the remaining troops if they would surrender. The soldiers of Baghdad went out, unarmed, and the Tartars killed them all with arrows. This is the Tartars' notion of honor."

"They will do the same to us!" shouted a cardinal. The pope slapped his palm loudly on the arm of his chair, and silence settled again.

"Hulagu Khan, the commander of the Tartar army, now entered the city and made the caliph serve him a splendid dinner. After dinner the khan demanded that the caliph show him all the jewels and gold and silver and other treasures that had been gathered by the caliphs of Baghdad over the centuries. Hulagu promised to let the caliph live, together with a hundred of his women."

This brought a loud cackle from under one of the red hats in the front row.

"Only a hundred women!" a voice followed the laughter. "Poor caliph! How many was he wont to have?"

"Seeing how ugly those Saracens women are, I would think one wife too many," another prelate called out.

Irritated, Simon wished he could silence them all. This was too serious a matter for such unseemly jokes.

The ribald jests continued, to Simon's annoyance, until Fra

Tomasso rang his bell. Then David, looking grimmer than ever, spoke to Ugolini, and Ugolini began to address the assembly.

"Next the Tartars commanded all the people of Baghdad to herd out onto the plain outside the city, telling them that they would be made to leave the city only while the Tartars searched it for valuables.

"When they had the people at their mercy they separated them into three groups, men, women, and children. When families are broken up, the members do not fight as hard to survive. The Tartars slaughtered them with swords and arrows. Two hundred thousand men, women, and children they killed that day, after promising them they would not be harmed."

Simon tried to imagine the butchering of those hundreds of thousands of people. He had never seen any Saracens, and so the victims in his mind's eye tended to resemble the people of Paris. He shuddered inwardly as he pictured those countless murders.

"The Tartars now entered the city whose people were all dead, and sacked and burned it. It had been such a great city that it took them seven days to reduce it to ruins."

Simon's heart turned to ice.

What if it were Paris? Could we fight any harder for Paris than the Saracens did for Baghdad?

Ex Tartari furiosi.

"They have a superstition that it is bad luck to shed the blood of royal personages. So they took the caliph and his three royal sons, who had seen their city destroyed and all their people killed, tied them in sacks, and rode their horses over them, trampling them to death."

"These deeds of the Tartars smell sweet in the nostrils of the Lord!" shouted Cardinal de Verceuil. There were cries of approval.

Without waiting for David to say more, Ugolini replied to de Verceuil. "Yes, Baghdad was the seat of a false religion. But it was also a city of philosophers, mathematicians, historians, poets, of colleges, hospitals, of wealth, of science, of art. And of two hundred thousand souls, as David has told us. Muslim souls, but souls nevertheless. Now *it does not exist*. And whoever thinks that the Tartars will do such things only to Saracen cities is a fool."

Simon hated to admit it, but Ugolini's words made perfect sense to him.

"They will do it everywhere!" cried someone in the audience. Now David said through Ugolini, "What is more, the Tartars who rule in Russia have converted to Islam. They still dream of the conquest of Europe and may return to the attack at any time. Perhaps while your armies are occupied in Egypt or Syria.''

Fra Tomasso raised his quill for attention. ''How would you describe the character of the Tartars, Master David? What sort of men are they?''

David answered and then looked about with his bright, compelling gaze while Ugolini translated. ''I have lived among the Tartars and traveled with them. The Tartar is unmoved by his own pain or by that of his fellows. The suffering of other people merely amuses him. His word given to a foreigner means nothing to him. He thinks his own race superior to all other peoples on earth.''

Fra Tomasso said, ''What you have told us has been most enlightening, Master David, because you have seen with your own eyes. But if your empire of Trebizond now trades with the Tartars, how is it that you come here to denounce them?''

''I came to Orvieto as a merchant bearing samples of silk from Cathay,'' said David. ''It is only, as Cardinal Ugolini has said, God's providence that I am here when you are deciding this great question.''

Fra Tomasso turned to Pope Urban. ''Holy Father, is there anything else you wish me to ask?''

Pope Urban shook his head. ''I believe I have heard enough for now. We do not want to sit here all day.'' Smiling, he turned to David. ''Master David, we thank you for coming all this way to bring us this warning.''

''Your Holiness.'' David bowed, a fluid movement that made Simon grunt with distaste.

Curse the luck! Why is there no one here who knows the Tartars to answer this David? How do we know he is not a liar? A Greek silk merchant is not the sort of person I would trust. He would say anything if he thought it would help him sell his wares.

But doubt cooled Simon's anger. He did not want to admit it, but Cosmas's and David's tales had frightened him. He thought of the hard, cold faces of John and Philip. He *could* see them beheading women, shooting children with arrows.

Do we want to ally ourselves with such creatures?

King Louis did. Count Charles d'Anjou, Uncle Charles, wanted the alliance. Simon had agreed to come here. How could he face Uncle Charles, what could he say, if he changed his mind?

A lifetime of scorn, that was what lay ahead of him if he were to turn back now.

David sat stiffly upright, his hands resting on his knees, as Cardinal Ugolini approached the pope, reaching out in appeal.

"Holy Father, your predecessor, Clement III of happy memory, declared a crusade against the Tartars after the battle of Mohi. I beg you to sound the alarm again, like that brave trumpeter of Krakow. A Christian prince should no more make a pact with the Tartars than with the devil. Let the nations of Christendom be warned in the sternest terms. Let us declare excommunicate any Christian ruler who allies himself with the Tartars."

Shocked outcries burst from all parts of the hall. Simon went cold. The thought of King Louis being excommunicated horrified him. But surely it would not come to that. King Louis was too loyal a Catholic to defy the pope. But that, then, meant that Simon's mission would fail.

De Verceuil jumped to his feet. "You, Ugolini! You should be excommunicated for even suggesting such a thing!"

"Cardinal Paulus, you yourself have had much to say out of turn," Pope Urban said testily. "I give you leave now to speak in favor of this proposed alliance."

De Verceuil took his stand in front of the papal throne, and Ugolini returned to his place in the pews.

If only the pope favored us more. He is a Frenchman, after all. What about this Manfred von Hohenstaufen? The pope needs French help there. But what a disaster for us that he asks de Verceuil to speak. If any man can turn friends into enemies, it is de Verceuil. We need Friar Mathieu. In God's name, where is he? He could answer this David of Trebizond.

De Verceuil quickly dismissed the Hungarian's testimony. All that, he said, happened a generation ago. Today the Tartars would not win such easy victories in Europe because we know more about them, and they would not invade Europe again because they know more about us. The Tartars have new leaders since those days, and that is why they have chosen to make war on the Mohammedans. Christian friars have gone among them, and many Tartars have been baptized. The wife of Hulagu Khan is a Christian. Wherever the khan and his wife travel, they take a Christian chapel mounted on a cart, and mass is said for them daily.

"Yes!" Ugolini cried from his seat. "A Nestorian chapel. The khan's wife and the other Tartars you call Christians are Nestorian heretics.''

"From what I have heard of your dabblings in alchemy and astrology, it ill behooves you to speak of heresy, Cardinal Ugolini," said de Verceuil darkly.

Ugolini stood up and advanced on de Verceuil, who was twice his height. "As for Christian friars going among the Tartars"—he held up a small book—"let me read—"

De Verceuil turned to Pope Urban. "Holy Father, you have given me leave to speak."

"True, but more than once you interrupted him," said Urban with a smile. "Let us hear this."

"The Franciscan Friar William of Rubruk, at the command of King Louis of France, visited the court of the Tartar emperor in Karakorum," said Ugolini. "This is his account of his travels in that pagan capital. He says the Tartars were so stubborn in their ways that he made not a single convert." He opened to a page marked with a ribbon. "Here is his conclusion, after years among the Tartars—'Were it allowed me, I would to the utmost of my power preach war against them throughout the whole world.' " Ugolini slapped the book shut and sat down, looking triumphant.

De Verceuil failed to respond immediately. What a poor advocate he was, Simon thought. If only Friar Mathieu were here. He, too, was a Franciscan like this William of Rubruk, and he might well have the answer to Rubruk's words.

"Friar William," de Verceuil said at last, "wrote years before the Tartars conquered Baghdad. As for me, I count myself happy to have heard the words of this merchant from Trebizond." He pointed a long finger at David, who stood in the crowd about twenty feet away from Simon. David looked back at de Verceuil with a rigid face full of raw hatred that reminded Simon of what he had read about basilisks.

"Happy, I say," de Verceuil went on, "to hear every detail of the utter destruction of that center of the Satanic worship of Mohammed. I was reminded of the rain of fire and brimstone that wiped out Sodom and Gomorrah. My heart sang with joy when I heard of the caliph, successor of that false prophet, trampled by Tartar horses. I hold that the Tartars are God's instrument for the final downfall of His enemies. What wonderful allies they will make as we liberate the Holy Land from the Saracens once and for all!''

"And who will liberate the Holy Land from the Tartars?" a cardinal, forgetting his Latin, shouted in Italian.

"Be still, you fool!" cried another cardinal in French.

The Italian advanced on the Frenchman. "Whoever says 'Thou *fool*!' "—he gave the French cardinal a vicious shove with both hands—"shall be liable to the *judgment*." Another shove.

Fra Tomasso rang his small bell furiously, but the furious prelates ignored him.

Now someone had seized the Italian from behind. Simon was shocked, having never dreamed the leaders of the Church could be so unruly. It seemed that anything the French cardinals were for, the Italians were against. And was the pope, though a Frenchman, likely to approve the alliance, with nearly half the cardinals against it? And even if he did, could it succeed in the face of that much opposition?

"Pax!" the pope cried, climbing a few steps toward his throne and lifting his arms heavenward. "Peace!" The angry sound of his voice and the sight of him slowly brought quiet to the hall.

Urban took them to task. The whole future of Christendom might be at stake, and they were brawling like university students. Perhaps he should treat them like students and have them whipped. Sheepishly the cardinals and bishops took their seats with much rustling of red and purple robes.

D'Aquino asked de Verceuil if he had finished. He said he had, and Simon's heart sank.

I promised Uncle Charles I would work to further the alliance. I want to believe in it.

But after listening to Ugolini's two witnesses and de Verceuil's feeble attempt to refute them, he was beset by frightening doubts.

He prayed he would not have to reverse himself. If he changed his colors now and repudiated the alliance, Count Charles might well feel himself betrayed and say that Simon was no better than his father.

"But did not a Franciscan named"—the stout Dominican consulted his notes on parchment—"Mathieu d'Alcon journey from Outremer with these Tartar ambassadors? Why is he not here to tell us what he knows about them?"

Hope leapt up in Simon's heart. Yes! If they would only hear Friar Mathieu, that might yet win the day for the alliance.

And it might help me to feel I am doing the right thing.

"I assumed, before this august body, my testimony would be

sufficient," said de Verceuil with a slight stammer. "After all, what could a mere Franciscan friar add—"

Fra Tomasso raised his eyebrows. "I remind you, Cardinal, that His Holiness has entrusted the conduct of this inquiry to a 'mere friar'—myself. And William of Rubruk, whose book was quoted here today, was a 'mere friar.' Can this Friar Mathieu be found, and quickly?"

De Verceuil spread his hands. "I have no idea where he is, Fra Tomasso. He parted company with us after we arrived in Orvieto and neglected to tell us his whereabouts."

A lie!

Friar Mathieu had told everyone he would be at the Franciscan Hospital of Santa Clara. Simon was honor bound to speak out.

Still, it took all his courage to force words through his throat—loud words at that, to make himself heard over the murmur of many conversations.

"Reverend Father!" he called out, and his heart hammered in terror as hundreds of eyes turned toward him, de Verceuil's first of all. "Reverend Father!"

Fra Tomasso turned toward Simon.

"I know where Friar Mathieu d'Alcon is," Simon called.

D'Aquino raised his eyebrows. "Who are you, young man?" When Simon announced himself as the Count de Gobignon, Friar Tomasso's smile was welcoming enough to reassure Simon a bit.

"Friar Mathieu is at the hospital of the Franciscans," said Simon. "He told me he wanted to work there until his services were needed for the embassy."

"His services are needed now," said d'Aquino. "Not summoning him here was an oversight." He glanced coolly at de Verceuil. "The hospital is not far away."

"I know where it is, Reverend Father." Simon had gone to the hospital to inquire about the man shot in the street by the Venetians, he who had died despite Friar Mathieu's urgent efforts.

"Then have the friar fetched at once, Count, if you please," said d'Aquino.

Simon shot a quick look at de Verceuil before he turned to leave. The cardinal was staring at him, his long face a deep crimson and his eyes narrowed to black slits. Their eyes met, and Simon felt almost as if swords had clashed.

Why was de Verceuil, who wanted the alliance, so angry?

I know. He wanted to be the authority on the Tartars. He wanted to carry the day for the alliance all by himself.

Hard to believe, Simon thought, but it seemed de Verceuil would rather see his cause lost than have someone else win credit for its success.

"I shall fetch him myself, Fra Tomasso," Simon said loudly.

To his relief, he found de Pirenne, expecting an outing in the country, with their two horses just outside the papal palace wall. Simon explained his errand, and together they made the short ride through the stone-paved streets to the Franciscan hospital. There the Father Superior hastily summoned Friar Mathieu.

De Pirenne relinquished his horse to the old Franciscan. Friar Mathieu's bare skinny shanks, when he hiked up his robe to sit in the saddle, looked comical to Simon.

"I knew the Holy Father had called a council today," said Friar Mathieu, "but I assumed Cardinal de Verceuil would send for me if I were needed."

"Better to assume that he will do the opposite of what is needed," said Simon. Friar Mathieu laughed and slapped Simon's shoulder.

The pope's servants were passing flagons of wine and trays of meat tarts when Simon and Friar Mathieu entered the hall. The arguments among the prelates had risen almost to a roar, but died down as men saw Simon escorting the small figure of Mathieu d'Alcon in his threadbare brown robe toward the papal throne.

Fra Tomasso spoke softly and respectfully to the elderly Franciscan. While de Verceuil glowered from the pews, Friar Mathieu stood before the pope, seeming as serene and self-possessed as if he were in a chapel by himself.

And why should he not? thought Simon. After what Simon had heard about the Tartars today, it seemed to him that anyone who could live for years among them could face anything.

D'Aquino quickly summarized what had been said so far. Hearing the clarity and simplicity with which the Dominican conveyed the arguments, Simon could see why he was thought of as a great teacher and philosopher.

"I must warn Your Excellencies," said Friar Mathieu, "that if you sent a thousand men to journey among the Tartars, you would get a thousand reports, each very different. Also, you must keep in mind that the Tartars are changing so rapidly that what was true of them a year ago may no longer be so today.

"Italy, France, England, the Holy Roman Empire—all have existed for hundreds of years. The Church has carried on Christ's work for over a thousand years. This city of Orvieto is even older. But a mere hundred years ago the Tartars were tribes of herdsmen, even simpler than the Hebrews of Moses' day. Now they rule the largest empire the world has ever seen."

How could such a thing happen, Simon wondered. It seemed almost miraculous. The Tartars must have had the help of God—or the devil.

"Imagine a baby with the size and strength of a giant," Mathieu said with a smile. "That is what we are dealing with here. Such a gigantic infant might, in a moment of ungoverned anger, kill thousands of people, destroy all manner of precious objects, even sweep away whole cities. But an infant learns rapidly, and so it is with the Tartars. The new emperor, or khakhan as they call him, Kublai, reads and writes and converses in many languages. And he does not destroy cities, he builds them. He is the brother of Hulagu, who sent the ambassadors here."

Simon began to feel relieved. Friar Mathieu's calm words washed over him, easing his fear that he was doing wrong by supporting the Tartar alliance.

Fra Tomasso raised a pudgy finger. "If the Tartars are so powerful and are gaining in knowledge, does this not make them even more of a danger to Christendom?"

"It could," said the old Franciscan. "Let me say, Fra Tomasso—and Holy Father"—with a bow to the pope—"I can tell you only what I have seen, and then with God's help you must judge what is best for Christendom."

Simon glanced over at the formidable David of Trebizond, who up to now had been the most expert witness on the Tartars. He stood stiffly, staring at d'Alcon.

There is a man sore vexed.

And De Verceuil, who should have been pleased at having this help, looked just as vexed.

Friar Mathieu outshines the cardinal, and he is furious.

"We have been told that the Tartars plan to conquer the whole world," said d'Aquino.

"For a time they thought they could," Friar Mathieu nodded. "But the world surprised them by going on and on, and now their empire is so huge they cannot hold it together. And they are such innocents, the nations they conquer are destroying them. They die in great numbers of the diseases of cities. In their prairie homeland they were not familiar with the strong wine drunk by farmers and city folk, and now many of their leaders die untimely deaths of drink. Also, as they grow wealthier and more powerful, they fight over the spoils they have taken. When they invaded Europe they were still united, and they were able to throw all their strength into that war. But now they have broken into four almost independent nations. So divided and extended, they are much less of a danger to Christendom.''

How could they hold their empire together, thought Simon, when they had been nothing but ignorant herdsmen a generation ago? Mathieu's discourse made sense.

''So,'' said Fra Tomasso, ''we are no longer dealing with a giant, but with a creature closer to our own size.''

''Yes,'' said Mathieu, ''and the proof is that only a few years ago, for the first time anywhere in the world, the Tartars lost a great battle. They were defeated by the Mamelukes of Egypt at a place called the Well of Goliath in Syria. If Hulagu's army had won that battle, the Tartars would be in Cairo, and they might be demanding our submission instead of offering us an alliance.''

''But you think it is safe for us to ally ourselves with them now?''

Friar Mathieu looked sad and earnest. ''If we and the Tartars make war on the Mamelukes separately, we will be defeated separately. And then, as sure as winter follows summer, the Mamelukes will take the few cities and castles and bits of land our crusaders still hold in Outremer, and all those generations of blood spilled for God and the Holy Sepulchre will have been in vain.''

Now Simon's relief was total. He felt like singing for joy. He was on the right side after all.

Friar Mathieu stopped speaking and there was silence in the hall. Gradually the prelates began talking. But there were no shrill outbursts from those who opposed the alliance. The voices of all were subdued, respectful.

The pope beckoned Friar Mathieu to his chair and spoke a few words to him, holding him by the arm. The old friar slowly lowered himself to his knees, bent and kissed Urban's ring.

Fra Tomasso called for silence, and Urban rose and blessed the assembly. Simon fell to his knees and crossed himself, thinking, *If I stay here very long, I shall get enough of these papal blessings to absolve me from punishment for a lifetime of sin.*

Accompanied by d'Aquino and a phalanx of priests, the Holy

Father left the hall by the side door. The arguments in the hall grew louder.

As he rose to his feet, Simon saw de Verceuil hurrying toward the front door, his small mouth tight with anger. A protective impulse made Simon look about for Friar Mathieu.

There he was, at the center of a small group of friars. Simon started toward him.

A figure blocked his way.

Even though he touched nothing palpable, he stopped as suddenly as if he had run into a wall. And the face he was looking into was hard as granite, eyes alight with the icy glow of diamonds. And yet it was not a cold face. There was something burning deep inside there, a fire this man kept hidden most of the time. That fire, Simon felt, could destroy anything in its path if allowed to blaze forth.

David of Trebizond was silent, but as clearly as if he had spoken, Simon heard a voice say, *I know you, and you are my enemy. Beware.* Simon realized that David had intended to meet him like this, intended Simon to seek the unspoken threat in his eyes.

He is trying to frighten me, Simon thought, and was angered. He held his arm still, but he knew that if his sword had been buckled at his side, nothing could have stopped him from reaching for it.

Simon looked the broad-shouldered man up and down, taking his measure. David, half a head shorter than Simon, stood relaxed but imposing, his hands hanging at his sides. That a man could appear at once so composed and so challenging was unique.

This man is no trader. It is not just an accident that he has come here to speak against the alliance.

Who and what is he—really?

Simon drew in a deep breath and said in gruff Italian, "Let me pass, Messere."

Slowly, almost insolently, David drew aside. "Forgive me, Your Signory. I was studying your face." He spoke Italian with a strange accent. "I thought I might have seen you a long time ago. But that is not possible, because a long time ago you would have been a child."

What does that mean? Is he trying to remind me that I am younger than he is?

"I am sure we have never met, Messere," Simon said coldly.

"Quite right, Your Signory," said David. "But no doubt we will meet again."

Simon walked past the man from Trebizond. His back felt terribly exposed, and he held his shoulders rigidly. He felt the enmity from behind him as sharp as a dagger's point.

XV

SIMON GUIDED THE BLACK PALFREY CAREFULLY DOWN THE ROAD into the wooded valley west of Orvieto. The path, like the streets of the city, was carved from rock and slippery.

When he needed to think, Simon liked to get out of doors, beyond any walls, and to feel a good horse moving under him. It was now a week since the day of the papal council, and its inconclusive outcome troubled him sorely. The pope had repeatedly postponed his audience with the Tartar ambassadors, pleading a sudden excess of phlegm. The Tartars were growing restless, pacing the courtyard of the Palazzo Monaldeschi, muttering to each other angrily and refusing to speak to anyone else.

The longer the negotiations were delayed, the greater the chance they would fail. The Tartars might even die. Friar Mathieu had said that the Tartars, coming from a land so distant and so different, were especially vulnerable to the diseases of Europe.

Charging de Pirenne and de Puys to keep careful watch over the two emissaries, Simon had ridden out into the hills to think what he might do to help his cause along.

But it is not my place to try to speed things up. My task is to guard the ambassadors, nothing more. If I do only that, I have done my duty.

But, as he rode out into the valley under the deep shade of huge old olive trees, he heard in his mind King Louis's voice.

And you, too, Simon, must do whatever you can, seize any opportunity, to further the cause of the alliance.

King Louis lay prostrate on the floor of the Sainte Chapelle, his face buried in his hands. Simon, impatient to speak to Louis about his mission to Italy, knelt on the stone a few paces away from the king's long, black-draped form. The two of them were the entire congregation this morning, far outnumbered by the twelve canons and fourteen chaplains chanting the royal mass.

Unable to keep his mind on the mass, Simon kept gazing up at the stained glass windows. Since the age of eight, when he had become part of the king's household, he had spent hundreds of mornings here in the chapel attached to the royal palace, but the building still amazed him. The walls seemed to be all glass, filled with light, glowing with colors bright as precious stones. What held the chapel up? Pierre de Montreuil, the king's master builder, had patiently explained the principles of the new architecture to Simon, but though Simon understood the logic of it, the Sainte Chapelle, most beautiful of the twenty-three churches of the Île de la Cité, still looked miraculous to him.

The mass ended and the celebrants proceeded down the nave of the chapel two by two, dividing when they came to King Louis as the Seine divides to flow around the Cité, each canon and chaplain bowing as he passed the prone figure.

When they were all gone, King Louis slowly began to push himself to his feet. Simon hurried to help him, gripping his right arm with both hands. The king's arm was thin, but Simon felt muscles like hard ropes moving under his hands. Though almost fifty, the king still, Simon knew, practiced with his huge two-handed sword in his garden. Age had not weakened him, though a mysterious lifelong ailment sometimes forced him to take to his bed.

Louis looked pained. "This is not one of my good days for walking. Let me lean on you."

Simon was grateful for the chance to help King Louis. The vest of coarse horsehair that Louis wore next to his body to torment his flesh—as penance for what faults, Simon could not imagine— creaked as he straightened up. He put his arm over Simon's shoulder, and Simon passed an arm around his narrow waist. He looked down at Simon with round, sad eyes. His nose was large, but blade-thin, his cheeks sunken in.

"Let us visit the Crown of Thorns," he said, pointing to the front of the chapel, the apse.

Louis was leaning all his weight on Simon as they walked slowly up to the wooden gallery behind the altar where the Crown of Thorns reposed. Even so, the king felt light. How could a man be at once so strong and so fragile, Simon wondered.

There was barely room on the circular wooden stairway for them to climb side by side. As they stood before the sandalwood chest containing the reliquary, Louis took his arm from Simon's shoulders. He took two keys from the purse at his plain black belt and used one to open the doors of the chest. Inner doors of gold set with jewels blazed in the light from the stained glass windows.

Louis opened the second set of doors with the other key and, with Simon's help, knelt. Simon saw within the chest, lined with white satin, a gold reliquary that contained the Crown of Thorns. It was shaped like a king's crown and set with pearls and rubies and stood on a gold stem and base, like a chalice. Simon was icy-cold with awe, almost terror, at the sight of it. To think that what lay within this gold case had been worn by Jesus Christ Himself, twelve centuries ago, at the supreme moment of His life—His death.

Still kneeling, Louis slowly drew the reliquary out of the chest, holding it with both hands. His eyes glowed with fervor, as bright as the pearls. Simon prayed he would not open the reliquary. The sight of the actual thorns that pierced Jesus's head would surely be too much to bear.

Louis kissed the lid of the case and held it out to Simon.

"Kiss this relic of Christ's passion, Simon, and beg His blessing on your mission."

Trembling, Simon touched his lips to the cool gold surface. Not one Christian in a hundred thousand had been this close to the Crown of Thorns. He felt ashamed, privileged far beyond what he deserved.

As they walked together out of the chapel, Louis limping and leaning on Simon again, said, "Baldwin, the French emperor of Constantinople, sold us two crowns after Michael Paleologos drove him out. I bought the Crown of Thorns, and my brother Charles bought the title of emperor of Constantinople. Which of us, I wonder, made the better bargain?"

Simon thought, did Count Charles actually hope to conquer Constantinople? And, if so, what did these dealings with the Tartars have to do with it?

"Is it your wish, Sire, as your brother, Count Charles, has told me, that I should guard the ambassadors from Tartary when they arrive in Italy?" he asked.

Louis stopped walking. They were almost to the doorway of the chapel. He turned his round eyes on Simon.

"Oh, yes, it is very much my wish." His thin fingers squeezed

Simon's shoulder. "For more than twenty years, ever since I took the crusading vow, I have wanted one thing above all else, to win Jerusalem back for Christendom. I led an army into Egypt, and it was God's will that the Mamelukes defeated me."

God's will and Amalric de Gobignon's treachery, thought Simon.

"Now, with the help of the Tartars, we could wrest the Holy Land from the Saracens' hands," Louis said.

"But if you wish to ally yourself with the Tartars, Sire, should I not bring the ambassadors directly to you instead of to the pope?"

"No, I cannot make a treaty with the Tartars without Pope Urban's permission. Only the Holy Father can proclaim a crusade. If he refuses to do that, I cannot recruit an army to join with the Tartars to rescue the Holy Land. Even if he does declare a crusade, raising an army will be terribly hard. Many of those who went with me last time and endured our terrible defeat and survived with God's help have told me they will not go again—or send their sons. I must have His Holiness's full support."

King Louis turned toward him fully now and put both hands on his shoulders. "You must help me, Simon. I am asking Cardinal Paulus de Verceuil to represent the cause of the alliance at the court of the pope. And Friar Mathieu d'Alcon will be there to testify that the Tartars may yet be won to Christianity. And you, too, Simon, must do whatever you can, seize any opportunity, to further the cause of the alliance."

Simon looked into the king's eyes. Their blue was slightly faded, and age and care had etched red streaks in the whites. Simon's whole frame was shaken by an overwhelming love for the man.

"Sire, I will do anything—everything."

Louis nodded. "I know how you have suffered all your life because of the ill deeds of—one I shall not name. I have tried to shield you from being unjustly punished. But even a king cannot control the hearts of men. In the end only you can win back for the house of Gobignon its place among the great names of France. This alliance with the Tartars, and what follows from it, the liberation of Jerusalem, can help you restore your honor."

Could a man have more than one father, Simon wondered. Surely King Louis had done more than anyone else to make him the man he was today.

"I will work for the alliance, Sire," he said. "Not for my family honor alone, but for you."

For King Louis he would guard the Tartars with his life. For King Louis he would do anything.

His horse slowed down to climb as the road rose along a steep slope opposite Orvieto, green with vineyards. Friar Mathieu had made a better witness than David of Trebizond, Simon thought. But the Italian cardinals remained vociferous in their opposition to the alliance. The pope might be French, but he had to live with the Italians.

Cardinal Ugolini was the key to it. He, it seemed, was the leader of the Italian party in the College of Cardinals. He was the cardinal camerlengo, after all.

Someone must try to reach Ugolini. It could not be de Verceuil, either, with his arrogance and bad manners. Even if the man were to try to talk to Ugolini, which was unlikely, he would doubtless make an even greater enemy of him.

Friar Mathieu should do it. He could speak to Ugolini as one churchman to another. But then Simon shook his head. So many of these princes of the church looked down on the mendicant friars.

Seize any opportunity.

Simon rode up the hillside, debating with himself. Just before the road passed between two rounded, green-covered peaks, it widened so that carters could pass each other. Simon swung his leg over the saddle and stepped down from his horse to enjoy the view. Against the hillside, under a peaked roof, a statue of Saint Sebastian writhed, his body pierced by arrows. The agony depicted on the saint's face made the countryside look all the more serene.

Oh, patron saint of archers, let no more harm come to innocent people from my crossbowmen.

Simon turned to look at Orvieto. It was like a city from some tale of faeries, a fantastic island on its huge rock. What was it the Italians called that gray-yellow stone? Tufa. Most of the churches and palaces and houses of Orvieto were also built of tufa. Beautiful.

The clatter of hooves interrupted his thoughts. He looked up to see four horsemen approaching from the north, followed by two heavily laden baggage mules.

Simon's mood changed at once from contemplation to tense alertness. His hands moved to check the position of his sword and dagger, making sure he could draw them quickly. You had to be careful of strangers in a strange country. As the men rode closer he saw that they also had shortswords and daggers hanging at their sides. Closer still, and he saw longswords slung over their backs, and crossbows hanging from their saddles.

Annoyed with himself for feeling afraid, he yet followed the dictate of prudence and mounted his own horse. He kept his hand near, but not on, the jeweled hilt of his scimitar as the men rode closer. Highwaymen would be willing to kill him just for that precious sword.

The man in the lead wore a soft velvet cap that draped down one side of his head. Under it, Simon saw, was curly black hair shot through with white. The stranger's grizzled mustache was so thick as to hide his mouth. But, courteously enough, he touched his hand to his cap where his visor would be if he were wearing a helmet.

"Buon giorno, Signore," he said in a deep but neutral voice.

Simon returned his salutation and the muttered greetings of the others, thinking he really should ask who they were, where bound, and on what business. In France, especially in his own domains, he would not have hesitated. But then, in France he rarely traveled alone. These men seemed not bent on troubling him, and it seemed wiser not to trouble them.

The other three men in the party looked younger than the leader, and there was insolence, almost a challenge in their dark eyes as they looked him over and rode on. It took an effort of will on Simon's part not to move his hand closer to his sword. But he sat stock-still until they were past and on their way down into the valley.

What business would bravos like that have in Orvieto? Perhaps they had come to join the Monaldeschi or the Filippeschi in their feuding.

Simon felt beleaguered at the thought of more bravos coming into town. Orvieto was already full of armed men serving the local families, as well as others in the retinues of the churchmen who had come here with the pope. Uneasiness made his spine tingle. Anything that added to disorder in Orvieto made it a more dangerous place for the Tartar ambassadors.

We must get this question of the alliance settled quickly.

Someone should speak to Cardinal Ugolini and find out if anything would persuade him to withdraw his objections. Simon wondered why de Verceuil had not already attempted it.

I could meet with Ugolini. He knows who I am. They all do, since the pope greeted me publicly. All I have to do is send Thierry around with a note asking for an audience.

At once he began trying to persuade himself to forget the idea. How could he talk a cardinal into changing his mind about such a great matter? Ridiculous! What could he possibly do or say? And what if this cardinal were one who knew of the shame of the house of Gobignon?

Seize any opportunity.

Cardinal Ugolini shrugged with his bushy grey eyebrows as well as with his shoulders. "The question had been thoroughly discussed, Count. Now it is up to His Holiness. I am delighted to meet you, but what have you and I to say to each other?"

The solar, the large-windowed room on the third floor of the cardinal's palace, was bright with light that streamed in through white glass. The floor was covered with a thick red and black rug, the walls decorated with frescoes of angels and saints lavishly bedecked with gold leaf. Simon's eye kept returning to a voluptuous Eve, no part of her nude body hidden by the leaves or branches artists usually deployed for modesty's sake. She was handing a golden fruit—it might have been an orange or a lemon rather than an apple—to a muscular and also fully displayed Adam. Simon found them disturbingly sensual though they dealt with a religious subject, and he was surprised that a cardinal should have such pictures on his walls.

Ugolini's small, elaborately carved oak table, set beside a window, was polished and quite bare. There were no books or parchments anywhere in the large room. Simon suspected that the cardinal used this room to receive visitors but did little work in it. A five-pointed star was carved in the back of the cardinal's chair above his head. Simon sat in a small, armless chair made somewhat comfortable by the cushion on its seat.

"I have come in the hope of presenting to you our French point of view on this proposed alliance," said Simon. That sounded impressive enough.

"And do you speak for France, young man?"

"Not officially, Your Eminence," said Simon, flustered. "I mean only that I *am* French, and that both King Louis and his brother Count Charles d'Anjou have deigned to share their views with me."

Ugolini leaned forward. His expression was earnest enough, but there was a twinkle in his eye that gave Simon the uneasy feeling that the cardinal was laughing at him.

"I am eager to hear what you have learned from the king and his brother."

"Quite simply," Simon said, "they look on the advent of the Tartars as a golden opportunity—one might say a God-given opportunity—to do away with the threat of the Saracens once and for all."

Ugolini nodded thoughtfully. "So it is not just a question of rescuing the holy places."

Am I giving away something I should not? Simon asked himself, suddenly panic-stricken. It was Count Charles, he now recalled, who had said that the alliance might make possible the complete destruction of Islam.

I am in this over my head.

But he had to go on.

"The Saracens believe they are called upon to spread their religion by the sword. They will continue to make war on us unless we conquer them."

Ugolini lifted a finger like a master admonishing a poorly prepared student. "The prophet Muhammad calls upon his followers to *defend* their faith with the sword, but he explicitly states that conversions made at sword's point are worthless and commands that Christians and Jews who remain devoted to their own worship be left in peace." He sat back and gazed as happily at Simon as at some well-fed mouse who had the whole granary to himself.

"I cannot dispute you, Your Eminence. Truly, I am quite ignorant of the Mohammedan faith." *Why study false religions?*—that had been the attitude of his teachers.

Ugolini nodded, his side whiskers quivering. "You and most of Europe."

"But Jerusalem, Bethlehem, Nazareth—those precious places we hear about in the Gospel," Simon argued. "We cannot leave them in the hands of Christ's enemies."

The cardinal shook his head. "Christ's enemies! Indeed, you know little of them, Count. The Muslim holy book, the Koran, reveres Jesus and His mother, Mary. Our sacred places are sacred to them also. Emperor Frederic von Hohenstaufen had the right idea. He made a treaty with the Saracens. If the crusaders in Syria had not broken it, pilgrims would be happily walking in the footsteps of Our Lord to this day."

Von Hohenstaufen. Simon remembered the hatred in the voices

of de Verceuil and le Gros when they spoke of the house of Hohenstaufen.

"The crusades were a mistake from the very beginning," Ugolini went on.

Having heard harrowing tales from men who had been there of
King Louis's disastrous defeat fourteen years before in Egypt, Simon found it hard to challenge Ugolini's assertion.

But history could not be undone, and with the help of the Tartars,
might this not be the one great crusade that would make any more
crusades unnecessary?

"We still hold Acre and Tripoli and Antioch and Cyprus," Simon said. "The Templars and the Hospitallers have their castles
along the coast. Think of all the men who have died just to get and
keep that much. And if we do not beat the Saracens now, they will
surely choose their moment and take those last footholds of ours."

Ugolini stood up and walked slowly, red satin robe whispering,
to a small door behind his table. The door was slightly ajar, and
Ugolini looked into the next room. Was there someone in there,
Simon wondered, listening to this conversation?

*I am getting in deeper and deeper. What if my words could some-
how be used against me, or against the alliance? I should never
have come here.*

Whatever he saw beyond the door seemed to satisfy Ugolini. He
turned, smiling.

"Count, I am going to suggest something to you that I am sure
will shock you at first: Perhaps we should leave the Holy Land in
peace."

Simon felt troubled, but, having heard much the same thing from
his parents—and, indeed, from some of the knights at the royal
palace when King Louis was out of hearing—he was not shocked.
But for himself he had never been able to reconcile such views with
his sense of his obligations as a Christian.

Even so, he began to see why de Verceuil had spoken of Ugolini
as if he were a heretic. How could a man with such opinions get to
be a cardinal?

"To leave the Holy Land in the hands of the infidels, Your Eminence? Would it not betray Our Lord Himself?"

Ugolini, unperturbed, continued to smile as he walked toward
Simon. "The whole world belongs to God. If Our Savior wished
the places where He was born, died, buried, and rose again to be
occupied by Christian knights from Europe, He would have per-

mitted it to happen. As it is, I truly believe that if we sent every able-bodied man in Christendom to fight in Outremer, we could not take Jerusalem back and we could not prevent the crusader strongholds from falling to the Muslims. The infidels, as you call them, are defending their own lands, and a people fighting for their homeland is always stronger than an invader. Another crusade, even with Tartar help, would be a tragic waste."

Ugolini stood before the seated Simon, and such was the difference in their heights that their eyes were almost on a level. Simon wanted to stand, but somehow he dared not move. He was beginning to feel desperate. He had walked into a trap that he had not anticipated. He had feared that he would not persuade the cardinal. He had not imagined that the cardinal might persuade him.

"But you would abandon the Christians who are there now to be overrun and slaughtered by the Turks?" Simon asked.

He reproached himself. It almost sounded as if he were conceding that there should be no more crusades.

The cardinal shook his head. "I would do everything in my power to bring them home."

He sighed and turned away. "You are a most impressive young man, Count Simon. I am glad we have had this chance to hear each other out."

Simon felt deeply shaken, as if he had been galloping in a tournament and had been ignominiously unhorsed. He had been foolish to think he could sway a man of Ugolini's eminence and intelligence.

Courtesy demanded, he supposed, that he take his leave. He could only hope that some of what he said would sink in and influence the cardinal's thinking in the future.

Ugolini, standing before him, thrust his small hand suddenly under Simon's nose, causing Simon to sit back, startled, in his chair. Then Simon realized the cardinal was offering him his ring to kiss. He slid out of the chair and dropped to one knee. He touched his lips to the round, blue sapphire which betokened Ugolini's rank as a cardinal.

While he still knelt, the door behind Ugolini swung open. Feeling awkward, Simon started to scramble to his feet.

As he did so, he saw the woman. Her features were delicate, her lips full, her eyes dark and challenging. She wore a yellow gown tied under her bosom by an orange ribbon. Simon stared at her, open-mouthed, until he realized he was in a half-crouching position that must look perfectly ridiculous. He shut his mouth. He slowly straightened.

"Buon giorno, my dear Sophia!" said Cardinal Ugolini. "Let me introduce our distinguished visitor."

He first presented Simon to the young woman and then presented her to him. "My niece, Sophia Orfali, daughter of my sister who lives at Siracusa, in Sicily."

It registered somewhere in Simon's mind that Sicily was part of the Hohenstaufen kingdom, and it occurred to him to wonder whether Sophia was of gentle birth. It struck him with much greater impact that she was an extraordinarily beautiful woman. Swallowing hard, he bowed over her hand. His fingertips pressing into her palm felt as if they were burning. His lips touched the back of her hand lightly; his eyes filled with smooth, cream-colored skin and the pale blue tint of delicate veins. As he stepped back he noticed that she gave off a faint scent of oranges.

She stood looking at him with a small, self-possessed smile, waiting for him to speak. All sorts of absurd phrases and sentences flooded into his mind—outrageous compliments, declarations of love. The upper part of her gown was pulled tight, and he had to make an effort to keep his eyes from her breasts. His face burned and his throat felt parched.

"Buon giorno, Signora," he choked out. "It is a great honor to meet you."

Her fine arched eyebrows lifted slightly and she answered him in French. "Why do you not speak your native language, Monseigneur?"

Simon's cheeks burned hotter. "I assumed you would prefer Italian, Madame."

She smiled, and Simon felt there was a shade of scorn in the smile. "I would prefer French, Monseigneur, to Italian as *you* speak it."

"Forgive me, Madame," Simon whispered.

"There is nothing to forgive," she said airily. Simon thought surely the cardinal would reprove his niece for her unkindness, but he stood there beaming like a master showing off a remarkably gifted scholar.

Ah, lady! thought Simon, *I pray you be merciful to me.*

Ringing a small bell that stood on his desk, much like the one Friar Tomasso d'Aquino had used to keep order at the pope's court, Ugolini summoned one of the priests on his household staff, and

Simon, his head still spinning from his unexpected encounter with Sophia, found himself being escorted out of the cardinal's mansion.

As Simon and the priest were walking through the gallery that led to the main entrance, the outer door swung open and a large gray boarhound trotted in. It was deep-chested, with long ears, a pointed, aristocratic muzzle, and intelligent brown eyes. The dog jumped at Simon, resting his forepaws on Simon's chest and looking up at him as if studying his face.

Simon, who had played and hunted with hounds all his life, took an immediate liking to the dog. He scratched the back of the animal's head.

"Down, Scipio," said a deep voice, and Simon saw the hound's master—the same swarthy man with grizzled, curly hair and thick mustache he had met on the road from the north three days before. The one leading the little company of bravos.

Again that tense, besieged feeling came over Simon, the same as when he met this man on the road. There was too much going on in Orvieto, almost all of it surprising and much of it seemingly dangerous. If he wanted to be sure the Tartars were safe, he would have to give up sleeping.

The dog dropped to all fours and stood beside his master.

The other did not acknowledge having seen Simon before. "Forgive us, Signore. I fear Scipio has gotten dust on your tunic."

"There is nothing to forgive," said Simon. He brushed off his plum-colored tunic. "Do you serve Cardinal Ugolini?" This time he would not let the man pass without questioning him.

"I am Giancarlo, Signore, a servant of Messer David of Trebizond." He bowed deeply.

Feeling angry because he was sure he was being lied to, Simon wanted to ask about the men with Giancarlo on the road, but decided it was better not to appear too suspicious.

Let them think I am a naive young nobleman, easily gulled. Not so far from the truth, anyway.

"Are you also from Trebizond, Messer Giancarlo?"

The dark brown eyes were watchful. "I am a Neapolitan, Signore. Messer David hired me when he arrived in Italy."

So it is David of Trebizond who is bringing bravos into the city. What for?

* * *

Out on the street, Simon looked at the spot where the crossbow-men had spilled two men's blood. He felt a weary anger. Two lives cut off because of that fool de Verceuil and his vanity.

Where the men had been shot there now stood rows of bowls and pots, from small to large. They were painted white, with pretty floral designs in red, blue, and green. A woman sat on the ground beside the display, painting a freshly baked jug. She looked up at Simon, then scrambled to her feet and stood, bowing deeply.

"Fine vases and plates, Your Signory? The earthenware of Orvieto is the most beautiful in the world."

Simon smiled. "No doubt, but not today, thank you." He must remember to bring some samples back to Gobignon, though, he thought. It was fine-looking ware, and it might give the potters of Gobignon-la-Ville some good ideas.

He turned and stared back at the mansion, a great cream-colored cube of the same tufa as the rock on which Orvieto stood.

From that rooftop, David of Trebizond had watched the heckling, the throwing of garbage and dung, the sudden killings.

Simon almost expected to see David appear on the roof now, but it remained empty. The cardinal's mansion remained flat and featureless, revealing nothing.

Simon sighed longingly. *Oh, for another glimpse of the cardinal's niece.*

But there was no sign of her, and he could not stand here any longer. Sighing again, he walked away.

XVI

THE DOOR LEADING FROM CARDINAL UGOLINI'S PRIVATE CABINET to the solar swung back, and David came in. As always when she first caught sight of David, Sophia felt her heart give a little jongleur's somersault. She loved the look of his hard eyes with their suggestion of weariness at having seen too much.

But now those eyes were turned toward her, and they were narrowed angrily.

"Why were you rude to him?"

His harsh tone, when she was so pleased to see him, hurt her. She had no ready answer for him. To give herself time to think, she walked to the small chair Simon had occupied and sat down in it.

Cardinal Ugolini, sitting at his carved oak table, spoke up.

"Sophia put him in his place by demonstrating to him that she could speak his language better than he could speak Italian, David. There is no end to the arroganzia of these French."

David was still looking at Sophia. The midday light streaming through the white panes of glass threw sharp shadows under his cheekbones, giving him the gaunt look of a desert saint.

God's breath, how I would like to paint his picture. At least I could have that much of him.

"Do you think I wanted you to meet him so that you could teach him better manners?" David demanded.

"Of course not," she said, "but you do not understand men."

David's laugh was as harsh as the planes of his face.

"Oh, yes," Sophia went on impatiently, "you have always lived with men, and you lead men and fight against men. But you do not understand how Christian men, especially Frenchmen and Italians, feel about women. You know nothing, for example, of l'amour courtois."

"Yes," said Ugolini. "The head of every young French nobleman is full of two things, honor and l'amour courtois."

David looked from Ugolini to Sophia and back again. "What is this l'amour courtois?" he demanded. "I should know about it. Why have you not told me?"

Ugolini lifted his shoulders in a gesture that reminded Sophia of a shopkeeper on the Mese.

"My dear fellow, we cannot guess where the gaps are in your knowledge of the Christian world. That is why it is so dangerous for you to go about in public."

David held out his hands in appeal.

"You have seen me testify before the pope himself. How can you still be afraid?" He curled his fingers in toward himself, inviting Ugolini to go on. "Tell me about courtly love."

How graceful his gestures are.

"It was begun many years ago by a number of noble ladies of France, and especially Queen Eleanor of Aquitaine, who led an absolutely scandalous life," Ugolini said. "She married the King of France, accompanied him on crusade. Costumed as an Amazon, rode bare-breasted in Jerusalem. Jerusalem! Divorced the King of France, married the King of England. Had lovers uncounted besides.''

If I had been born into the nobility, I might have been a woman like that, Sophia thought wistfully.

David shook his head as if buzzing flies circled it. ''But what has this to do with Simon de Gobignon?''

''As His Excellency said, this Simon comes out of a world shaped by courtly love,'' Sophia answered. ''There are many strict rules about how men and ladies should behave toward one another. One of the most important is that the woman rules the man.''

David smiled thinly. She had rarely seen a full open smile on his face, but she remembered what a glorious sight it had been and wished he would smile that way now.

''So, by scorning the way he spoke Italian, you believe you are making yourself more attractive to him?''

''Far better than I would by letting him put his foot on my neck, the way your harem women do.''

''You know nothing about our women.'' But his eyes were crinkled with laughter. ''Less than I do about your courtly lovers. And what do you think of *my* Italian?''

''Better than his,'' she said, and was rewarded with a broader smile.

She felt a warmth inside as if her heart were melting. Trained from childhood to hide her feelings, she turned her gaze toward the wall paintings of the nude Adam and Eve.

A loud knock shook the outer door of the solar. At Ugolini's summons the door swung inward. Sophia briefly saw the tops of the sun-dappled palm and lemon trees in the inner court, beyond the arches and columns of the galleria. Then the door closed again behind Lorenzo, Scipio at his side. He carried a small parchment scroll in his hand.

''I met the Count de Gobignon at the entryway just now,'' he said. ''Three days ago I was bringing men back from Castel Viscardo, and I encountered him, not knowing then who he was, on the road.''

David muttered something in the Saracen tongue. It could have been a curse or a prayer. But before he could speak, Ugolini's fist struck the desk.

''He saw you bringing bravos to Orvieto?'' he cried at Lorenzo. ''You will get us all killed. I see it now. De Gobignon did not come here to persuade me to change my mind about the Tartars. He came here to spy on us." His voice was shrill with fear.

Scipio growled at the cardinal, and Lorenzo slapped him sharply on the head, then on the rump. The dog fell silent at once and trotted off to the corner of the room farthest from Lorenzo. Ugolini and David both eyed the animal with distaste.

"Perhaps the count should be killed, then," said David, "before he can use against us what he has learned."

Oh, no, please don't kill him!

Sophia felt an urge to cry out, to do something to protect Simon. And with that protective feeling she saw him again—the glossy, dark brown hair that hung in waves almost to his shoulders—the startling blue eyes in an angular, intelligent face. The tall, slender body.

And that name—Simon. Was there an omen of some sort in that? Did not this Simon even look somewhat like her painting of Saint Simon Stylites, carried with her all the way from Constantinople? As the saint might have looked when he was a young man?

As Sophia Orfali meeting the Count de Gobignon, she had felt almost half in love with Simon.

"How can you talk of killing him?" Ugolini cried, his voice almost cracking. "The French cardinals and their men-at-arms would tear the city apart. It might be enough to bring Charles d'Anjou or King Louis himself down here with an army. Sooner or later they would trace it back to us. And then, if you want to know your fate"—his finger moved in turn from David to Lorenzo to Sophia— "go see what they do in the Piazza del Cattedrale to that poor wretch this count captured."

Sophia felt a sickening, falling sensation in her stomach at this reminder of the danger she was in. Usually she managed to keep calm by refusing to think about what would happen if she were caught. She cursed Ugolini for taking her defenses by surprise.

Lorenzo whirled suddenly on Ugolini. "Get hold of yourself, Cardinal. How can a man think, with you shrieking away like a crazy old nonna?"

Good for you, Lorenzo, she thought.

"I am a prince of the Roman Catholic Church," Ugolini shouted. "You will show respect!"

Unabashed, Lorenzo turned to David. "Despite his hysterics, I do think the cardinal is right. If de Gobignon were murdered, the city would be in an uproar. We could not go on with our work."

"Dear God, why did You send these people into my life?" Ugolini groaned.

Lorenzo offered the scroll in his hand to David. "This prince of the Church has been making such a commotion, I nearly forgot this. A man with a clerical tonsure brought it to the door just after the young count left."

David's dagger seemed to leap into his hand. The man could move so fast, Sophia thought. He cut the black ribbon tying the scroll and slipped the dagger back into its scabbard. He unrolled the parchment and studied it with a frown.

"This is in Latin," he said, handing the scroll to Ugolini.

Red-faced and breathing heavily, Ugolini took the scroll and read it, moving his finger along the lines. He shut his eyes as if in pain.

Whatever this message was, thought Sophia, it was upsetting him still more.

Ugolini looked up with fear-haunted eyes. "It is from Fra Tomasso d'Aquino. He invites you to visit him at the convent of the Dominicans. He says he wants to hear more about your travels."

David nodded. "Excellent. I have been wanting to find a way to meet privately with him."

Ugolini threw the paper to the floor and shook both fists. "Mother of God! Do you not understand that this is a trap? The Dominicans are in charge of the Inquisition. They are called the domini canes, the hounds of the Lord. They can *smell* heresy."

David laughed. "They will not smell it on me. I am a good Muslim."

Though Sophia felt inclined to share Ugolini's fear, she delighted in David's humorous courage. She could not take her eyes from his golden head as he stood in the middle of the room with the light from the window shining on him.

"That, d'Aquino will find even easier to detect than heresy," said Ugolini.

A small, amused smile played about David's lips. "Do you not think I have prepared myself for such a conversation? We need a respected man who can write letters and give sermons warning Christendom against the Tartars. If Fra Tomasso can be convinced the Tartars are dangerous, and if I can offer him something he wants badly enough, he might be the man."

"He and his fellow Dominicans will eat you alive," Ugolini moaned.

"I can accomplish nothing hiding here in your palace." David gazed down at the cardinal, unruffled.

Sophia sat perfectly still, hands folded in her lap, looking down at Ugolini's beautiful Persian carpet. But the quarreling made her writhe inwardly. If they could not agree, if they were not careful in their planning, if they started to hate one another, they surely would end by being torn to pieces on the public scaffold.

"Let us speak about the young French count," she said. "He, too, might be a man we can use. I did my best to attract him to me today."

If he thinks there is hope of my seducing Simon, he will not be so quick to want to kill him.

David's eyes held hers for a long moment. "That is what I want you to do. That was why I was angry, not understanding this courtly love." His face was somber. "That is what I brought you here for."

She nodded, thinking, *If only you could be my lover. There would be nothing courtly about it, and it would bring us both great happiness.*

But only a moment ago, had she not been thinking of Simon, fearing for Simon's life? Had she not almost felt love for him?

What is happening to me?

Her hands in her lap clutched at each other. She felt dizzy. It had happened so easily, so quickly. Was she becoming more than one person, like someone possessed by spirits? How could you know who you were unless you had a place and were firmly attached to other people?

Now, looking at David, she was aware of the feelings Simon had aroused in her as if they were the feelings of another person. Sophia Karaiannides wanted David. Her longing for him had been growing in her ever since their eyes first met in Manfred's audience hall months before.

"What is troubling you?" David said, frowning.

She felt flustered. "Nothing." When he looked skeptical, she added, "I am not certain how he feels about me."

David glowered at her. She tried to read his expression. He looked angry. Was he angry at her for being willing to take Simon as a lover?

He probably thinks I am nothing but a whore.

She liked to think of herself as a woman who was able to move easily in many circles, a woman who involved herself in affairs of state. But was she not deceiving herself? Was it not that all men valued her for was her body in bed? And David did not even want that; he just wanted to use her body to ensnare Simon de Gobignon.

Then why did he look at her so angrily?

"How will you find out what he feels for you?" David said. "Will you wait for him to make the next move?"

"I will send him a small favor, something he recognizes as mine. Then we will see how interested he is."

"Good," said David briskly.

As if dismissing her, he turned to Lorenzo. "Speaking of ladies and love, our young friend Rachel is still living here. I want you to escort her to Madama Tilia's house this afternoon."

Sophia stifled a gasp. She felt as if she had been struck from behind. She wanted to cry out in protest, but she knew it was useless.

"Must I?" said Lorenzo, and Sophia saw pain in his eyes.

"Remember your promise to me in Rome," David said, fixing him with a grim stare.

Lorenzo sighed. "I remember."

Sophia's heart, already bruised by her gloomy thoughts about herself, ached even harder for Rachel. She had tried to save her from being sent to Tilia's, but there was no more she could do. If Ugolini was right about their being in such terrible danger, Rachel might be safer at Tilia's than here.

How could she help Rachel, she thought desolately, when she herself was a stranger among strangers?

XVII

THE BEAUTY OF ORVIETO, SIMON THOUGHT, WAS THAT, ISOLATED as it was on its great rock, it was as big as it ever could be—and a man could go anywhere in the city quickly on foot. Those of wealth and rank often rode, but a horse or a sedan chair was a mark of distinction rather than a necessity. A bird looking down on the city would see a roughly oval shape, longer from east to west. One might get lost in the twisting side streets but otherwise could walk along the Corso from one end of Orvieto to the other while less than half the sand trickled through an hour glass. From Ugolini's mansion on the south side of the town, Simon reached the Palazzo Monaldeschi, near the northern wall, so quickly, he barely had time to think over the events of the day.

David of Trebizond was a trader, after all, and traders needed armed men to protect their caravans. Why worry about the three men with swords and crossbows he had seen with Giancarlo? They were far from being an army.

But was David actually sending out any caravans?

If I could put someone in the enemy camp . . .

Before entering the Palazzo Monaldeschi, he surveyed it with a knight's eye. It was a three-story brown stone building with a flat roof crowned by square battlements. In each of the four corners of the palace there were small turrets with slotted windows for archers. Above the third story rose a block-shaped central tower.

Even as he looked up, he noticed a figure on the battlements, a helmeted man with a crossbow on his shoulder. He looked down at Simon, touched his hand to his helmet, and walked on.

It was good to know that the Monaldeschi family maintained a constant guard on their palace. The hidden enemy of the Tartars could get at them here only by a full-scale siege.

Simon walked around the building. If there were two archers in each turret, their overlapping fields of fire would cover every possible approach. He noted that the piazza in front of the palace and the broad streets on the other three sides allowed attackers no cover. The city wall was nearby, though, he saw. Archers could fire on the Monaldeschi roof from there, and at least two of the city's defensive towers were so close that stone casters set up in them could score hits on the palace.

What if the enemy were to attempt a siege?

We must control that section of the city wall and make it our first line of defense. The buildings around the palace would be our second, and the palace itself the third. To control all that, we really need another forty crossbowmen. But how to pay and feed them and keep them under discipline? I will have to make do with my knights, the Venetians, the Armenians, and the Monaldeschi retainers.

And he felt the weight of responsibility pressing on his back like a boulder. He had studied siege warfare under veterans. But how good, he asked himself, would he be in real combat?

His entire experience of battle consisted of one siege that ended as soon as the rebellious vassal saw the size of Simon's army, one encounter in his private forest with poachers who ran away when he drew his sword, and one tournament, two years ago, in Toulouse.

And yet, if the Monaldeschi palace were attacked, he would be expected to assume command. The thought made his stomach knot with anxiety.

He scrutinized the palace itself. He saw no windows at all on the ground floor, but there were cross-shaped slots for archers. The second story had narrow windows covered with heavy iron bars. On the highest level the windows were wider and the grills that protected them of a more delicate construction. On that floor were the apartments of the Monaldeschi and their more distinguished guests. The darkness and cramped quarters one had to endure in the palace because it was so well-fortified were a measure of the fierceness of the street fighting that had been going on in Orvieto, as in most of the cities of northern and central Italy, for generations.

We French are better off doing most of our fighting in the countryside. City fighting is a dirty business.

There were only two ways into the palace. On the west side a postern gate for horses and carts was protected by a gatehouse with two portcullises and doors reinforced with iron. In front, facing the piazza, a two-story gatehouse with a peaked roof and arrow slots jutted out from the center of the building. The doorway was in the side of the gatehouse on the second floor, and to reach it one climbed a flight of narrow stairs.

Why plan for a siege that probably will never take place? Simon asked himself.

Because I have tried to go beyond my duty this day and accomplished nothing. I had better be sure I can do what I am expected to do.

The door swung open as Simon reached the top step.

"Oh, you look too serious, ragazzo caro. Don't frown so—it will put wrinkles in your smooth brow. Surely your life is not so melancholy as all that?" Fingernails stroked his forehead and then his cheek.

Simon recognized the voice, but after the bright sunlight of the street it took his eyes a moment to adjust to the darkness inside the doorway and actually to see Donna Elvira, the Contessa di Monaldeschi.

She took him by the hand and led him through the inner door, which, in the time-honored practice of fortified buildings, was set at right angles to the outer one. The hallway that ran the length of the second floor was dimly illuminated through the barred windows. Unlit brass oil lamps hung at intervals from the ceiling.

"I saw you from my window and came down to let you in myself." The contessa's nose was sharp and hooked like a falcon's beak. It might have been handsome on a man, but it gave her an unpleasantly predatory look. Simon felt distaste at the short silky hairs on her upper lip and uneasiness at the bright black eyes that looked at him so greedily. She gave off a strong smell of wine. How old was she, he wondered. At least eighty.

He politely bowed over her bony knuckles and kissed them quickly. She held his hand longer than necessary.

"Your greeting does me too much honor, Donna Elvira," Simon said, easing his hand away from hers. "I was frowning because I was thinking of what we must do to protect the ambassadors from Tartary. I am happy to see that you have a guard posted on the roof."

"Always." The contessa held up a clenched, bejeweled fist. "But surely you are not afraid for the emissaries. Who would want to hurt those little brown men? No, I am ever on guard against my family's ancient enemies, the Filippeschi."

Simon felt the boulder on his back grow a little heavier.

Something else to worry about.

"Is it possible that the Filippeschi family might attack us here?"

The contessa nodded grimly. "They have wanted blood ever since my retainers killed the three Filippeschi brothers—the father and the uncles of Marco di Filippeschi, who is now their capo della famiglia. They caught them on the road to Rome and cut off the heads of all three, to my eternal joy. Six years ago, that was."

"My God! Why did your retainers do that?"

There was more than a little madness, Simon thought, in the bright-eyed, toothless grin the contessa gave him. "Ah, that was to pay them back for the death of my husband, Conte Ezzelino, twenty years ago, and my son Gaitano, who died fighting beside him, and my nephew Ermanno, whom they shot with an arrow from ambush twelve years ago." She held up bony fingers, totaling up the terrible score. "They cut out my husband's tongue and his heart."

"Horrible!" Simon exclaimed.

"Now there remain only myself and my grandnephew, Vittorio, a ragazzo of twelve, to lead the Monaldeschi."

"What of Vittorio's mother?" Simon asked.

The contessa shrugged. "She went mad."

Well she might, thought Simon.

The contessa's face turned scarlet as she recounted her injuries. "Now that canaglia Marco would surely love to finish us by killing Vittorio and me. But he is not man enough. And one day I will cut out *his* tongue and *his* heart."

"Might the Filippeschi attack John and Philip, thinking it would hurt you?" Simon asked.

The contessa thought for a moment and nodded. "Ah, that is very clever of you. Certainly, they would treat any guest of mine as an enemy of theirs." She smiled. "At any rate, you need not worry about protecting the Tartars today. They are not here."

Simon felt as if a trapdoor had opened under his feet. "Where are they?"

The contessa shrugged. "Riding out in the hills. They left hours ago. They took their own guards and the old Franciscan with them. He told me they were restless."

God's wounds!

Simon remembered the bloody fight between the Venetians and the Armenians. He remembered Giancarlo and his bravos. He thought about what the contessa had just said about the enmity of the Filippeschi.

He pictured the mutilated bodies of the Tartars sprawled on a mountain road.

"Did my French knights go with them?"

The contessa shrugged. "They are in the palazzo courtyard, practicing with wooden swords."

Simon ground his teeth in rage.

The idiots! Training themselves for some future battle while their charges go off to face God knows what dangers!

"Which road did the Tartars take? I must go after them."

The contessa was by now rather obviously annoyed at his lack of interest in her. "I do not know. Perhaps Cardinal Paulus knows. He spoke to them before they left."

Simon bade the contessa a polite good-bye. She insisted on embracing him. He wondered if he had looked as foolish to Sophia as Donna Elvira now appeared to him.

* * *

For the second time that day Simon found himself sitting in a chair that was too small for him. The back of this one came to an abrupt stop halfway up his spine, and his shoulders ached even though he had been sitting for only a few moments. He had taken off his gloves and tucked them in his sword belt, and he sat with his fists clenched in his lap.

De Verceuil strode across the room and stood over Simon. "I may yet demand that you be sent home. I cannot imagine why the Count of Anjou entrusted such a stripling with a mission of this importance."

"Your Eminence may not approve of my visiting Cardinal Ugolini," Simon said, keeping his voice firm, "but can you show me where I have done wrong?" He did not want to talk about Ugolini; he wanted to find out where the Tartars were. But de Verceuil had not even given him time to ask.

"You could have gone wrong in a thousand ways," said de Verceuil, staring down at Simon. "Both the king and Count Charles have confided in you. Rashly, I believe. You might have revealed more about their intentions than you should have."

Simon remembered how Ugolini had reacted at once to the idea that the purpose of the alliance was to conquer Islam completely. Saying that might indeed have been a blunder. He felt his face grow hot.

Discomfort and anger pushed Simon to his feet. De Verceuil had to take a step backward.

"Why have you allowed the ambassadors to go riding in the hills with only six men to escort them?" Simon demanded. "That is negligence, Your Eminence. A good deal more dangerous than my visit to Cardinal Ugolini. Where have they gone?"

De Verceuil whirled, the heavy gold cross on his chest swinging, and paced to the mullioned window, then turned to face Simon again. His face, a deep crimson, seemed to glow in the light that came in through the translucent glass.

"Guarding the ambassadors is your responsibility, Count." He spoke in a low, relentless tone. "I did not bother to inquire where they were going. If you think they should not have gone out into the countryside, you should have been here to stop them." His voice rose to a shout. "Not waiting upon Cardinal Ugolini!"

Simon's face grew hot with shame. De Verceuil had him. Even if he had not done anything wrong by visiting Ugolini, he should have first made sure the ambassadors would be safe while he was gone. He could have left explicit orders with Henri de Puys or with Alain de Pirenne.

"I will go after them now." Simon started for the door.

"I have not dismissed you."

Rage boiled up within Simon. "I am the Count de Gobignon. Only the king can command me."

De Verceuil crossed the room to thrust his face into Simon's once again. "God can command you, young man, and the Cardinal-Archbishop of Verceuil is God's spokesman. Have a care, or I doubt not God will show you how fleeting is worldly rank."

Is he trying to use God to threaten me? Simon thought, dumbfounded.

"If you overstep your bounds again," de Verceuil went on, "I promise you my messenger will fly to the Count d'Anjou, demanding that you be removed from this post. If the count must choose between you and me, I have no doubt he will choose the more experienced head and the one more influential with the pope."

"Do that," said Simon, his voice trembling with fury. "And I will make my own report to the count."

He turned on his heel, and de Verceuil's shout of "What do you mean by that?" was cut off by the slam of the heavy oak door.

It seemed to Simon as if the air were filled with motes of gold. He, his equerry, Thierry, and de Pirenne and de Puys were riding high on the western slope of a mountain thickly clad with pines. Shadow drowned the valley below. The horizon to the west was an undulating black silhouette. From beyond that range, the platinum glow of the setting sun dazzled his eyes.

"Look ahead, Monseigneur," said Alain, griping Simon's shoulder and pointing toward a dark green hill with a rounded top to the north. Simon's stomach tightened as he saw a party of riders strung out along the road. They rode in sunlight, and he recognized the flame-colored tunics of the Armenians.

At last, he thought, sighing and smiling. The Tartars' party had ridden far. He had followed their trail most of the afternoon, and found them only now because they were coming back.

He squinted, trying to see the Tartars. He clucked to his palfrey and spurred her lightly from a walk to a trot. His three companions did the same.

Two carts with high sides lurched down the road behind the

Armenians. A single mule pulled the cart in front, two drew the second. A man in a red tunic drove each cart. Where the devil were the Tartars? Bringing up the rear of the party on the back of a donkey, he saw a figure in brown. Friar Mathieu. Simon began to feel panic again.

"Do you see the Tartars?" he asked his men.

De Puys snorted. "They are probably too lazy to ride. They are sitting in one of those carts, fancying themselves lords of the earth."

"Tartars think it unmanly to be carried when they can ride," Simon told de Puys, annoyed at the old knight's ignorance.

"But I see horses without riders," Alain de Pirenne said. "Four of them."

Simon squinted again and saw that each of four Armenians on horseback was leading a riderless horse.

Even though it was a warm evening, he felt as if a sudden blast of cold wind were blowing right through him. He sat frozen in the saddle.

Dear God, are we too late?

"Follow me," he snapped, kicking his palfrey hard.

Riding as quickly as they dared down the rocky, unfamiliar road, they heard church bells chiming out the Angelus. The shadow cast by the hills to the west rose to engulf them as they descended.

The Armenians had gathered on the other side of a meandering river at the very bottom of the valley and seemed to be trying to decide where to cross. Simon still saw no sign of the Tartars, but it was too dark to make anyone out clearly.

In his dread he rode his horse straight into the river. She stumbled on the rocky bed a time or two, and once plunged into a deep place where she had to swim. It being the end of August, all the streams hereabout were at their lowest level. Even so, when Simon got across he was soaked up to his waist.

He saw the Armenians unslinging their bows and nocking arrows. "It is I, de Gobignon!" he shouted. He heard Friar Mathieu call something to the men, and they lowered their bows. Good that they were alert, he thought, but what might have happened to them on the road to make them so?

He rode in among the Armenians, and felt a hollow pit in his stomach as he saw the rich saddles on two of the riderless horses, silver and mother-of-pearl inlays glistening even in the darkness of the forest.

"Simon!" Friar Mathieu, on donkeyback, called.

Simon turned to the nearest cart and looked in over the shoulder of the driver, one of the Armenians, who stared at him from under heavy brows.

There, on a bed of straw, lay two bodies. They had the short, broad build of the Tartar ambassadors. Simon's heart stopped beating.

"Mary, Mother of God!" Simon whispered. He got down from his horse.

Mathieu was beside him, gripping his arm. "Did you come looking for us, Simon?"

Simon was sick with despair. He gestured feebly at the two bodies.

"What happened to them?"

"You might call it a mischance due to their inexperience. I tried to warn them, but they would not heed me."

"Mischance? What sort of mischance?" Did it matter, Simon wondered, how this had happened? He had failed utterly and absolutely, that was all that counted. His foolish decision to go to Ugolini had led to this disaster. Another stain on the house of Gobignon.

He put his hands to his face. "If only I had stayed with them this morning."

Mathieu patted his arm. "Do not reproach yourself. No one will blame you. It would probably have happened just the same even if you were there."

Simon felt the old friar's words like a blow in the face. What shame, to be thought so useless that even his presence would not have saved the Tartars. But, he told himself, turning the knife in his own guts, it was true. Anyone stupid enough to let something like this happen *would* surely be useless in a moment of danger.

"Did you not know how dangerous these hills could be?" he asked.

"They were determined on a long ride," said Friar Mathieu. "Tartars are used to vast distances and great spaces. You cannot imagine how miserable they were feeling, cooped up in a hill town surrounded by a wall on top of a rock. I felt sorry for them. In fact, I even feared for their health."

Simon was indignant. "Feared for their health! The devil you say! Now look at them."

Friar Mathieu squeezed Simon's arm. "Do not mention the devil. He may come when you call. As for them"—he waved a hand at the two inert forms in the cart—"this is embarrassing, to be sure, but we need not blame ourselves."

"Embarrassing? Embarrassing! Is that all you call it?"

One of the bodies on the straw moved. As Simon stared, it lurched to its knees. He heard a few slurred words in the guttural speech of the Tartars. The figure crawled on hands and knees to the side of the cart, lifted its head, and vomited loudly and copiously.

"They are not dead!" Simon cried.

"Dead drunk," said Friar Mathieu.

Relief was so sudden and stunning that for a moment Simon could not breathe. He caught his breath and gasped. The gasp was followed by a roar of laughter. Simon stood, his head thrown back, helpless with laughter. He pressed his hands against his aching stomach.

Friar Mathieu had gone to attend the sick Tartar. He wiped the man's face with the sleeve of his robe, went to the stream and washed the sleeve, then came back and pressed the wet wool to the Tartar's brow.

"Can you not stop laughing?" he said on his second trip to the stream. "The Armenians do not like you laughing at their masters."

"Dead drunk!" Simon shouted, and went into another spasm of laughter.

It started innocently enough, Friar Mathieu explained as they rode back together. He himself had proposed to take the road to Montefiascone, along which he had heard there was a particularly impressive view of Orvieto. Simon remembered the spot. He had been enjoying that same view when David of Trebizond's servant— what was his name?—Giancarlo, came along with those three heavily armed men.

The Tartars had been pleased enough with the view, but they wanted to ride on. Friar Mathieu felt some trepidation that they might encounter highwaymen in the hills. But he had confidence in the Armenians, too, and so they pressed on along the mountain road.

"They observed everything and talked to each other in such low voices I could not hear them." Mathieu turned to give Simon a pained look. "I think they were discussing how an army might be brought through these hills."

Simon was appalled. He pictured a Tartar army, tens of thousands of fur-clad savages on horseback, sweeping through Umbria on its way to Rome, burning the towns and the farms and slaughtering the people. Simon shook his head in perplexity. If such a thing happened, he would have helped to bring it about.

By the time the Tartars and their entourage reached the little town of Montefiascone, Mathieu went on, in the heart of vineyard-covered hills, they were all hungry and thirsty. They took over the inn—the black looks cast by the Armenians were enough to drive out the other patrons—and proceeded to drink up the host's considerable supply of wine.

"The wine of Montefiascone is a great gift from God," Mathieu said. "Very clear, almost as light as spring water, just a touch sweet, just a touch tart. And the host brought it up from a stone cellar that kept it deliciously cold. Not strong wine, actually, but the Tartars drank *all there was*."

Friar Mathieu pointed to the young Armenian leader, Prince Hethum, who was now riding beside Alain de Pirenne, at the head of their procession back to Orvieto. The prince was carrying the Tartars' purse, now somewhat less fat with gold florins. The host at the inn had been delighted to serve his thirsty guests, but when his supply of wine was gone, the Tartars turned ugly. Philip Uzbek, the younger Tartar, grabbed the host by the throat. The Armenians, who were careful to drink sparingly, fingered their bows. The innkeeper left his wife as a hostage and went out to the nearby farms, and after a tense hour arrived back with a cartload of wine barrels. This time the wine outlasted the Tartars.

"They have no head for wine, you see," Mathieu said. "Poor innocent world conquerors. They drink a beverage called kumiss, which is fermented mare's milk. Very mild, but it satisfies their desire to get drunk. When they conquered the civilized lands, for the first time they could have as much wine as they wanted. They have an ungodly appetite for it."

When the Tartar ambassadors collapsed, unconscious, Mathieu and the host had both sighed with relief. With the Tartars' gold, Mathieu bought two carts and three mules, and they loaded John Chagan and Philip Uzbek in one and the remaining barrels of Montefiascone wine in the other.

"Montefiascone may be the only town in the world that can say it has been invaded by Tartars and profited," said Mathieu. Simon laughed.

He had thought to bring flint, tinder, a lantern, and a supply of candles with him, and now Thierry rode at the head of the party with the lantern raised on the end of a long tree branch, giving them a little light to follow. At least this way the Tartars would not go over a cliff in their cart in the dark.

"If I could have found you this morning, I would have asked you to come along and bring some of your Frenchmen," the old friar said. "But you were meeting with Cardinal Ugolini, were you not?"

When Mathieu mentioned Ugolini, Simon immediately found himself thinking of the cardinal's beautiful niece. He wondered, was she older than he? How would she react if he tried to see her again? He wished he could forget Tartars and crusaders and Saracens and devote himself to paying court to Sophia. Of course, if he went anywhere near Ugolini's establishment again, de Verceuil would undoubtedly think he was trying to continue the forbidden negotiations.

"My efforts went badly," he told Friar Mathieu. Before going on, he peered as far along the road ahead as he could see. De Pirenne and de Puys were both riding at the head of the party, just behind Thierry with his lantern. Hethum and the other Armenians came next, and they understood no French. Simon and Friar Mathieu were at the end of the line, behind the two carts. There was no risk in talking.

"Cardinal Ugolini nearly convinced me that our efforts to liberate the Holy Land are futile. And then de Verceuil knew that I had gone to Ugolini, and he was furious. How did he know where I had been?"

Friar Mathieu smiled. "He had you followed."

"That snake!"

The Franciscan reached over and laid his fragile hand lightly on Simon's. "Hush, Simon. The cardinal will answer to God one day for his worldly ways."

Simon shook his head. "I tell you, Friar Mathieu, between Ugolini's persuasion and de Verceuil's bullying, I was nearly ready to leave Orvieto today."

But he would not have left under any circumstances, he knew. Especially not after meeting Sophia. He recalled her smoldering eyes and full red lips. And her splendid breasts. Ah, no, he must stay in Orvieto and became better acquainted with Sophia Orfali.

XVIII

A SWOLLEN YELLOW MOON APPEARED OVER THE TREETOPS, AND Simon was grateful for its light. Now they would have less trouble following the road.

Friar Mathieu said, "It is not an easy thing for so young a man to match wits with two powerful churchmen skilled in dialectic. I congratulate you on doing it at all."

Simon felt a hollow in his stomach. He saw himself going back to France, sneered at not only for his family's disgrace but for his own incompetence.

"Our mission *must* succeed," he said, clenching his fist. His voice rose above the creak of the wagon wheels, surprising even himself with his vehemence.

"God has His own ideas about what ought to succeed or fail," said Friar Mathieu. "Do not try to take the whole burden on yourself."

"I must," said Simon, feeling tears burn his eyes.

The voice in the semidarkness beside him was soft, kindly. "Why *must*?"

"Because of who I am," Simon said in a low voice.

"What do you mean, Simon?"

Can I tell him, Simon wondered. Ever since, seven years ago, his mother and Roland had told him the secret of his birth, questions of who he really was, questions of right and wrong, had assailed him, and there had been no one to ask. He loved his mother and he admired Roland, but they were too close to it all. But to tell anyone else would bring calamity down on all three of them.

There had been times during the years Simon had lived with King Louis that the king had seemed ready to listen. But Simon had also known that King Louis believed in doing right no matter whom it hurt.

Friar Mathieu, though, seemed to have more of a sense that life was not a matter of simple rights and wrongs. He could see the Tartars for the ferocious creatures they were, and yet feel kindly toward them. His wisdom and worldly experience could help Simon sort things out.

Then, too, there was a way to bind Friar Mathieu never to speak of this to anyone.

But when Simon tried to speak, his chest and throat were constricted by fear, and his voice came out in a croak. He felt as if he were under a spell to prevent him from uttering his family secrets.

"Father, may I confide in you under the seal of confession?"

The old Franciscan tugged on the reins of his donkey, so that they fell farther behind the rest of the party. Simon slowed his palfrey to fall back beside Mathieu.

"Is it truly a matter for confession, or just a secret?"

Simon's hands were so cold he pressed them against his palfrey's neck to warm them. How could he tell everything to this priest he had known only a few months? Perhaps he should just apologize and say no more.

But he thought a little longer and said, "It is a question of right and wrong. And if I am doing wrong, I am committing a terribly grave sin."

Friar Mathieu looked around him. "Very well, then, what you tell me is under the seal of the sacrament of confession, and I may repeat it to no man, under penalty of eternal damnation. Make the sign of the cross and begin."

Simon touched his fingertips to forehead, chest, and shoulders. For a moment he hesitated, his mouth dry and his heart hammering. He had promised his mother and Roland never to tell anyone about this.

But I must! I cannot have it festering inside me for the rest of my life.

What, though, if Friar Mathieu disappointed him? What if he had nothing useful, or even comforting to say on learning Simon's secret? Well, there was a way to test him.

The secret was really twofold. One part of it was terrible enough, but already known to the king and queen and many knights who had been on the last crusade. Simon could tell Friar Mathieu the lesser secret safely enough, then weigh his response and decide whether to tell him what was known to only three people in the world.

"I said I must make this mission succeed because of who I am. What have you heard about the last Count de Gobignon?"

By now the moon had risen high, and Simon could see the old Franciscan's face quite clearly. Friar Mathieu frowned and stroked his long white beard.

"Very little, I am afraid. He was a very great landowner, one of the five Peers of the Realm, as you are now, and he was zealous in putting down the Cathar heretics in Languedoc." He cast a pained look at Simon. "I spent the years when your father was prominent wandering the roads as a beggar, then studying for the priesthood, and I am afraid I paid very little attention to what was happening in the world."

Friar Mathieu's reply brought a sad smile to Simon's lips.

"That you, like most people, know so little of Amalric de Gobignon I owe to the generosity of King Louis and those close to him. The man whose name I inherited was a murderer, an arch-traitor, a Judas. But when King Louis came back from that failed crusade in Egypt, he decreed that Count Amalric's deeds not be made known."

"I well remember my horror when I heard that the king was captured and his army destroyed," said Friar Mathieu. "I fell on my knees in the road, weeping, and prayed for him and the queen and the other captives. What joy when we learned they were ransomed and would be coming back to us."

"It was Count Amalric's treachery that caused the calamity." It seemed to Simon that Nicolette, his mother, and her husband, Roland, had told him the story hundreds of times. They wanted him to know it by heart.

"He believed that the Cathars had murdered his father, Count Stephen de Gobignon, my grandfather," Simon went on. "King Louis advocated mercy toward heretics. Count Amalric had a brother, Hugues, a Dominican inquisitor, who was killed before his very eyes by an assassin's arrow in Beziers while he was presiding over the burning of Cathars."

"Ah, those heresy-hunting Dominicans." Friar Mathieu shook his head.

"When Hugues was killed, Count Amalric blamed the king's leniency toward heretics. After that, it seems, a madness possessed the count. He came to believe he could overthrow the king and take his throne."

"He must have been mad," said Friar Mathieu. "Never has a King of France been so loved as this Louis."

"Count Amalric went on crusade with King Louis, taking my

mother, Countess Nicolette, along with him, even as King Louis took Queen Marguerite. I was a very young child then. They left me in the keeping of my mother's sisters. The crusaders captured Damietta, at the mouth of the Nile, left the noncombatants there and marched southward toward Cairo.''

Simon hesitated, feeling himself choke up again. These were the crimes of the man everyone believed was his father. It was agony to give voice to them.

But he plunged on. "At a city called Mansura, Count Amalric led part of his own army into a trap, and most were killed. He tricked the rest of the army, including the king, into surrendering to the Mamelukes. He alone escaped. He went to Damietta, supposedly to take charge of the defense. He made a secret promise to the Sultan of Cairo to deliver Damietta, together with the ransom money, if the sultan would slay the king and all the other captive crusaders.''

Friar Mathieu gasped. "Why in God's name would a French nobleman do such dreadful things?''

"With the king and his brothers dead, he would be the most powerful man in France,'' said Simon. "He might have succeeded, but for two things. First, the Mameluke emirs, led by the same Baibars who now rules Egypt, rose in revolt and killed the sultan with whom Count Amalric was bargaining. Baibars and the Mamelukes preferred to deal honorably with their prisoners.''

"Ah, yes, Baibars,'' Friar Mathieu nodded. "The Tartars hate him and all of Outremer fears him.''

"And then a knight-troubadour captured along with the king, one who had an old grudge against the Count de Gobignon, offered to go to Damietta and meet the count in single combat. After a fierce combat he slew Count Amalric. The king and the surviving crusaders were saved and they ransomed themselves. The troubadour's name was Roland de Vency.''

"I never heard of him,'' said Friar Mathieu.

"No, just as you never heard of Count Amalric's treason. The king wanted the whole episode buried in an unmarked grave along with the count.''

There was silence between them for a moment. Simon listened to the cart wheels creak and looked up at the moon painting the Umbrian hillsides silver. Soon they would round a bend and see the lights of Orvieto.

Simon, torn by anguish, wondered what Friar Mathieu thought

of him. Did he despise him, as so many great nobles did? He remembered that Friar Mathieu had once been a knight himself. How could he not hate a man with Amalric de Gobignon's blood in him? His muscles knotted as he waited to hear what Friar Mathieu would say.

He looked at the old Franciscan and saw sadness in his watery eyes.

"But what happened does not lie buried, much as the king and you would wish it to."

Simon felt tears sting his eyes and a lump grow in his throat. He remembered the sneers, the slights, the whispers he had endured. Such heartbreaking moments were among his earliest memories.

He shook his head miserably. "No. What happened has never been forgotten."

"You are ashamed of the name you bear." The kindness in Friar Mathieu's voice evoked a warm feeling in Simon's breast.

I was not mistaken in him.

"You are—how old—twenty?"

Simon nodded.

"At your age most men, especially those like you with vast estates and great responsibilities, are married or at least plighted."

Pain poured out with Simon's words. "I have been rebuffed twice. The name of de Gobignon is irrevocably tainted."

Friar Mathieu rubbed the back of his donkey's neck thoughtfully. "Evidently the king does not think so, or he would not have honored you with so important a task."

"He did everything possible to help me. When my mother and my grandmother fought over who should have the rearing of me, the king settled it by making himself my guardian and taking me to live in the palace. Then his brother, Count Charles d'Anjou, took me for a time as his equerry."

"Why did your mother and grandmother fight over you?"

The hollow of dread in Simon's middle grew huge. Now they were coming to the deepest secret of all.

"My mother married the troubadour, Roland de Vency. My grandmother, Count Amalric's mother, could never accept as a father to me the man who slew her son."

He felt dizzy with pain, remembering his grandmother's screams of rage, his mother's weeping, Roland facing the sword points of a dozen men-at-arms, long, mysterious journeys, hours of doing nothing in empty rooms while, somewhere nearby, people argued over his fate. God, it had been horrible!

Friar Mathieu reached out from the back of his donkey and laid a comforting hand on Simon's arm. "Ah, I understand you better now. Carrying this family shame, fought over in childhood, no real parents to live with. And the burden of all that wealth and power."

Simon laughed bitterly. "Burden! Few men would think wealth and power a burden."

Friar Mathieu chuckled. "No, of course not. But you know better, do you not? You have already realized that you must work constantly to use rightly what you have, or it will destroy you as it destroyed your father."

Yes, but . . .

Simon thought of the endless fields and forests of the Gobignon domain in the north, what pleasure it was to ride through them on the hunt. How the unquestioning respect of vassals and serfs eased his doubts of himself. He thought of the complaisant village and peasant girls who happily helped him forget that no woman of noble blood would marry him. He reminded himself that only three or four men in all the world were in a position to tell him what to do. No, if only the name he bore were free of the accursed stain of treachery, he would be perfectly happy to be the Count de Gobignon.

Friar Mathieu broke in on his thoughts. "You feel you must do something grand and noble to make up for your father's wickedness. Listen: A man can live only his own life. The name de Gobignon, what is it? A puff of air. A scribble on a sheet of parchment. You are not your name. You are not Simon de Gobignon."

Simon's blood turned to ice. *Does he know?*

But then he realized Friar Mathieu was speaking only figuratively.

"But men of great families scorn me because I bear the name de Gobignon," he said. "I will have to live out my life in disgrace."

"God respects you," said Friar Mathieu quietly and intensely. "Weighed against that, the opinion of men is nothing."

That is true, Simon thought, and great chains that had weighed him down as long as he could remember suddenly fell away. He felt himself gasping for breath.

Friar Mathieu continued. "The beauty of my vows is that with their help I have come to know who I truly am. I have given up my name, my possessions, the love of women, my worldly position.

You need not give up all those things. But if you can part with them in your mind, you can come to know yourself as God knows you. You can see that you are not what people think of you.''

Tears of joy burned Simon's eyelids. *Thank you, God, for allowing me to meet this man.*

"Yes," Simon whispered. "Yes, I understand."

"But," said Friar Mathieu, a note of light reproof in his voice, "I know you have not told me everything."

Caught by surprise, Simon was thankful that the lantern up ahead started swinging from right to left, a ball of light against the stars.

De Pirenne's voice came back faintly to Simon. "Orvieto!"

From the cart in front of Simon, the one carrying the Tartars, came the sound of loud snoring. An Armenian chuckled and said something in a humorous tone, and the others laughed. Simon pretended to be intensely interested in what the Armenians were saying and in the view up ahead.

"Simon," said Friar Mathieu.

If he has relieved me of one burden, can he not take away the other, the greater?

"Patience, Father. We are coming to the spot where the road bends around the mountain, and we will be able to see Orvieto. Everyone will be gathering to rest a bit. Let us wait until we are spread out on the road again."

Friar Mathieu shrugged. "As you wish."

Across the valley the silhouette of Orvieto loomed like an enchanted castle against the moonlit sky. The yellow squares of candlelit windows glowed among the dark turrets and terraces. The tall, narrow windows of the cathedral church of San Giovenale were multicolored ribbons of light. Simon found himself wondering where Sophia, the cardinal's niece, was right now, and what she was doing.

When they were stopped by the shrine of San Sebastian, Simon took the lantern and peered down at the Tartars. The stench of wine and vomit hung heavily over their bed of straw, and both of them were snoring loudly. Aside from being in a stupor, they seemed well enough. The stringy black beard of the younger one, Philip, was clotted with bits of half-digested food. Friar Mathieu produced a comb from his robe and cleaned the beard. Simon rode to the head of the party.

"What are you and the old monk gabbling about back there?" asked Alain.

"He is hearing my confession," said Simon lightly.

Alain laughed. "If you have done anything you need to confess, you've been clever about hiding it from me."

When they were back on the road, Simon and Friar Mathieu took up their position at the end of the line.

"How did you know there was more, Father?"

"You asked me to keep what you have told me secret under the seal of the confessional," said Friar Mathieu. "But you have told me nothing that is a sin on your part."

Guilt pierced Simon's heart like a sword, twisting in the wound as he thought how he was betraying his true father and his mother.

I have sworn to Nicolette and Roland never to tell this to anyone.

He took a deep breath.

But I may never again have a chance to talk about it with a wise person I can trust.

Another deep breath.

And then: "The truth of it is, Amalric de Gobignon was not my father."

Friar Mathieu was silent for a moment. "The man who slew Count Amalric. The man your mother married soon after the count was dead." His voice was soft and full of kindness.

"Yes," said Simon, almost choking. "And now you know my sin. The world thinks I am the son of a traitor and murderer, which is bad enough. But I am not even that man's son. I am an impostor, a bastard, and I have no right to the title of Count de Gobignon."

Simon flicked the reins, and his palfrey started picking her way down the road into the Vallia de Campesito. Mathieu clucked to his donkey and kept pace with him.

"Do you believe that you are committing a grave sin by being the Count de Gobignon?"

"My mother and Roland say no, but I do not think they are very good Christians. They are full of pagan ideas. I am Count Amalric's only male heir. And the blood of the house of Gobignon does flow in my veins. I am not the son of Count Amalric de Gobignon, but I am the grandson of his father, Count Stephen de Gobignon."

Friar Mathieu clapped his hand to his forehead. "I am lost in the tangle of bloodlines. What in heaven's name do you mean?"

Simon's entire body burned with shame as he thought how accursed his family would seem to anyone hearing this for the first time. The bastard son of a bastard son. The usurper of his half uncle's title. Tangled, indeed. Twisted was a better word for it.

In his agony he whispered the words. "Roland de Vency, my true father, is the bastard son of Count Stephen de Gobignon, sired by rape in Languedoc. Roland and Count Amalric were half brothers."

"God's mercy!" exclaimed Friar Mathieu. "But then you do have some claim by blood to the title. To whom else could it go?"

"I suppose the fiefdom could go to my oldest sister, Isabelle, and her husband. He is a landless knight, a vassal of the Count of Artois. My three sisters married far beneath their stations—because of what Count Amalric did."

Friar Mathieu sighed. "Would any great evil come of it, do you think, if you were to give up your estate?"

"My mother and father—my true father, Roland de Vency—would be exposed as adulterers. We would all be charged as criminals, for defrauding the kingdom and the rightful heirs, whoever they might be." He saw his mother kneeling with her head on a chopping block, and a chill of horror went through him.

"Simon, this is no easy question you have set before me this night. The lives of thousands of people, even the future of the kingdom, could be determined by who holds the Gobignon domains. I think it is not so important that the Count de Gobignon be the *rightful* person as that he be the *right* person. Do you take my meaning?"

"I think so," said Simon. What Friar Mathieu was saying gave him a faint feeling of hope.

"I know you well enough to know that the people of Gobignon are blessed to have you as your seigneur. When a bad man inherits a title, we say it must be God's will, and those who owe him obedience are bound to accept him. Might we not say that when a man like you is invested with a title, regardless of how he came by it, that is God's will, too? In any case, Simon, we cannot settle this question tonight. There is too much at stake, and we must proceed thoughtfully."

"But what if—if something happens to me while I am in sin?" Simon pictured himself lying in a street in Orvieto, blood streaming from his chest as Sophia watched, weeping, from a distant window. And then he saw grinning Saracen-faced demons in hell jabbing him with spears and scimitars.

"I can give you absolution conditional on your desire to do whatever is right," said Friar Mathieu. "Promise God that you will make all haste to determine His will in this matter and that when you know what He wants, you will faithfully do it, whether it be to give up the title or to keep the title and the secret. I need hardly remind you that God sees into your heart and knows whether you truly mean to set things right. Say an Act of Contrition.''

The weight of shame seemed as crushing as ever, and Simon did not think Friar Mathieu's speaking Latin words while he himself spoke the formula of repentance would take the burden away. But he began the Act of Contrition.

His voice as he uttered the prayer was barely audible over the clicking of the horses' hooves on the stony road, the rumbling of the two carts and the rustling of the pines on the hillside. He repeated what Friar Mathieu had said to him about being ready to follow God's will. Then the old Franciscan made the Sign of the Cross in the air.

The road narrowed now so that there was not enough room for horses side by side. Simon fell behind Friar Mathieu.

Roland and Nicolette need never know I told anyone.

The only way they would find out would be if he felt called upon to reveal the secret to the world.

He felt as if his whole body were plunged into icy water. He realized that by his promise to Friar Mathieu—to God—he was embarked on a course that could end in ruin or worse for his mother and father as well as himself. Their pretense that Simon was Amalric's child was a crime. He saw them all brought as prisoners before King Louis.

How could he bear to face the king, whom he admired more than any other man in France, even more than his own true father?

What punishment would the king mete out to them? Would they spend the rest of their lives locked away in lightless dungeons? Would they have to die for their crime?

Surely God would not ask that of him.

And then, Simon might decide, with God's help, that he had the best right of anyone to the count's coronet. If he kept it, and kept the secret of his parentage, it would be through his own choice. No mortal would thrust that choice upon him.

He began to feel better. He started humming a tune, an old crusader song Roland had taught him, called ''The Old Man of the Mountain.''

Until now other hands had shaped his life. From this moment on he would hold his destiny in his own hands.

* * *

"May I disturb you for a moment, Your Signory, before you retire?" The Countessa di Monaldeschi's chief steward was a severe-looking man with long white hair streaked with black.

Simon had just set foot to the steps leading to the third story of the Monaldeschi palace, where his bedchamber waited. He most definitely did not want to be disturbed this evening. But the steward had shown gravity and discretion arranging for the drunken Tartars to be bundled off to bed, and Simon felt that whatever he might say would be worth listening to.

"Late this afternoon a vagabondo came to our door. He claims to be a former retainer of yours. He begs an audience with you—most humbly, he says to tell you. He waits in the kitchen. We can keep him till tomorrow. Or we can put him out in the street. Or you can see him. Whatever Your Signory desires."

A former retainer? A sour suspicion began to grow in Simon's mind.

"Did he at least tell you his name?'

"Yes, Your Signory. Sordello."

Simon felt hot blood pounding at his temples in immediate anger.

Has that dog had the temerity to follow me all the way to Orvieto?

"Send him away," he said brusquely. "And do not be gentle about it."

The steward's stern face remained expressionless. "Very good, Your Signory." He bowed himself away. A good servant, thought Simon. He showed neither approval nor disapproval. Simon started up the stairs.

What the devil could Sordello have to talk to me about?

Do not call upon the devil. He may hear you and come.

Halfway up the stairs Simon felt the itch of curiosity growing stronger and stronger. Perhaps Sordello had been to see Count Charles and had some word from him. The feeling was like a scab Simon knew he should not pick but could not let alone.

He turned. The steward was almost invisible in the shadows at the end of the long hallway.

"Wait. I will go to him."

In the kitchen on the bottom floor of the Palazzo Monaldeschi, under a chimney in the center of the room, a cauldron big enough to hold a man simmered over a low fire. From it came a strong smell of lamb, chicken, onion, celery, peppers, garlic, cloves, and other ingredients Simon could not identify. Beyond the cauldron a trapdoor covered the stairs to a locked cellar pantry where, Simon knew, the Monaldeschi hoarded possessions as costly as jewels— their collection of spices imported from the East.

Simon had just a glimpse of the ruddy face with its broken nose before the crossbowman-troubadour fell to his knees and thumped his forehead on the brick floor.

Perhaps I could pop Sordello into that cooking pot and be done with him for good and all.

"Thank you, Your Signory, for being willing to see me," came the muffled voice from the floor. "You are far kinder than I deserve."

"Yes, I am," said Simon brusquely. "Get up. Why have you come to me?"

Sordello rocked back on his heels and sprang to his feet in a single, surprising motion. Simon told himself to be wary. It was all very well to be gruff with Sordello, but he must keep in mind that the man was a fighter, a murderer. And one with a vile and overquick temper, as he had proved in Venice.

"I have no one else to go to." Sordello spread his empty hands. He had grown a short, ragged black beard, Simon noticed. He wore no hat or cloak, and his tunic and hose were stained and tattered. His tunic hung loose, unbelted. No weapons. That made Simon feel a bit easier. The toe of one boot was worn through, and the other was bound with a bit of rag to hold the sole to the upper.

"I thought you would see the Count d'Anjou." And Simon had half expected Uncle Charles would send Sordello back with a message insisting Simon take the fellow back into his service.

Sordello laughed and nodded. "Easy to say 'see the Count d'Anjou,' Your Signory. Not so easy to do when you are a masterless man with an empty purse. The count likes to move about, and quickly at that. But I caught up with him at Lyons. He already knew the whole story."

"I wrote to him," said Simon.

"Well, your letter must have been most eloquent, Your Signory, because the count refused to take me back into his service. He called me a fool and a few other things and told me I deserved exactly what I got. Told me if I wasn't out of the city in an hour he would have me flogged."

"I assumed that the count reposed great confidence in you, and I felt I must convince him that I had done the right thing in dismissing you.'' He sounded in his own ears as if he were apologizing. He reminded himself firmly that the scoundrel had no right to an apology.

"You convinced him, all right.'' Sordello's manner was becoming less humble by the moment.

He is either going to attack me or—worse—ask for his position back. I must not be soft with him.

"Once a man as well known as the Count d'Anjou has expelled you from his service, you can't find a position anywhere in France or Italy,'' said Sordello. "Not if your only skills are fighting and singing. I sold my horse in Milan. I walked from there on. I ran out of money in Pisa. I starved and slept in ditches to get here.''

"And stole here and there, too, I'll wager,'' said Simon, determined to be hard with Sordello. "Well, here you are, and why have you come?'' He knew the answer perfectly well, and was determined, no matter how the troubadour tried to play on his sympathies, to send him on his way. Even if he had wanted to take Sordello back into his service—and he most definitely did not—the Armenians and the Tartars would never permit his presence among them. At any rate, regardless of what Sordello claimed, he would not starve. He could sing for his supper in inns. And Italy's street-warring families and factions could always use a dagger as quick as Sordello's.

"I could throw my lot in with the Ghibellini, Your Signory, but their prospects are poor,'' said Sordello, as if aware of Simon's thoughts. "The day is coming when all of Italy will be in the power of the Count d'Anjou. I want to get back into his good graces, and the only way I can do that is through you, Your Signory. If you take me back, he will take me back.''

David of Trebizond's servant, Giancarlo! Just today, was I not wishing I could put someone in the enemy camp?

Simon stood staring into Sordello's eyes, deliberately making him wait for an answer. The troubadour's eyelids wrinkled down to slits, but he held Simon's gaze.

"I was going to tell you I had nothing for you.'' Simon saw Sordello's face brighten at the hint that Simon would offer him something. "But there is a way you can serve me.''

Sordello began to smile.

"It does involve throwing your lot in with the Ghibellini,'' Simon said, "but you will be serving me and, through me, Count Charles. Does that interest you?''

Sordello dropped to his knees, seized Simon's hand, and kissed it with rough lips. "To spy upon them? Your Signory, I was made for such work. Thank you, thank you for letting me serve you. Command me, Your Signory, I beg."

XIX

"ARE THERE ANY GREAT COLLECTIONS OF BOOKS IN TREBIZOND?" Fra Tomasso leaned forward intently, and his belly, swathed in the white linen robe of his order, pushed the small black writing desk toward Daoud.

Fra Tomasso's dialect was easy for Daoud to understand. It was the same as Lorenzo's, since the friar came from southern Italy. It was the dialect Daoud had learned in Egypt.

But in another sense, conversing with d'Aquino was not at all easy. His body tense, Daoud sat on the edge of his chair, alert for any question that might be meant to trap him. And at the same time, he burned for a chance to persuade the stout Dominican to oppose the Tartar alliance. He was both hunted and hunter today.

"Yes, Father. The basileus of Trebizond—the emperor—has the biggest library, with the monks of Mount Gelesias not far behind. Several of the great families have large collections of very old manuscripts. I am afraid I cannot tell you what is in any of those libraries. I know more about spices and silks than I do about books. Is there a particular book you are interested in?"

Daoud, relieved, watched the round face glow as the Dominican seemed to relish the possibilities. It would never have done to admit it to Ugolini, but Daoud was not without fear. He realized that a slip might lead to his arrest and torture, the end of his mission, and, finally, death. His head had begun to ache from the effort of posing and answering all questions with care.

But now he sensed a way of reaching d'Aquino. More than anything else, the man would want books—books that would help him write more books of his own. Perhaps his huge physical appetite was but a reflection of his hunger for knowledge.

"Ah, Messer David." He smiled, and Daoud realized that his mouth was not small—it only looked small because of the round cheeks on either side of it. "There is one book I have heard of that I would give everything I possess—if I possessed anything—to own. You are familiar with *the* philosopher, Aristotle?"

Daoud nodded. How wise it had been of Baibars, he thought, to command him to spend months with a mullah from Andalus who was versed in the philosophies of the Christians and of their Greek and Roman predecessors. Daoud had even read works by Aristotle in Arabic.

"Much of my work, like that of my colleagues, is based on the writings of Aristotle," d'Aquino went on. "He has been called the Master of Those Who Know. I call him *the* philosopher. His thought encompassed every subject under the sun—and the sun itself, I believe. The ancient writers refer to a book by Aristotle called in Latin *De Caelestiis, Of the Heavens.* In it *the* philosopher writes about the movement of heavenly bodies, the sun, the stars, and the planets, and their relations with one another. That book disappeared during the long wars that led to the downfall of the Roman Empire. Every time I meet a traveler from some distant part of the world, I ask him about *De Caelestiis.*"

"Does it tell how the planets rule men's fates?" Daoud asked.

"That is a ridiculous, irrational, and superstitious notion." Fra Tomasso waved the suggestion away with a stubby-fingered hand. Daoud felt a cold wave of terror. Had he said something that gave him away?

But Fra Tomasso, leaning back in his squeaking chair, seemed unperturbed. And Daoud remembered that Ugolini studied the influence of the stars on human lives. So it could not be such an un-Christian belief.

The Dominican pointed over his shoulder to the window of his cell, a large rectangle cut in the curving whitewashed wall. This was one of the few rooms Daoud had entered in Italy that was not covered with idolatrous or obscene paintings, and he liked its austerity. Except, of course, for the ubiquitous figure of Jesus the Messiah, crucified, hanging opposite the window. Daoud tried to avoid looking at the crucifixes because they reminded him of his childhood, but they were everywhere in Orvieto.

"Aristotle reasoned about the relations of the heavenly bodies to one another," Fra Tomasso said. "One account of the *De Caelestiis* declares that he believed that the sun does not move."

"But we see it move," Daoud said, surprised.

"We think we see it move." D'Aquino smiled. "But have you ever stood on the deck of a galley as it was pulling away from the quay and had the feeling that the quay was moving while the ship was standing still? Well then, what if the earth is moving, just like a ship on whose deck we stand, while the sun remains fixed?"

Daoud thought about the vast and solid earth and the daily journey of the sun like a bright lamp across the sky. It was self-evident which one of them moved. But he sensed that Fra Tomasso was in love with this idea. He had best not argue too strenuously against it.

"Ingenious," he said.

Ridiculous, he thought to himself. *This man dismisses astrology and approves greater absurdities.*

"I myself suspected that the sun might be stationary while the earth moves long before I learned that Aristotle might also believe so." Fra Tomasso waved a hand toward the window again. His cell was the top floor of one of the towers fortifying the Dominican chapter house, an anthill of constant, mysterious activity. D'Aquino's window overlooked the north side of Orvieto's wall. There was no covering on the window, and the shutters were open to let in the cool mountain air. Daoud gazed upon the rolling hills, bright green in the sunlight, beyond Orvieto's battlements. This was a lovely country, he thought. Back in Egypt the hills would be brown this time of year.

"Look how much light and heat we get from the sun," Fra Tomasso went on. "Yet, the sun appears small—I can hide it with my thumb."

Your thumb could hide four or five suns.

"Perhaps it *is* small," Daoud said.

"If it is as big as it must be to produce such light and heat, it must be very far away—thousands of leagues—to appear so small. But if it is that far away, it must be bigger still, for its heat and light to travel such a distance. The bigger it is, the farther away it must be—the farther away it is, the bigger it must be. Do you follow? There must be a strict rule of proportion."

Daoud told himself to ignore this nonsense and concentrate on the important thing—that Fra Tomasso badly wanted a book by this pagan philosopher Aristotle. That book might be the means of winning Fra Tomasso. Not that he could be crudely bribed, but certainly such a present would favorably dispose him to what Daoud had to say.

And he saw another way to make the point he had come to make.

"It may be, Your Reverence, that the book you want has been lost forever. When I spoke of the destruction of Baghdad the other day, I should have mentioned that the Tartars burned there a library rivaled only by the great library of Alexandria in its prime."

His flesh turned cold. That was a mistake. In his zeal he had momentarily forgotten that it was Christians who had destroyed the library of Alexandria. As the story was often told in Egypt, when the Muslim warriors took Alexandria from the Christians, they found that most of what had once been the world's greatest collection of books had been used to fuel the fires that warmed the public baths.

But, to Daoud's relief, Fra Tomasso only shut his eyes and shook his head, his cheeks quivering gently like a bowl of frumenty. "God forgive the Tartars."

"God will certainly not forgive *us*, Fra Tomasso, if we help the Tartars to destroy Damascus and Cairo. Or Trebizond and Constantinople."

The Dominican opened his eyes wide. "Constantinople?"

"In the Far East they have taken greater cities and conquered much larger empires."

Fra Tomasso crossed himself. "But it is God's will, even as Augustine tells us, that cities be destroyed and empires rise and fall. The Tartars may be the builders of a Christian empire that embraces the whole world."

God forbid it! Daoud was becoming exasperated with the fat Dominican's "perhapses" and "maybes." *Perhaps the earth moves and the sun stands still. Maybe the Tartars are God's means of making the whole world Christian.*

He warned himself not to let his anger show. This might seem to be a pleasant conversation, but actually he was tiptoeing around the edge of a pit of quicksand.

Still, if this clever, restless mind could be recruited to work against the alliance, how persuasive it would be. Daoud had already noticed that most of the leaders of Christendom listened when d'Aquino spoke. But Daoud dared not argue against the belief that God decided the fate of nations. He recalled a teaching of his Sufi master, Sheikh Saadi. He framed it in his mind to offer to d'Aquino.

"Your Reverence, truly we must accept as the will of God that which has happened. But to think we can guess what God wills for the future is sinful pride. We can be guided only by the knowledge of right and wrong He has implanted in us."

D'Aquino let his folded hands rest on the great sphere of his belly. His blue eyes gazed off at a point somewhere behind Daoud, whose muscles tightened as he waited for the friar to speak. He watched through the open window as a flock of crows circled in the deep-blue sky. They chose a direction and dwindled to a cloud of black dots over the green hills.

Daoud realized he had been holding his breath. He let it out just as the last crow disappeared.

"That is well stated," said Fra Tomasso. "I can find no objection to that."

Elated, Daoud pressed on. "And it follows that if we think the Tartar destruction of civilization is wrong, we must fight against it." He hoped he did not sound too eager. D'Aquino would surely be suspicious if he saw how badly Daoud wanted his cooperation.

"I will have to consider that," said Fra Tomasso judiciously. "But perhaps we could teach the Tartars the value of civilization. If we made allies of them, we could make it a condition that they not destroy any more of the great cities of the Muslim world. Indeed, our missionaries will be among them. They can point out what should be saved."

Daoud's breathing quickened as rage rumbled up inside him. It sounded exactly as if Fra Tomasso meant that the Tartars could slaughter all the people of Islam as long as they left the libraries intact. Using the Hashishiyya technique called "the Face of Steel within the Mask of Clay," he walled off his anger.

He would not contradict Fra Tomasso's last idea. He would try instead to make the beginning of a bargain.

"Those libraries of Trebizond you asked me about," Daoud said. "I am sure there are many books in them that exist nowhere else in the world. Perhaps even the book you mentioned, that rare book of Aristotle. Would you write down its name for me, Fra Tomasso? I will inquire about it in my next report to my trading partners."

The Dominican leaned forward until most of his belly disappeared below the horizon of his desk. In that position he was able to pull the desk closer and search it for a blank slip of parchment. He dipped his quill ceremoniously in his inkpot, wrote briefly, then carefully poured fine white sand from a jar to absorb the excess ink. Daoud rose to take the parchment from him.

Now, if only such a book exists somewhere in the lands where Baibars's power runs. And if only the weather on the Middle Sea allows us to get the book here quickly. And if only it has the effect on Fra Tomasso that I want.

So many ifs. Far too many. The outcome of a battle would be easier to predict. For the thousandth time Daoud wished he were leading troops in the field rather than intriguing in the chambers of enemy leaders.

"I understand it will be possible to meet the two Tartars when the Contessa di Monaldeschi gives a reception in their honor next week," said Daoud. "Will Your Reverence be attending?"

Fra Tomasso nodded. "But I also intend to talk with them privately as I have with you." Daoud tensed inwardly as he heard that. "It will be interesting, though, to see how they comport themselves in a gathering," the Dominican went on. "Yes, I shall come to the contessa's. And you?"

"As Cardinal Ugolini's guest," said Daoud with modesty. "And what of the execution of the heretic who threatened the ambassadors in the cathedral? Will Your Reverence witness that? I understand it should be a most edifying spectacle." He folded Fra Tomasso's bit of parchment and thrust it into the pouch at his belt.

Fra Tomasso shook his head. "The good of the community demands that we make an example of the poor creature. He refuses to admit his errors. Still, I cannot stand to see a fellow human being suffer. I will not be there."

So, thought Daoud contemptuously, the fat Dominican was one of those who could justify the shedding of blood but could not stand to see it shed. And in the same way, d'Aquino might decide to be for war or for peace and never see the consequences of his decision. Daoud might wish to lead troops in battle, but he reminded himself that it was in studios like this, where men of influence thought and read and argued, that the real war was being fought.

XX

THE MADMAN HAD A LOUD VOICE. DAOUD COULD HEAR HIM LONG before he could see the victim and his torturers. The people around Daoud jostled and craned their necks toward the sound of the screams.

The heretic, in accordance with his sentence, had been dragged through every street in the city and tormented at every intersection, but most of Orvieto's citizens had been waiting in the Piazza San Giovenale to see his final agonies before the cathedral he had desecrated. The piazza was so packed with people it seemed not another person could squeeze in.

Daoud had positioned himself at the foot of the front steps of the cathedral. He faced a wooden platform, newly built in the center of the piazza, on four legs twice the height of a man. Above the platform rose a tall pole. The whole structure was of white wood, unseasoned and unpainted—which was only sensible, since it would shortly be destroyed. Bundles of firewood were piled under it.

Daoud's arms were wedged so tightly to his side by the crowd of people standing about him that it was an effort for him to wipe his face with his sleeve. He had expected Italy to be cooler than Egypt now, in the middle of the Christian month of September, but the damp heat of summer lingered. Thick gray clouds hung low over the city. Sweat streamed from under Daoud's red velvet cap, and he wished he could wear a turban or a burnoose to keep his forehead cool and dry.

At the top of the cathedral steps, in a space cleared by papal guards, stood six red-robed cardinals. Ugolini was among them. He had not wanted to witness the execution, but Daoud had persuaded him to go. His presence, like Daoud's, might counter the suspicion that those who opposed the alliance with the Tartars were connected with the disturbances against them.

Near Ugolini stood Cardinal Paulus de Verceuil, the Tartars' chief supporter in the Sacred College, in a scarlet robe trimmed with ermine, and a broad-brimmed red hat. He looked disdainfully down at another cardinal who Ugolini had pointed out to Daoud as Guy le Gros, also a Frenchman. Every so often de Verceuil would cock an ear to the screams, which were coming closer, or he would glance that way with bright, eager eyes.

Behind the cardinals stood a man-at-arms holding a staff bearing the pope's standard, a gold and white banner blazoned with the crossed keys of Peter in red. Ugolini had learned from the pope's majordomo that His Holiness would not attend. Like Fra Tomasso, Urban had neither need nor desire to see this execution.

One who did have to witness the torture and death of the heretic stood with folded arms on the cathedral steps. He was stocky and much shorter than the two guards in yellow and blue, the city colors, who stood holding halberds on either side of him. His face was grim, and there were deep shadows around his eyes. A small, thin mustache adorned his upper lip. Daoud knew him to be Frescobaldo d'Ucello, podesta of Orvieto.

Daoud's eye moved on. There was the young hero, the man who had captured the would-be assassin. Count Simon de Gobignon stood a little apart from the churchmen and the podesta, speaking to no one. It seemed he had brought none of his Frankish henchmen with him. The black velvet cap he wore and his long dark-brown hair contrasted with the pallor of his thin face. His dress was rich but somber, his silk mantle a deep maroon, his tunic purple. His gloved left hand played nervously with the hilt of his sword, that very sword that had stricken the blade from the heretic's hand.

It was surprising, Daoud thought, that the count's sword was a long, curving scimitar with a jeweled scabbard and hilt. What was the boy doing with a Muslim sword? A trophy of some past crusade, no doubt.

Not enjoying your triumph here today, are you, young Frank? Born to rank and power and wealth, with castles and knights and servants and lands all around you. You have probably never seen a battle, much less fought in one. And yet, knowing not what war is, you try to bring together the Tartar hordes and your crusader knights that they may lay waste my country, kill my people, and stamp out my faith.

Recalling how he and de Gobignon had faced each other at the pope's council, Daoud once again felt rage boil up within him and wondered why he hated the young nobleman so. Was it because he intended to use Sophia to spy on de Gobignon and corrupt him, and that she must bed with him? But that was her work, Daoud tried to tell himself, just as warfare was his.

But was this warfare? To pander to a fat friar's yearning for an old book? To send a lovely woman to the bed of a spoiled young nobleman? To incite a poor fool, maddened by God, into getting himself tortured to death? Daoud wished he could fight openly— draw his sword and challenge de Gobignon. To drive him to his knees, to cut him down, to strike and strike for the people he loved and for God.

To kill him before all, as I did to Kassar.

Daoud, like de Gobignon, was alone. Lorenzo dared not come; the condemned man might recognize him and call out to him. Daoud would never bring Sophia to witness such a sight, even though there were many women, and even children, in the crowd.

The previous night Tilia had told him that she had rented for the day a house overlooking the piazza, from which some important patrons would enhance their pleasure with Tilia's women by watching the pain of the heretic. Daoud looked around at the colonnaded façades of the palaces around the square, wondering which were the windows through which Tilia's depraved clients watched.

A howl went up from the crowd in the square, the people around Daoud shouting so loudly as to deafen him. He saw a cage made of wooden poles rocking into the piazza. People cheered and laughed. Two executioners in blood-red tunics, their heads and faces covered with red hoods, stood on either side of the cage, each man holding in his hands a pair of long-handled pincers. Standing on tiptoe, Daoud saw on the platform of the cart a black iron dish from which ribbons of gray smoke arose.

The prisoner, squatting in the cage, was silent for the moment. Even at this distance Daoud could see his shoulders shaking spasmodically with his panting. He was naked, and all over his flesh were bleeding, blackened wounds.

The executioners thrust the ends of their pincers into the coals and held them there. When they raised them out and brandished them, the claws were glowing red. They turned to the prisoner, who started screaming at once. One executioner thrust his pincers through the front of the cage. The prisoner tried to back away, but the cage was too small. He only pressed his buttocks against the bars behind him, where the other executioner had crept and now dug the jaws of his pincers into the man's flesh as the crowd roared with laughter. Daoud heard the sizzle. The man's scream rose to a pitch that made Daoud's ears ring. The executioner held up his pincers with a gobbet of burnt flesh caught in them for the crowd to see, then slung them so that the bit of meat flew through the air. Daoud saw people reach up to grab at it.

This man is dying horribly because of me. The thought bit into Daoud's heart like the red-hot claws. When Sophia had said as much accusingly to him, he had shrugged it off. Now he had to face the fact.

Let your guilt pierce you through the heart. Do not armor your-self against it. Do not run away from it. Above all, do not turn your back on it. So Saadi had advised him after he avenged himself on Kassar.

The sands of the Eastern Desert were the color of drying blood. The hooves of Daoud's pony sank into them with each step, and he wished he had a camel to ride.

Their training troop had never traveled this far south, and Nicetas had been a fool, Daoud thought, to go hunting in unknown and dangerous country with only a pony to ride. No wonder he had not come back yesterday. Probably, the sun had killed the pony, and Nicetas was crouched in some wadi waiting to be rescued.

I should have gone with him.

But they had been friends, and more than friends, for two years, and from time to time each needed to be alone. They both under-stood that. And so, when the naqeeb Mahmoud gave them a day of rest after the trek down from El Kahira, and Nicetas said he wanted to go out alone to get himself a pair of antelope horns, Daoud simply hugged him and sent him on his way.

Daoud felt the murderous heat of the noon sun on his head through his burnoose. Ten times hotter here than at El Kahira, now a hun-dred leagues to the north. The wind filled the air with red dust, and he had wrapped a scarf over his nose and mouth. Only his eyes were exposed, looking for Nicetas.

Antelope horns! Not even a lizard could live in this desert.

He should get into the shade, but he did not want to stop search-ing. If Nicetas were hurt and lying out in this sun, it would burn him to death. Daoud saw a line of sharp-pointed hills off to his left. There was shade there, and Nicetas would try to reach shade. He tapped his pony's shoulder lightly with his switch and turned its head toward the hills.

Nearly there, he saw what looked like a black rock half-buried ahead of him. Could it be a body? For a moment his heart hammered. No, it was too big. His pony floundered on through the sand till they reached the dark shape.

It was Nicetas's pony, dead. Windblown sand half covered it, but he was sure of it. Nicetas's pony was black.

Daoud swung down from his horse, looping the reins around his wrist so it could not run off, and knelt to examine the dead pony. He brushed away sand from the forehead. Three white dots; he knew those markings well.

He scooped sand away from the dead pony and found an arrow jutting out of the chest. In spite of the fiery sun his body went cold. Wild Sudanese were said to prowl this desert.

He jerked on the arrow. It had gone in deep, and the head must be broad. It took him long to tear it free.

The head was wedge-shaped and made of steel, with sword-sharp edges. Sudanese tribesmen had no such arrows. Even Mamelukes had only a few. Each Mameluke carried two or three, to use against a well-armored opponent.

"Oh, God, help me find Nicetas," he prayed.

Nicetas was out there somewhere. Daoud pushed out of his mind the thought that he might be dead.

Was this punishment for their sin of loving each other, he wondered as he mounted his little horse. God frowned on men lying with men, the mullahs said, but everyone knew that men, especially young men far from women, often took comfort in one another.

He pulled his burnoose farther down over his eyes to shade them better against the sun. He wanted water, but he would not let himself drink until he had reached the hills. He might find Nicetas there, and Nicetas might need the water.

The hills thrust abruptly out of the sand in long vertical folds. Half blinded by the glare, he could see only opaque blackness where the sun did not strike them.

He thought he saw movement in one shadow. He kicked the pony, driving it to struggle faster through the sand, keeping his eyes fixed on the spot.

A deep crevice sliced into the hillside. Daoud rode into it cautiously. Whoever killed Nicetas's mount might still be somewhere about.

Once out of the sun, he slid down from the saddle. He saw no water, but there was a dead tamarisk, its branches like supplicating arms, at the mouth of the crevice. He tied the pony to a limb and moved, slowly, deeper into the shadow.

He looked down at the floor of the crevice, paved with drifting sand and tiny pebbles. He felt a pain in his heart as he saw a trail of dark circular spots, each about the size of his hand. It could be a wounded animal, he told himself.

Then he saw a palmprint, the same dried color, and the pain in his heart sharpened.

He saw the movement again, at the far end of the crevice. A figure lay with its legs stretched out before it, its back propped against the brown stone. Pale hands were clasped over its stomach.

He heard a low, moaning sound, and realized it was coming not from Nicetas but from his own mouth.

Daoud ran and fell to his knees beside him. The half-open eyes widened and the amber gaze turned in his direction. The Greek boy's face was reddened with dust that clung to his sweat. His lips, partially open, were so dry and encrusted they looked like scabs. Daoud put his hand on Nicetas's cheeks. His face was burning.

Now the hurt in Daoud's heart was like death itself.

I am going to lose him.

But this was no time to wail and weep. He must do everything he could. It might yet be God's will that he save his friend.

Let him live, oh God, and I will never sin with him again.

"I knew you would come." The voice was so faint Daoud could barely hear it above the wind whistling past the mouth of the crevice.

Daoud sprang to his feet and ran to his pony to get his water bottle. He untwisted the stopper over his friend's mouth.

The Greek boy shook his head. "I cannot swallow. Just pour a little in my mouth to wet it." Daoud saw deep red cracks in Nicetas's lips. The water trickled out the corners of his mouth and streaked his dusty cheeks.

A hundred half-formed thoughts crowded Daoud's mind. His eyes burned, and pain pounded at his chest.

All he said was "What happened to you?"

"It was Kassar," Nicetas whispered. "He got me with his first arrow. Then he shot the pony and it fell on me. He rode me down. He took my bow before I could get free."

After all this time! Daoud thought. Kassar had said nothing, done nothing, since the day Nicetas beat him at casting the rumh.

Two years Kassar had waited.

He bent forward to take Nicetas in his arms, but the Greek boy shook his head. "Do not move me. It will hurt too much."

"Where are you hit?"

"In my back. Still in me. I broke off the shaft."

Why was I such a fool, to think we were safe?

"It can't be a very bad wound."

Nicetas closed his eyes. "Bad enough that he could use me for his pleasure and I could not fight him off."

A dizzying blackness blinded Daoud. His skull felt as if it were going to burst.

"By God and the Prophet, I will kill him."

"I want you to."

"Did he do any more to hurt you?"

"Yes, he got me here." He parted his hands and raised them from his stomach. His white cotton robe was caked with black blood, and there was a tear in the center. The wound was not wide, but Daoud knew that it must be very deep.

"He made sure to use his rumh, you see."

"Because that was how you beat him."

Daoud wanted only to hold Nicetas and cry, but he sensed that what would most comfort the Greek boy would be talking about what happened to him.

"After the rumh, I lay very still and held my breath. He thought I was dead. He left me lying there with the pony. Took my weapons and my water bottle. I crawled here. In the sun. Yesterday afternoon. I bled and bled."

He is going to die, Daoud thought. He did not want to believe it. For a moment he was angry at Nicetas. Why had he been such a fool as to come out here alone? And then at himself. Why had he let him go?

And then at God.

Why did You let this happen? Do You hate us because we love each other?

"I knew you would come for me, Daoud. I stayed alive to greet you."

Daoud took Nicetas's hand. "I will take you back."

"No. Bury me out here. Let him think you never found me. Bide your time, as he did. Give him no reason to fear you. He fears you already, or he would never have done it this way."

"Before the year is out, you will look down from paradise and see him burning in hell."

"I'm sorry. I was never strong enough to be a Mameluke."

"No. You *are* strong."

"Not strong enough to live," said Nicetas, so faintly Daoud could hardly hear him. "Good-bye, Daoud. Remember the Greek I taught you. You may meet someone else who speaks Greek."

"I will never meet anyone like you." The tears spilled out over his eyelids, and he did not try to brush them away. The hand he held squeezed his, weakly, then relaxed.

Daoud bent forward and touched his mouth to the split, dust-coated lips. No breath came from his friend's body. A curtain of shadow swept before his eyes, and he thought he was going to faint.

He thrust himself to his feet as Nicetas's head fell to one side.

He threw his arms over his head and screamed.

Arms still upraised, he dropped to his knees.

"Oh, God!" His voice echoed back from the walls of the crevice. "God, God, God!"

The pain in his heart was as if a rumh had impaled it. He felt that he must die, too. He could not bear this loss. Never to see his friend smile again, never to hear his laughter. That body he had loved, nothing now but unmoving, empty clay.

He looked over at Nicetas, hoping to see a movement, the flicker of an eyelid, the rising of the chest. Nothing. Daoud would never again look on in admiration as the Greek boy rode wildly, standing in the stirrups shooting his arrows at the gallop or casting his spear unerringly at the target. They would never, as he had dreamed, ride side by side into battle.

Daoud crumpled to the ground in the position of worship, his forehead pressed against the sharp, broken stones. But he was not worshipping. He simply did not have the strength to hold himself upright.

It seemed hours later when he at last stirred himself. Sobbing, he carried Nicetas out to a place near the mouth of the crevice, where the sand had drifted in, and with his hands he dug there a grave. All along the base of the hillside were many loose brown stones, chipped away by the eternal wind. With bleeding hands he piled the stones high over Nicetas's body, but tried to make the pile look like a rock slide, so that no one would know someone was buried here. He knelt, weeping and talking to Nicetas's spirit, until the sun was low in the west.

* * *

As Nicetas had told him to do, Daoud had pretended, when he came back from the desert, that he had no idea what had happened to his friend. The naqeeb had declared that Sudanese tribesmen or wild animals must have gotten him. Daoud was not alone in his grief. Many of the boys in the troop had liked Nicetas.

Even Kassar had said words of sympathy, his face expressionless and his slanted eyes opaque. Daoud held in his rage, a white-hot furnace in his heart, and in a choked voice he thanked Kassar.

At first he went about in a daze, unable to think. He told himself that in spite of his dissembling, Kassar would be on guard. He would have to choose a time to take his revenge when Kassar would be preoccupied. And Daoud himself must be alert at all times. Kassar might not be satisfied with killing only Nicetas. In spite of these warnings to himself, Daoud's mind remained numb. He was, he told himself, like a mall ball, hit one way by grief, the other way by rage, unable to take control of his destiny.

That thought of mall gave him the beginning of a plan.

He let three months go by from the day he found Nicetas. His plan was very simple. It left much to luck, and it might fail utterly— Kassar might anticipate what he was going to do and turn the moment against him, killing him and claiming he was defending himself. Kassar's friends might thwart Daoud.

He would have only this one chance. If he failed, he would be dead or crippled. Or worst of all, cast out of the Mamelukes to spend the rest of his life as a ghulman, a menial slave. But if he succeeded, Nicetas would be avenged before Baibars and Sultan Qutuz and all Daoud's and Nicetas's khushdashiya.

Whatever punishment might befall him then, he thought he could bear it for Nicetas's sake.

The Warrior of God is a man who would give his life for his friends.

On the day Daoud decided to act, the Bhari Mamelukes, the slaves of the River, rode out to play mall. Emir Baibars al-Bunduqdari led them across the bridge from Raudha Island to the Nasiri race course, their training and playing ground, within sight of the great pyramids built by the ancient idol-worshipers of Egypt. The people of El Kahira watched with shining eyes as their guardians assembled on the field. Baibars's tablkhana, his personal mounted band, playing trumpets and kettledrums, cymbals and hautboys, rode before them. Sultan al-Mudhaffar Qutuz came down from the citadel of El Kahira to watch the games as the guest of his Mamelukes.

The troops of julbans, Mamelukes in training, brought up the rear of the parade on their little ponies, with their naqeebs riding before them, the oldest boys in the lead and the first- and second-year boys on foot at the end. They wore plain brown shirts and white cotton trousers and caps. No special marks of rank were allowed these young slaves until they became full-fledged Mamelukes.

Daoud's troop, the boys in their fifth year of training, rode immediately behind the Mamelukes. Each boy carried a mallet, which was as much part of his equipment as his bow, his rumh, his dabbus, and his saif. The mallets were made of cedar and were large and heavy. They had to be, to drive a wooden ball half the size of a man's head.

Slaves had pulled perforated water barrels in carts over the field to lay the dust. Baibars and the sultan and the highest-ranking emirs seated themselves on cushions in an open pavilion facing the center of the field.

Daoud's teammates chattered excitedly. They loved mall, and to play before the sultan was a special honor. Kassar, the captain of their team, boasted that he would make ten goals that day. Theirs was to be the second match.

Hefting his mallet, Daoud watched the first match, also between two teams of fifth-year trainees. Each team of eight riders tried to drive the wooden ball between a pair of stone pillars painted with red and yellow stripes, defended by the other team. With every crack of a mallet against the ball, a roar went up from the watching Mamelukes.

A judge with an hourglass called time halfway through the match, to let the field be watered again and the teams change ponies. By the end of the match, the dust was so thick Daoud could not see who had won. But he did not care. He felt utterly calm. He was past anger and past fear. He thought only of watching for the right moment.

Now it was time for their team.

Kassar, Daoud, and the other six riders lined up on the east side of the field, the eight members of the troop they were playing against forming on the other side.

The judge set the wooden ball, yellow with a bright red stripe around its middle, in the center of the field. The sultan held out a blue silk scarf and dropped it. Kassar and the captain of the other team raced at the ball from opposite goals, screaming their war cries. Kassar whirled his mallet over his head, and his pony's legs were a blur in the dust. He reached the ball an instant before his opponent. His mallet slammed into the ball with a crack like the splitting of a board, and the ball flew halfway toward the enemy goal.

The ball was in play, and now the other riders could join in.

You will make not even one goal today, Kassar, Daoud thought as he galloped across the field with his team.

The players on the other side were trying to hit the ball away from their goal. Kassar had ridden into their midst, his pony nimbly following the ball. He held his mallet low to hit through the legs of the opposing team's ponies. Two of the opponents had stayed back by their goalposts to deflect the ball should Kassar hit it.

Kassar was on top of the ball. Daoud kicked his pony's ribs hard and galloped after him.

As Kassar swung low from his saddle to hit the ball, Daoud drove in on him. Kassar glanced up, fear flashing across his broad face. Whatever passed through his mind was his last thought. Daoud swung his mallet up from the ground, smashing it into Kassar's jaw. The force of the blow knocked the white cap from his head. His pony ran free of the melee. Kassar reeled, unconscious, but his horse nomad's instinct held him in the saddle.

Daoud jerked his pony around to race after Kassar. In an instant he was beside his enemy.

He was about to kill a khushdashiyin, a barracks comrade, in open defiance of the code of the Mamelukes and in front of his emir and his sultan.

I am a dead man, he thought as he swung the mallet high.

His body felt cold as death, and he hesitated. As he did so, Kassar turned his head, and Daoud saw consciousness struggling to return to his glazed eyes.

This was Daoud's last chance to avenge Nicetas.

He heard a distant roar of command from the naqeeb Mahmoud, but he ignored it.

He brought the mallet down with all his strength on the Kipchaq's glistening black hair. The shock of the contact ran up his arm and into his shoulder. Kassar started to fall. Daoud struck again with the mallet.

Kassar pitched from his pony's back. As he struck the ground, Daoud smashed the mallet into his head a third time, just as if he were hitting a ball. He tried to hit hard enough to knock Kassar's head right off his neck. Daoud saw the head suddenly distorted, flattening, and knew the skull was crushed. Kassar lay on the ground on his back, only the whites of his eyes showing, his mouth hanging open. Dust half obscured his body.

Daoud heard shouts from the bystanders, but he paid no attention to what they were saying. He saw riders, the other players, racing toward him.

A silence fell on the playing field.

"Get down from your horse." It was Mahmoud, who had run out into the field on foot.

As Daoud and Mahmoud walked across the field, the naqeeb said, "You will answer to El Malik Qutuz and to Emir Baibars for this. Fool, whatever your quarrel was, could you not have settled it in private? Have you forgotten that Baibars is a Kipchaq? He will not forgive you."

Despite his joy at seeing Nicetas's murderer dead, Daoud now felt terror clutching his throat as he approached the two seated figures in their splendid robes at the side of the field. Now that the deed was done and could not be undone, he dreaded facing these two mighty judges.

Baibars is a Kipchaq, but it was Baibars who bought me for the Mamelukes, Daoud thought. *I wonder which will mean more to him this day.*

Baibars and Qutuz sat side by side on cushions in the shade of a silken canopy. Baibars wore an egret's plume, symbol of valor, on his green turban. His wide, harsh mouth was tight under the red mustache, his good eye as empty of feeling as the blind one that was crossed by a vertical saber scar.

Beneficent God, if I must die for what I have done, let it be a quick and clean death. And then I will join Nicetas.

El Malik al-Mudhaffar Qutuz, Sultan of El Kahira, a Mameluke of a Kurdish tribe, was somewhat older than Baibars. His face was criss-crossed with tiny wrinkles. His beard, greased so that it jutted like the prow of a galley, was such a flat back that it must surely be dyed. He wore a large black turban and full black robes with gold embroidery.

Daoud fell to his knees and prostrated himself before the sultan.

"Get up and take off your cap," said Qutuz without preliminary. Daoud rose to his feet, lifting his cap from his head.

"Look at that blond hair," said Qutuz wonderingly. "I thought he had the look of a Frank about him, Bunduqdari."

"I could have told you that," said Baibars flatly. "He belongs to me. He is known as Daoud ibn Abdallah. His parents were Franks. We took him when we freed Ascalon." He talked to Qutuz, Daoud noted, as if they were equals.

Baibars turned his one eye on Daoud. "Why did you do this?" he said softly. "You are not a fool, and you would not kill out of foolishness."

"Effendi, he killed my friend," said Daoud, making himself stand straight and look levelly at Baibars. The emir might sentence him to death, but he would show himself a true Mameluke. He would not cringe or beg. He would honor Nicetas.

"How do you know?"

Daoud told Baibars how he had found Nicetas in the desert and what he had said to him. He kept his voice level, trying not to let his fear show.

"You should have reported this to me!" shouted Naqeeb Mahmoud, his white beard quivering. The naqeeb would bear some blame, Daoud thought, for this breach of discipline.

But Daoud only turned to him and threw his own words back at him, "Among Mamelukes, he who is strongest rules."

Perhaps he should not be so defiant, he thought. Both the sultan and Baibars liked to show themselves to be men of great generosity.

Yes, but not to a julban who has broken the law.

"He cannot kill his comrade and go unpunished," said Qutuz. "He should be beheaded."

At the words, even though he had thought himself prepared for them, Daoud felt something shrink with dread inside him. He felt the blade slicing through his neck. The sultan had spoken. His life was over.

"He is too valuable to be beheaded," said Baibars. "Believe me, My Lord."

Valuable?

Daoud felt as if he had fallen from a cliff and a strong hand had reached out and was dragging him back. He was breathless with a relief he barely dared to feel. He tried to keep his face and body still as the two great ones debated his fate, but he could not stop his fists from clenching.

The sultan's eyes narrowed, and a deep crease appeared between his brows as he turned to Baibars. "Is this Frankish murderer a protégé of yours, then?"

Baibars nodded. "I have seen reason to take a personal interest in him, if it please My Lord."

What did that mean? What had Baibars seen in him that day in the slave market, and why had Baibars come there that day?

I have long watched for such a one as you, who could have the outward look of a Christian knight but the mind and heart of a Mameluke. One like you could be a great weapon against the enemies of the faith.

"It does not please me," said Qutuz shortly. "There is too much breaking of rules among the Bhari Mamelukes." He spoke, Daoud thought, as if he were not originally a Mameluke himself.

"There is a law among Mamelukes more binding than any lesser rule," said Baibars quietly. "He who feels himself greatly sinned against must strike back. If he cannot do that, he is not enough of a man to be a Mameluke. Even as this foolish boy said, the strong must rule."

Daoud saw grave approval in Baibars's brown face and realized that it did not matter at all to Baibars that Kassar was a Kipchaq. His joy grew as he realized that he had Baibars on his side.

Daoud remembered Nicetas's dying words—*I am not strong enough to be a Mameluke.*

But together we were strong enough to do what had to be done.

Qutuz said, "If all Mamelukes believed only in the rule of the strongest, we would have chaos."

"Only if it were not certain who *is* strongest," said Baibars quietly.

Baibars and Qutuz sat looking at each other in a grave and thoughtful silence that seemed to stretch on forever. Finally, Qutuz turned away.

"I must allow you to discipline the Bhari Mamelukes—or not discipline them—as you see fit, Bunduqdari. That is your responsibility."

"Thank you, My Lord," said Baibars with just a hint of sarcasm. He turned to Mahmoud. "Take him away."

Daoud crossed the field, walking beside Mahmoud, wondering how his khushdashiya, clustered together around what had been their goal, would greet him.

I have killed Kassar, Daoud thought. *I have taken a life.* It was the first time, and he felt glad and proud.

But he would gladly give up this proud moment to have Nicetas back. His grief for Nicetas was sharp as ever, not at all eased by vengeance.

Is it wrong to have done as I did and to feel this way?

A sharp voice rang out behind them. "Mahmoud!"

Daoud and the naqeeb turned together, and Daoud was amazed to see that Baibars, splendid in his red satin robe and green turban, was approaching them. Daoud and Mahmoud rushed to stand before him, rigid and trembling.

"Mahmoud," Baibars said, "when we return to Raudha Island tonight, you will issue this fool the steel helmet of a full-fledged Mameluke, trimmed with black fur."

He swung that searching blue eye back to Daoud. "Tonight at the Gray Mosque I will perform the ceremony that frees you. You will be a part of my personal guard from now on."

Dizzy with exultation, Daoud fell to his knees and pressed his forehead to the cool brown earth before the emir. Tears burned his eyes and dripped to the ground.

"May God praise and bless you, Emir Baibars!" he cried.

"Get up," Baibars said briskly. "Had you let your friend go unavenged, I would no longer be interested in you."

As he scrambled to his feet, Daoud saw Mahmoud smiling through his beard.

"You learned well the lesson I tried to teach you."

Dizzy, Daoud tried to grasp what had been going on in the minds of these men without his realizing it.

Baibars said, "Now you must learn to kill with more grace and subtlety. I shall see that you are trained by masters, as I did when I sent you to Sheikh Abu Hamid al-Din Saadi."

And I must go to Sheikh Saadi again, thought Daoud. *That he may tell me if I did wrong.*

Now it was over ten years since Kassar had killed Nicetas and Daoud had killed Kassar. And though Daoud had never felt guilty for killing Kassar, he understood what Saadi meant about facing guilt.

If he had not understood, he might have told himself that it was not his fault, it was these Christian brutes who chose to torment the poor madman in this way. He might have told himself that Lorenzo, not he, had found the man and brought him to Orvieto. He might simply have said, as he had said to Sophia, that in war there must be innocent victims. He might have reminded himself that he and Lorenzo thought that the man would only raise a commotion in the church, not that he would draw a knife.

And if he consented to any of those thoughts, he would have been pinching off a fragment of his soul, just as the executioners pinched off bits of this man's body.

He forced himself to watch as the cage moved slowly into the piazza and the executioners tore again and again at the victim's body with their red-hot pincers. He saw now that six laughing, well-dressed young men were pulling the cart. Of course. No beast, its nostrils assailed by the smell of burning flesh and its ears by the victim's howls of agony, could remain calm and pull a cart through this frenzied crowd.

These were the same people who had rioted against the Tartars a month ago, the day this man was arrested. Now they cheered and jeered at the death of the Tartars' assailant. And that meant, Daoud thought, that the man's death was in vain.

The cage drew near him now as it approached the scaffold. Daoud held his breath at the thought that the condemned man might look him in the eye. *How could I bear that?* But the man's eyes, he saw, were squeezed shut with fear and pain.

And guilt continued to cut into Daoud like the twisting knife blade of a Hashishiyyin.

A better man than I would have found a way to stir the people and keep them stirred, so that lives would not be wasted.

The two red-garbed executioners had set aside their red-hot pincers and were dragging the heretic up the ladder to the scaffold. His feet dangled on the rungs. On the platform stood another man waiting for the victim.

Daoud felt his eyes open wide and his lips begin to work silently when he saw who the third executioner was.

His face was left bare by the executioner's black hood, whose long point hung down the side of his head past his chin. No use to mask this man's face; his body made him instantly recognizable to anyone who had ever seen him before.

He smiled a serene, almost kindly smile down at the moaning man who was being dragged up the ladder toward him. He held a cook's knife in one hand with a blade as wide as his wrist and as long as his forearm. If he were not holding the knife up to display it to his victim, the tip of it would have rested on the platform, because the executioner's back was bent forward as if it had been broken in some accident long ago.

The firewood seller at Lucera!

Daoud's head swam as he tried to fathom how the crippled dwarf who had been part of the crowd of tradesmen entering the great Hohenstaufen stronghold with him, who had witnessed Daoud's arrest by Celino at the gate and even seemed to pray in his behalf, could be here conducting a public execution in the city of the pope. He must have been a Guelfo spy, by coincidence infiltrating Lucera at the same time as Daoud.

He had been in Manfred's pastry kitchen. Had he really been sleeping, or had he seen Manfred, Lorenzo, and Daoud walk through together?

If he sees me here in the crowd, he will expose me! The people around Daoud, their breath reeking of onions and garlic, pressed him so tightly he could barely move. Twisting his body, he managed to get his back turned to the scaffold. This put him face-to-face with a broad-shouldered man in a mud-brown tunic, with a thick black beard and mustache. The man laughed at him.

"Would you turn away? Have you no stomach for Erculio's holy work?"

Daoud fixed the man with a stare, thinking of what he would like to do to him. He realized, though, that if he tried to fight his way out of the piazza, the little man on the scaffold would certainly notice him. If he simply stayed where he was and watched, his would be one face in thousands, and the dwarf obviously had more pressing business. He reached up to the soft cap on his head, making sure it covered most of his blond hair. Without a word to the man in brown, who had shrunk from his stare, Daoud turned and faced the platform. He was just in time to see the bent dwarf—Erculio, was that his name?—bless himself, just as he had at Lucera.

Daoud's heart pounded as he imagined himself and Lorenzo and Ugolini suffering as this naked, bleeding blistered heretic was.

And Sophia! God forbid! I would cut her throat myself before I let anything like this happen to her.

The thought of Sophia being tortured in public was such agony that he wanted to scream and fight his way out of the piazza. He did Sufi breathing exercises to calm himself.

They had tied the moaning victim down on a wooden sawhorse. Lying on his back, he was low enough that the bent man could easily reach any part of him. One of the executioners in red held the victim's mouth open, and the little man reached in with one hand, pulled forth the tongue and sliced it off. Like a jongleur producing an apple from his sleeve, he waved the severed tongue at the crowd, then threw it. A forest of hands clutched at it. Common people everywhere, Daoud recalled, believed that parts of the bodies of condemned men could be used in magic.

It took a moment for Erculio to saw the heretic's nose off. With tongue and nose gone, the condemned man's screams no longer sounded human. They were like the bellowings of a steer being clumsily slaughtered.

Daoud realized that he was grateful for the problem that the little man presented. It gave him something urgent to think about other than what he was watching.

Erculio now stuck the knife, point down, in the platform and used both hands to tear the heretic's eyeballs out. The tormented man was silent now. He must have fainted. The little man danced about him, jabbing him repeatedly with the knife until the screams started again.

Were the nobles and churchmen enjoying this as much as the common folk, Daoud wondered. There seemed to be fewer prelates in red and purple on the church and steps when he looked. Ugolini stood with his hands behind his back, turning his eyes away from the scene in the piazza. De Verceuil stared right at the victim, his little mouth open in a grin showing white teeth. D'Ucello stood stolidly between his guards, his arms folded. He did not seem to have moved or changed the expression on his face since Daoud first saw him.

Simon de Gobignon was pale as parchment, and even as Daoud watched, the young man turned and hurried into the cathedral.

Weakling! It is because of you, too, that this man suffers, but you cannot face it.

Erculio, dancing, grimacing comically under his black mustache, feinted repeatedly with his knife at the condemned man's groin. When the shouts of the crowd had reached a crescendo, he fell upon his victim and sliced away testicles and penis with quick strokes. The heretic gave a long, shivering howl of agony, then was silent. The little man tossed the bloody organs into the air. An executioner in red caught them and threw them to the other one, who in turn hurled them into the crowd.

I hope dozens of them are killed in the scramble. God forgive me for the pain I have caused this man.

The two men in red untied the condemned man and heaved him

to his feet, his face and body so running with blood that he, too, seemed dressed in red. The crowd began to back away from the scaffold, and Daoud felt himself irresistibly carried back with them. The executioners tied the limp form of the heretic to the stake jutting up from the center of the platform.

The black-clad dwarf scuttled like a monkey to the edge of the platform, and someone handed him a flaming torch. He danced with it. He whirled it in great circles around his head, and Daoud heard it hissing even over the cheers of the crowd. He swung the flame between his legs and leapt over it. He threw it high in the air, the torch spinning under the thick gray clouds that hung low over Orvieto. Erculio neatly caught it when it came down. For a man so badly deformed, his agility was eerie.

Erculio turned toward the cathedral, holding up the torch. Daoud followed the dwarf's gaze and saw d'Ucello, the podesta, his face a white mask, give a wave of assent.

Spinning on his heels, the dwarf scurried to the ladder, scrambled down a few rungs, and threw the torch into the tinder piled under the platform. Then he turned and leapt out into space. The other two executioners had left the platform and stood at the bottom of the ladder, and one of them caught Erculio and swung him down.

The flames shot up with a roar, a red and gold curtain around the heretic. Daoud heard no more cries of pain. Perhaps he was already dead of his wounds. Daoud prayed to God that it be so.

The smoke did not rise in the hot, moist air, but coiled and spread around the scaffold. People coughed and wiped their eyes and drew back farther from the blaze. Daoud was close enough to feel the heat, and on such a sweltering day it was unbearable. But now, he discovered, he could move. The crowd was dispersing. There was nothing more to see. The heretic was surely dead, and the smoke and flames hid the destruction of his body.

Daoud looked up at the cathedral steps. There were no red or purple robes there, and the papal banner was gone. The Count de Gobignon had reappeared and was staring at the fire. As Daoud watched, the count stumbled down the steps, his arms hanging loosely at his sides.

Daoud turned to go back to Ugolini's.

"Well, Messer David, do they do as thorough a job on heretics in Trebizond?"

Daoud's path was blocked by a man in a scarlet robe. From beneath the wide circular brim of a great red hat, the long, dark face of Cardinal de Verceuil glowered at him. Thick red tassels hung down from the hat all around the cardinal's head.

Immediately behind de Verceuil stood two attendants. One held high a white banner blazoned with a red cross and a gold flower shape in two of the quarters; the other man, a sturdy, shaven-headed young cleric in black cassock, carried a long golden rod that curved into a tight spiral at the top. That was called a crosier, Daoud recalled, and was the cardinal's staff of office. Behind them were four men-at-arms who looked hard at Daoud, as if expecting him to give offense to their master. Daoud wondered if the cardinal would consider having him killed here in public. Daoud stared at him through the smoky air, measuring him, looking for those small signs of tension to be found in a man about to order an attack. The man seemed too relaxed for that.

"No, Your Eminence, we only stone our heretics to death."

De Verceuil smiled. "That may be a better way of disposing of them. After a burning, the unpleasant thought always occurs to me that I am carrying the heretic away in my nostrils and lungs."

Sickened inwardly at this reminder of the rancid smell that had come from the heretic's pyre, Daoud smiled at the grisly jest, as he assumed the cardinal expected him to. He remained silent, waiting for de Verceuil to reveal the reason for this encounter.

"Ordinarily we merely burn heretics," the cardinal went on. "We had this man tormented first because he threatened our guests, the Tartar ambassadors, and disturbed a service in the cathedral with the pope himself present. We had to be severe with him."

"Assuredly," said Daoud, still smiling. De Verceuil's Italian sounded strange to him. He must be speaking it with a French accent.

"But perhaps, since you seem to think the Tartars are such a danger to Christendom," said de Verceuil in a voice that was lower and more menacing, "you approve of what that man did." He gestured toward the burning scaffold. The stake and whatever was left of the body bound to it had fallen through the platform into the pile of faggots. A breeze had sprung up and was blowing the smoke away from Daoud and the cardinal, for which Daoud thanked God.

"I came here today to see justice done," Daoud said firmly.

"You profess the Greek Church," said de Verceuil, eyeing him coldly. "That makes you a heretic yourself."

The men-at-arms behind the cardinal shifted restlessly, and Daoud wondered again if de Verceuil meant to provoke a fight leading to a killing. Or perhaps have him arrested. He looked past de Verceuil and his men and saw that some curious citizens had formed a circle around himself and the cardinal. And there was de Gobignon, standing watchfully only a short distance away at the foot of the cathedral steps. Was his sword, too, at the cardinal's command?

"If you are concerned about justice, it is too bad you chose to be Cardinal Ugolini's guest during your stay in Orvieto," de Verceuil said. "You will hear only a corrupt Italian point of view in his household."

Praise God, de Verceuil was not pursuing the matter of Daoud's heresy.

Daoud shrugged. "I have seen what devastation the Tartars do, Your Eminence. With respect, let me say to you that they are as much a danger to your country, France, as to Italy."

De Verceuil essayed what he may have thought was an ingratiating smile, but his small mouth made him look sly and sour.

"I invite you to come to live at the Palazzo Monaldeschi. I have spoken to the contessa, and she would be most happy to receive you. The Monaldeschi are the wealthiest family in Orvieto, and they have connections with other great families in the Papal States. If you wish to find good customers for your silks and spices here, it is the contessa you should see. And if you would trade with France, perhaps I can help you there."

The possibility of spending some days and nights in enemy headquarters was intriguing. But would it be prudent to put himself into de Verceuil's and de Gobignon's hands?

Daoud shook his head with what he hoped was a regretful smile. "Forgive me, Your Eminence. Your offer of the contessa's hospitality overwhelms me, but I have already promised to remain with Cardinal Ugolini, and he would be deeply offended if I were to leave him."

De Verceuil glowered. "Ugolini is from Hohenstaufen territory. The Monaldeschi have always been loyal to the pope and have great influence with him. Just as I have with King Louis of France and his brother, Count Charles. Come to us, and when you go back to your own land you will be a wealthy man."

"Could it be that Your Eminence hopes I might change my testimony about the Tartars?"

Daoud felt close to laughter as the cardinal's cheeks reddened.

De Verceuil shot back, "Could it be that your enmity to the Tartars is more important to you than your profit as a merchant?"

Daoud's heart beat harder. That was too close to the mark. It was foolish of him to jest with a man who had the power to condemn him and his friends to be tortured and burned like that poor madman.

"I regret that I have offended Your Eminence," he said. "I have seen what I have seen, and I am honor bound to speak the truth. And profit will do me no good if the Tartars slaughter us all."

"You are ignorant of our ways," de Verceuil said ominously, after a long pause during which Daoud felt raindrops strike his face. "Have a care that you do not slip into pitfalls you cannot possibly foresee."

First de Verceuil joked, then he threatened, then he offered hospitality, then he threatened again. He seemed to have no sense of how to deal with men.

Even if we were on the same side, I would hate him. What a trial he must be for his allies.

But Daoud was eager to get away without creating any deeper enmity between himself and the cardinal. "I thank you again for your offer of hospitality, Your Eminence. Even if I cannot come to live at the Monaldeschi palace, I do hope to meet the contessa. She has graciously invited Cardinal Ugolini to her reception for the Tartar ambassadors, and I shall accompany him."

"Do not think you are free to do as you please in Orvieto," said de Verceuil angrily. "You are being closely watched." He turned abruptly and strode off. Daoud bowed politely to his scarlet back. Casting ugly looks at Daoud, the cardinal's men followed.

Daoud told himself that it would be wise to be frightened. But what he felt was more a profound disdain for Paulus de Verceuil.

As a man of religion or of power, how can this squawking bird in red plumage compare with Sheikh Saadi and the Imam Fayum of the Hashishiyya?

The rain was coming down harder. It hissed in the still-burning heap of wood and bones.

A movement near the cathedral steps caught Daoud's eye. He turned and saw Simon de Gobignon looking at him. Why was he alone? Had he, like Daoud, not wanted any of his comrades to see this horror?

How infuriating it must be for that proud young Frank to have to work closely with a man like Cardinal de Verceuil. The cardinal was so arrogant, so overbearing, so crude as to turn people *against* any cause he might support, no matter how worthy.

As the rain fell on him, Daoud hardly noticed it. He saw a new plan shimmering like a mirage on the horizon of his mind.

XXI

"BONSOIR, MESSIRE. I HAVE NOT SEEN YOU SINCE THE DAY THE heretic was burned. I trust the spectacle did not disturb you?"

Simon had deliberately addressed David of Trebizond in French, to find out whether the trader spoke that language in addition to Greek and Italian. He might be from the other side of the earth, but there was something very French-looking about him.

They stood facing each other a little apart from the crowd gathered in the sala maggiore, the great hall of the Palazzo Monaldeschi. The large room was lit by hundreds of candles. Four musicians in a distant corner sawed away energetically at vielles of different sizes held between their knees, while two others blew on hautboys. Tables were piled high with meat and pastry along the sides of the hall. Servants circulated, refilling goblets from pitchers of wine. Neither Simon nor David was holding a goblet.

The big blond man, who had not been looking at Simon, turned and stared at him. Simon detected a pallor under his tan. David did not react to the sound of French like a man who had heard an unfamiliar language. He looked more as if he had heard the voice of a ghost.

David bowed. "Pardonnez-moi, Monseigneur. I had not expected to be addressed in French."

Simon was surprised to hear in David's northern French the harsh accents of the English Channel coast.

"Where did you learn my tongue, messire?" Simon asked.

David shrugged. "Since the Crusades began, many of your countrymen have passed through Trebizond."

Many Crusaders had been Normans, Simon thought. It made

sense. But it was odd that this man David, who claimed to be a Greek, not only spoke like a Norman, but looked like nothing so much as a big, blond Norman knight. Simon had seen just such faces—square, with long, straight noses and cold gray-blue eyes—everywhere in Normandy and in England when he had accompanied King Louis on a state visit to the realm of his vassal, King Henry of England.

But David did not dress like a Norman, Simon noted. His apparel was gaudy in the extreme. He wore a white cap with a bloodred feather, a short cloth-of-gold cape, particolored hose—light green and peach—and forest-green boots.

Simon, who, in emulation of King Louis preferred somber colors, had chosen for tonight a brown velvet singlet and maroon hose. The brightest thing about him was the jeweled handle of his prized scimitar.

"I hope that you were not upset by the bloody execution of that heretic last week," Simon said once again.

"Oh, no." David smiled. "But I saw you there, and you seemed to be."

God's wounds, how true that is! was Simon's first thought. He had held himself rigid throughout the heretic's horrible death, afraid that he would throw up.

But how disturbing to discover that this Greek merchant, apparently an enemy, had seen right through Simon's effort to appear imperturbable. Of all the people in Orvieto, this man was the last Simon would want to reveal himself to. He cursed himself for giving David such a perfect opening.

How could I be such a fool? And I thought I was so clever, addressing him in French.

Simon had been anticipating his next encounter with David with a mixture of eagerness, fear, and anger, almost as if it were to be a battle. Now he wished he had stayed away from the man.

"I felt sorry for the poor devil, as I believe a Christian should," Simon said. "Did you not?"

There was a baleful look in David's eyes, as if he hated Simon for his answer.

But the man from Trebizond only shrugged and said, "I have seen much blood and pain in my life."

A broad figure in a white robe billowed up to Simon and David. Simon remembered him from the pope's council—Fra Tomasso d'Aquino, the distinguished Dominican. The friar's belt of rosary beads rattled as he walked. It would take a week, Simon thought, to recite all the Our Fathers and Hail Marys that encircled Fra Tomasso.

"Count, I trust you will forgive my interrupting you. I have already had the pleasure of meeting Messer David of Trebizond, but I have wanted to speak to you ever since you arrived in Orvieto. As a seminarian I studied for a year in Paris under your uncle, Hugues de Gobignon. A friar of great renown. His murder was such a tragedy."

Simon felt uneasy at reminiscence about the uncle who was not really his uncle. As he chatted with Fra Tomasso, his eyes roved through the large room. He noticed the crowd gathered around the Tartars, John and Philip, who were seated in large, comfortable-looking chairs placed near a crowned swan at the center of a serving table. He saw a servant pour wine into a silver cup John held out to him. More of that wonderful wine of Montefiascone?

Beside the Tartars stood a woman named Ana from the land of the Bulgars, territory now ruled by the Tartars. Anything, thought Simon bitterly, to keep Friar Mathieu from achieving too much importance. De Verceuil had found her and had taken her along as interpreter when the Tartars had their first private audience with the pope.

Another group stood around the seated Pope Urban, many of them in the red and purple of cardinals, archbishops, and bishops. There was de Verceuil, of course, as near to the pope as he could get. The cardinal's vanity, as usual, had made him choose layman's garb, a tunic of gold-braided silk and a cape of aquamarine satin trimmed with red-dyed squirrel fur. And between two prelates' shoulders Simon could just make out the top of Cardinal Ugolini's fuzzy gray head.

If Ugolini was here, had his niece Sophia come tonight as well? Yes, there she was, halfway across the hall, talking to the Contessa di Monaldeschi. The pale violet of Sophia's gown made her skin look darker. The poets always sang of *fair* ladies, but Simon found her dark complexion wondrously attractive. She had let her embroidered silk shawl fall away from her bare shoulders, and he marveled at their sweet delicacy. Under her gauze veil the pearls in her headdress twinkled like stars against hair that was black as night.

"Excuse me, Fra Tomasso, Messer David. I have promised to deliver a most urgent message to the contessa."

Fra Tomasso, in the middle of an anecdote about Friar Hugues's subtlety as an inquisitor, gave Simon leave to go. As David bowed, his eyes met Simon's, and his look was at once both knowing and bitter. He, too, was a guest in Ugolini's house, thought Simon. Was he, too, attracted to Sophia? Who would not be?

As Simon moved toward Sophia, the contessa's majordomo strode to the center of the sala maggiore and called in a deep voice, "Signori e madonne, tables, game boards, and cards are set for your amusement in the inner galleria."

Then Simon was bowing before the contessa, acutely aware of Sophia standing beside her. He kissed the old lady's shiny knuckles, hoping he would have an opportunity to kiss Sophia's hand as well.

"My dear boy, did you hear the announcement? Do you enjoy cards or backgammon? I understand your pious king forbids such amusements at his court. And yet our Holy Father himself loves to play alii." She saw Simon staring at Sophia and smiled.

"You see, my dear?" the contessa said to Sophia. "Does this splendid young Frenchman look as if he is interested in cards or dice? Or in you? Enough of your modesty."

Sophia lowered her eyelids and blushed. How beautiful her olive complexion was, tinted with rose!

"The contessa is merciless," she said in a low voice.

"Merciless!" the contessa cackled. "My dear, if I were the envious sort, then indeed would I show you no mercy. By San Giorgio, I would have you poisoned. But I made up my mind many, many years ago, when I saw my looks beginning to fade, that I had to choose between hating the beauty of other women or enjoying it. I was already spending all my hatred on the odious Filippeschi. So I decided that when I saw beautiful women I would rejoice at their presence in the world and delight myself by remembering my own youth and imagining the pleasures they must be experiencing."

She put her hand on Simon's arm. "What do you think, Count Simon? Would you like me to present this young lady to you?"

"A thousand thanks, Contessa," said Simon, falling into the extravagant style of speaking the occasion seemed to call for. "I have already had the great pleasure of meeting Madonna Sophia at her uncle's mansion."

The contessa nodded. "Ah, you have called upon Cardinal Ugolini. I am glad to hear that. I would have told you to if you had not done it on your own." She turned again to Sophia. "Your uncle and I have been friends ever since the Holy Father moved the papal household to Orvieto. I deeply admire and respect him. When he reads the stars for me, his insights and predictions are remarkably accurate. His remedies for my body's complaints always achieve their purpose, which is more than I can say for other physicians I have consulted. And best of all, he finds time for a lonely old lady, when others who should be more attentive make excuses."

"My uncle is a marvelous man, Your Signory," Sophia murmured. "I am most fortunate to be his niece. Otherwise I could never hope to be present on this magnificent occasion, to meet and talk with you."

"And to be waited upon by this handsome cavaliere," the contessa finished for her, smiling broadly.

The contessa really is enjoying this, Simon thought. The old lady was beaming with pleasure.

Sophia turned to Simon.

"I am most pleased to see you again, Count." Her eyes seemed to shine at him. Was it his imagination?

She held out her hand. His whole body felt more intensely alive as his fingers touched hers. He noticed as he bent over her hand that she wore one ring, a garnet of a red so deep as to be almost black. His lips touched the creamy skin of the back of her hand, and he thought he felt her tremble slightly.

Contessa Elvira eyed both of them, sighed happily, and said, "I think it is time for me to find someone to play rota with. Perhaps I will ask your uncle to tell my fortune with the cards. He reads the cards as well as he reads the stars."

They bowed as she moved off. As she turned her back, Simon noticed that her long blue velvet gown had threadbare patches in the rear. She was so old and so powerful, Simon thought, that such things did not matter to her. Perhaps it was a favorite gown from the days when she was young and beautiful, like Sophia.

But he doubted that she had ever been as beautiful as Sophia.

"May I bring you some wine or something to eat, Madonna?" he asked Sophia.

"Thank you, I am not hungry. But"—she gestured as if to free him from obligation to stand with her—"perhaps you—"

"Oh, no, I am quite content. A hand of cards, then?" Simon hoped she would see that he was making it his responsibility to entertain her.

She took a deep breath, and Simon felt a small thrill as he watched her bosom rise and fall under the fine silk of her violet gown. "What I would really like, Count, would be a stroll in the garden. This room, big as it is, is so hot and crowded. And even though it is September, this evening it is very warm, do you not think so?"

"Very warm," said Simon, delightedly taking her arm.

As Fra Tomasso chatted with him, Daoud watched de Gobignon and Sophia stroll across the brightly candlelit hall to the door leading to the inner galleria.

De Gobignon spoke to me in the language of my parents.

Sire Geoffrey and Dame Evelyn Langmuir, he knew, were of English stock. But Daoud's father had once told him that all the English nobility spoke French.

Tonight was the first time since Daoud landed in Italy that he had heard French or had spoken it. When he first heard himself addressed in French, he had experienced a strange and frightening sensation, as if his dead father were speaking to him. He hated de Gobignon for doing that to him.

And I hate him because he will enjoy the woman I want for myself.

The voice of Fra Tomasso faded away. Black rage filled Daoud's skull, deafening and blinding him. He pictured Sophia naked in Simon de Gobignon's arms, and his body trembled.

And when he did become Sophia's lover, the puppy would have no understanding of how much of a woman he was possessing. To him she would be the sweet Sicilian niece of a cardinal. He would have no idea of the woman behind that mask.

Sophia, Daoud had come to realize, had known suffering and loss. She had survived at the very bottom of the world, and she had risen to be the intimate of an emperor and a king.

She occupied his thoughts, Daoud sensed with some uneasiness, far more often than did Blossoming Reed back in El Kahira.

Simon would know Sophia Orfali, not Sophia Karaiannides, who had told Daoud more than once, he thought with a grim smile, how much she hated Franks. She would make a fool of this Frank.

Fra Tomasso was rambling on about the one sea voyage he had ever taken, from Normandy to Naples. "One would think going around the continent of Europe like that would take much longer than making the same journey overland. It took us only a month, whereas on land it would have taken at least three. The sea is a two-dimensional surface. On land one is traveling over a three-dimensional surface and can encounter many obstacles."

Yes, and a carrier pigeon travels much faster than a ship. In a month or two Daoud's request for the book Fra Tomasso wanted would have reached Baibars, and a few months after that, if Baibars could obtain the book, the Friar's pudgy hands would be holding it.

Listening with half an ear, Daoud looked about him at the marble pillars that ran up to the gilded beams of the ceiling, at the paintings of angels and saints on the plaster walls, at the fragments of old Roman statues that stood here and there—mostly nude torsos. Idolatry, yes, but beautifully done. The arts of the Christians and their pagan predecessors were not altogether as barbaric as he had imagined them.

Ugolini suddenly appeared at Daoud's elbow to interrupt his thoughts and Fra Tomasso's discourse. "Excuse me, Fra Tomasso, but His Holiness wishes a word with David."

The little cardinal's eyes darted about nervously. Obviously, the idea of a conversation between Daoud and the pope terrified him.

"Have you had any wine?" said Ugolini in a low voice as they crossed the room to where Urban, in his white cassock, a red cloak wrapped around his shoulders, was sitting in a large, high-backed chair. The spiritual father of all Christians was dressed heavily for such a warm evening, Daoud thought. A sign of ill health.

"I never drink wine if I can avoid it," he answered Ugolini.

"Well, you will not be able to avoid it tonight. But remember, you have no head for it."

Daoud was about to retort sharply, but he swallowed the impulse. Such unnecessary advice was the cardinal's way of allaying his terror. He had never told Ugolini about the training in resistance to drugs he had undergone with Sheikh Saadi. Al-koahl, the intoxicating element in wine, could affect his body but not his mind.

"This is a very dangerous practice," Sheikh Saadi said as he crouched over a small cooking pot suspended on a tripod above a low fire. "But it is now a necessary one for you."

Whatever was bubbling in the pot gave off a strange, cloying odor that Daoud found frightening and seductive at the same time. They were in the inner garden of Saadi's small house in al-Fustat, the oldest quarter of El Kahira.

Daoud half sat, half reclined on a pile of cushions. He leaned back and saw that the stars were fewer and the sky was lighter. They had been up all night drinking kaviyeh.

The liquid Saadi was brewing now smelled nothing like kaviyeh. Studying the simmering, sweet-smelling liquid, Saadi seemed satisfied. He took the pot off the fire and set it on a stone.

Still on his knees, the sheikh swung around to smile at Daoud. In the firelight his face was many shades of brown and black. But his beard, in the years Daoud had known him, had gone from gray to a white as pure as the wool from which the Sufi took their name.

"Kneel and compose your mind," said Saadi.

Daoud rose from a sitting position to his knees. As Saadi had taught him, and as he had practiced for many years, he visualized his mind as an empty pool, walled with tiles. A fountain sprang up in the center of the pool and filled it slowly with clear water. The walls of the pool disappeared, and there was nothing but clear water in all directions, stretching away to infinity.

Saadi seemed to know when Daoud had reached the vision of infinity, and he spoke again.

"Think of God."

Daoud saw a mountain, a flame, the sun. None of those were God. At last he saw the blackness of the spaces between the stars. There in the infinite lightlessness was the dwelling place of God, like the Black Stone in the Qa'aba. He saw the darkness that veiled God, and he locked the idea of God in his mind.

"Now, hold the thought of God, and drink."

Saadi held a silver cup to his lips. The liquid was sweet and thick. He swallowed, and it burned the lining of his stomach.

"What is it?"

"Wine mixed with hashish."

Daoud was shocked.

Filth, spiritual poison!

Saadi himself had taught him that. And now Saadi had tricked him into sipping the vile stuff.

He swayed on his knees, feeling dizzy and angry. Saadi held up a warning hand.

"Remain in the Presence of God. He will protect you from the ill effects of the poison. This is the practice."

Daoud struggled back to the infinite emptiness that hid God, and as he did so he felt his mind clear. The drugs were spreading like tiny flames through his body, but his body was far away. Too far away for him to feel the heat.

Beside him, Saadi said, "Everything made by God has two sides, a useful side and a harmful side. That which is sometimes a poison can at other times be a medicine. Even kaviyeh, which we drink in such great quantities to give vigor to our minds, can be a poison. If a substance is taken in the right amount, on the right occasion, with the right attitude, it can unlock doors in the mind. Our lord Baibars, peace be upon him, has told me he plans to send you to the Hashishiyya for further training. This practice will help you to gain more from their teachings—and protect you from being corrupted by them. In the months to come you will learn to take in every kind of intoxicating substance and keep your mind free. This is not magic. This is a power of the spirit. What are you feeling?"

"The drug devours my body, but my mind is in the Presence of God."

"One day, when you have learned all you can from the Hashishiyya, I will teach you the secret of the most powerful drug of all—soma, the drug that is made by the mind and does not harm the body at all."

No head for wine? No man in this room is less susceptible to wine.

De Verceuil still stood beside the white-bearded pope. His gloomy face tightened as his eyes met Daoud's.

Daoud dropped to one knee before the pope and kissed the heavy gold ring that bore a tiny engraving of a man in a boat. He saw that the old man was wearing white satin slippers.

Daoud felt so dizzied by the wonder of this moment that the tiled floor seemed to shake under him. He held in his hand the hand of the Pope of Rome, successor to those popes who had sent wave after wave of crusaders crashing against the walls of Islam, whose words had caused the deaths of thousands and thousands of the faithful. He, Daoud ibn Abdallah, once David Langmuir, had penetrated to the very center of Christian power.

Was there ever a moment like this before in all of time, when a servant of the true God and a believer in the word of the Prophet held the hand of a pope in his?

"Messer David of Trebizond, the Venetians have just raised the prices of saffron, curry, ginger, and cardamom," said the pontiff in a deep voice. "All of which are indispensable to my kitchen. Can you furnish me with spices more cheaply?"

It took all of Daoud's self-control to hold in a burst of laughter. *A Mameluke comes face-to-face with the pope, and what do they discuss? The price of spices!*

But he sobered as he realized how useful the pope's interest in spices could be to him. As a purveyor of spices to the papal palace, his position in Orvieto would be more respected and more secure.

"If you deal with us, Holy Father, you are dealing with the people from whom the Venetians get those spices," said Daoud with a smile as he stood up. "This is exactly the purpose of my visit."

"Good, good. Have Cardinal Ugolini arrange an appointment for you with my steward."

As they walked away, Daoud said softly to Ugolini, "Would it not be amusing if the Sultan of Cairo were to furnish the spices for the pope's kitchen?" The irony of it once again struck him as funny. What a tale for the bazaars of El Kahira.

Ugolini stared at him, side whiskers quivering. "Not amusing at all."

Ugolini is right to be afraid. I saw what they did to that man in the piazza. I must not make jokes. Ugolini needs to feel he can rely on me.

Celino emerged from the circle around the Tartars to stand before Daoud. At Daoud's insistence the Sicilian wore garments tailored specially for this evening, mostly in white, with gold embroidery on the edges of his waist-length ermine-trimmed cape and his satin tunic.

"What are the Tartars doing?" Daoud asked.

"Sitting and drinking and mostly talking to each other," said Celino. "There is a crowd of curious people around them, asking them questions."

"Where is that Friar Mathieu who interprets for them?"

Celino shrugged. "Not here. There is a woman from some eastern country translating."

Daoud felt a tingle of excitement, like a hunter who had sighted prey.

He surveyed the room. Simon de Gobignon— *may his right hand rot and wither*—had already left with Sophia, as Daoud and Sophia had planned. De Verceuil still hovered near the pope.

"Celino, you heard the contessa's servant announcing games in the next room? See if you can draw Cardinal de Verceuil into a game with you."

"He favors backgammon," said Ugolini.

"All the French dote on backgammon," said Celino.

"Keep him entertained," said Daoud.

"To entertain de Verceuil you will have to bore yourself," said Ugolini. "He prefers a game whose outcome is never in doubt."

Daoud and Ugolini turned to the serving table, and Daoud began methodically to work his way through the various dishes the contessa's servants had set out for her guests. There were eels steeped in a strange, almost rotten-smelling sauce, there were small, tender lobsters and large, meaty ones. There were baby birds meant to be eaten bones and all. There was white bread and there were fine cakes. Daoud filled his stomach, forcing himself to eat even those foods that repelled him, while he watched Celino join the group gathered with the pope.

Daoud used his dagger to cut himself a slice of roast veal. It was juicy and tender, and he cut himself another. The meat tasted as if the calf had been killed that same day; it was not heavily spiced. How pleasant to dine at the home of a wealthy woman. By the time he finished his fourth slice, Celino and de Verceuil were in conversation.

Daoud chatted with Ugolini about astrology. In the cardinal's opinion it was an auspicious night, and that assessment of the heavens helped calm the bewhiskered little man somewhat.

It being harvest season, the contessa's tables were laden with fresh fruits. Daoud enjoyed apricots and grapes, and sliced open an orange. He watched Celino and de Verceuil move toward the galleria, where the contessa's guests were playing games.

Daoud eyed the two brown-skinned men in their shimmering robes sitting at their ease in the sala maggiore in the midst of a circle of curious people. Their chief guardians, de Verceuil, de Gobignon, and Friar Mathieu, were all elsewhere.

Daoud, as was customary among these people, dipped his hands in a basin of water and wiped them on the table linen. Then he began to push his way into the ring of people around the Tartars.

After a few moments he found himself staring down at them. They were laughing together over some private joke, speaking to each other in their chirping language.

Fra Tomasso was part of the group around the Tartars, as were several bishops and two cardinals. A stout, middle-aged woman stood beside John, the older of the two. She wore a stiff, brocaded blue gown, and her hair was tightly wrapped in a net of gold thread.

"Madonna Ana," said Fra Tomasso, "ask Messer John Chagan for me whether the city called Karakorum is still the capital of the Tartar empire."

The woman turned to the white-bearded John and repeated the question in rapid-flowing Tartar speech.

John bowed and smiled to Fra Tomasso and spoke to the woman. Daoud almost felt envy at the sight of John's gorgeous ankle-length silk robe—white, printed with flowers having massive, many-petaled crimson and purple heads, along with clusters of green leaves and wispy gold clouds. He gestured as he spoke, and his hands were square, short-nailed, and hard-looking. Daoud had no doubt that those hands had taken many lives.

"Messer John says the capital of their empire is wherever the Great Khan makes his home," said the Bulgarian woman in a flat tone. "It used to be Karakorum. But now the Great Khan is building a city in the land of Cathay. The city is called—Xanadu."

"And how long would it take to travel from Baghdad to this Xanadu?" Fra Tomasso asked.

"Messer John says for a party of Christians to go to Xanadu from Baghdad might take as long as a year. But for the Tartar post riders it takes two months."

"Two months!" exclaimed Fra Tomasso. "For a journey that would take ordinary men a year? How far is it?"

"Permit me to answer that, Father," Daoud interrupted, "because the Tartars do not know your system of measurements. The roads between Baghdad and the great cities of Cathay are tortuous, and vast deserts and huge mountains stand in the way. But our geographers in Trebizond estimate that a caravan going over that route would travel a distance of three thousand leagues."

"And the Tartars cover that in two months? Do they fly?" The fat monk's jowls quivered. Daoud noticed that the front of his white tunic was stained with what appeared to be spots of gravy and wine.

Daoud turned to Ana. "Kindly ask the ambassadors to explain to Fra Tomasso how their riders cover such a distance so quickly."

After some conversation between Ana and the Tartars, Fra Tomasso had his answer. "The fastest riders and horses in our empire carry messages in relays over the major routes. A message never stops traveling, night and day, until it reaches its destination. At night, runners with torches guide the riders."

The Italians looked awed. Daoud felt unimpressed. The Mamelukes also had post riders. They could carry a message from El Kahira to Damascus in four days.

"How intelligent!" said Fra Tomasso. "I will warrant we would be better governed here in Europe if we had such a system."

The note of admiration in Fra Tomasso's voice made Daoud uneasy. A servant passed, offering cups of wine on a tray. Daoud took a goblet. John and Philip raised the empty cups they held, and Ana refilled them from a pitcher on the table.

"Your empire is so vast, is it not," Daoud said to the Tartars through Ana, "that even messages that travel swiftly cannot hold it together?"

Philip, the black-bearded Tartar, answered that, smiling. "Fear of the Great Khan holds our empire together," Ana translated.

"Is the Great Khan feared even in the lands of Kaidu Khan and Baraka Khan?" Daoud asked, naming the two rebels who did not recognize Hulagu Khan's brother Kublai. He strove for a tone of innocent curiosity.

The faces of the two Tartars remained expressionless, but Daoud, schooled by his Hashishiyya masters to notice signs of emotion in the most guarded of men, observed the flush creeping into their brown cheeks, the slight quickening of their breathing, and the twitching of their fingers. Until he asked his disturbing question they had answered Daoud readily, almost casually, as they would any of the contessa's other guests. Now, in silence, they studied him. Waiting for them to finish their inspection, Daoud held out his wine cup to Ana, who filled it from the pitcher on the table. The pitcher was almost empty, and she signaled to a servant to bring another.

John Chagan said, and Ana translated, "I do not believe we have had the honor of being presented to you, messere."

Daoud turned to Fra Tomasso, who was following the conversation closely. "Will you be good enough to introduce us, Your Reverence?" Any opportunity to involve himself with the Dominican philosopher could be useful.

While Fra Tomasso presented him and Ana translated, Daoud stared at the Tartars with deliberate challenge, draining his wine cup. Philip caught the meaning of the gesture at once, and drank deep from his silver goblet as well. John followed suit.

"Trebizond," said John. "Not far from our borders." Daoud had wondered whether any of the Tartars' sponsors had told them of David of Trebizond and his testimony against them at the pope's council.

"Your khan, Hulagu, has already pressed our emperor for tribute and submission," said Daoud, refilling his cup. He tensed, wondering whether he was pushing the Tartars too far, too quickly. If they grew insulted and refused to speak to him, he would have accomplished nothing.

He sipped his wine. Before tonight, the taste of wine had always puckered his mouth, and he had had to force himself to drink it. But this straw-colored wine was as sweet as spring water. John and Philip seemed to enjoy it, too. They quickly emptied and refilled their cups.

Daoud watched the two Tartars closely as Ana translated his last remark. A suggestion of amusement played about the eyes of the white-bearded John Chagan. John, he guessed, must be about sixty years of age. Old enough to have ridden under the founder of the Tartar empire, the ruler called Genghis Khan. Philip, whose face was fuller, was probably half John's age.

"We are at peace with Trebizond," said John. "We have exchanged ambassadors." He took a gulp of wine and emitted a deeply satisfied sigh.

"How can a people who believe that the whole world belongs to them remain long at peace with anyone?" asked Daoud. He watched the woman, Ana. If she were to dull the edge of what he said in translating it, his effort would fail. But she seemed unmoved by what he said and repeated it quickly in the Tartar tongue.

But now the two Tartars were glaring at him, Philip in open fury, John with a cold hostility as if Daoud were an insect that needed to be stepped on.

How much farther could he press them, he wondered as he took another sip of wine and stared back.

XXII

SOPHIA FELT COOLER HERE, IN THE ATRIUM OF THE PALAZZO Monaldeschi, than she had in the sala maggiore. A breeze blew through the archway that led to the rear courtyard of the palace, but it did not blow hard enough to keep the mosquitoes away. Nor did the essence of lemon in the wax candles in lanterns that lit the

atrium repel the whining little pests, though it scented the air pleasantly, mingling with the sachet of dried orange cuttings she wore
under her gown, between her breasts.

To protect herself from the insects, Sophia wrapped her shawl
around her bare shoulders and drew her gauze veil over her face.
She thought it made her look more mysteriously attractive as well.
Perhaps that was the real reason Muslim women were willing to
wear veils. She wondered whether Daoud had a lover or a wife back
in Cairo.

Probably half a dozen of each.

She glanced over at the young French count, walking solemnly
beside her with his hands clasped behind his back. The mosquitoes
did not seem to bother him, or at least he did not slap at them.
Well, he was a tall, thin man with sharp features, dark hair, and
pale skin. She imagined the blood of such a man might taste sour
and not draw mosquitoes. He was good to look at, surely, but there
was a bitterness about him. She saw at once that he was not a happy
man.

"Perhaps I should not walk alone with you like this, Madonna,"
he said. Actually, his Italian was not difficult for her to understand;
she had criticized it only to throw him off balance when she first
met him. Probably her French was no better than his Italian, but
he had been too gallant to say so.

"Do you fear for your virtue, Your Signory?" she asked lightly.

He smiled, and even in the dim lantern light his face took on a
sweetness that was quite at odds with his previous solemn appearance. "My virtue, such as it is, is yours to dispose, Madonna."
She felt warmed within by his words and the beauty of his smile.

They paused by a square pool in the center of the atrium. He
bent and dipped his cupped hands, then held them out to her filled
with water.

"The contessa has told me that the pool is fed by an underground
spring," he said. "The water is the purest I have ever tasted. Try
it."

"Do the Monaldeschi keep fish in it?" She hesitated, thinking
of Cardinal Ugolini's vivarium.

"No. This is their drinking water. Taste it." She lifted her veil
and lowered her mouth into his hands. The water was pure and
sweet, just as he had said. As a lover, she thought, Simon would
be like this water—sweet, not bitter.

The water was gone and her lips touched his palm. Deliberately she paused a moment before drawing back.

He moved toward her, holding out both hands, but she turned as if she had not noticed and took a step away from him on the gravel, dropping the gauze veil before her face.

"You have not explained to me why you think you should not be walking alone with me, Your Signory."

"Ah—well—" He had to gather his thoughts, she saw. Such a *boy*. She'd had a middle-aged emperor and a splendid young king as lovers. She now felt herself in love with a strange Saracen warrior, a Mameluke, who was subtle, ruthless, kindly, mysterious, daring—so many things, it dizzied her to think about him.

But Simon's simplicity brought back memories of Alexis, the boy she had loved when she herself was as innocent as Simon now appeared to be.

Simon said, "Because your uncle leads the faction here in Orvieto that opposes the Tartars. And because the chief witness against them has been the merchant David, who dwells, as you do, in the cardinal's house."

He hates David. She heard it in his voice.

"What has that to do with you and me, Simon?" This was the right moment, she thought, to call him by his name. "I care nothing for affairs of state. In Siracusa we have better things to do with our time than worry about alliances and wars."

"Everyone will be affected by what happens here concerning the Tartars," he said. "Even the people of Siracusa."

She tried to look impressed. "If *you* think it would be so good for Christians and Tartars to fight together against the Saracens, I cannot imagine why my uncle is against it."

"I do not understand that either," said Simon. "Or why he brought this man David to Orvieto to cause so much trouble."

She shrugged. "I hardly ever see the man from Trebizond. My uncle's mansion is so big, people can come and go without ever meeting." She hoped the suggestion would take root. It was vital for him to think there was no connection between David and herself.

"This is a God-given opportunity for us to rescue the Holy Land," he said.

"Perhaps I can help you," she said.

"Would you?" His face brightened.

"I could try to find out why my uncle opposes your cause. If you will tell me why we Christians *should* ally ourselves with the Tartars, I will repeat your reasons to him. I will not say they came from you. Hearing the arguments in private, coming from a loved niece, he might open his mind to them."

Simon's eyes opened wide in amazement. "You would do all that? But why are you so willing to help me, Madonna, when your uncle is so opposed to my cause?"

"Because I would like"—she hesitated just for a breath, then put her hand on his arm—"I would like to see more of you."

She was on dangerous ground. The tradition of courtly love, in which he had doubtless been reared, called for the woman to be aloof and for the man to beg for meetings. But Daoud had told her she did not have the time to allow this inexperienced young man to proceed at his own pace.

He appeared overwhelmed with happiness. Her answer had just the effect she had hoped for.

"But you must help *me*," she said with the satisfied feeling that she was now closing the trap. "You must teach me what to say to my uncle. As I said, it would be easy for you to come to me without anyone knowing. Will you visit me when I send for you?"

"Oh, Madonna! Command me." His eyes were huge now, and his smile was like a full moon shining into the atrium.

"I command you to come over here with me," she said.

She took him by the hand, and, as a light rain began to fall, led him into a shadowy corner of the open gallery that surrounded the garden. He pressed her back against a column. She lifted her veil and let him kiss her fiercely as the rain pattered down on the lemon trees.

She became entirely Sophia Orfali and tasted his kisses hungrily, dizzy with joy at having won the love of a splendid young nobleman.

"Of course I fought in Russia and Poland," Ana said, speaking for John Chagan, while the old Tartar threw out his arms in a sweeping gesture. "Everyone went."

Daoud smiled and nodded, leaning back in the chair someone had brought for him, his right leg crossed over the left. He tried to look relaxed, though his heart was beating fast. He felt like a man climbing a cliff, whose slightest misstep might bring a disastrous fall.

He was feeling the effects of the al-koahl—a hissing sound in his ears, a numbness in his face, a difficulty focusing his eyes, an urge, difficult to suppress, to splash the contents of his wine cup in John's ugly face. But his mind was untouched, he knew, and that meant he was under better control than these two savages whom he had drawn into telling stories of their wars.

"Was that your first campaign?" he asked.

John made a lengthy speech in answer to Daoud's question, striking his chest many times and reaching for more wine. Finally Ana translated. She seemed made of iron, this Bulgarian woman. She did not drink, she did not get tired, she did not even sit down, and she did not seem to care what anyone said.

John assured David that as a young man he had participated in the destruction of the Khwarezmian empire. Khwarezmia, Daoud remembered, a Turkish nation, was the first Muslim land to fall to the Tartars.

He glanced around and saw that Ugolini and a number of other cardinals, both French and Italian, had gathered to listen. The contessa was there, too. And even as Daoud looked, the circle parted for Pope Urban. Two servants hurried over, carrying a chair for him, and he sat down heavily.

The Tartars had turned Khwarezmia into a desert, but this audience would not care overmuch about that. Daoud wondered if he could turn the conversation back to what they had done in Christian lands.

"What about Moscow?" he said. His voice sounded to him as if his ears were stuffed with cotton. He worried that John might realize that he was being led to talk about what he had done against Christians.

"Moscow?" said John. "That was much later." Strange, how John's voice seemed to be coming from Ana's lips. "I was in command of my own tuman there, ten thousand men, under our great commander Subotai Baghadur. Ah, yes, we killed off all the people of Moscow."

Daoud felt like leaping from his chair. Just what he had hoped to hear. He made himself slump down still more and look sleepier.

"I never could understand how it is possible to kill off the population of a whole city," he said, affecting a tone of cool curiosity. "It must take days and be very tiring."

Philip Uzbek laughed when this was translated. Clearly he thought it a foolish remark. His round, flat face reminded Daoud of Kassar, and with the thought a red mist of rage passed before Daoud's eyes.

John responded to Daoud's remark. "Not at all tiring. We had five tumans at Moscow. There were about fifty thousand people living in the city, and many had died in the siege. Subotai gave the honor of the killing to the most valorous tuman, which happened to be mine. We just divided them up. Each of us took about five of them. You can kill five people in no time. It is not like fighting. Some we shot with arrows. Others we cut their heads off. The women are especially easy. You just pull their hair to stretch their necks so the sword will go through easier, and chop!" Ana, imperturbable even now, repeated the slicing gesture John made with his hand.

"The children run away sometimes, and you have to chase them," John chuckled. "It is best to use arrows on them. But the adults are so terrified, they just stand there."

Daoud looked again at the circle around them. Several people looked a bit sick. The mouth of the elderly contessa hung open, revealing the absence of two or three lower front teeth. Pope Urban leaned forward in his chair, his face expressionless.

Driven by his growing hatred for the Tartars, he pressed them to reveal more of themselves. He should be pleased, he thought, at this much success, but he wanted to destroy them utterly.

"You do not mind killing children?" he asked.

John seemed puzzled by the question. "What else could we do with them? With their parents dead they would only starve to death. Or if they lived, they would grow up hating us, and we would have to fight them."

You could make slaves of them, said a voice inside Daoud, and the red mist swelled into a cloud of fury billowing up inside him. He had to sit motionless, his fist clenched on the stem of his silver goblet, waiting for the feeling to pass. Thank God for Saadi's teaching. It was painful to look directly with the inner eye at the disorientation of his senses and at the anger surging through his body, but it saved him from any fatal mistake.

Philip said, "At Baghdad I found a whole house full of babies, maybe thirty or forty. I slit all of their throats. Their mothers were dead already. I suppose they left the babies behind when they went out of the city to be executed, hoping they would survive. But with no one to suckle them, the babies would have starved to death. Killing them was an act of mercy."

Remembering what he had seen of Baghdad, Daoud felt his rage grow cold and towering as the mountains of the Roof of the World. Those were his Muslim people. He wanted to draw the dagger at his belt and slash the throats of the two gloating, drunken savages before him. He bit down hard on his lower lip to keep himself under control.

"When we shot people with arrows," said John, "we went around and pulled the arrows out of the bodies afterward so we could use them again. We do not waste anything."

He is trying to show how admirable they are.

Daoud watched the stout Bulgarian woman Ana speak John's words in Italian, still expressionless, still standing motionless. But to his surprise he saw rivulets of tears on her round cheeks.

She had been in Bulgaria when the Tartars came, he thought. She had seen what Christians called "the fury of the Tartars." She must have been among the survivors who submitted to their rule, but she had not forgotten. Perhaps translating John's and Philip's words exactly as they spoke them was her way of taking revenge.

John held out his goblet, and Ana refilled it. He laughed softly at nothing in particular and drank more.

"But why do this to city after city?" Daoud asked.

"When we invade a kingdom, the rulers and people are determined to resist us," said John. "To fight them might cost us the lives of thousands of our warriors. But when we wipe out one or two whole cities, they become terrified. They lose their will to fight and surrender quickly. It saves many lives on both sides."

Philip grinned broadly. "It shows that we have power like no other people on earth." He shook both fists. "We can level whole cities. This teaches all men that Eternal Heaven has given us dominion over the whole earth."

Daoud heard whispers from the people around him, and Pope Urban coughed softly.

Daoud could hardly believe his luck. Not luck, he thought. God had delivered the Tartars into his hands.

"The whole earth?" said Daoud. "Even Europe? Even the Christian lands?"

Philip threw out his arms expansively. "The whole earth. All there is. Every corner."

Daoud's earlier rage had subsided. Instead, he felt wild triumph, and he had to grip the seat of his chair to hold himself down.

Daoud heard Cardinal Ugolini declare, "You see? Exactly what we have been saying."

"You say Eternal Heaven gives you the right to rule the world?" Daoud asked. "Do you mean God?"

John shrugged. "Eternal Heaven is what our ancestors called Him. Now that we are Christians we call Him God."

Fra Tomasso suddenly cut in. "But surely you realize that the sky, or whatever you worshiped before you became Christians, is not the true God."

After Ana translated this, John questioned her, squinting at the Dominican as he did so, apparently wanting to make sure of Fra Tomasso's meaning.

"Would God have neglected us before Christian priests found their way to our land?" John said through Ana. "Of course He has spoken to us. Has He not made us the most powerful people on earth?"

"Perhaps He has done so in order that you might *now* hear His word," said Fra Tomasso.

"I am not a priest," John said with a sudden broad grin. "But we have the highest priests of the Christian faith here tonight. Let them say whether Eternal Heaven and God are the same." He bowed his round head and held out his hand in invitation.

A silence fell. The little band of musicians playing vielles and hautboys in one corner of the room suddenly sounded very loud. Daoud turned to look once again at the audience his dialogue with the Tartars had drawn. The Contessa di Monaldeschi, Fra Tomasso, at least half a dozen cardinals. And Pope Urban himself. Their figures swam before Daoud, and he knew the wine was overcoming him—bodily, at any rate. The faces of the Christian leaders looked very grave, though, and the grimmer they looked, the more pleased he felt.

Fra Tomasso especially, he hoped, had heard enough to sway him.

He turned back to the Tartars. They, too, seemed aware of the uneasy, unhappy silence. The pope appeared not to feel that John's inquiry deserved an answer. The older Tartar's smile faded, and he carefully set down his wine cup. Philip's eyes darted this way and that.

John said something to Philip in a low voice, probably a warning to say no more. John had the look of a water buffalo beset by village curs, his eyes smoldering, his white-wreathed head turning from side to side. Daoud sensed, because he often felt the same way himself, how alone John must feel, surrounded by enemies.

He does not have ten thousand warriors at his back now.

Daoud heard a stir behind him, and turned to see the crowd parting to let Pope Urban leave, the broad back of Fra Tomasso following close behind him. A priest-attendant in black was coming from a corner of the room with a cloth-of-gold outer mantle for the pope. The contessa rustled after Urban, who turned and offered her his hand to kiss. As the aged hostess knelt unsteadily before Urban, Daoud rejoiced at the troubled, abstracted expression in the pope's aged eyes.

Daoud heaved himself out of his chair and stood, swaying. For a moment his eyes would not focus, and he thought he was going to fall. Then he saw John Chagan giving him a look as piercing as a Tartar lance. Now, Daoud saw, John understood what he had done to him. As for Philip, he sat slumped, only half awake, his empty wine cup held loosely. The stout, dark-haired Ana stood impassive, hands clasped in front of her, as if content to remain there all night. Her cheeks were now dry.

We defeated your army at the Well of Goliath, Tartar, and now I have defeated you at Orvieto.

"Monsters!" It was the voice of the contessa, and Daoud turned to see her, losing his balance and having to put out a foot to catch himself.

He saw de Verceuil as well, coming across the hall almost at a run, just ahead of the contessa, his aquamarine cloak flying. His eyes were wide, his little mouth tight with fury. The contessa, looking just as angry, was hurrying to keep up with him and tell him what she thought.

"You have brought monsters into my house. Everything bad I have heard about them they have now admitted. In a year or two they will be at the gates of Rome. They are the Huns all over again." Her eyes were huge, and her nostrils flared with passion. Daoud suppressed an urge to laugh aloud with deilght.

De Verceuil checked his rush to get to his Tartar charges, and turned to the contessa. "Your Signory, I beg you to understand. They have been drinking. They did not know what they were saying. Old soldiers' boasting. Exaggerated tales of their exploits. The Tartars are given to that sort of thing."

"It is not exaggerated," the old lady cried shrilly. "We have heard tales before of their massacres. Now I have heard the same from their own lips. These very men whom I have welcomed into my house—their hands drip with the blood of children. One of them told how he slit the throats of forty babies. And they are proud of what they have done. They feel no remorse. Old soldiers' boasting? Old soldiers boast of overcoming strong enemies. These—these bestioni gloat over the slaughter of the helpless. Perhaps they look at my palazzo and think that one day it will be theirs. And you have brought them under my roof.''

''Donna Elvira,'' de Verceuil pleaded, ''let me find out the truth about what has been happening here.''

Daoud's heartbeat quickened. He should slip away now. Drunk as he was, he would be too vulnerable to de Verceuil.

The French cardinal was shouting at the Bulgarian woman. John the Tartar was smiling as if de Verceuil's appearance were enough in itself to extricate him from the consequences of his too-free speech. Philip's fleshy chin rested on his chest and his eyes were fast shut.

Something white moved in the corner of Daoud's eye, and he looked toward the doorway leading to the inner galleria, where the gaming had been going on. Lorenzo was just sauntering out. He was all the way across the room, and Daoud's vision was too blurred to see his expression, but he was probably smiling. He walked closer, seeming to be looking at Daoud for a signal, but Daoud could think of none to send.

Well done, Lorenzeo. How badly, I wonder, did you have to play at backgammon to keep de Verceuil occupied all this time?

''How could I stop them from speaking, Your Eminence?'' Ana was protesting. ''I am here only to translate what they say. This man came up to talk to them, and I simply repeated what they said to him and what he said back to them.''

''What man?'' de Verceuil asked the question almost in a whisper, and Ana's eyes turned toward Daoud.

Too late. Now I must face him.

''You,'' de Verceuil said in the same low voice.

Daoud swayed, and it came to him at once how best to respond. He would pretend to be too drunk to understand what was happening.

''You provoked these indiscretions,'' the cardinal ground out. The jeweled cross hanging on his chest winked and glittered as it rose and fell with his deep breathing.

Daoud put out a hand to grasp the back of his chair. Smiling at the cardinal, he leaned heavily on the chair and circled it methodically. He sat down heavily on the arm, almost tipping the chair over. Then he slid into the seat with a thump.

He looked up at de Verceuil and said, "What?"

The cardinal's hands—they were very large, Daoud saw—clenched and unclenched.

He wishes he could strangle me.

"Why have you tried to embarrass these ambassadors?" de Verceuil demanded. HIs voice was a good deal louder now.

Daoud let his head loll. He caught sight of Lorenzo again. The Sicilian was much closer. Daoud shook his head ever so slightly and jerked his chin.

Go away.

He let his head fall forward.

De Verceuil moved closer. Raising his eyes while keeping his head lowered, Daoud found himself staring at the cardinal's belt buckle, a gold medallion displaying an angel's head with wings growing out of its curly hair.

"I have embarrassed no one," Daoud mumbled thickly. "I know John and Philip's people. They are our neighbors." He laughed, and let the laugh go on too long. "We talked about things everybody knows."

He felt those big hands seize the front of his tunic and jerk him to his feet. De Verceuil's flushed face was less than a hand's width from his own. The cardinal's eyes were huge and dark.

Daoud felt his muscles bunch, and he forced them to relax. He felt fear. Not fear of de Verceuil, whom he could easily kill, but fear of losing control of himself, of letting the Face of Steel show through the Mask of Clay. Such a revelation could put an end to his mission.

"Who the devil are you? What are you doing in Orvieto? Answer me!" De Verceuil shook Daoud violently. Daoud's head rocked back and forth, and he saw two faces of de Verceuil.

Had there been no wine in his blood, it would have been easier for Daoud to control his fear and his anger. He knew he must play at being a merchant who would be terrified at having provoked the wrath of a prince of the Church. But, as it was, he felt himself caught up in a whirlwind of rage, and his hands came up, going for the cardinal's throat. Just in time he changed the move into a cringing, self-protective gesture.

"I could have you killed!" de Verceuil shouted. "And I will if you do not answer me."

"Stop!" The small body of Cardinal Ugolini was beside them, almost between them. "David of Trebizond is my guest." Daoud glanced down at Ugolini and saw that he was trembling violently.

He thinks I might do something that would expose us all.

"Trebizond!" De Verceuil spat the word. "This man is a damned schismatic Greek who has come here to betray Christianity!"

"On the contrary," said Ugolini, "he may yet save Christendom from a terrible error. De Verceuil, I demand that you take your hands off him."

Daoud let his body go suddenly limp, so that de Verceuil was holding up all of his weight by his tunic. At the jerk on his arms, de Verceuil gave a snort of disgust and let go, pushing Daoud away from him. Daoud collapsed into his chair.

"I am only a trader," he said plaintively to the room in general. "I am sorry I ever said a word to the damned Tartars. It has meant nothing but trouble for me. Why did I not remain silent?" Adding a strong flavoring of drunkenness, he imitated the gestures of Greek merchants he had seen in the bazaars of El Kahira. He turned his head from side to side, surveying the onlookers. He could not see Sophia, which was good. He wanted her, like Lorenzeo, far away. Perhaps she was still in the garden with de Gobignon.

No. Daoud saw the young French count's head. He was pushing his way through the audience.

The Contessa di Monaldeschi, her hands nervously smoothing down the front of her blue velvet gown, confronted de Verceuil.

"Eminence, leave this man alone. He is a guest in this house. As you are, which is a thing I begin to regret."

"Contessa, this is all a mistake," said de Verceuil pleadingly. Daoud suspected he feared the ignominy of finding the ambassadors and himself out in the street.

"It is not a mistake." Ugolini seemed to have plucked up his courage now. "My esteemed colleague of the Sacred College is trying to punish David because the Tartars spoke frankly to him. David made no accusations. The Tartars accused themselves."

The contessa seized Ugolini's arm. "Oh, Your Eminence, will God be angry with me for harboring these demons?"

Ugolini patted her hands. "You cannot be blamed, dear Contessa. You acted in good faith at the request of His Holiness himself.

He, having heard what the Tartars said tonight, may also regret this affair.''

Ugolini looked accusingly at de Verceuil, who, purple-faced, looked as if he wished he could tear his little colleague of the Sacred College limb from limb.

Now Simon de Gobignon, having broken through the circle of onlookers, declared, ''This would not have happened if Friar Mathieu had been here interpreting for the Tartars, guarding them against indiscretions. Instead, you found this woman who is altogether ignorant of what is at stake here. You had her translate for the Tartars because you begrudge Friar Mathieu his share of the honor of this diplomatic accomplishment. Except that there will be no accomplishment, because of your bungling.''

Tall as de Verceuil was, de Gobignon was taller. Righteous anger made the French boy's blue eyes flash.

Daoud wanted to laugh aloud at the count's fury and de Verceuil's utter embarrassment. But he decided he should be too stupidly drunk to understand what was going on.

''You have no right to criticize me!'' de Verceuil shouted.

''Be sure that the Count d'Anjou will hear of this,'' Simon answered.

De Verceuil offending Fra Tomasso would be even better than de Verceuil shouting at de Gobignon. If there were a way I could make that happen. Sophia, working through de Gobignon?

Even though his Sufi training helped him keep his mind clear, puzzling out this new idea was beyond his present powers after all the wine he had drunk.

Daoud let his head fall forward, and his eyes met the penetrating black gaze of John Chagan. John was drunk, and he did not speak the language of these people. But Daoud saw understanding in the crinkled brown face. John could not know Daoud was a Mameluke, but he knew him for an enemy. He looked at Daoud with the same icy determination to annihilate all enemies as Daoud had seen staring at him from under the fur-and-iron helmets of the Tartars at the Well of Goliath.

And Daoud, slumped in his chair, felt the same implacable resolution he had felt that day, to fight back until the last invader was driven from the Dar al-Islam, the Abode of Islam.

* * *

The Tartar army appeared as a darkness across the eastern horizon, deepening as it spread. Curry-colored clouds towered above the gray-black line like mile-high djinns.

The distant thunder of hooves reached the Mameluke commanders as they halted in the plain between the hills of Galilee and the mountains of Gilboa near a village called Ain Jalut, the Well of Goliath. A fierce sun beat down on yellow grass and dusty tamarisks.

El Malik al-Mudhaffar Qutuz was mounted on a milk-white stallion from Hedjaz in the midst of his emirs. Baibars al-Bunduqdari rode a fawn-colored half-blood mare, part Arabian and part steppe pony. Daoud, in his early twenties and risen through the ranks of Baibars's personal guard to be second in command of the orta, fifteen thousand strong, sat on his sturdy Yemenite stallion before the other emirs. His red turban shaded his face and shielded his steel helmet from the sun. His chest was encased in the breastplate of an emir, steel inlaid with gold.

The Mameluke emirs, bashis and muqaddams wore their fortunes into battle—gold bracelets and belts, jeweled rings, necklaces of coins. Jewels sparkled on their belt buckles and the scabbards and hilts of their scimitars, on their turbans, on the toes of their boots, on their fingers. Over their mail shirts and gold-inlaid breastplates the emirs wore velvet vests and long khalats of crimson or gold satin, lined with white silk, fastened with gold buttons, trimmed with silver thread at the collars and cuffs and hems. Silk turbans were wound around their helmets, red, blue, yellow, pinned with jeweled clasps and adorned with the plumes of rare birds. Tied tight around their waists were wide shawls printed with stars and crescents. Their boots were of soft leather, crimson-dyed, with silver spurs, gold buckles, and pointed toes.

And all that I have, Daoud thought, *may be torn from me in an instant today.*

From Daoud's neck hung the silver locket given to him by his first, and so far only, wife, Baibars's daughter Blossoming Reed. It was, she had told him, a magical thing.

The Mamelukes were now the last defenders of Islam. The Tartars having conquered Baghdad and Damascus, El Kahira was the only remaining center of Muslim strength. If the Tartars overcame the Mamelukes, all that remained of the Dar al-Islam would lie open to the invaders, even the holiest place of all, Mecca, the house of God.

''We are a hundred thousand and they not a fourth of that,'' said

Qutuz almost petulantly, his eyes fixed on the oncoming Tartars. "How can they dare to turn and fight us?"

"They are Tartars," said Baibars. "They do not fear the numbers of their enemies."

"Being a Tartar yourself, you can tell us how they think," said Qutuz. Daoud heard a faint undertone of contempt in the Kurd's voice. Baibars must have heard it, too; Daoud saw his lord's cheeks darken slightly.

Looking into the sultan's set face, Daoud realized that Qutuz, despite his apparent disdain, had already given up the battle. His lips, almost hidden in his oiled black beard, were pressed tight, in an effort to keep them from trembling.

The Mamelukes might outnumber the Tartars today, but the Tartars had never been defeated anywhere in the world. The sultan must have led the army to what he saw as certain death, for himself and all of them, only because he knew his Mameluke emirs would depose and kill him if he did not.

How can a Mameluke fear death, or even defeat? Qutuz has been sultan too long.

"With the help of God, my brothers," said Qutuz, his voice hollow, "let us ride forth and slay them. I will command the center, Kalawun the left wing, and Baibars the right. When you see my green banner dip, we will advance to surround and destroy them."

He does not believe that God will help him, thought Daoud. *And he does not believe he can help himself.*

Riding over the dusty field to rejoin the men under his command, Daoud yearned for the fighting to begin. His body felt tight, as if it were being pressed inward from all directions, and his heart seemed to swell in his chest, trying to break out of the pressure.

If I must die today, let me first do a great deed for God!

By the time the oncoming Tartars were clearly visible, Daoud was back with the right wing of the Mameluke army, at the head of his own troop. The Tartars came on at an unhurried trot, spread out in a series of long ranks, one behind the other, and he could see their fur-trimmed helmets, their waving lances, their colored signal flags. He could hear their shrill war cries and the braying of their horns. Above their front rank flew their savage standard, rows of long black tails of animals waving from crossbars mounted on a tall pole.

Drawn up across the plain behind Baibars's yellow banner were dark ranks of Mameluke heavy cavalrymen armed with tall spears and wearing steel chain mail and helmets.

Daoud saw Qutuz's green flag, small and far to the west, dip, heard Baibars's cry, relayed the shout to his men.

In a moment the parched earth of the plain of the Well of Goliath was trembling under the hooves of fifteen thousand Mameluke horses. The kettledrums of Baibars's tablkhana, his camel-mounted band, thundered, and the trumpets blared, sending Daoud's blood racing.

Daoud drew his double-curved bow of horn and sinew out of the case hanging from his saddle and nocked an arrow as the galloping hooves of his horse jolted his body. He let his voice pour out of him in a long scream.

The braying of the Tartars' signal horns floated over the plain. They, too, were galloping, bent over the necks of their ponies. The Tartar horses were short-legged, their barrel-shaped bodies encased in leather armor.

Ugly little horses, Daoud thought.

The ponies of the Tartar unit passing him all appeared to be white with black spots. The Tartars' tunics were brown, their trousers gray, and their fur-trimmed iron helmets painted red.

Ahead of him Daoud saw Baibars's yellow standard fluttering against a sky gray with dust. Baibars's wing and the Tartars were riding past each other. The emir was leading his men eastward. To Daoud's left, across an empty space of grassy plain, the Tartar army was passing them, charging to the west. Arrows flew from the Tartars, but singly, not in volleys. Daoud loosed an arrow of his own at the passing horde. It arced over the bare strip between the two armies and fell in the Tartar mass without result that he could see.

He looked back toward the center of the Mameluke host and saw small figures in white robes striding through the grass. They were holy men, he knew, dervishes dedicated to death. As they marched on foot and unarmed against the Tartars, they were calling on God to avenge the martyrs of Islam. Arrows flew at them from the Tartar lines, and in an instant it seemed the dervishes vanished as they crumpled into the tall grass.

They are showing all of us how to die, thought Daoud. By going joyfully to their deaths, the dervishes reminded the Mamelukes that each warrior who died here today would be a mujahid, one who fell in holy war for Islam. Such a one was destined for paradise.

But he also realized uneasily that he had seen a demonstration of Tartar marksmanship.

Signal flags, yellow, green, and red, fluttered among the Tartar horsemen, and horns bellowed. Daoud heard the pounding of a great battery of drums. From twenty thousand Tartar throats at once there rose a long, terrifying scream. Daoud turned in the saddle to see the entire Tartar army, now in a wedge formation, the beast-tail standard at the point of the triangle rushing upon the green banner of Sultan Qutuz.

A blue flag fluttered beside Baibars's yellow one. The signal to halt. Daoud raised his arm and shouted the order to his troop. The Mameluke right wing rumbled to a stop and turned their horses to face the fighting that had just passed them by. Reining up his horse, Daoud put his bow back in its case.

He blinked as bright bursts of light flashed above the distant ranks in the center of the Mameluke army. Swiftly that part of the field was enveloped in thick clouds of brown smoke. A moment later he heard popping sounds like the cracking of innumerable boards. The dim shapes of horses plunged and reared in the smoke.

He heard his men muttering to one another behind him.

They think it is sorcery.

Daoud, having seen the Tartar army in action when he visited Baghdad disguised as a Christian trader, recognized the fiery noisemakers.

He turned and shouted, "It is not magic. I've seen this before. It is like Greek Fire, but it does not hurt. It just makes noise and smoke."

He saw smiles of relief among those who had heard him. They would pass the word to the others farther back, and the troops would settle down.

He peered anxiously into the chaos of smoke and dust and horses and men, trying to see the Tartar standard, with its long black tails, and Qutuz's green banner. They had been close together when he last saw them. Now he could not find them.

A movement near the western horizon caught his eye. He saw a bit of green waving just below the blue Galilee hills that separated this plain of Esdraelon from the coast. Qutuz's banner, smaller, farther away.

Despair clutched at Daoud. But Qutuz could be feigning a retreat to lure the Tartars into spreading themselves too thin. Then he saw the black Tartar standard, much closer, in the midst of a furious melee of fighting men and falling horses half obscured by dust. Qutuz would not leave part of the center behind to fight the Tartars unless he were running away. Daoud remembered the tightness he had seen in Qutuz's face before the battle, the hopelessness in the sultan's voice.

He is fleeing in terror. We are all dead men. Islam is lost.

Daoud looked to the east and saw that Baibars was still sitting motionless, a small figure at this distance on his fawn half-blood, the bearer with the yellow standard sitting behind him.

Daoud turned in the saddle and swept his gaze over the long line of his own troop. Their red turbans bobbed up and down as their horses danced. The wind was from the north, and their scarlet cloaks fluttered behind them. The bearded faces in the front rank were grave, but there was no fear. There was no murmuring now, no questioning. Their mounts, brown, white, and black, the finest steeds in al-Islam, stood with necks stretched and ears laid back, eager for the charge.

An orange pennant beside Baibars's standard summoned the commanders to confer with their leader.

"I go to the emir for orders," Daoud said loudly, so they would not think he was fleeing the field.

By the time he reached Baibars, a half circle of five emirs and ten bashis had formed around their commander. Daoud could hear Baibars muttering to himself in his boyhood Kipchaq tongue. Curses, no doubt.

Far to the north Daoud saw horsemen riding westward, away from the battlefield. The left wing, under Kalawun. The Tartars had come nowhere near them. They must have given way to fear when they saw the center fall back.

Daoud saw no fear in Baibars's brown face. His wide mouth with its thin lips was formed in a half smile. The expression around his eyes, the blue one that saw so deeply and the opaque white, was calm and confident. He pulled on his reins to turn his half-blood so that his back was to the field of battle.

"Most of our army has fled." His voice was deep and so full of confidence Daoud almost thought he heard laughter in it. "The Tartars think they have won. Now, therefore, let us ride against them."

The commanders looked at one another in wonderment.

Buoyed up by Baibars's calm strength, Daoud felt himself despising the officers under his and Baibars's command.

They think Baibars is mad. To the devil with them. Even if he is mad, I will follow him and die with him.

The thought occurred to him that if Baibars should fall—God forbid!—then he would have to lead these fifteen thousand men. For a moment he was seized by fear, whether of his lord's death or of having to lead alone, he was not sure.

Baibars saw the disbelief of his officers. "You do not deserve to ride with me," he said, and now there was scorn in his tone. "Have you not always risked death in battle? Can the Tartars do more to you than kill you? I tell you, if we are defeated, better to die here than live as fugitives. Now go to your troops. In a moment you will see my standard move against them. Do as you will, follow or run away as you choose, and God will reward you accordingly. If I must, I will ride alone."

Daoud felt the blood rush to his head in dizzy excitement.

"You will not ride alone, Lord," said Daoud fiercely.

"No, Bunduqdari, no," said another emir, Bektout, a Kipchaq like Baibars. "Let us offer our lives to God and ride out with light hearts."

The other officers shouted their eagerness to die for Islam. Daoud felt full of gratitude. Baibars had put the spirit of war back into them. He had done what Qutuz could never do.

After the other emirs had ridden back to their troops, Baibars said quietly to Daoud, "I truly believe I will win. Until the instant that they kill me, I will know that I am winning."

Back at the head of his own troop, Daoud watched Baibars and waited. For a moment a silence fell over this part of the field. The drumming of hooves, the clash of steel, and the screams of men carried clearly from far to the west.

Baibars on horseback sat a short distance in front of the long dark ranks of Mamelukes. He turned and beckoned to his standard bearer, who trotted forward bearing the yellow silk banner inscribed with the words of the Koran in black letters, "For the safety of the faith, slay the enemies of Islam."

Baibars took the banner in his right hand and held it high, then lowered it till its end rested in a leather socket beside his foot. In his left hand, his sword hand, his long, curved saif, inlaid with gold, flashed in the sunlight. His fawn half-blood pawed the air with her front hooves.

"Oh, God, give us victory!" he shouted. "Yah l'Allah!"

An echoing roar came back from the ranks of the right wing.

Half standing in his copper stirrups, guiding his mare with the pressure of his legs, Baibars sent her into a headlong gallop. Daoud struck his spurs into his own horse's flanks and raced after him. He squinted into the wind that blew his beard back against his neck.

The dark blur of struggling Tartars and Mamelukes grew rapidly larger. Qutuz's banner was nowhere to be seen, but the beast-tail Tartar standard rose up in the west, and Kalawun's black banner was waving far to the north.

They were coming on the Tartar horsemen from the flank and rear. Daoud was close enough to see faces turn and Tartars wheel their ponies to meet the attack.

Daoud drew his bow out again, picked a big Tartar with a drooping black mustache, and loosed an arrow at him. The Tartar fell back over his gray pony's rump, and the pony slowed, trotted out of the Tartar formation, and stood nibbling on the tall dead grass while its dead master lay nearby.

Three Tartars peeled off from their formation and charged at Daoud. His arrows took two of them, and an arrow from one of his men struck down the third.

Elated, he whispered a prayer of thanks to God. Baibars's yellow standard changed direction. Following it, Daoud pulled his horse around and raced away from the Tartars. He stood in the stirrups, bow and an arrow in hand with a steel-tipped armor-piercing arrow nocked. Resting his right knee against his heavy wood and leather saddle, he turned until he, was looking over his horse's rear and took careful aim. To steady his aim, he fired the arrow just after his horse's four feet struck the ground. He saw a Tartar thrown off his pony by the force of the arrow, and he laughed aloud.

He saw files of Tartars pulling away from the main formation, which was pursuing Qutuz and Kalawun. Baibars's attack was pulling the Tartars apart.

Love for Baibars surged within him. The Tartars were said to be masters of warfare, but Baibars could out-general even them.

Following the yellow standard, Daoud rode back and forth over the field. He lost all sense of the progress of the battle. For brief moments he took his eyes off the enemy warriors to glance up at the sun, a pale disk visible through a haze of smoke and dust, to see in which direction he was riding.

Many times he shot his last arrow, got down from his horse and, standing in the grass with horsemen galloping all around him, refilled his quiver from those of fallen Mamelukes and from the bodies of Tartars.

Mounted or on foot, he felt as if no arrow or sword could touch him. He seemed, when he had ridden out to battle, to have left fear somewhere behind.

He recognized Mamelukes from other ortas riding beside him, and his hopes leapt at the sight of them. They must have come back to join the battle from the shattered left wing and center.

Following the yellow standard, he saw that the Tartars were now always on his left. For the most part, he kept his eyes on them and stayed close to the other Mamelukes. The plain was almost featureless, but glancing to his right from time to time, he noticed certain twisted trees and black boulders he was sure he had passed before.

The sun was halfway between the zenith and the western horizon when the yellow standard halted. The Mamelukes turned to face the Tartars, whose standard rose from their midst. Looking to either side, Daoud saw curving lines of mounted Mamelukes stretching until they disappeared around the edges of the packed Tartar mass.

What had happened? Baibars's refusal to abandon the field and the greater numbers of the Mamelukes must have tipped the scales. Daoud's heart pounded with joy as he realized that they had ground down the numbers of the Tartars and surrounded the survivors.

Baibars, down the Mameluke line, called out, "Finish them. One by one. Hand to hand."

He still held high the banner of the orta. He raised his curved saif and pointed it at the Tartars.

He turned toward Daoud for a moment, and Daoud saw the exaltation in his face. Baibars's face was coated with gray dust. His gold khalat was streaked with blood, and none of it, Daoud was sure, was his. An angel must be riding on his shoulder.

With another wave of his saif Baibars charged into the mass of Tartars. Howling in an ecstasy of fury, the rest of the Mamelukes rushed after him.

Daoud reached over his shoulder and pulled his curving, double-edged saif from its leather-covered scabbard. He tried to ride near Baibars, but a wall of Tartars rose up between them. While he fought for his own life, Daoud could only pray that God would protect Baibars.

And then he was no longer fighting many Tartars, but just one.

They had chosen each other out of the struggling multitudes, like partners in a dance.

Daoud saw his man as vividly as if he had been staring at him for hours. Red ribbons fluttered from the sides of his fur-trimmed iron helmet. The ends of his black mustache hung down on either side of his mouth like whiplashes. His cheeks and chin bore the ridges of thick scars he seemed to have cut into his flesh. His nose had been crushed in some past battle, and it was a shapeless lump between his jutting cheekbones. His eyes were hard and expressionless.

Daoud rode at the Tartar eagerly, rejoicing that for now the battle was between himself and this one man. For him now this Tartar was all Tartars.

The scarred brown face was utterly concentrated on a single purpose, to kill Daoud. The Tartar reminded Daoud of a tale told by a storyteller in a bazaar at El Kahira of invincible bronze warriors, statues brought to life by a magician.

Daoud's Yemenite stallion leapt at the Tartar as Daoud brought his saif down.

The Tartar raised his round leather-covered shield and easily caught the blow of Daoud's sword while swinging his own scimitar around at Daoud's chest. The blade struck Daoud's ribs on the left side. The cunningly woven rings of Damascene steel under Daoud's tunic stopped the edge of the blade, but the blow sent a shock of pain through his body.

Daoud struck downward again with his saif and chopped a deep gash in the Tartar's shield. The force of the blow hurt Daoud's arm. His tall Yemenite and the Tartar's piebald pony pranced in a cloud of dust as their riders slashed at each other. The Tartar's brown tunic hung in ribbons.

Daoud saw a spot of sunlight reflected from his silver locket flash in the Tartar's eyes. The Tartar glanced at Daoud's chest, his eyes caught by the light. In that instant Daoud thrust straight at the his enemy's throat.

He thought he had no chance of hitting the right spot, but the point of his saif went in just below the Tartar's chin and above his high leather collar. Blood poured after the sword's point as Daoud jerked it out.

Praise God! Daoud thought with delight as he saw that he had won. And he thought with thankfulness of Blossoming Reed, for her gift of the locket.

For the first time, an instant away from death, an expression of feeling crossed the Tartar's face. His lips parted and the corners of his mouth pulled down in a grimace of pain and disgust.

Daoud had to parry one more blow of the scimitar before the Tartar slumped over in the saddle and slid to the ground, disappearing in the dust kicked up by the hooves of a dozen milling horses. In his last moment the Tartar had still been trying to kill him.

"We have destroyed them!" a voice cried near him. It was Mahmoud, naqeeb of Daoud's old training troop. He now wore the plain gold belt buckle of an emir of drums, in command of forty mounted warriors. His beard was whiter now, but he rode easily and held his scimitar with a young man's strength.

Mamelukes rode forward on all sides of Daoud, their saifs stabbing the air.

The victory whoops of his fellow Mamelukes were, for Daoud, a draft of elixir from paradise filling him with new strength.

"Great Baibars, honor to his name, has defeated those who never knew defeat!" Mahmoud exulted.

As the last word left his lips, a Tartar arrow, long as a javelin, thudded into his chest. He gasped, and his pain-filled eyes met Daoud's. He dropped his scimitar and his hand reached out to grasp Daoud's arm.

"A good moment," he grated. "Praise God!" He slumped in the saddle, the flowing white beard fluttering in the east wind.

Grief shot through Daoud like the Tartar arrow that had pierced his old naqeeb.

Daoud knew what Mahmoud's last words meant. It was the best of moments to die. A moment of triumph.

But a moment of grief for me, Mahmoud, because I have seen you die.

Daoud rode forward over dead Tartars to the place where the enemy had planted their standard, on a small hill. Bunched together, the last few Tartars fought on foot.

A fierce joy swept Daoud. Victory! He had believed that God would not allow Islam's last defenders to be defeated, but the wonder of a triumph over the invincible Tartars was so overwhelming that he almost fell from his saddle.

In the midst of the Tartars one man dashed this way and that, shouting orders to the few dozen men as if they were still thousands. He wore a gold tablet stamped with symbols on a chain around his neck, the badge of a high-ranking Tartar officer. Scouts had reported that this Tartar army was commanded by one called Ket Bogha. This must be he.

Ket Bogha shot arrows into the tightening circle of Mamelukes until he had no more arrows left. He threw javelins. Then he stood with his sword held before him, not the usual Tartar saber, but a two-handed sword that he swung ferociously at anyone who approached.

With a single swipe of his sword Ket Bogha cut off the foreleg of a horse that rode at him. The horse toppled screaming to the ground, and the rider barely managed to jump free and run away as Ket Bogha slashed at him.

The battle ended for Ket Bogha as six naqeebs clubbed the Tartar general to the ground with the butt ends of their lances.

He deserved better than that, Daoud thought sadly.

But the momentary sympathy for his conquered enemy was swept away in the ecstatic floodtide of triumph. Now the battle was truly over! And the Mamelukes had won over the Tartars.

The naqeebs bound Ket Bogha's arms. Baibars himself dismounted and took the Tartar general's great sword and tied it to his own saddle, then lifted the gold tablet from around his neck and dropped it into his saddle pack. Smiling, he spoke to Ket Bogha in the language of the Tartars and tied a rope around his neck. Then he mounted his own fawn-colored mare and led the defeated general past heaps of Tartar and Mameluke dead and clusters of rejoicing Muslim warriors. Daoud, and then Baibars's other emirs and bashis followed.

The standard of Qutuz was back on the field, looking more black than green with the afternoon sun behind it.

"Can it be? Can it be that we have truly won?" Mamelukes cried, running beside Baibars's horse.

"Baibars! Yah, Baibars!" cried the warriors as Baibars rode slowly over the field.

"Tell us, Baibars, that we have won!"

As an answer Baibars gestured grandly to his captive stumbling along behind him.

"Baibars, bringer of victory!"

The sultan's servants were already setting up his gold silk pavilion on the edge of the battlefield. When Baibars rode before Qutuz, pulling Ket Bogha, a deafening roar went up from the emirs, the bashis, the muqaddams, the naqeebs, the troopers.

Daoud glanced at Qutuz and saw that his eyes were wide and his face pale. He must still be dazed by the outcome of this battle.

But the sultan stepped forward to peer at Ket Bogha as the Tartar general was freed from Baibars's rope. Qutuz gestured to his men to untie Ket Bogha. A circle of emirs formed around Qutuz and the Tartar commander, to hear what they would say to each other.

Qutuz had found time at the end of the battle to have his black beard combed and oiled and to robe himself afresh. His black and gold khalat glittered in the hazy sunlight. The Mamelukes had stripped Ket Bogha of his armor, and he stood before the sultan in a dirty, bloodstained tunic that had once been a bright blue. His shaven head was round as a ball, and, like most Tartars Douad had seen, his short legs were bowed from a lifetime in the saddle.

Once again Daoud felt sorrow for the Tartar leader, who looked like a lonely island in the midst of a sea of joy.

Since Baibars spoke both Tartar and Arabic, he stood between the sultan and the Tartar general to translate.

"You have overthrown kingdoms from the Jordan to the Roof of the World," said Qutuz through Baibars. "How does it feel to be defeated yourself?"

Released from his bonds, Ket Bogha paced furiously back and forth before Qutuz. He started to talk so rapidly the interpreter could not keep up with him.

Daoud was amazed to see that he actually seemed to be laughing at what Qutuz had said.

He still feels the excitement of the battle, Daoud thought. *And by walking and talking as he does, he keeps at bay his grief at the loss of his army. His words are as much for himself as for the sultan and the emirs.*

"Defeat?" said Baibars, speaking Ket Bogha's words. "Oh, Sultan, do not play the fool by claiming this skirmish as a victory. You rashly chose to overrun this handful of men, but the harm you have done to Hulagu Khan is that which a gnat does to an elephant. You have not hurt him. You have angered him. The men and horses he has lost here, the wives of his soldiers and the mares in his paddocks will make up in a single night."

"You talk like some old storyteller in the marketplace who tries to frighten children," said Qutuz in a shrill voice.

The amazement all of us feel, that we are not only alive but victorious, must be even stronger in Qutuz. Most of my Mameluke

comrades may think that their sultan planned for victory all along.
But he himself knows better.

Ket Bogha stopped pacing and pointed a stubby finger at Qutuz.
"Soon Hulagu Khan will return from beyond the Oxus and the
hooves of his horses will trample your land all the way to the Nile
and beyond. He will do to your Cairo what he did to Baghdad."

Qutuz laughed harshly. "Your faith in your master is touching,
but I will have your head carried before me on a spear when I ride
back to Egypt. He cannot save you from that."

"I would rather die for my khan than be like you, one who rose
to power by murdering his rightful lord!" Ket Bogha cried.

Baibars smiled wryly as he repeated the Tartar's words in Arabic.

Qutuz went white with fury. "Take him away and cut his head
off," he ordered. "And you, Baibars, how dare you repeat such a
slander to me? I never murdered anyone."

Qutuz's command revolted Daoud. After the poor part the sultan
had played in the battle, he had no right to take the head of a brave
enemy. Daoud heard Baibars give a little snort of disgust, and the
emir strode to Qutuz's side.

Baibars spoke in a low voice, but Daoud heard him. "My Lord,
this is not worthy of a sultan in his hour of victory. This is a brave
commander, and I repeated all that he said because you wished me
to."

Qutuz glared wildly at Baibars. "Be still! I will not spare your
fellow Tartar."

Qutuz, Daoud thought with smoldering wrath, was not worthy
to be sultan.

Baibars turned his back on Qutuz. The brown face was impassive, but in the one blue eye Daoud saw death.

XXIII

THE RATS SCAVENGED IN THE GARBAGE AND THE CATS HUNTED
the rats. And cats and rats scurried out of the way of the two men

who staggered beneath a waning moon through the streets of Orvieto.

"I was truly drunk," said Daoud. "But only my body was drunk. It is still drunk." He walked with one arm thrown over Lorenzo's shoulder to steady his steps. It must have rained during the evening. The streets were slippery, and the clean, vaporous scent of drying rain was stronger than the usual odor of rotting rubbish piled between the houses in the spaces the Orvietans called quintane.

"You feign the extremity of drunkenness quite well," said Lorenzo. They had met by prearrangement on the street outside the Monaldeschi palace. Sophia and Cardinal Ugolini left earlier and separately, carried in sedan chairs and escorted by the cardinal's guards.

"What hour is it?" Daoud asked.

"Past the third nocturn. Do you know what that means?"

"It was explained to me once, but now my memory seems to be drunk."

"Simply, dawn is not far off," said Celino. "The third nocturn is between midnight and dawn. The contessa's reception began at the first nocturn, between sunset and midnight. Tell me, did you never experience wine in Egypt?"

Daoud decided that, much as he liked Lorenzo, he did not want to confide any of Saadi's most secret teachings to an atheist.

"Many times we stayed up all night, drinking kaviyeh, talking and watching the dancers. But we do not drink wine."

"Really?" said Lorenzo, glancing at him. "Permit me to be skeptical. I know many Muslims who drink wine."

Daoud shook his head. "Most Mamelukes do not drink wine. When Baibars became sultan, he closed all the wine shops in El Kahira." He also decided not to tell Lorenzo that in private Baibars enjoyed the Tartar drink kumiss, made from the fermented milk of mares.

Lorenzo grunted. "Then you Mamelukes are stricter in your observance than many others who were born to Islam."

They passed the cathedral of San Giovenale. It was lit within, and the narrow stained glass windows glowed red, yellow, blue, and white.

You go into a Christian church during the day, and the windows are all alight with colors. At night the windows are black if you are inside the church but brightly lit if you are outside. As if the church is calling to those outside in the darkness.

"So beautiful," Daoud said, "even if the images were idolatrous."

"You should see some of the new cathedrals up near Paris. The windows are much bigger, and the figures are more lifelike."

"Do you admire the Christian churches?" Daoud asked.

"I admire beauty wherever I find it. On Sicily, there are beautiful stained glass windows in many synagogues."

"We are building a mosque in El Kahira that will be the wonder of the world. But when were you in Paris?"

"Four years ago, on a mission for King Manfred."

Four years ago I was battling Tartars in Palestine.

As they passed the open front doors of the cathedral, Daoud looked up the steps. He saw the bright yellow light of massed candles and heard a chorus of male voices raised in song. The voices seemed thin and high, as if reaching up into the night sky. He had heard such singing before—a long time before. He felt a catch in his throat.

"Why are the priests singing so late at night?"

"Those are the priests of the cathedral chapter. It is the beginning of day for them. They are chanting lauds, the dawn prayer of the Church."

Listening to the voices, Daoud felt hot tears running down his face.

Lorenzo glanced at him and chuckled. "I see you are not so impervious to the attractions of Christianity."

Daoud was embarrassed, but he could not stop the flow of tears. "It is the wine."

He was remembering high mass in the chapel of the castle, with his father's hand on his shoulder as they knelt and the chief priest in dazzling white and gold cope raised the white wafer toward heaven. His father whispered, "Jesus is come down among us," and then his strong tenor voice joined in "Veni Creator Spiritus."

I weep now for my father because I had no chance to weep for him when he was killed.

"Suppose he is in some Christian heaven looking down at me. What would he think?"

Daoud started at the sound of his own words.

I must be drunk. I would never speak so in front of Lorenzo—or anyone—otherwise.

"Who is looking down at you?" Lorenzo asked. His shoulders were hard and broad under Daoud's arm, and he seemed to bear

Daoud's weight without the least difficulty. They were past the cathedral now, following a straight, fairly wide street that gently sloped downward. Broken clouds drifted away from the half moon. Like a watchman's lantern it hung over the center of the street, between the overhanging second stories of the houses.

"My father," said Daoud, and a sob bubbled up in his throat as he softly spoke the word, albeit in the unfamiliar tongue of Italy. "How he must hate me and curse me for fighting for Islam."

Lorenzo halted his stride and lifted his head. Then he started walking again. He raised his hand and gripped the wrist Daoud was resting on his shoulder.

In a very low voice he said, "Someone is following us."

Now Daoud stopped, tensing. He called on the power of his mind to resist the wine. His tears dried on the instant.

"Walk on," said Lorenzo in a low voice. "Keep your arm over my shoulder. Keep talking to me." In a louder voice he said, "I do not believe people's souls go to a heaven of any sort."

"Can they hear us?" Daoud said softly. De Verceuil, he thought. He must have decided to have me killed. HIs body felt cold. His journey from Egypt and all his work, despite tonight's triumph, might end here on a rain-wet street. And what would happen to Sophia if he were killed?

"They cannot hear what we say. But careful, they might be able to tell from the tone of our voices whether we are aware of them. Can you fight?"

"Not well. Not well at all." The Scorpion, the small crossbow hidden in his cloak, he thought, might account for one or two of them, if he could see well enough to aim it. He blinked his eyes. He saw two moons hanging over the street, blinked again, and saw one.

"Do not Jews believe in an immortal soul?" he asked in a normal voice, keeping up the pretense of conversation.

He cursed his lack of foresight. Why had he not thought to arrange for some of their bravos to meet them and escort them back to Ugolini's palace? Because he did not want himself connected with the fighting men Lorenzo had brought to Orvieto. That it had been a sensible precaution did not ease his anguish now.

"Maimonides writes that men and women live on after they die only in the memory of others," said Lorenzo. "Of course, orthodox rabbis say that Maimonides was a heretic."

"If the dead live on only in memory, then my father is truly dead, because I have done nothing for his memory, and I fight against all that he fought for.''

Daoud realized that his wine-numbed mind was hardly working. He was relying on Lorenzo to think of some way to get them through this. He hated having his life depend on another man's cleverness. He tried to free his thoughts from the poisonous grip of al-koahl. It had been easier earlier this evening, but he was very tired now.

''I prefer to believe that people become more broadminded after they die,'' said Lorenzo. ''They come face-to-face with the truth, whatever it is, and they see how each of us, Turk and Jew and Christian, has been struggling to uphold a dimly glimpsed version of what they see plainly. If they do not feel sorry for us, then probably they laugh at us.

''And now, this way. Move as silently as you can.''

Abruptly, holding tight to Daoud's wrist, Lorenzo made a sharp left turn into an alley so narrow it was almost invisible. It was scarcely more than a quintana, a tunnel rather than an alley; the overhanging second stories of the houses on either side actually had a wall in common.

Lorenzo pulling him, Daoud broke into a trot. All around them was a hot blackness reeking of decay. Daoud could hear creatures scrabbling out of his way. Ahead was a bluish oblong—the end of the tunnel and the moonlit space beyond it.

They stopped abruptly. Lorenzo swung Daoud's arm down and stepped away from him, gripping him briefly by the shoulders to brace him.

''Now you must clear your head, Messer David. I hear them coming. I think they saw us duck in here. Get out your sword or your dagger, whatever suits you best, and get ready to fight.''

Daoud heard the sound of running boots. He tried to guess how many pursuers there were, but his head was not clear enough of wine fumes for that. He fell against the rough plaster wall. Could he and Lorenzo break through a doorway into a house and hide there? No, the people within would probably give them away.

He heard the slithering sound of Lorenzo's sword being drawn. He decided not to use the Scorpion. It would take too long to load and cock it, and if he fumbled, he would be cut down without a second chance.

His mind was fairly clear of the toxic power of al-koahl, but his body, still in its grip, felt half dead to him.

How can I fight, as dizzy as I am? Thou hast said it, O God, wine is an abomination. Forgive me for drinking it, and help me now.

He reached for his sword, the handsome new one he had bought in Orvieto. He drew it out slowly, as quietly as he could, and hefted it in his hand. A bit late now to wonder how it would stand up in a fight.

The running footsteps stopped suddenly. Looking at the end of the alley, Daoud saw figures silhouetted by the moonlight. He heard voices murmuring. Then the figures seemed to fill the rectangular mouth of the alley. There seemed to be six of them. They moved slowly, cautiously.

"Capons," whispered Lorenzo. "Afraid to charge us. Let us move to where there is light to fight by."

He pulled Daoud after him. Daoud felt his head clearing. He could hear better and, despite the darkness, see better. But he staggered as they ran out of the alley.

They found themselves in a campiello, a courtyard surrounded by houses. In the center, on a small pedestal, was a statue, one of their saint idols, with arms outstretched. Daoud looked quickly around him. There seemed to be no way out but the alleyway they had entered through.

He heard a loud thump to his right. A dark figure suddenly stood there. Another thump on the left, and another in front. Men were jumping down from the rooftops.

In a moment, four men in a rough semicircle faced Lorenzo and Daoud. Blades gleamed silvery in the moonlight.

The six others who had been pursuing them rushed out of the alley.

Filled with a despairing rage, Daoud clenched his teeth and raised his sword.

XXIV

RACHEL'S BODY FELT COLD. SHE KNEW THE NIGHT OUTSIDE WAS warm despite the lateness of the hour, and the room was stifling, with all its candles and the heavy silk draperies that held in the heat. But her feet and hands were icy. It was fear that chilled her so as she sat half listening to Tilia. She huddled in a corner of the big bed, her feet tucked under her, her hands clenched in her lap. She wanted to jump out the window.

Only, she was here of her own free will. And anyway the window was barred.

"We will be watching through spy holes in the walls," said Tilia. "There will be at least three of us. If he hurts you in any way, we will be here in a trice to rescue you."

Tilia Caballo had a face like a frog, Rachel thought. The fat old woman was trying to be reassuring, but just now Rachel hated her. She could not believe Tilia would interfere with a wealthy client's pleasure no matter how badly a girl of hers was being hurt.

The skepticism must have shown in her face, because Tilia had said, "I know this man. He has been here five times. He is not the kind that likes to hurt women. I do have patrons of that sort. For them I supply women like Olivia. Sometime when you are not so frightened I may tell you what Olivia likes men to do to her. Of course, she pretends not to like it. Her clients would get no pleasure if they knew Olivia *wanted* them to do what they do. But no matter how I gain my livelihood, I am still a woman of honor." She glowered fiercely at Rachel, jowls quivering slightly. "I do not allow certain things to take place in my house. I do not allow my women to be mistreated."

"I know," said Rachel. "That is why I have not run away."

"You need not speak of running away," said Tilia loftily. "The door will be open for you whenever you wish to walk through it." Rachel believed that, just as she had believed gruff Lorenzo Celino when he told her she did not have to go to Tilia's house. But she also knew that if she had not come here, or if she chose now to walk out that door, these people would do nothing more for her.

Staying, much as she might hate what would happen to her, was better than wandering alone on the roads of Italy.

She looked up at the canopy over the bed. It was peach-colored, as were the bed curtains. The walls of the small room were hung with yellow silk drapes framing frescoes showing nude, smiling women fleeing from creatures that were half man and half goat, with things that stuck out before them like spears.

"Real men do not have pizzles as big as that," Tilia had said when she first showed Rachel the room, pointing with a grin at a bright red organ. "Although it may look that big to you the first time you see one in all its glory." Tilia had stopped joking then, and had carefully told her exactly what would happen on this night.

I am better prepared, Rachel thought, *than many a woman is on her wedding night.*

Indeed, her own mother, months before she died, had already explained much of this to Rachel. But the thought of her mother fairly broke her heart now. Her mother would cut her own throat if she could see Rachel in this place, about to let a man do this thing to her for money.

Her body shrank with dread.

She would rather, far rather, be the ignorant bride of a carpenter or a traveling merchant like her poor Angelo, who had been her husband in name only, or even the wife of a butcher, than to lie here in this gorgeously decorated room and give her most precious gift to a stranger who had bought the right to deflower her.

She found herself wishing poor old Angelo had asserted his right as her husband so that she could not now let her virginity be defiled.

Thank God Angelo is not alive to see this! But if he had lived, I would not be doing this.

God will never forgive me.

But if God does not want me to do what I am doing, why did He let this happen to me?

Tilia sat beside the bed in a big chair with a curved bottom. The jeweled cross she wore—which reminded Rachel that she was among Christians here and therefore not safe—rested on her bosom, half covered by the gold lace bordering the neckline of her gown. The cross quivered minutely with Tilia's heartbeat.

"You are probably wondering, child, whether you are doing the right thing."

"Yes." Rachel was so choked with fear that she could only whisper the word.

"Well, I can tell you there are thousands of women who would give anything to be in your place."

"In my place? To become a putana?"

Tilia laughed. "You think most women are contentedly married, with husbands to take care of them, with children who love them and neighbors who respect them—while only a few like me and the women who work for me are putane, whom the rest look down on. Well, listen to me, little one, other women *envy* us. A married woman sells herself, body and soul, to be some man's slave for life. And she gets damned little in return. We rent out this little part of our anatomy"—she patted her lap—"for a moment, and we keep the profit for ourselves. If we are clever, as I have been, we learn how to keep and increase our money. So when we no longer have youth and beauty to sell, we can take care of ourselves. And I tell you that a woman in her later years is likely to be a better friend to herself than any husband."

She speaks with conviction. But I cannot trust her, either. I have not had a true friend in this world since Angelo was killed.

Rachel sighed. "It is just that after tonight there is no turning back. This is for the rest of my life."

"That is right," said Tilia. "You will give up something that you can lose only once. When you have a commodity as unique as that, my child, you owe it to yourself to get the most you can for it." Her eyes hardened. "Every man wants to be the first to pierce a woman and hear her cry out and make her bleed. But what woman gets anything worth having in return? She gives it away on a dark night to some furfante with a smooth tongue and a handsome leg, or else the tonto she married takes it from her and then tells her to go wash the bed linen." She turned to stare at Rachel. "Do you know what I got for my virginity?" Her cheeks were red with anger.

"What did you get, Signora?" The heat with which Tilia spoke reassured Rachel. This was what the woman really felt. She was not just talking to lead Rachel astray.

"Blows and slavery." Tilia thrust her face close to Rachel's to underline her words. "Blows and slavery. The Genoese, may leprosy devour their limbs and may their prickles fall off in their hands, raided Otranto. They raped me—that was how I lost *my* virginity. They sold me to the Turks.''

"You were a slave to the Turks?'' Rachel gasped. "Where?'' And how did she escape them and come to Orvieto and grow so rich and fat?

Tilia looked away. "Never mind. It would take too long to tell you.'' Rachel sensed that there was something here Tilia did not want to talk about. But she resolved to pry the story out of her one day.

Tilia's head swung back to face her. "Have I told you what you are getting this night for giving this man this proud moment of possessing a virgin?''

"I—I do not remember.'' Tilia had named a figure, but it had been so outrageous and Rachel had been so frightened by the prospect that she had promptly forgotten it.

"By the five wounds of Jesus, you truly are a child, not to remember something so important! Well, fix it in your mind this time, and think of it when you are wondering whether you are doing right. Five hundred golden florins. Five hundred, newly minted in Florence. That is your share. That is half of what he is paying. The other half is mine, as is only just. Think of it. He pays the price of a palazzo for you because you are a very young, beautiful virgin, and that is what he most desperately desires. Compare that with what most women get when they let a man have them for the first time.''

That is far more money than Angelo ever saw in his whole life. Who is this man who will pay so much to have me? Rachel supposed Tilia would tell her who the man was if she asked, but she had decided it was better not to know anything about him ahead of time. That way she could imagine that he would be someone kind and gentle.

"I do not know what I will do with all that money,'' Rachel said softly.

If I lose it, all this will have been for nothing.

Tilia's wide mouth stretched even wider in a grin. "I will show you how to plant it.''

"Plant it?''

"Yes, and then watch it grow. There are many many fields in which to plant money. You can place it with the Templars or certain Lombards or men I know among your own Jews, and they use it, and when they give it back to you there is more. Miracolo! Or you can buy beautiful and valuable things with it, whose worth increases as they get older. Or you can buy shares in a ship of Venice or Pisa, or even''—she spat—''Genoa, or a German caravan, and when the caravan or the ship comes back, if it comes back, you get your money back tenfold. That is risky, but it is the quickest way to great wealth.''

Rachel felt a momentary excitement. Then she remembered how she was going to get the money. Her body felt colder than ever, cold as death. This, she thought, must be the way that poor man they killed last week felt when he was waiting for the torturers to come for him. She shuddered and hugged her knees tight against her chest under the gauzy gown Tilia had given her to wear.

Tilia must have seen the sudden darkening of her mood. She moved over to the bed and sat down beside Rachel, making the frame of the bed groan alarmingly. She put a hand lightly on Rachel's arm.

''Listen, Rachel. I was raped. I will not be party to the rape of another. You do not have to do this. Just tell me that you do not want to.''

A sudden heat rushed through Rachel's body. She was no longer cold. She burned with anger.

''Stop saying that!'' she screamed. ''Will you leave me alone?'' Being reminded over and over again that she was doing this of her own free will was an even worse torture than imagining what the man would do to her.

Oh, God, I am going to cry and make myself ugly, and he will not want me and I will not get the five hundred florins.

She pressed her hands against her face, trying to stop tears.

''I was asking you to think, not carry on,'' said Tilia reprovingly. ''If you want to walk well in life, you had better learn not to burst into tears when you have an important decision to make.''

Rachel took deep breaths to calm herself.

''I decided days ago that I could not do any better for myself than this, Signora Tilia. But I am so afraid. Perhaps the man will not want me when he sees how afraid I am.''

Tilia grinned broadly. ''Nonsense. The more innocent and timid you appear, the more you will delight him.''

Rachel heard a light tapping at the door, and her heart beat so hard she thought it would burst.

Tilia rose, brushing down her green satin gown. ''The signal that he has arrived. I thought he would never get here. It's almost morning. I must go down and greet him, child. But remember, I will be watching everything."

I do not really like that.

Tilia winked and pushed on what looked like a plaster panel between two gold-painted beams in the wall. It swung away from her and she squeezed through.

Rachel sat in the bed, drawn up into the corner of it that was farthest from the door, and waited. She played nervously with fingers that felt like icicles.

A short time later she caught a glimpse of Tilia pushing open the door, but her eyes fixed on the man standing in the doorway.

She drew in a deep, gasping breath. She wanted to scream.

The man standing in the doorway was short and broad. He wore a long, brightly colored silk robe. His skin was brown, his eyes little black slits. A white mustache drooped below his flat nose. A thin white beard like a goat's hung from his chin.

She had seen this man once before, when she watched from the window of Sophia's room at Cardinal Ugolini's, the day he arrived in Orvieto in a great procession.

Rachel's breath, so long held, burst out of her in a moan.

The man who had come to take her virginity was a Tartar.

"It was as much by my choice as the cardinal's that I did not attend the contessa's reception," said Friar Mathieu, yawning. "How could a Little Brother of San Francesco stay up till all hours with people stuffing themselves with rich food and drinking wine? And gambling, and kissing each other in dark corners?"

The old Franciscan's eyes were watery with sleepiness, but the corners of his mouth quirked with humor under his white mustache. He sat on the edge of the cot, which, as he had insisted when he moved into the Palazzo Monaldeschi, was the only piece of furniture in the room. Simon paced the floor, unable to stand still.

Simon felt the barb in the mention of kissing, but he did not mind it. When he routed Friar Mathieu out of his narrow bed in a remote corner of the palace, he admitted at once that he had been in the atrium with Ugolini's niece, Sophia, while David of Trebizond was so disastrously baiting the Tartars.

"I was wrong to pay court to the cardinal's niece." He could still feel her lips under his, still taste them, and his body tingled at the remembrance. "I am as much at fault as de Verceuil. But it was he who found that ignorant woman to replace you as interpreter, and then he went off to gamble—with David's servant, of all people—and left the Tartars alone and unprotected."

Friar Mathieu shook his head. "Yes, and drinking that wine of Montefiascone. I wonder why God chose to make those particular grapes so irresistible."

Simon pounded his fist into his palm. "We must confront de Verceuil, Friar Mathieu."

A deep crease appeared between the thick white eyebrows. "At this hour?"

Simon saw the fatigue in Mathieu's wrinkled face and felt guilty. "I am most heartily sorry for awakening you at this ungodly time of night. It was just—"

"Just that you could not sleep yourself." The friar laughed. "But it is a most Godly time of night. The fact is, I would have had to get up soon to say the first part of my office. Were I living with my brother Franciscans—as I wish I were—I would be up chanting lauds with them. But I fear the cardinal will be neither willing nor able to talk to us if we go to him now."

"So much damage has been done, Friar Mathieu. The contessa is furious. I could not begin to reason with her. She went on and on, talking about murderers of babies. I would not be surprised if tomorrow morning she ordered us to leave her palazzo."

The old man raised a hand. "Pope Urban would not let her do that. It would be an insult to the ambassadors."

"Cardinal le Gros told me the pope looked pale and shaken when he left. He might not care whether the ambassadors are insulted. We can have no more of de Verceuil's blundering."

Or mine.

Friar Mathieu shook a finger at him. "What happened tonight is not the cardinal's doing. None of this is accidental. What happened tonight shows that Ugolini will do everything in his power to block this alliance."

"But Ugolini did nothing tonight. It was all that man from Trebizond."

"That is like saying that the ax chops the tree down, and not the woodsman wielding it. Ugolini brought David to the contessa's reception. He brought David's servant, an accomplished gambler as well as a recruiter of brigosi. And he brought his niece, Sophia."

At the mention of Sophia a sharp pain went through Simon's chest.

Sophia cannot be part of it. Not when I have just found her.

Was it possible that the passion she had showed in their time together in the atrium was a sham? That would be too cruel. And yet, how could he prove that she was innocent?

"It is just a coincidence that Sophia is here in Orvieto now," he said. "She is as undecided about this matter of the Tartars as the pope himself is."

But is the pope still undecided, Simon wondered as he spoke.

The wrinkles around Friar Mathieu's faded blue eyes deepened a little. "Well, I would not expect you to say otherwise. A knight does not doubt the honor of a lady he has kissed."

Simon sensed Friar Mathieu's skepticism, but he could not bring himself to believe that Sophia had knowingly been the cardinal's agent. This woman had made Italy a place of enchantment for him.

Friar Mathieu went on. "We both agree, do we not, that the luring of Cardinal de Verceuil by David's man, Giancarlo, was planned by Ugolini?"

Glad to be on safer ground, Simon nodded vigorously. "We agree on that, to be sure."

"But we cannot simply go to de Verceuil, as you proposed, and denounce him for having left the room with Giancarlo. Not when he can at once point out that you also left the room—with Sophia."

Simon turned his back on Friar Mathieu and stared out, almost unseeing, toward the window. It had neither glass nor shutters nor parchment, only a gauze curtain to discourage insects, iron bars to keep out larger intruders. He felt furious with himself.

The mention of Giancarlo reminded him that he had heard nothing from Sordello. By now the old mercenary should have insinuated himself into the band Giancarlo was gathering. Perhaps through Sordello Simon could prove Sophia's innocence.

He noticed now that some light was coming through the curtain, and he thought he heard birds singing. He had been up all night.

"Then you think it pointless for us to confront de Verceuil? I suppose you do not think I should write to Count Charles, either."

"I think it very unlikely that Count Charles would give the cardinal's responsibilities in this to someone else. I think it very likely that Cardinal de Verceuil has his intriguers around the count who would learn of your message and might set themselves to do you harm. No, I do not think we can rid ourselves of the cardinal. But I agree that we should meet with him."

Simon was bewildered. "To do what?"

Friar Mathieu shrugged. "No man is beyond redemption. He

must realize that because of his blundering tonight—our blundering—the mission is perilously close to failing. Perhaps we can convince him that in the future we must work together. Otherwise there will be no glory for him to steal from us.''

The old friar had been sleeping only in a robe of gray frieze. He pulled a sleeveless brown mantle over his head and tied a white cord around his waist, and he was dressed for the day. Simon envied him the simplicity of his apparel. It took him a good deal longer to dress himself in the morning, and he knew noblemen who spent hours in their wardrobes, with servants to help them, before they felt ready to face the world.

''We will go now, then?'' he asked.

''Well, you are up. If the cardinal is as upset about this disaster as you are, he may well have spent a sleepless night, too. Let us go and see.''

They walked side by side down dim corridors cluttered with battered old chairs and tables, past walls covered with tattered hangings, dented shields, and rusty coats of mail. The Monaldeschi family, it seemed, never threw away anything. The rooms set aside for the cardinal and his entourage were on the third floor of the palazzo, where the windows were larger and set with white glass. A man wrapped in a blanket lay on a sack of straw outside the door to the cardinal's rooms. The top of his head, shaved in a tonsure, gleamed dully in the light of the one fat candle that illuminated the corridor. A cleric in minor orders, no doubt. Simon shook him.

''No, Your Signory,'' the cleric said, yawning and stretching as he stood up to bow properly to the count. ''The cardinal is not sleeping, but neither is he here. After the contessa's reception he and the Tartars and their guards all went out. His Eminence did not choose to tell me where they were bound.''

Simon felt the wind knocked out of him, as if he had been running full tilt and tripped. He looked at Friar Mathieu, who wore a pained, even sad expression.

After everything else that had gone wrong, how could de Verceuil take the Tartars into the streets late at night? They might run afoul of bravos or some of the wild young men of Orvieto's feuding families. Why would de Verceuil take such a risk?

Then Simon understood the reason for Friar Mathieu's look of sadness. Men would leave the Palazzo Monaldeschi at this hour for only one reason—loose women.

Simon had heard that in the darkest hours a corrupt, secret world glowed brightly in Orvieto, hidden behind discreet walls. Rumor told of high-ranking churchmen who ventured behind those walls; indeed, it was said that the secret world existed because of the patronage of such men. Of course de Verceuil would be a patron of that sinful night world. And of course he would draw the Tartars into it. Barbarians that they were, they no doubt expected the attentions of harlots as their due.

That I am surprised only proves, I suppose, what a bumpkin I am, thought Simon, annoyed at himself and disgusted with de Verceuil.

He must pray, he thought with a chill, that the Tartars' guards were well armed and alert.

XXV

SWORDS DRAWN, DAOUD AND LORENZO STOOD BACK-TO-BACK IN the shadowy courtyard. Lorenzo faced the six men who had emerged from the end of the alley and were now fanning out to surround them. Daoud confronted the four who had jumped down into the campiello.

A shutter opened on the overhanging second floor of a house, and Daoud glanced up to see a face. The shutter slammed with a finality that declared the householder wanted nothing to do with what was going on below.

It was too dark to see the faces of the men before him. They wore dark capes, and two of them carried long daggers in one hand and swords in the other. One shadowy figure stepped forward now, and Daoud wondered if they were going to challenge him.

"Messere, let us speak quickly. You are David of Trebizond, are you not?"

The man had asked the question in an urgent but respectful tone.

Feeling a bit more hopeful, Daoud answered, "Yes, I am David."

"Who the devil are *you*?" called a voice from behind Daoud.

The man addressed his answer to Daoud. "I am Andrea Sordello of Rimini, Messer David. These three men are my comrades. It would honor us if you would accept our service."

"Accept his service," Lorenzo said at once from behind Daoud. "We have nothing to lose."

Daoud made himself decide at once. "If you are willing to help me, I am grateful."

"Be off with you, Messer Sordello," called one of the original pursuers. "This is no quarrel of yours."

"And what is *your* quarrel with these men?" Sordello replied.

"That is no affair of yours, messere!" It was the voice of a very young man, intense, passionate.

Daoud turned to face the young voice. At once Sordello moved to take a position at his side.

Daoud realized that he could see better; the first hint of dawn. And not only was there more light, but his head was clearer as well. The heat of his body, aroused to fight, was burning away the intoxicating spirits in his blood.

The men opposite were spread far apart. The one who spoke for them was slender and wore a cap that fell over one ear. A silver badge glittered on the cap.

Sordello spoke again. "Since you will not say, Messere, I will tell *you* what your affair is. You are of the famiglia Filippeschi. You saw these gentlemen leaving the Palazzo Monaldeschi and decided that any guest of the Monaldeschi must be an enemy of yours. And so you decided to hunt down and kill these good gentlemen, who have done you no harm and are not even citizens of Orvieto, for the offense of having enjoyed the hospitality of your rivals."

Filippeschi. Daoud had been wanting to make contact with them ever since his arrival in Orvieto. Now he had met them, and—accursed luck—they wanted to kill him.

"Lorenzo, they are Filippeschi," he muttered. "Talk to them."

"There is no talking to *them*, Messer David," said Sordello. "They are out for your blood."

"Be still," said Daoud. The man had offered his services. Let him confine himself to serving, then.

Lorenzo stepped out in front of Daoud, his sword still out before him, but angled toward the ground.

"Messeres, at least you should know who it is that you have set out to kill. I am Giancarlo of Naples, and this is my master, David. He is a merchant from Trebizond, which is very far away. Much too far for him to have any connection with the quarrels of Orvieto."

One of the Filippeschi bravos, a short man standing to the left of the slender leader, said, "You spin a tale to try to fool us. Anyone can see your master is a Frenchman. Too many damned French in Italy. The Monaldeschi are toadies of the French. Death to the Monaldeschi, and death to the French!"

What a bitter fate it would be, Daoud thought, if his Frankish looks, which caused him to be sent here, earned him his death in a stupid street fight.

"There are six of you," said Lorenzo. "But now that these four men have joined us, there are six of us. Bad odds for you, because no matter how much you harm us, you will certainly come out of this quarrel worse off than you went into it." Lowering his sword even more, he stepped closer to the young man with the silver badge on his cap. "Signore. Which of these men are you willing to lose, to pay for the privilege of hurting us?" With his free hand he pointed from man to man in the circle of six. "That man? That one? That one? Yourself?"

"We will start with you!" the short man shouted.

He lunged at Lorenzo, his sword thrusting straight for Lorenzo's chest.

Lorenzo's sword was up in an instant, parrying the short man's attack. At the same moment, out of the corner of his eye Daoud saw Sordello's arm flash up, then down.

The short man gave a cry and stumbled. He staggered a few steps, then collapsed in a heap at the feet of one of the other Filippeschi bravos.

Lorenzo stepped back so that he and Sordello flanked Daoud. Sordello's three men moved up beside them, one to the left, two to the right.

"You may see to the man who is hurt," said Lorenzo. "Unless you want to continue."

"If he is only hurt, I should retire to a monastery." Sordello laughed. Indeed, Daoud saw that the man on the ground was not moving.

I do not like this Sordello, Daoud thought. *He comes out of nowhere wanting to work for me. He kills in haste and boasts about it.*

The young man with the silver badge on his cap knelt by the

fallen bravo and felt under his cape. "Morte," he said harshly, and stood again.

"Well, Messeres," said Lorenzo, "we are now six to five. We did not choose to quarrel. We still do not wish to fight. In fact, we ourselves are at odds with the Monaldeschi."

"How might that be?" said the young man.

"Are we done fighting? I wish to make a proposal to you."

The Filippeschi spokesman glanced at his fellows. "What say you?"

"Alfredo was my cousin," said a tall bravo in a rust-colored cape. "But I cannot avenge him alone."

"Alfredo was impetuous," said the young man. "He acted before I gave an order."

"You are no leader, Marco, if you will not undertake the vendetta for one of your men."

The vendetta. These Italians are like the desert tribesmen. Kill one of them, and you have his family to deal with.

"I will show you what kind of a leader I am if you speak that way to me again," said Marco.

"Enough, enough," said one of the other bravos, and the man in the rust-colored cape shrugged.

It was now almost daylight, and Daoud studied the face of the young man called Marco. He could not be more than seventeen, Daoud thought, looking at his smooth cheeks and downy black mustache.

Marco! He had heard that the head of the Filippeschi family was a young Conte Marco di Filippeschi.

"What do you propose, Messere?" said Marco.

"Meet me in front of the Church of Sant'Agnes," Lorenzo said. "This evening at Compline. Come alone, as I will. There are things we can discuss, I think, to our mutual profit."

Marco bowed to Lorenzo. "I shall expect you, Messere." He gestured, and the man in the reddish cape and one other picked up the body of Alfredo.

"Momento, Messeres," said Sordello, moving to the body in three quick strides. He bent down, reached under the body, and with a jerk of his hand pulled free a long, thin throwing knife, which he wiped on his cape.

"I can ill afford to lose so well-balanced a knife as this."

Alfredo's cousin, holding the body by the shoulders, said, "I know your name, Andrea Sordello, and your face. You will not need that knife much longer."

Sordello made a mock bow. "Be assured, Messere, this knife will not miss *you*, if we should meet again."

A moment later the Filippeschi and their burden had disappeared into the alley.

Daoud studied the dark irregular stain where the fallen man had bled on the rain-damp paving stones of the campiello. It was dawn, already past Fajr, the time for morning prayer.

God is great. In the name of God, the Beneficent, the Merciful. All praise be to God, Lord of the Worlds.

"I advise you not to have any dealings with the Filippeschi, Messeres," Sordello said suddenly. "They'll betray you."

Even though he had given no outward sign that he was praying, Daoud was angered at being interrupted. He eyed Sordello. The man was shorter than he, about fifty years of age, Daoud judged. His hair was a good deal grayer than Lorenzo's, and it hung lankly down to his jawline under a shabby maroon cap. The bones of Sordello's nose and brows were thickened and flattened, as if they had been broken many times. It was the face of an old fighter, the sort of face that usually commanded Daoud's respect, be it borne by Christian or Muslim. But when Daoud looked at him, Sordello stared back fixedly, unnaturally, as if it were an effort to look Daoud in the eye.

"Was your advice asked, Messere?" Lorenzo growled.

He feels about the man as I do, Daoud thought. Now, Daoud thought, Sordello would bluster about saving their lives, and he would ask for employment.

"Forgive me," Sordello said. "I presumed too much." He pulled off his cap and bowed to the surprised Daoud. Either he was a better man than he seemed at first glance, or he was much more devious.

"Forgive *us*," Daoud said, bowing back, though not as deeply, and drawing a disapproving grunt from Lorenzo. "We owe you our deepest gratitude. How came you leaping down from the housetops when we needed help so badly?"

"I have been looking for a chance to meet Messer Giancarlo. Tonight I waited outside the Monaldeschi palace, hoping that you would emerge from the reception in a good mood. While I and my fellows were hanging about the palace, we chanced to see those brigosi lurking in the shadows nearby. When you came out, it was you they chose to follow, so we followed them. When you went down this alley, we took to the rooftops, the better to surprise your enemies."

"Why were you looking for me?" Lorenzo asked gruffly.

"I heard that you pay well for men who are adept with sword and dagger and who ask no questions about what they might be hired for."

"I also like a man who does not talk much," said Lorenzo. "You talk a great deal."

"Yes, Messer Giancarlo." Sordello lowered his eyes. Again, that disarming humility.

The man was resourceful and quick-thinking. He was arrogant one moment, humble the next.

"How did you come to Orvieto, Sordello?" Daoud asked him.

"I served Sigismundo Malatesta, governor of Rimini, until his death," said Sordello. "Since then I have not found a suitable master. I was traveling south, thinking perhaps of offering my sword to King Manfred, when I heard of you, Messer Giancarlo, while passing through Viterbo."

Daoud felt uneasy, hearing that Lorenzo's recruiting expeditions were being gossiped of in the cities around here. And how easily Sordello had been able to make the connection between Giancarlo and David of Trebizond. Just as Tilia had said, it was impossible to hire men without attracting attention.

He realized Lorenzo was waiting for him to speak.

"You may walk with us to Cardinal Ugolini's mansion," Daoud said.

When they emerged from the alley, there was no sign of the Filippeschi. Two of Sordello's men walked in front of Daoud and Lorenzo, and Sordello and the other man followed behind them. The wine had worn off altogether, but Daoud felt a throbbing pain behind his eyes and a great need to sleep.

"Well?" Lorenzo said, keeping his voice low. "The man wants us to hire him."

"We need more men, and we want clever street fighters," said Daoud. "He is that."

"Yes, but he is the type of man I detest," said Lorenzo. "I did not need him to kill that Filippeschi bravo for me. He acts before he thinks."

"After tonight we may not have to attack the French directly," Daoud said. "On the other hand, we are sure to have further need of bodyguards, and I think Sordello and his three companions would suit. Let us give ourselves time to think. Tell him you will meet him and give him our answer in two days.''

XXVI

IT COULD NOT BE WORSE, RACHEL THOUGHT. SHE COULD NOT BE more degraded. An old man, and a Tartar. Were the Tartars even human, she wondered, or was she about to commit the further abominable sin of mating with an animal?

The door had closed behind him with a terribly final sound, and he was standing in front of it, showing his teeth, large and strong and very white, in a broad grin.

She wondered if he could see her knees and hands trembling. If only she had accepted Signora Tilia's offer to release her from this. Was it too late? Could she rush past the Tartar to the door and pull it open and run away? If she did that now, doubtless the Tartar would be insulted. From what she knew about these creatures, it would be very dangerous to make him angry.

I will pretend to be sick. When he is not looking, I will stick my finger down my throat and throw up. That will disgust him so, he will leave me alone.

Or it might antagonize him enough to kill her. Her body broke out in a cold sweat. Her eyes were shut, but she heard the monster coming closer. She thought of what he would do to her, and her stomach heaved—she would throw up even without trying to. She hoped he *would* kill her. Better that than his animal's thing inside her.

She opened her eyes, to see that he had stopped halfway between the closed door and the bed.

Actually, he was not so hideous. He had a round brown face and bright black eyes, and his beard was white, as Angelo's had been.

Ah, Rachel, Rachel, the joy of my old age, Angelo would say. *My beard was white before you were born.*

He would not rejoice in his old age if he could see me now.

The Tartar's beard and mustache were not full and flowing, as Angelo's had been, but stringy. The beard almost seemed like a false beard, pasted on that small, sharp chin.

He said, "Buona sera, berra feeria." He had learned some Italian. But it was not evening. It was almost morning. And what was he trying to say—"bella figlia?" Beautiful daughter? He had probably asked someone what he should say, and they had told him the wrong things.

"Buona sera, Mio Signore," she answered, inclining her head slightly. Her voice was a terrified whisper. When she heard how frightened she sounded, she became more frightened still and huddled into the farthest corner of the bed, wishing she could squeeze through a crack in the wall beside her and disappear.

The Tartar tapped his chest, smiling and nodding. "John." He wore a crimson silk tunic that fell to his knees, and over it a pale green gown, open in front, with wide sleeves. When she had stood by a window in the cardinal's palazzo and watched the Tartars' arrival in Orvieto, he and the other Tartar had worn foreign-looking silk robes, blood red, covered with blue birds with long golden tails. Now he was dressed like an Italian.

He was still nodding at her, with a questioning look on his face. He wanted her to say her name.

"Rachel," she said, touching her chest. How small her breasts were, she thought. He could not possibly want a girl with such small breasts. He certainly would not want to devour them. She felt sick to her stomach again.

"Reicho. Buona sera, Reicho." He could not pronounce the letter *l*.

"Buona sera, John," she answered. She was about to smile, but she checked herself. If she seemed to be encouraging him, he would come at her. Cold sweat broke out over her skin.

He is going to come at me anyway.

A silver pitcher of wine with two silver goblets stood on a small marble-topped table beside the bed. Wine might make this easier for her. Except that too much wine would make her sick. Well, was that not what she wanted? She stretched a trembling hand toward it.

"Will you take some wine, Messer John?" *Where on earth did he get a name like John?*

She poured the wine, carefully filling the goblets only two-thirds full so her trembling hands would not spill their contents.

The Tartar crossed the room and sat in the round-bottomed chair Tilia had occupied a short while earlier. Rachel held out a goblet to him, and her hand shook so badly she almost dropped it. He did not seem to notice. Maybe he was used to being waited on by trembling women. He smiled and nodded.

Tilia was watching all this, Rachel remembered. She drained her cup quickly, the silver giving the wine a slightly metallic taste. She poured a second cup for herself, and looked at him. He barely sipped from his goblet before setting it on the table, holding his hand palm down over it. Too bad, she thought. She had heard that men who drank too much could not get stiff enough to go into women.

John started talking to her in his own tongue. He spoke for a long time with many gestures, some toward himself, some toward her. She tried desperately to guess what he was saying. She did not want to respond the wrong way and anger him.

He seemed quite at ease, and he laughed occasionally, as if he were telling her funny stories that amused him as well. She saw webs of fine wrinkles in the brown skin around his eyes and thought, *He could be older than Angelo.*

He began to make a strange sound, a long-drawn-out moan. Perhaps he was in pain. Perhaps *he* was going to be sick. Her heart leapt hopefully. Then the moan changed pitch, and his mouth began to shape words. They must be Tartar words. He was singing to her. It was unmistakably a song, but it was strange and shrill to her ears. She almost burst out laughing, but immediately felt terror at the thought of offending him.

It began to dawn on her, though, that John was not behaving like a brute, as she had feared he would when she first saw him in the doorway. If she looked behind the black slits that were his eyes, under the tanned-leather skin, he seemed a pleasant old man. His language might be gibberish to her, but it was clear that he was trying to entertain her, even woo her.

But she hated the thought of what he was trying to woo her *for*.

He ended his song by clapping his hands rhythmically—she counted nine handclaps. He followed that with more eager smiles and nods. He actually wanted to know whether she liked his song. She relaxed a bit.

She smiled and nodded back. "Yes. Very good, John. Che

bello!'' Perhaps she could get him to sing more, and put off the moment she dreaded.

But he stood up with a look on his face that froze her heart in her chest. There was nothing ferocious or cruel in it or even lustful. There was neither kindness nor pity in it, nor anything that recognized her as a person. It was the satisfied smile of a man looking upon a possession.

He slipped off the wide-sleeved gown and unbuckled his belt. She began to tremble uncontrollably.

Daoud sat slumped with exhaustion on the carpeted floor of Ugolini's cabinet. The long night just past had drained him of all his energy. He wanted to sleep, but first he must see to it that Ugolini made good use of the advantage they had gained at the contessa's reception.

A strong, rich, familiar smell filtered into his nostrils, and his head lifted, as if a powerful hand had gripped it. The door opened, and a servant carried in a tray laden with six small porcelain cups, one each for Ugolini, Daoud, Sophia, and Lorenzo and two extra, as well as two pitchers. Ugolini pushed aside a pile of parchment on his work table, and the servant set the tray down.

As the door closed behind the servant, Daoud drew a deep breath to identify the smell and felt a glow of surprised pleasure.

''Is it possible?'' he said to Ugolini. ''You have found kaviyeh?''

Ugolini, sitting in the big chair behind his work table, just his head and shoulders showing, smiled benignly. ''You may hate the Tartars for invading the Islamic lands, my friend, but it means that we Christians can now trade with that part of the world. The Venetians have been importing the beans from the uplands of Persia in small—and very expensive—quantities. I was saving this for a special occasion. This morning, after your triumph over the Tartars and your narrow escape from death, seemed appropriate.''

Daoud found the strength to stand up and pour the steaming black liquid from the pitcher into a cup. He held the cup to his face with both hands and sniffed deeply. He felt happier than he had in a long time.

Sophia, sitting on a padded bench against the wall opposite Ugolini's table, said, ''What is that?'' Daoud heard shrill alarm in her voice.

She must suspect it was some sort of drug, thought Daoud with amusement.

The cardinal chuckled amiably. "Only a beverage, my dear. Long used in the Orient by sages and poets. It produces a heightened state of alertness and vigor."

Daoud sipped the hot liquid. The taste was wondrously bracing after months of deprivation, but it was not quite strong enough.

"This is very good, and I am your grateful slave forever," he said. "But you should tell your servants to boil it longer."

Having sensed that Sophia feared his pleasure, he wanted to share it with her that she might see how harmless it was. He went to her and held out his cup.

"Try this. Be careful, the cup is hot."

She took the cup from him, her fingers brushing his. He felt a tingle in his arm. She raised the cup, sniffed suspiciously and grimaced, but took a small sip.

He was disappointed to see her mouth pucker. She did not like it. Well, he could not expect her to take to it at once. He had been drinking it ever since he was a child. Even his crusader family had drunk kaviyeh.

"A very interesting taste," she said, handing back the cup. A Byzantine comment, he thought. He heard Lorenzo chuckle.

A pang of jealousy shot through him. He could not expect her to like kaviyeh any more than he could expect her to love him. Especially not after she had been alone in the Monaldeschi atrium with that damned French count.

His longing for Sophia made his heart ache. If only he could have her for himself, and not be forced to throw her at Simon de Gobignon. But she was no more his than that emerald Baibars had entrusted to him.

Resignedly he told himself he must find out what she had accomplished.

"How did you deal with the Frankish count?"

"As you wished me to."

He walked back to the cardinal's table and turned to face her. Her amber eyes were fixed on him. She must have been watching him cross the room.

"Does he want to see you again?" David demanded.

She shrugged. "He did when I left him. But by now he and Cardinal de Verceuil will have talked together and may well realize my part in what we did to them."

"Well," said Ugolini, rubbing his hands together. "There will be no more need for you to pursue Count Simon, my dear, or for

Messer Lorenzo to play backgammon with the French cardinal. And no need for our illustrious David to risk further verbal jousting with the Tartars.''

Daoud felt a stab of exasperation. Just as he had feared, Ugolini wanted to believe that with last night's triumph over the Tartars, their work was done. Would he be able to persuade the cardinal to realize this was only the beginning of a long struggle—one in which he, Ugolini, must play the chief part?

"De Verceuil is a clever but sloppy player," Lorenzo interjected. "He kept leaving blots less than six points away from me. But I managed to lose eighty florins to him. That kept him interested. Once he decided I was not a skillful player, he kept doubling the stakes and pressing me to do the same when the choice was mine." He went over to Ugolini's work table and poured himself a cup of kaviyeh.

Ugolini laughed. "He must now think his winnings eighty costly florins indeed." He filled a cup from another pitcher, sprang up, and carried the cup across the room to Sophia.

"You will enjoy this spiced milk more than the Muslim kaviyeh. It is my favorite morning drink."

"You think it is all over, then, Cardinal?" Daoud growled. "I can go away and leave you in peace—and richer?"

From the suddenly outraged face Ugolini turned toward him, Daoud thought the cardinal might well be wishing the Filippeschi had finished him off.

"Was last night not a victory?" the cardinal asked in a choked voice.

"Do you know the difference between winning a battle and winning a war?"

"What more can the French do?" said Ugolini.

"We must talk about that," said Daoud. "Even though, in spite of this good kaviyeh, my body screams for rest." He drained the cup, put it down, and stretched his arms. With difficulty he brought his anger under control. He must win Ugolini, not turn him into an enemy.

Ugolini had sat down in the high-backed chair behind his work table. His slender fingers restlessly polished the dome of the skull with the diagram painted on its cranium that lay before him. He looked as gloomy as if he were contemplating the day when he himself would be reduced to bones. Lorenzo quietly got up and poured himself another cup of kaviyeh.

Daoud turned to Sophia. "How do you think de Gobignon feels

toward you?'' He hated to ask the question. He watched her face closely. What he really wanted to know was how *she* felt about de Gobignon.

Her eyes were heavy-lidded. Even with Hashishiyya-trained senses, he could not guess what was behind that damnably unrevealing mask.

''I think I persuaded him that the cardinal's niece neither knows nor cares anything about alliances and crusades. I—believe he could come to love me.''

Rage throbbed in his temples. What, in his sheltered existence, could the young count have learned of love?

''Love you? Unlikely,'' Daoud challenged her.

He saw with quick regret that he had hurt her feelings. She recoiled as if struck.

''Do you not think me worthy of a nobleman's love?''

Daoud crossed the room in three quick steps and stood over her. ''Such pampered creatures as he are not capable of love.''

The mask was back. She shrugged.

''Love or lust, he is drawn to me. Do you mean to make some use of it?''

''Send him a note by one of the cardinal's servants asking him to meet with you in a few days time.'' Daoud turned and walked to the celestial globe beside Ugolini's table and spun it absently as he studied Sophia. ''Let him pick the place, so he feels secure.''

Again he had a glimpse through the mask. Her eyes widened in fear. She thought he meant to kill de Gobignon. That angered him. Did she care so much for the Frenchman, then, that his possible death made her lose her composure?

To Daoud's surprise, Ugolini jumped from his chair and advanced on him, shaking his finger and crying, ''All of France will be down on us like an avalanche if you harm that boy.''

Daoud checked an impulse to laugh. Ugolini was such a comical figure in the flapping white robe he had donned on returning to his mansion.

To Daoud, who had lived most of his life among men for whom death was as common as fear was rare, the little man's tendency to panic seemed contemptible. But, anew, he reminded himself that he needed Ugolini and must treat him with respect.

''Please, Your Eminence,'' he said. ''If I meant to have de Gobignon killed, I would not involve Sophia. I want her to tell him what we are supposedly doing. I hope to create conflict among the supporters of the alliance.''

"But Sophia takes a great risk meeting with him," said Ugolini. "What if de Gobignon attempts to force the truth out of her?"

The thought of de Gobignon laying violent hands on Sophia angered Daoud, and he spoke impulsively.

"*Then* I will kill him."

"God help us!" Ugolini went back to his work table and sat down behind it, his hands over his face.

At once Daoud regretted what he had said. But was there no way to instill courage into this man?

"There is much work for you to do, Cardinal," he said. "You must not falter now."

"Then let there be no more talk of killing," said Ugolini fiercely, taking his hands from his face.

Daoud poured himself another cup of kaviyeh and stood looking down at Ugolini.

"With so much at stake, surely you know I would not do anything rash."

"You need not think of *doing anything*," Ugolini said, a plea in his eyes. "As long as the pope delays his decision about the Tartars, your people are safe."

True enough, Daoud thought. Delay was a large part of his mission. But, despite what Ugolini might think, it was not enough. For the safety of Islam, an alliance between Tartars and Christians must be made impossible.

"Your Eminence, will it please you to visit the cardinals who heard the Tartars condemn themselves last night?" He tried not to make it sound like an order.

"I see no need for that," said Ugolini.

Of course, Daoud thought. The little cardinal's mind was so full of fear that he could not see at all.

"But I am hoping that you can organize a delegation of cardinals to go to the pope and urge him to give up the idea of an alliance with the Tartars. After all, you are the cardinal camerlengo. Your word has weight."

Ugolini made a bridge of his interlaced fingers and rested his forehead against them, as if his head ached.

"I have attacked the Tartars at the pope's council." He spoke down at his table, barely loud enough for Daoud to hear him. "I have introduced you into the highest circles in Orvieto. I have let you recruit criminals and instigate riots while you live in my mansion. I hear you plotting murder.'' He looked up suddenly, wild-eyed. ''Basta! Enough!''

Despair made Daoud feel weak. He knew this sick feeling came partly from being awake all night, poisoning himself with al-koahl, and nearly getting himself murdered. He told himself it did not matter how he felt. He was Sufi-trained, and could control his feelings. He was a Mameluke, and must remain on the attack.

But he chose not to meet Ugolini's refusal directly.

''I also hope that you will be able to persuade Fra Tomasso d'Aquino to write an open letter, to the pope or to the King of France, denouncing the Tartars. Copies of the letter can be circulated to men of influence throughout Christendom.''

Ugolini shook his head, whiskers fluttering. ''Fra Tomasso is neutral and wants to stay that way.''

But if I can, I intend to push Fra Tomasso away from his neutrality.

''Surely he could not have failed to be moved by what he heard last night,'' said Daoud. ''I could see that he was.''

''It will take more than one incident to move Fra Tomasso,'' said Ugolini.

Now I have him! Daoud glanced at Lorenzo, who nodded encouragingly.

Daoud leaned forward, pressing both hands on the table. ''There! You yourself have said the very thing I have been trying to tell you. Last night was just one incident. It was not enough to move Fra Tomasso *or* the cardinals *or* the pope. We must do more. You can accomplish everything we want by persuasion and cunning and subterfuge. If you do, I will never have to put my hand to my dagger, and you will have nothing to fear.'' He shook his open hand at Ugolini. ''Take the lead yourself.''

Ugolini sat staring at the skull while Daoud held his breath.

The little cardinal pulled at his whiskers and looked up at Daoud. ''What must I do?''

Daoud let his breath out. Strength surged back into his body, and despair fled before it.

''Tell me,'' he said, ''if Fra Tomasso were to turn against the Tartars, what do you think the Franks would do about it?''

Ugolini frowned. ''I think that then the only way to reach him would be through the Dominicans. If his superiors commanded him to change his opinion on the Tartars, or to be silent, he would have to obey.''

"And who, of the alliance's chief supporters, would speak to the Dominican order for the French?'' Daoud pressed.

"Count Simon lacks the authority,'' Ugolini said. "Friar Mathieu is eloquent and knows the Tartars well, but I cannot imagine that the chief Dominicans would pay any attention to an ordinary Franciscan priest.''

"What of de Verceuil?'' Daoud asked.

Ugolini nodded. "As a cardinal, de Verceuil can speak as an equal to the head of the Dominican order.''

"Good,'' said Daoud. "That is what I hoped you would tell me.'' He turned away from Ugolini. He had accomplished as much as he could for the moment. Exhaustion struck him like a mace on the back of his head.

"Lorenzo, when you meet that bravo Sordello, tell him that I have decided he and the three with him can join us. I am going to bed.''

"I have a bad feeling about him,'' said Lorenzo.

Daoud paused to consider this. It was precisely for such advice that he needed Lorenzo.

He put his hand on Lorenzo's shoulder. "If he is spying on us, we need to know who sought to place him in our camp. Let him feel he is secure with us. Then start keeping a close watch on him. See to whom he leads us.''

Daoud turned from Lorenzo to look at Sophia. She was looking at him intently, but he could not tell what she was thinking or feeling. Tired as he was, he wished she would come to bed with him. If only she were willing. If only he could invite her.

Rachel lay with her face to the wall, crying silently. She wanted not to weep because she was still afraid of offending the Tartar, even though it was all over.

She realized that her gown was still above her waist, and she lifted her hips to pull it down. But what was the point of modesty for her anymore? Especially with this man, who had taken her virginity.

She heard the rustling of silk as he dressed behind her. He had not taken all of his clothes off, just enough to bare his member. It had been smaller than she imagined. Once, in a stable in Perugia, a boy had shown himself to her and tried to rape her, but she had run away. That stableboy's thing had been much bigger.

John said something to her, but she understood only his "Reicho." He was probably telling her to stop crying.

Even though he had been kindly before getting into the bed with her, she had expected that he would become like the wild, savage Tartars she had heard about. His weight on top of her, even though he was a small man, had frightened her, but he had entered her slowly, and stopped and waited when she cried out. In the end it had been she, wanting in desperation to get it over with, who finished the piercing by pressing upward with her hips. His few quick thrusts and his shout of pleasure—a drawn-out horseman's yell—followed in a moment. And that was all there was to it.

She sobbed aloud suddenly and bit into the pillow. The thought that her whole future had been decided by a moment that had not lasted even as long as it takes to light a candle was too much to bear.

Angelo would say I am not a good woman anymore.

The Tartar spoke again, and tapped her on the shoulder. His voice was soft and kind. Quieting her sobs with one last, deep, shuddering sigh, she rolled over to look at him. More smiles and nods from him. Yes, he wanted to cheer her up. She sensed that he knew something about women, and what he knew had come not just from rapes committed on the battlefield. He must have a wife in the faraway land he came from, and he must, long ago, have done to that wife what he had just done to Rachel. More than one wife, she reminded herself, and more than one deflowering, because according to Tilia, the Tartars took several wives, as the Muslims did. He was probably a grandfather many times over back in that land.

He stood beside the bed, fully dressed. He had even tucked back and knotted his hair behind his head. His grin broadened when she looked at him. Rachel had not seen a Jewish or a Christian man as old as John with such good teeth.

He untied a small bag from his belt. He held it out to her. Should she take it? Of course she should. Was not getting paid the whole point of what she had just gone through? Was not money what her body was to be traded for from now on?

"Thank you, Messer John," she said, and reached out her hand. But he came closer and rubbed the soft leather of the bag against her cheeks, to dry her tears. She understood what he was trying to tell her—that this money should pay her for her pain. Being a pagan, he could not understand the greater pain of her soul because she had sinned, because she had shamed her family and dishonored herself forever.

But I have no family—none living. That is why I am here.

John put the bag into her hand and closed her fingers over it, then pushed her hand against her chest. The bag was very heavy for its small size. He frowned, put his finger to his lips, and waved his hand. He was trying to tell her, she thought, that this was a special present for her, that she was not to tell Madama Tilia about it. He did not know that Tilia had been watching everything they had done together.

He pressed the callused palm of his hand against her cheek and said something, then turned and quickly walked out of the room.

And Rachel was alone with her desolation. She wanted to sleep. There were no windows in this room, but it must have been morning by now. She realized that she did not feel sleepy, although she was tired. She felt a dull ache down inside herself, where he had broken the seal of her virginity. The bag of money lay heavy in her lap. Perhaps if she drank some wine it would help her sleep.

She heard men's voices, loud and rough, in other parts of the house. A man laughed, and then a woman laughed. How many men had come with the Tartar? She felt too tired even to crawl to the edge of the bed and pour herself the wine. She picked up the money and pushed it under a pillow. Perhaps Tilia had not seen him give it to her. She had done this for money, and she ought to get as much as she could for it.

The door swung open and Tilia was standing there, her wide mouth stretched in a broad smile, and her hands rose in benediction. "You were just what he wanted. He seemed most pleased."

Rachel tried to smile. "It was not as bad as I thought it would be."

Tilia shrugged. "Men who are terrible in warfare are sometimes kinder in bed. I thought his zipolo rather small, did you not? That was lucky for you."

Rachel felt her face grow hot. "I have seen only one other—when it was hard like that. And it *was* bigger."

"Well," said Tilia, "small as this Tartar was, he was able to mount you twice, and that is remarkable for a white-haired man who has been up drinking all night." Then she laughed. "Ah, but you should have seen the French cardinal who came here with this

Tartar. He asked for three women, and he swived each one of them mightily. Those French! I care not for their high-horse airs, but they are a lusty lot.''

Rachel felt herself smiling. Was it so easy to begin to think like a whore and laugh at whores' jokes?

"Well," said Tilia, "we must get you washed out at once. You do not want to be giving birth to a little Tartar in your first year as a woman, do you?'' She went to a cabinet and drew out a grayish-white bladder with a tube coiled beside it.

"Peculiar-looking if you have never seen one before," said Tilia. "But there is nothing to worry about. It does not hurt. We just fill the pig's stomach with warm water and squeeze it, and the water goes through the vellum tube and up inside you. The women of Rome used them centuries ago when they did not want to get pregnant. I suppose that is why the barbarians finally overran Italy.''

Rachel looked at the thing Tilia laid on the bed beside her and felt sick.

"Oh, by the way," said Tilia as she went back to the cabinet and got out a basin and a pitcher, "I will let you keep the purse he gave you. He looked so happy when he left here, I think you deserve it.''

The Tartar could come and go as he pleased, thought Rachel, but she must stay. Even now, with over five hundred florins, more money than she had ever had in her life, she was alone. She knew how to travel; she had traveled for two years with Angelo. But she also knew the terrors and dangers of the road, dangers that ultimately had killed Angelo.

The best she could hope for was to endure this life for a year or two, get what she could from it, let it make her rich. When she did leave, she would have enough money to hire guards to accompany her. She would make up an elaborate story about her past. She would go where no one knew her, Sicily perhaps, and begin a new life as a wealthy woman, venturing into banking or trading for herself.

The hope of a wealthy new life—that was the raft that would bear her up when she felt she must drown in sorrow.

XXVII

DAOUD'S TIRED EYES BURNED. HE SHUT THEM, AS HE ENTERED HIS bedchamber, against the bright light coming through the white window glass. But, tired as he was, sleep did not come. Perhaps he was too tired.

He had missed the proper time for morning prayer, but he poured water into a basin and washed his hands and face, then turned toward the risen sun and humbly addressed God, first bowing, then kneeling, then striking his forehead on the carpet.

When I pray, I am at home no matter where I am.

After praying, he pushed open the iron casement with its diamond-shaped glass panels to let in air and then pulled the green velvet curtains across the window to shut out light.

He moved now in a cool dimness, as if underwater. He must rest, to be strong for the next battle.

Crossing the room to his sleeping mattress, which lay on the floor Egyptian-fashion, he stripped off his sweat-soaked tunic and threw it down. He unbuckled his belt and laid it carefully on the mattress. Then he kicked off his boots and dropped his hose and his loincloth. He splashed water over his body and felt cleaner and cooler.

There was another way to be home. He had been waiting for the first time he could feel he had triumphed. He knew all too well what that way could do to a man in the aftermath of defeat—sharpen his misery till he could ease the pain only by destroying himself.

But last night he had unmasked the Tartars before all the great ones of Orvieto, and he had survived a street encounter with bravos who intended to kill him. And so this morning he could allow himself this.

He had brought a cup of kaviyeh from Ugolini's room. He set it on the black marble table beside his sleeping mattress. Then from his traveling chest he took the dark brown leather pack that had accompanied him here from Lucera. He felt for the small packet and drew it out. Unwrapping the oily parchment, he looked at the small black cake, a square about half the length of his finger on a side. He drew his dagger out of its sheath—the dagger that would have been poor protection for him earlier if he had had to fight those Filippeschi men. Carefully he shaved peelings from the cake to the polished black marble. With the sharp edge of the dagger he chopped at the peelings until he had a coarse powder. He held the cup of cooling black liquid below the edge of the table and scraped the powder into it. He stirred the kaviyeh with the dagger's point.

Holding the cup up before him as if he were offering a toast, he spoke the Hashishiyya invocation: "In the name of the Voice comes Brightness."

He put the cup to his lips and sipped it slowly. The lukewarm kaviyeh masked the other taste, but he knew it would begin to work as soon as it reached his stomach. He peered into the bottom of the cup to make sure he had missed no precious grains, then set it down.

The magic horse that flies to paradise, so the Hashishiyya called it.

From Sheikh Saadi he had learned how to resist the power of drugs. From Imam Fayum, the Old Man of the Mountain, he learned how to use them, when he chose.

Naked, Daoud lay back on his mattress with a sigh that sounded like a roar in his ears. If the Filippeschi came upon him to kill him now, he would greet them with a smile and open arms. Lying on his back, his head resting on a feather-filled cushion, he let his senses expand to fill the world around him. His eyes traced the intricate red-on-red floral pattern of a damask wall hanging. The humming of a large black fly that had blundered in through the open casement and the closed curtains resounded in his ears like a dervish chorus chanting themselves into an ecstasy.

Odors swept in through the open window—clean mountain air with the scent of pines in it, but from nearby the swampy foul reek of every kind of filth produced by thousands of human beings living too close to one another. It had rained last night, but not enough to clean the streets, and the scavenging pigs—Daoud's heightened senses could hear and smell them, too—could not keep up with the garbage and sewage produced by the overcrowded people of Orvieto.

But he need not remain in Orvieto. He raised his head and lifted the chain that held the silver locket about his neck. Turning the little screw that fastened the lid of the locket, he let it fall open. It covered most of the palm of his right hand. Holding the crystal disk backed by silver close to his eyes, he saw his face reflected back at him from the convex surface. His image was broken up by a pattern etched into the transparency, a five-part webwork of interlocking angles and boxes, spirals and concentric circles. The pattern formed a maze too complex for the eye to grasp. He believed that the man who used a stylus, doubtless diamond-pointed, to cut the design into the crystal must have gone blind in the course of his work. No mosque bore a more intricate—or more beautiful—pattern on its walls.

His eyes, as they always did when he looked into the locket, tried to follow the pattern and became lost in it. As the drug extended its empire within him, it seemed that he could actually see his eyes, coalesced into a single eye, staring back at him from the net of lines and whorls that entrapped it.

The captive eye means that the locket now controls what I see.

He saw the face of Sophia Karaiannides. Her dark lips, luscious as red grapes, were parted slightly, showing even, white teeth. Her thick-lashed eyelids were half lowered over burning eyes. Her hair hung unbound in brunette waves on either side of her face. She had splashed water on her face, and the droplets gleamed on her cheeks and brow like jewels.

Daoud had no doubt that he was seeing her exactly as she was at this moment, somewhere else in the cardinal's mansion. The locket had that property.

But I do not want to see Sophia. I want Blossoming Reed.

Then Sophia spoke to him. "Oh, David, why will you not come to my bed?"

Her voice was rich as velvet. His muscles tensed with a sudden hunger, a long-felt need that Francesca, the woman he bedded with now and then at Tilia Caballo's, could never satisfy. Sophia, he realized, could give him what he wanted, what he missed so terribly since leaving home.

No! Let me see Blossoming Reed.

He shut his eyes, and Sophia was still looking at him. The locket and the drug together could show a man things he did not want to see, make him feel things he did not want to feel. Things that were inside him that he did not want to know.

The knowledge you run from is the most precious of all, Saadi
had said.

*I know I want Sophia. I do not hide that from myself. But I cannot
have her. Let me therefore see my wife, Blossoming Reed, she who
gave me this locket.*

Sophia's image faded now, and he saw again the crystal and its
pattern that caught his soul like a fish in its toils. Gradually the
pattern became the face of Blossoming Reed. Sparks flashed from
her slanting eyes, painted with black rings of kohl. Her wide mouth
was a downturned crescent of scorn. The nostrils of her hawklike
nose flared proudly. There was a message in her face. What did
she know, and what was she trying to tell him?

Blossoming Reed, daughter of Baibars and a Canaanite wife Baibars had stolen from the crusader stronghold in Sidon. It was ru-
mored that Blossoming Reed's mother practiced a kind of sorcery
that was ancient even when the Hebrews were in bondage in Egypt.
But would Baibars, the mightiest defender of the faith since Saladin,
allow devil-worship in his own house? Daoud could not believe it.

And yet, what was this locket if not the work of some evil magician? He would not have touched the thing, much less worn it,
had it not come from Blossoming Reed, whom he loved.

Blossoming Reed, betrothed to him at twelve, married to him at
fourteen, whose breasts were like oranges and whose nails flayed
his back in their lovemaking. Blossoming Reed, Baibars's gift of
honor to him, seal and symbol of eternal friendship between Baibars al-Bunduqdari and Daoud ibn Abdullah.

Blossoming Reed, who now spoke to him in anger out of the
magic of hashish and the locket.

Go back to the Well, Daoud!

Back to the Well?

To the Well of Goliath?

He saw again the plain of tamarisk, thorn bush, and grass, and
the long black line of charging Tartars. Eagerly Daoud leaned forward in the saddle. Tightly he gripped his bow.

Now, devils, now you will pay for Baghdad!

He had relived that day, the greatest battle of his life, hundreds
of times in thoughtful moments, in dreams, in hashish visions.
What he saw now were moments that seemed to leap at him out of
the darkness.

* * *

Screaming a war cry and brandishing a scimitar, a Tartar galloped at him. They were in open ground. Daoud circled away, sheathing his saif and pulling his bow from its case. The Tartar chased him, guiding his horse with his knees and firing arrow after arrow at Daoud. But he was in too much of a hurry. He was not aiming carefully, and all the arrows whistled over Daoud's head.

The muscles of the black Yemenite stallion bunched and stretched under Daoud as its hooves thundered over the plain. He stood in the saddle. He turned and took aim along the shaft of his arrow at the center of the Tartar's chest. The arrow went low, to Daoud's annoyance, and struck the Tartar in the side of the stomach. But he must have been wearing light leather armor, for the arrow with its steel point went deep into him. The Tartar gave a short cry and dropped his bow, then fell, like a stone, from the saddle into the sand.

Daoud wheeled his Yemenite about, then jerked the horse to a stop and jumped from the saddle with his saif out. The Tartar had somehow risen to all fours, but was vomiting blood into the sand. Daoud kicked him with his red-booted foot and rolled him over on his back.

Holding his saif high, he looked into the face of Nicetas, contorted with pain and fear.

"Oh, God!" he whispered. "Oh, God, no!"

He stood paralyzed. Their eyes met.

Nicetas said, "You have to."

"God be merciful to me," Daoud said, and brought the saif down.

XXVIII

LORENZO'S EYES ACHED AS HE STARED THROUGH A PEEPHOLE IN the doorway of a storeroom into the common room of the inn called the Angel. Alternating his left and right eye at intervals, he stared at a bench by the opposite wall, where a hooded figure sat alone, holding a cup of wine in his lap. As Lorenzo had instructed him, the tavern keeper had put a lighted candle in a sconce near where Sordello was sitting, so that Lorenzo could watch his quarry.

The candle beside Sordello was one of only four in the common room—just light enough for the innkeeper to be certain he was paid in honest coin while making it hard for his patrons to see the color of his wine. It was early evening, and there were only about six men and women in the room. All of them except Sordello sat on benches at the one long table near the wine barrel. Sordello, leaning against the rough-hewn wooden wall, had to set his cup beside him.

The mercenary's square hand lifted the painted pottery cup into the shadow of his hood. Lorenzo knew Sordello was under the tightly drawn hood only because he had followed him diligently through the tangle of Orvieto's streets from the house where a dozen of the brigosi Lorenzo had recruited were quartered.

Daoud's secret army was growing. The evening after the contessa's reception Lorenzo had sealed a bargain with Marco di Filippeschi, who was ready to help Daoud against the alliance if it meant striking a blow against the Monaldeschi.

Before any plans were made, though, there remained the question of Sordello.

A stout woman in a black gown came into the common room of the Angel and went straight to the hooded man. The lower part of her face was covered by a black scarf. Anyone watching the hooded Sordello and the veiled lady would think theirs was just everyday wickedness—an adulterous couple meeting for an assignation. She sat beside him on the bench. Their heads drew together, and Lorenzo, behind a door across the room, was too far away to hear.

Lorenzo heard a scratching behind him. He turned, but it was too dark even to see movement.

Rats, he thought. *This work continually brings a man into the company of rats. Four-legged rats and men like Sordello.* He put his eye to the peephole again, just in time to see a slip of paper disappear into the woman's deep sleeve. Whoever Sordello was reporting to, he was putting it in writing. Interesting that the man *could* write. That put him a cut above the average bravo, in education, at least.

The innkeeper came over to offer the woman wine, but she waved him away without looking at him. She stood up, brushing the seat of her gown fastidiously, like one who was used to sitting in cleaner surroundings. Without a gesture or a handclasp she left Sordello as quickly as she had come. Nothing loverlike about those two.

Lorenzo decided to follow the woman, and left by the bolthole the tavern keeper had shown him. He doubted that the old bravo would do anything other than sit there and get drunk.

He had to run through the alley beside the inn to catch a glimpse of her going around a corner. She was hard to see. The darkness of night was made deeper by the jutting upper stories of the houses, and she was wearing black.

He kept running, his footfalls muffled by the mushy layers of moldering refuse that paved the streets. A woman going through the byways of the poorest part of town after dark was taking a great chance with her purse and her honor. She was either well paid or very dedicated.

Lorenzo, whispering breathless curses, twice had almost lost her in the maze before she emerged onto a wider street, the Via di San Remo. There, lights from windows made her easier to follow. Now he was quite sure where she was going, and was not at all surprised when she hurried up the stairs leading to the front door of the Palazzo Monaldeschi. The door opened. There was a blaze of torchlight, and she pulled down her scarf to identify herself. Even from across the street Lorenzo knew her.

Ana, the woman who interpreted for the Tartars.

Sophia entered Cardinal Ugolini's cabinet holding a letter written by Simon de Gobignon. It had been pressed into her hand by the French count's young scudiero when she was out walking. She had read it over and over again before bringing it to David.

He was alone in the room. As he looked up from his seat on a pile of cushions on the floor, she caught her breath. In that white light coming through the translucent glass panes, David's grayish eyes took on an opalescence.

The cardinal's cabinet on the top floor was the best-lit chamber in the mansion. When Ugolini was not using the room, David often came here to study, write, and meditate. And when neither David nor Ugolini was there, Sophia sometimes came to draw and paint.

She felt as if David were a magician, and that his eyes had cast a spell on her. In Ugolini's cabinet it was easy to think of magic. She had always associated magic with darkened chambers and cellars, but Ugolini practiced his magic at the top of his mansion, in a room with many windows.

"The long-awaited answer from Simon has come," Sophia said, tossing the opened scroll down before David.

David spread Simon's letter on his lap and read it, while Sophia looked around the room. On a table near a window lay that painted skull Ugolini kept toying with. On one wall were two maps of the heavens. Sophia recognized the constellations in one of them, but the other was utterly strange. One arrangement of stars in the second map seemed to take the form of a Latin cross. She studied with interest the paintings on scrolls nailed to the walls, of plants and animals so odd-looking that she thought they might be an artist's inventions. One was a bird without wings, another a spotted animal that looked like a deer but had an enormously elongated neck. It might be pleasant to try painting such creatures herself.

As David's eyes ran over Simon's letter, his lips curled in a faint smile. Was it a smile of contempt for Simon's passionate outpouring, which she had, in her delight with it, all but memorized?

> Lady, I cry you mercy. You know it not, but your gentle eyes are more puissant than a mighty host. From those eyes have flown such bolts as wound but do not kill, and they have pierced my heart. I will bleed forever within my breast where none can see, and all will wonder at my pallor and my weakness that have no outward cause.
>
> The physick for any wound or illness, sages tell us, must be like that which caused the hurt. Thus only you, who have delivered this wound, can cure it. Let me come to you, I beg, under cover of night. Let me but adore you in secrecy for a moment, and my strength will return. . . .

"He is almost as good as an Arab poet," David said mockingly as he handed her back the letter. Did it bother him, she wondered, that Simon wrote words of love to her? David, she saw, was working on a letter of his own on a tiny, thin scrap of vellum on a writing board which he now laid over his knees. As if to show her that Simon's letter was of no moment to him, he added to his own, writing rapidly with a quill dipped in an inkpot—but from right to left.

"You write backwards?" she said, seating herself beside him on the floor to look at his work.

"No, Christians do," he said with a faint smile. He covered what he was writing with his hand, but she caught a glimpse of lines that wavered and curled like tiny black snakes.

"Why bother to cover it? Do you really imagine that I could read that?" Lightly she touched the hand that covered the writing, noticing the fine yellow hairs on its back.

"I have to keep up the habit of secrecy." He gave her one of his rare full smiles, and she wanted to reach out and hold his face between her hands. They were so close, she thought, sitting side by side here on the floor. And alone. They had but to stretch out on this thick Arabian carpet and wrap their arms around each other. But, of course, Ugolini or one of his servants might come in at any moment. Her longing for David was a constant ache. She had not thought of Manfred, save as a figure in the background of their lives, in weeks. And as long as she did not have to meet with Simon, she was fully Sophia Karaiannides, and not troubled by the yearning of Sophia Orfali for the young French count.

If only David did not insist on keeping her at a distance.

"Do you still want me to let Simon de Gobignon visit me secretly?" she asked.

There was a momentary silence between them.

Then, "Have I told you of any change in plans?" he said gruffly. He looked down at his scrap of parchment with the tiny crawling lines.

"What shall I let him do when we are together?" she asked quietly.

I know David is jealous, and I am goading him. I want to hear his jealousy.

He stood up abruptly and put his writing board on a table. He walked to an open window and stood looking out, rolling his thin parchment tightly between his fingers.

She hated this conversation. It turned him into a panderer and her into a whore. And she sensed that he hated it as much as she did.

"Do what you think is necessary," he said coldly.

"Necessary to what?" she demanded through gritted teeth.

He turned toward her and held up a finger. "To win his trust." He held up a second finger. "To hear and remember anything he may let slip." He held up a third finger. "Most important, to tell him things."

"Tell him what?"

"Tell him that Cardinal Ugolini has persuaded Fra Tomasso d'Aquino to oppose the alliance of Christians and Tartars."

"And if Simon believes you have won over Fra Tomasso, what will that accomplish?"

"The unbelievers are already desperate to repair the damage I have done to the reputation of the Tartars," David said. "If they

think they have lost Fra Tomasso, they may be provoked to do
exactly the wrong thing.''

"What would that be?'' Sophia had heard that Muslims were
devious. She certainly could not follow Daoud's mind in this.

"Not knowing Fra Tomasso is actually trying to remain neutral,
they will use every means they have to try to win him back, as they
think, to their side. I am hoping they will try to bring Cardinal de
Verceuil's influence to bear. If de Verceuil goes to Fra Tomasso—
or, even better, to Fra Tomasso's superiors—he may well drive the
learned friar over to our side.''

"What if you are wrong? What if de Verceuil and the other
Franks do persuade Fra Tomasso to support the alliance? Would it
not be better to leave him where he is, neutral?''

Daoud shook his head. "At least this way we are trying to control
what happens.''

She smiled. "I thought you Muslims believed in leaving things
up to fate.''

"The efforts of men are part of the workings of fate.''

She would probably never understand his Muslim way of thinking. Perhaps he would not accept her love because he saw her as
an unbeliever. It made her angry to think he might hold himself
aloof from her because of her religion, and he not even a Muslim
born.

"The Turks killed your parents,'' she said. "How can you be a
Muslim?'' It was something she had never understood and had
wanted to know ever since she learned what he was, but she asked
it now to hurt him.

He gave her that silent, burning stare, and she began to wonder,
with a rippling of fear in the pit of her stomach, if she was in danger.

"That was my fate,'' he said. "I had to lose my mother and
father to find God.''

Before she could catch herself, she started to laugh with a kind
of wildness, a touch of hysteria. She had been angry at him and
had goaded him and feared his striking back, and instead he made
a statement that was utterly absurd.

*I lost my mother and father, and I gained nothing from it. I
became nothing, neither daughter, nor wife, nor mother.*

At her laughter, he took a step backward, as if she had struck
him, and his tan face reddened. Now she felt terror. This time she
had surely gone too far.

"Forgive me. Your answer surprised me. It sounds so strange for a man of your profession to talk of finding God."

"What profession?"

"Well, you are a warrior and a spy, not a holy man."

"We do not need to speak of this." He turned away from her to stare out the window. She looked past him at red-tiled rooftops. A flock of pigeons circled in the distance.

"No," she said. "And as an unbeliever I suppose I would not understand."

Surprisingly he approached her and looked down with eyes that were serious and free of anger. "If you ever, in sincerity, want to know about Islam, come and ask me, and as best I can I will answer your questions. But do not speak foolishness. And do not laugh."

She thought she understood a bit better. The Muslims had captured his body, but then in his enslavement he had freely given his soul to their religion. He did not serve the Turks. He served the God they called Allah. How this had come about she could not imagine. But she knew a little better why his sultan had entrusted him with this undertaking. He was perfect for it.

"I must go," he said, as if eager not to talk anymore.

"To deliver your message?" She gestured toward the clenched fist that held the fragile parchment. "Is there truly someone in Orvieto who can read it?"

He smiled again. Oh, that smile! It so easily overcame her anger and fear.

"There is no harm in my telling you. It goes to my sultan, by carrier pigeon and ship." He must be proud, she thought, of his swift and secret courier system.

"And do you get messages back in the same way?"

"It takes over a month each way, so I have received but one message from the sultan since coming to Italy."

"Does the cardinal keep the pigeons?"

He had taken a tiny leather capsule out of his belt purse and was inserting the message into it now. "Madama Tilia keeps the pigeons."

"Then are you going to her house?" Sophia remembered with a feeling of guilt that she had not thought of Rachel in some time. "Please, David, will you see how Rachel is while you are there?"

David looked at her quickly and glanced away. She felt a coldness in her chest.

"What has happened to her?" she demanded. She seized David's arm, lest he turn away from her.

He did not try to pull free. "She is well. She is already wealthy, in fact." His eyes did not meet hers at all now.

"Oh, my God! A man has had her!" She let go of David and turned her back on him.

There was another silence while fury churned in Sophia. She wanted to turn on David, to scratch his face with her nails. She wanted to tear her clothing in anguish, in mourning for Rachel's lost innocence. She hated herself for her part in the child's degradation.

"Sophia." David's voice came from behind her, soft, a little uncertain. "Were you so much older than Rachel when you—became a woman?"

Wrath overpowered her other feelings, and she turned on him. "Do you think *that* is what makes a girl into a woman? And you complain about speaking foolishness?"

"How old, Sophia?" His voice was more confident now, as if her anger had put him on firmer ground.

She thought of Alexis, the boy she had loved, and the long afternoons they had spent together hidden under an old broken arch covered with vines and lapped by waves on the Aegean side of Constantinople.

She shook her head. "Yes, I was her age. But I was in love. Doing it for money or for my city came later, when I was alone in the world and older."

There was appeal in his look. "But you know what it is to be alone and in need. Just as you freely chose to serve the Emperor of Constantinople with your body, so Rachel freely chose to sell her virginity for a fortune in gold."

His obtuseness made her more angry than ever. "You know nothing about freedom or women. Rachel was no more free to keep her virginity than you were free to remain a Christian after the Turks captured you. As for me, at least I know enough to hate the murderers of my parents."

His fingers dug into her shoulders until they hurt and the fire in his eyes terrified her. But she held her face frozen, refusing to show fear or pain.

"Say no more," he whispered in a strangled voice. "Not another word."

Saint Simon, protect me.

Simon.

She could see the struggle in David's face and body. She had enraged him to the point where he wanted to hurt her. But he was not going to let himself do it. She thought she must have taken a hundred breaths before he released his grip on her shoulders, pushing her away a little.

Again she wondered what he had been through that would give him such iron self-control. She stood looking at him, breathing heavily in the aftermath of her terror.

I am a fool to despise anything as powerful as what he has.

He raked her with his eyes, then turned toward the door.

"Do not bother to find out about Rachel for me," she said. "I will go myself."

He stopped, and the fury in his face made her brace herself again for an attack.

"You cannot go. You cannot be seen going into Tilia's."

"Do you think I have served great men for years without learning how to move about a city unnoticed?"

"Go, then." His normally fair face was scarlet with rage. "And learn from Rachel's own lips what the Tartar did to her."

For a moment she seemed to go blind and deaf. She felt hot and cold at once. Her body had reacted to the meaning of his words before her brain understood them.

"*Tartar!* The man was a Tartar? You let a Tartar have her?" Sophia seized the first object near her hand and threw it at him. She saw as it struck him that it was the painted skull. It hit his chest with a thump, and he took a step backward.

"You filthy bastard!" she screamed. "Pig of a Turk!"

Expressionless, he turned without another word and left her, closing the door of Ugolini's cabinet behind him.

She sank weeping to the floor.

Rachel, Rachel, how could they do this to you? With a Tartar. Oh, no!

She sat there until her tears stopped and her thoughts began to make some sense. The skull, lying on its side, seemed to look back at her.

Thank you, David. You have made my decision for me. Simon de Gobignon shall have me.

XXIX

THIS WAS A FEARSOME PLACE, THOUGHT DAOUD AS HE GAZED around the underground chamber hewn out of the yellow tufa on which the building stood. Lit with torches, its vault was festooned with ropes and chains, one wall lined with whips, rods, and scourges hanging from hooks, pokers and branding irons heating in smoking braziers, a rack in one corner, a ring of wood and iron six feet in diameter suspended in the center of the room, on which a man could be spread-eagled. A veritable bazaar of torture instruments. Its door was of solid oak reinforced with criss-crossed strips of iron, designed to dash any hope of escape.

Daoud sat in a thronelike chair painted black—Tilia said it had once belonged to a pope—on a raised platform against a wall. If the damned chair had a few cushions in it, it might almost be comfortable. This place, Tilia had told him, was for patrons of hers who liked to torture—or be tortured.

It was perfect for his purpose. But could he himself be as perfect as the room? This was a hard and wily man he had to deal with tonight. It would be difficult to dominate him.

Beside Daoud, a preparation of wine, hashish, and the distilled juice of the Anatolian poppy simmered in a pot held on a metal tripod over a candle flame. He sniffed the faint steam that rose from the warm potion. He warned himself to do no more sniffing, or he would be unable to conduct the night's proceedings with a clear head. He glanced down at one broad arm of the throne, where a small brass bowl lay. In the dish rested a steel needle as long as a forefinger, its tip covered with a black paste.

A nervous anticipation tingled in the pit of his stomach, but he held himself very still.

Daoud heard Lorenzo's voice, and a moment later the oak-and-iron door swung open. A man stumbled through, his head covered with a black hood, his hands tied behind him, his ankles chained close together with hobble-gyves. Two of Tilia's mute black slaves held his arms. Behind him walked Lorenzo, a broad-bladed dagger held at waist level.

Daoud sat straighter in the throne, resting his hands on the arms. The door boomed shut, and at Lorenzo's command the slaves untied the prisoner's wrists and pulled the hood off his head.

Sordello stood before Daoud, blinking and staring angrily around him. Daoud watched, pleased, as the sight of the irons and chains and scourges bore in on Sordello and the anger on the bravo's face changed to alarm.

"Why have you done this to me? What the devil is this place?"

An appropriate question, Daoud thought. "You are in hell," he said.

Sordello squinted at Daoud. "And who are you supposed to be, Messer David, the Prince of Darkness? Is this some sort of miracle play?"

The man's defiance dismayed Daoud. He had hoped that the mere sight of the chamber would set Sordello to babbling and begging. He needed to be frightened more.

"Have them chain him to the ring, Lorenzo."

Sordello aimed a kick at one of the slaves following Lorenzo's orders. The African gave Sordello's arm a quick twist and got a howl of pain out of him. Soon the aging bravo, arms stretched out, legs spread apart, was suspended upright in the great hoop. The ring of iron hung from the ceiling on a single chain wrapped around a huge beam, allowing it to rotate slowly. Daoud imagined how helpless Sordello must feel hanging there.

Lorenzo took hold of the ring and gave it a spin. Face and back, face and back, face and back, Sordello whirled before Daoud. His eyes bulged.

"Figlii di cagne!" he shouted.

Still more angry than frightened. But perhaps he is just good at concealing his fear.

Daoud made a small hand gesture, and Lorenzo stopped the spin of the ring so that Sordello was facing Daoud.

Daoud studied Sordello, looking for the subtle signs that would reveal his true feelings. His eyes gleamed like a caged hyena's, full of hatred for Daoud.

Lorenzo had kept Sordello locked in a pitch-black cubicle in Cardinal Ugolini's mansion for a day and a night before bringing him here. Daoud studied the man. It was obvious from his pallor, his red-rimmed eyelids, and his sagging mouth that Sordello had lain awake much of the time in the darkness. Daoud could see the fear, too, in the clenching and unclenching of Sordello's jaw muscles.

Daoud flicked a finger at Lorenzo. "Read the love song you found on this trovatore when you seized him."

Lorenzo unfolded a square scrap of parchment and read:

> Your Magnificence:
> On Thursday last Donna Sophia left the Cardinal's mansion alone, on foot and heavily veiled. As she clearly did not want to be seen, your servant thought much was to be gained by following her, and so did. I regret to say she spent the afternoon wandering in the craftsmen's market, shopping for gloves, purses, and other adornments. Before Nones she went to the Church of Sant' Andrea, where she prayed a while, then went to Confession. Your servant attempted to approach close enough to overhear, but was unable to do so without being seen.

Lorenzo looked up and shook his head. "What a furfante you are! Trying to eavesdrop on penitents." He went on with the reading.

> David of Trebizond has spent his days riding about Orvieto, meeting with the fattori of various trading houses that deal in silks and spices. Your servant adds a list below. The cardinal sleeps most of the day and works through the night behind the locked door of his cabinet on the top floor of the palazzo. Sometimes he mounts to the roof and studies the stars with the aid of magical instruments. Of the servant Giancarlo I am unable to make report, having not seen him all this week.

Lorenzo laughed. "That is the only true statement in this list of lies. You did not see me all week because I have been constantly at *your* back."

Sordello spat at Lorenzo's feet. "Ladruncolo! Sneak!" At this Lorenzo and Daoud broke into laughter, while Sordello glared at them helplessly. The hoop on which he was splayed turned slowly one way and then back the other.

"You are indignant at being spied upon?" Lorenzo chuckled. "Then imagine how we feel. And what is worse, you do not even tell the truth about us."

"I piss in your teeth," Sordello snarled.

"For instance, what you write about Madonna Sophia," Lorenzo went on, unperturbed. "You lost her a mere three streets from the cardinal's mansion. She knew you were following her and took pains to rid herself of your unwanted attentions. But you could not admit to your master what a buffone you are, so you made up all that about her buying gloves in the bazaar and going to church.''

Actually, Daoud thought, that was the afternoon Sophia had come here, to Tilia's house, to see Rachel, and it would have been disastrous if Sordello had followed her. They would then have had to kill him, which would have been unfortunate, since this way of handling him was so much better.

Of course, they might still have to kill him. He already knew enough about them to send them all to the stake if he ever spoke out. He must be brought under control, to serve their purposes, or he must quietly disappear.

"So, you not only spy on us, but you lie about us," said Daoud. "And to whom do you send these lies? When the Bulgarian woman Ana takes your weekly reports back to the Palazzo Monaldeschi, to whom does she deliver them? De Verceuil? De Gobignon?"

"Go peddle your silks and spices, Messer David." The man was so ill-tempered he had not the sense to try to protect himself by hiding his anger and defiance.

Daoud gritted his teeth in frustration. Sordello was not breaking quickly enough.

Daoud sent Lorenzo a signal with two fingers. Lorenzo sprang at Sordello with his blade, a dagger so big it was almost a short sword, and slashed at his tunic, belt, and hose. The blacks grinned. Sordello roared his protests. A last flick of the blade cut away his grimy loincloth. In a moment Sordello hung naked on the ring, his shredded clothes hanging from his ankles or lying on the flagstone floor. His body was wiry and muscular, with only a small paunch at the waist. The flickering torchlight picked out the shadows of scars crossing his chest and belly. Daoud stared with curiosity and faint distaste at the uncircumcised penis peeping from its thicket of grizzled hair.

Daoud put his fingertips together and casually crossed his legs, lounging back in the throne, letting the contrast between his position and Sordello's sink in. He prayed that the man might succumb. His soul must be made of sand; how could it be otherwise?

The ring slowly rotated. Sordello twisted his head to look over his shoulder at Daoud.

"If you kill me, he will know." There was the faintest quiver in his voice.

Daoud chose not to ask the obvious question—who "he" was—but said, keeping his voice soft and kindly, "What will he learn from your death, Sordello?"

Before Sordello could answer, Lorenzo burst out, "We are not going to kill him for a long while, are we, Messer David? You promised me I could have some sport."

"Quiet, Giancarlo," said Daoud, narrowing his eyes. "You shall have your sport."

"Why torture me? Why kill me?" There was a plea in Sordello's voice now. "I have told nothing that could hurt you."

"You have told *us* nothing, Sordello." Daoud stood up. The platform on which the throne chair stood gave him impressive height, and the torches high in the wall behind him threw his shadow across the room.

"I admire your fidelity to your master, whoever he is," Daoud said with a smile. "What a pity he will never know about it. As I told you, this is hell, and you are dead already. You will just vanish, like a bit of rubbish washed out of the city by the rain. Your master will probably think you deserted him, as your sort of wandering ladrone so often does."

"I am not a highwayman!" Sordello's cry echoed against the stone vault. "I am a man of honor. I am an educated man, a trovatore."

"You are feccia!" Lorenzo shouted, and slapped Sordello's face hard.

"For that I will one day slice open your guts," Sordello growled.

Exasperated, Daoud saw that hurting Sordello only made him angrier. If they hurt him enough, certainly, they would have him begging for mercy, but by then they might have injured him so badly he would be of no use to them.

"Let him be, Giancarlo," Daoud snapped.

"I saved your life," Sordello said to Daoud. "I killed a man for you. Is this how you repay me—letting this pig strip me and beat me?" His narrowed eyes gave a hint of slyness. "I could be worth ten of this Neapolitan mezzano to you."

"You dare call me a pimp!" Lorenzo lunged at Sordello again, this time aiming the point of the huge dagger at his belly. Sordello twisted his body in the chains and gave a cry of fright.

"Giancarlo!" Daoud shouted sternly. "Back!"

Sordello hung rigid in his chains. Sweat ran down his face. His whole body was covered with sweat, glistening in the torchlight, and Daoud suspected he would be cold to the touch. Sordello's eyes rolled from Lorenzo, who stood frozen with the dagger outstretched, to Daoud and back again. The two blacks stood behind Lorenzo, smiling broadly.

"You are worth nothing to me at the moment, Sordello, because you refuse even to give me the one harmless piece of information I ask for. You will not tell me who set you to spy on me. So I might as well give you to Giancarlo here for his amusement." He held a hand out to Lorenzo, as if giving him leave to proceed.

"It is Simon de Gobignon!" Sordello cried. "It is to him my messages go."

Daoud's heart leapt with exultation, and he allowed himself a satisfied little sigh. A flicker of a finger told Lorenzo to lower his knife. Sordello had made the first surrender, on which all further success with him depended.

But—de Gobignon. That was a surprise. Daoud had been sure it would be Cardinal de Verceuil who would try to place a spy in his camp. A Frankish knight like de Gobignon would prefer the frontal attack, the pitched battle, to trickery. That was why the Franks were gradually losing their grip on the land they called Outremer. The French cardinal was another story. Daoud had seen in him a combination of pride, ambition, and lack of scruple that would use any means to defeat an enemy.

How to find out the truth? He ground his teeth.

"You are lying," Daoud said firmly. "It is Cardinal de Verceuil you serve. Giancarlo—" Daoud gestured, and Lorenzo went over to the brazier and slowly drew out an iron. The tip of it glowed red in the dim light of the chamber. His teeth flashing white under his thick mustache, Lorenzo advanced on Sordello.

"No! It is the truth!" Sordello shrieked, the chain that suspended the hoop rattling as he tried to pull himself away from Lorenzo and the smoking metal rod he held. As Lorenzo slowly approached, Sordello babbled out a tale of having been sent to Venice by Charles d'Anjou, brother of the King of France, to recruit and command archers for Count Simon. He had gotten into a brawl and wounded an Armenian prince who had come to Venice with the Tartars, and Simon had sent him away.

"I cannot serve Count Simon openly because the Armenians still want my blood," Sordello explained. "So he set me to spy on you instead."

The frantic haste with which Sordello spilled out his story gave it the sound of truth. This was going much better. Daoud's tense jaw muscles were relaxing.

Daoud picked up the bowl with the needle in it, gestured Lorenzo back, and slowly strolled across the chamber to Sordello. He gave the bowl to Lorenzo to hold, and drew closer until his face was only a hand's width from Sordello's, until he could smell the inner rot on the man's breath. Sordello's eyes rolled sideways, trying to watch the needle in the bowl Lorenzo was holding.

"What does de Gobignon say of me?" Daoud whispered. "What does he think I am?"

"He thinks you are a foreigner brought here by Ugolini to thwart the French plans for a crusade," Sordello gasped. "He says Ugolini is an agent of the Hohenstaufen king. He thinks Giancarlo is gathering a band of men to murder the Tartars. Please, for the love of God, do not hurt me, Messere." His eyes would fall out of his head if he stared any harder at the needle.

"Give me a candle, Giancarlo," said Daoud. He reached out without looking, and Lorenzo pressed the lighted candle into his hand. Taking a step back, he held the flame before Sordello's sweating face. His lips trembling, Sordello turned his head away.

"Look at the flame, Sordello," said Daoud softly. "Just look at the flame and listen to me. Look at the flame, and I will tell you what I really am." Daoud passed the candle back and forth before Sordello's face, murmuring reassurance. Sordello's eyes followed the candle.

He wondered if this would work. It seemed too much like magic. He had seen it done by Hashishiyya imams, but he had never done it himself.

"I am a sorcerer, Sordello, a mighty wizard. I can pass through any obstacle. I can see what people are doing thousands of leagues away. I can bring the dead back to life. I told you that you are a dead man, Sordello. You are truly dead, but you have nothing to fear, because my power can bring you back to life."

The bravo hung lax in the chains, his half-shut eyes still moving from right to left, following the candle flame. His knees had buckled and his belly sagged.

Daoud handed the candle to Lorenzo and beckoned to one of the Africans, who took the simmering pot of drugged wine from the tripod, holding it by a wooden handle, and gave it to Daoud.

"Where are you, Sordello?"

"I am in hell."

"And what are you?"

"A dead man."

"And I?"

"A mighty wizard."

"Very good. Now drink this." Daoud felt the lip of the pot to make sure it was not too hot, then brought it to Sordello's mouth. Obediently Sordello lifted his chin and opened his lips, allowing Daoud to pour the warm wine into his mouth, and then swallowed. Daoud poured more into him and then gave the pot back to Tilia's servant.

"Now you will truly know my power, Sordello. Prepare yourself for the most wonderful night of your life. You will make a journey from hell to heaven. Close your eyes and raise your head." Lorenzo held out the brass bowl with the needle, and Daoud took the needle, holding it firmly with his thumb and first two fingers. Gesturing to Lorenzo to bring the candle close to Sordello's throat, he searched out a vein just where the neck met the shoulder.

"You can feel nothing. You can feel no pain at all."

Daoud took a deep breath and prayed to God to guide his hand. He jabbed the needle into Sordello's neck. The bravo remained utterly motionless, and Daoud heard Lorenzo gasp in amazement. Daoud left the needle stuck in the pale, pink flesh. He watched Sordello closely and put his palm before his lax mouth. He could feel Sordello's breath on his palm, slow and steady, the breath of a sleeping man. After a time the craggy block of a head fell forward, and the body hung limp in the chains.

So far, all was working as he had hoped. But the man was stronger than he had thought. He had been harder to break. There was always the danger that somewhere deep in his soul a part would remain free. Daoud had heard of such things happening, of slaves of the Old Man of the Mountain who suddenly rebelled. The methods of the Hashishiyya were not perfect.

He would have to chance it. It was in God's hands now.

"Are you sure he is not dead?" Lorenzo said in a low, awed voice.

"Look for yourself. He breathes. His heart beats."

Lorenzo shook his head. "What is that stuff?"

Daoud pointed to the two Africans, who stood calmly by, awaiting orders. "*They* know. In the jungle below the great desert, where it is very hot and wet, a body can rot in hours. Tiny men, less than half our size, live there, and they hunt large animals for their meat.

They smear this stuff on their darts. It comes from a mushroom that grows in their forest. The animal struck is paralyzed and unconscious, but it lives. They have time to carry it back to their village, which may take days, and then they can slaughter it and butcher it.''

''But what a blessing this could be for the wounded and the sick,'' said Lorenzo. ''Why does the world not know of it?''

Daoud shrugged. ''The tiny men kill those who venture into their forests. What little is brought back by Arab traders is kept as a precious secret. Only sultans may permit its use.'' He turned to the two blacks. ''Take him upstairs now.''

XXX

WELL SATISFIED WITH WHAT TILIA HAD ACCOMPLISHED, DAOUD gazed about at the frescoed moons, stars, and suns scattered across the dark blue walls of the apartment. A cool night breeze blew through the rooms from windows hidden by screens and gauzy curtains. In the large central chamber an oval pool gave off a scent of roses. Hangings of violet, silver, and azure turned the rooms into a maze that baffled the eye.

Everywhere Daoud looked he saw beds and divans and cushions. The floors were covered with soft rugs and the tables laden with pitchers of wine and plates of peaches, grapes, and melon slices.

In a corner of a smaller room, its walls covered with maroon and black drapes, the flame of a large candle warmed a solution of wine and hashish in a green earthenware bowl. A single silver cup stood beside the candle.

''All this for one lousy traditore?'' said Lorenzo.

''After he has experienced what I have prepared for him tonight, he will no longer be a traitor,'' said Daoud. ''His very soul will be mine, and that will be worth—all this.''

He watched the two silent black men lug in the naked body of

Sordello, and he pointed to a forest-green divan beside the pool. Gently they laid Sordello there.

Tilia Caballo appeared from behind a curtain. At a gesture from her, the two black men bowed to Daoud and left.

Three women followed Tilia into the room.

"Goddesses!" whispered Lorenzo, staring.

Daoud, who had chosen them, agreed. Two of them, Tilia had told him, were sisters whose specialty was working together with one man. They had hair the color of honey, olive skin, and Grecian profiles. Each had a gold fillet in her hair and wore a short tunic of pure white linen. Each tunic left one delicate shoulder and one perfect breast exposed. On Orenetta the uncovered side was the right, and on Caterina the left.

The third woman was tall, taller than most men, and her bare shoulders were broad. But her body, tightly wrapped in a gown of black silk that stopped just above her breasts, was magnificently female. Her long unbound hair was lustrous and black as her gown, her skin pale as snow. A gold collar that appeared to be woven of spiral strands encircled her neck. Maiga, Tilia said, was from Hibernia, an island west of Britain, and she spoke no Italian and did not need to.

Daoud felt a fluttering in his chest as the sight of the three women, and the scent of the simmering wine brought back memories of his own initiation at the hands of the Hashishiyya.

It had been the Tartars, indirectly, who had made it possible for him to take that training. They had besieged and destroyed Alamut, the great Persian fortress of the Sheikh al-Jebal, the Old Man of the Mountain, and kicked him to death after he surrendered. The Old Man's surviving followers scattered across the lands of Islam. It was inevitable that some of the highest adepts came for protection to Sultan Qutuz of El Kahira.

After they were settled, Baibars had gone to them with the proposal that certain Mameluke emirs be initiated into the secrets of the sect. Fayum al-Burz, the new Sheikh al-Jebal, saw an opportunity to infiltrate the highest levels of the Mamelukes and was only too pleased to comply.

And so it had come about that Daoud, already trained by Saadi to resist the power of hashish, passed through the gates of paradise and learned, in time, how to administer the same experience to others.

Of course, Sordello, after he went through this, would be no adept. He would learn no secrets. He would be the lowest of the low—a tool, like the fedawi, the devoted killers who were the source of the Sheikh al-Jebal's power.

"This is a lucky man," said Tilia, her big mouth splitting her face in a lascivious grin. "He will experience delights here tonight that many of my most distinguished patrons have never enjoyed. His pleasures will be limited only by what his body can endure."

She walked over to Sordello, asleep on the divan, and ran caressing fingers down his bare chest and belly. "And he looks to be a strong man for his age. These scars. Quite the veteran bravo, eh?"

Though the room seemed cool to Daoud, sweat ran over Tilia's bare bosom down into the deep square collar of her purple gown. Her deadly pectoral cross lay heavily against the purple satin between her breasts. She might need that cross tonight, Daoud thought, if anything went wrong with Sordello.

"I begin to envy the man," said Lorenzo. "Ill-treated as he has been up to now."

"Surely you are not such a fool," said Daoud brusquely. But then, he thought, Lorenzo had no real idea what initiation into the Hashishiyya did to a man.

A few last soft words of instruction to Caterina, Orenetta, and Maiga, and Tilia led Daoud and Lorenzo to a wall panel which swung open at the pressure of her finger on a spring. The room they entered was as cool as the one they had just left, its large open window covered over with fine netting to let in air and keep out insects. But it was darker. Only a single fat candle burned in a large stick enameled green, red, and white.

Francesca, the woman Daoud had lain with on his previous visits to Tilia's, rose with a smile and came to him. As Daoud took her hand and kissed it, she squeezed his fingers. The polished, carved beams that ran up the walls and across the ceiling of this room were the same color as Francesca's hair, a dark brown. Opposite the window there was a small fireplace, dark and empty.

"Here, here, and here are the places from which you can watch what goes on in there," said Tilia, marching along one wall and pointing to tiny circular openings, each one ringed with a little *O* of wood. Under each opening was a couch, and the openings were low enough in the wall so that one could sit, or even lie down, and still look through them. The light in this room had to be lower than in the room where Sordello was, Daoud realized, or the peepholes would be visible on the other side of the wall.

"Francesca is here for your pleasure, should you find what is happening on the other side of this wall arousing," said Tilia, dabbing with a handkerchief at the pool of sweat that kept forming at the top of her cleavage. It must be her weight, Daoud thought, that made her perspire so much.

"You have thought of everything, Tilia," said Daoud.

"There is more," she said with a smile, and pulled on an embroidered strip of purple velvet hanging from the wall. Daoud heard a bell ring somewhere beyond the wall. Then through the door to the outer gallery came two more of Tilia's black servants. The first one bore a wide silver tray, and Daoud smelled a familiar and savory odor that filled the air of the room. As the servant laid the tray on a round table, Daoud saw slices of roast kid garnished with shredded cheese on a bed of rice with peppers.

"Roast yearling!" Daoud exclaimed, delighted.

He bit into a sliver of kid. It was delicious. The meat was accompanied by sliced boiled lemons sprinkled with nadd and scented with ambergris.

"But where did you learn to prepare such a dish?"

The stout little woman rolled her eyes. "There is much you do not know about me. If I find you deserving I will tell you, one day. Meanwhile, partake! And you, Lorenzo. And Francesca. Levantine cookery will not poison you."

The second servant set a platter of peaches and figs and a flagon of kaviyeh beside the lamb. A good meal for a long night, thought Daoud.

He sat on one of the couches to peer through a peephole. He could see the three women gathered around Sordello's inert form. They were massaging him gently, as instructed.

But it would be a while yet before he woke and found himself with three beautiful women, every pleasure they gave him enhanced by hashish.

"In the south we know and love Saracen dishes," said Lorenzo with a grin as he licked his fingers after helping himself to the kid. "But, Madama Tilia, am I to have food only? Shall I not have a companion to help me endure this night's work?"

Tilia reached up and pulled at the end of his grizzled mustache. "Only rarely does a Sicilian bullock set foot in my house. I am saving you for myself."

"Meraviglioso!" Lorenzo exclaimed. "Instead of one of the handmaidens of Venus I shall have Venus herself."

Lorenzo's wit was itself meraviglioso, thought Daoud. But for him, something other than the games of Venus was uppermost in his mind. Ever since his angry words with Sophia of a few days before, he had been troubled by the thought of Rachel. And especially tonight when, even as he passed the time here at Tilia's, Simon de Gobignon was visiting Sophia. Sophia had been to see Rachel herself, but had refused to talk about her. He wanted to reassure himself that Sophia had been wrong to condemn him and that all was well with the girl.

"While we wait, Tilia," he said, "I would have a private word with you."

When they stepped out of the room Daoud said, "I want to see Rachel."

Tilia frowned and was silent for a moment. "In all honesty, she is well and happy, and richer by nearly two thousand florins. Your companion Sophia visited her and found nothing amiss. And the roast kid will get cold."

Two thousand florins. Nearly enough, Daoud reckoned, to buy a mansion like Ugolini's. But what of Rachel herself?

"Just take me to her, Madama."

When he first saw Rachel's surprised smile, he thought that she was indeed well and happy, as Tilia had said. But then her dark gaze was averted, her straight brows drawn together in a little frown. She started playing with the gold lace on the hem of her white satin gown.

Daoud said. "Well, Rachel. You look like a queen sitting there."

Each woman at Tilia's had her special room, Daoud knew. The hangings in Rachel's room were cream-colored, the tables and chairs and the bedposts painted ivory, and the canopy over the bed was cloth-of-gold. She sat in one corner of the bed, with her legs curled under her.

It must have been on this bed that the Tartar had her.

"I am so pleased to see you, Messer David," she said in a low voice. "How can I serve you?" She smiled at him, but his trained eye saw that it was a false smile. And the hint of defiance he had noticed on first meeting her in Rome was gone.

"Rachel, I only wanted to see with my own eyes that you are content here and well treated."

Her eyebrows lifted slightly, and she shrugged. "I have never till now known such comfort, Messer David."

Daoud realized that he should ask her about the Tartar. Tilia herself had given him an account of Rachel's first night with John Chagan. The pain Daoud felt at hearing what he had delivered Rachel to was relieved only slightly by knowing that the Tartar had been surprisingly gentle with her. At first, though, he had hated Tilia for being willing to risk Rachel, and, impulsively, he had resolved to kill John. That made him feel a little better, until, a moment later, he remembered that hating Tilia and killing the Tartar would be no help whatever to Rachel. And he, as much as anyone, was guilty of what had happened to her.

Since John Chagan's first visit, Daoud knew, he had been back twice more, paying a thousand florins each time to spend part of the night with Rachel. He seemed much taken with her, and continued to be careful and kindly in his use of her body, Tilia reported. Watching them, Tilia had learned nothing that Daoud could use. But there were things Rachel might have noticed, useful things Tilia could not have observed through a spy hole.

Not tonight. I will ask her for information another time.

One thing he must know, though, was whether Tilia had been telling him the truth. "Have you been hurt in any way?"

Rachel looked at him, looked away and sighed. How enormous her dark eyes were, Daoud thought, how soulful. Her stare made him uncomfortable, and he was thankful that she soon looked away. She kept on toying with the hem of her gown.

"Everyone has been very kind. You need not worry about people hurting me. After all, Messer David, you are a merchant, as my Angelo was, and you understand that goods must be kept in the best possible condition to obtain the best price. Everyone here understands that, too."

There was no mistaking the bitterness and despair in her voice. Had he felt any differently after the Turks captured him, raped him, beat him, and sold him in the slave market?

"You are being given the money you have earned?"

She nodded, not looking up. "My share is five hundred florins for each of his visits. And he gave me a purse of three hundred the first time. A bonus, because I was a virgin. Madama Tilia keeps it for me, but I am allowed to look at it and count it." She looked up suddenly and said earnestly, "I could not have fallen into better hands than Madama Tilia's." But there was a deadness in her eyes that belied what she said.

"We did not force you to give yourself to the Tartar," he burst out.

A light came into her eyes then, the fire of anger. "Thank you for reminding me that I became a whore of my own free will. Is that why you came to see me, Messer David? To tell me that this is all my own fault?" Her lips stretched in a ferocious grin. "Pay me enough and I will say anything you want to hear."

Rachel's eyes were fixed on his, and his on hers, and they stayed that way, frozen, until Daoud shut his eyes and slowly turned away.

He could not even think of a word to say in farewell. As he closed the door to her room behind him, his eyes burned and there was an aching heaviness in his chest. Remorse. He felt as if he had killed a child—two children. Not just Rachel, but the boy David who had always lived inside him. The pain was unbearable. He longed to escape it.

XXXI

TILIA EYED DAOUD APPREHENSIVELY. "IS IT NOT AS I HAVE SAID—she is well and happy?" She lifted the pectoral cross to raise its gold chain away from her bosom and mop her flesh with a square of pale green silk. He remembered the blade in the cross, and wondered if she was afraid he might attack her.

He wished he could hate her for what had happened to Rachel. But all Tilia had done was introduce Rachel to a way of life that Tilia herself had found rewarding.

"She is as well as I could have hoped," he said, hearing in his own voice the deadness he had heard in Rachel's. He sat down heavily on a divan.

Lorenzo looked at him searchingly. His big mustache hid his mouth when it was in repose, but his eyes were wide, and they glistened wetly in the light of the one candle that illuminated this small room. The Sicilian's hands lay limp in his lap, the hands of a man in pain and unable to do anything about it.

Through a peephole Daoud saw that Sordello had awakened. The gray-haired bravo was staring about him in wonder, only six feet away from Daoud's eye, while Maiga gently pressed his shoulders back against the divan, Orenetta stroked his chest and whispered to him, and Caterina's blond head rose and fell between his legs.

Francesca sat on the divan beside Daoud, offering him a slice of kid. He took it and chewed it, but even though Tilia had cooked and seasoned it perfectly, it was tasteless to him.

It was not only Rachel's fate that troubled him, he realized. It was what was happening on the other side of this wall—those three lovely women ministering like houris of paradise to that old ruffian. They would do it with skill and even with the appearance of enthusiasm because they had no choice. They did not even think of choosing. They just did as they were told. Their orders came, through Tilia, from Daoud. Francesca, here beside him, would do whatever he wanted, not because it was what *she* wanted, but because she, too, had no choice.

And he had never really thought what it meant for women to live this way until he saw, tonight, what had happened to Rachel.

God is a flame, Sheikh Saadi used to say, *and each human soul a spark from that flame. When we treat our brother or sister like a thing, we trample God Himself.*

They were all slaves in this house of Tilia's. He had sent Rachel here to become a slave.

I, too, was once a slave.

But as a full-fledged Mameluke he was free. These women did not have that way of escape. As long as they could, they must perform the act of love, as it was called, with whoever paid them, or starve.

Baibars had done well to close the brothels of El Kahira. It was the very meaning of love that it was freely given. Love was free submission to another, just as Islam was free submission to God. Daoud had first experienced love when he and Nicetas gave their bodies to each other. And later with Blossoming Reed, even though theirs was an arranged marriage, that, too, was love.

He could not lie with Francesca tonight. It would be too much like lying with Rachel. He could not watch what Orenetta, Caterina, and Maiga would do with Sordello. The thing he was having them do to Sordello was an abomination. Despicable though Sordello was, he, too, had a soul, and tonight Daoud was trampling upon God in the person of Sordello.

And yet he must see that all went as planned tonight. Did he want his homeland destroyed?

But I have to get away from here.

He stood up suddenly. "I must go back to Cardinal Ugolini's." Tilia, Lorenzo, and Francesca stared at him.

Tilia recovered first. "But you were to stay the night here. What about—" She gestured toward the wall.

Daoud shook his head. "I am not needed. And I have an important matter to discuss with Ugolini."

"Which you just remembered," Lorenzo said, eyeing him sourly.

Daoud pressed his lips together. "Those three women know what to do. There is no need for anyone to intervene unless he starts to resist. And then you can kill him as easily as I can."

Lorenzo stood up and bowed formally. "Thank you for your trust, Messere."

If I am right in thinking that he hates this as much as I do, then he hates me for making him stay here.

The thump of Daoud's boots on the cobblestones echoed against the fronts of the huddled houses. Armed with sword and dagger, his head clear, and keeping to the wider streets, Daoud felt safe from attack, even though it was well past midnight. Besides, the Filippeschi had been won over, so he need no longer fear them. Fear, he thought, was the wrong word for it. Tonight he would welcome battle.

And he had the Scorpion with him tonight. He no longer ever made the mistake of going about in the streets of Orvieto at night without carrying the Scorpion in a concealed pocket in his cloak.

He walked past the cathedral church of San Giovenale, and once again from the open doors heard the pale voices of the priests of the cathedral chapter. A heavy odor of incense, carried on the moist night air, filled his nostrils.

Pain crushed his heart as he passed beyond the pool of light that spilled out the cathedral door. He seemed to feel a heavy hand on his shoulder, and looked up. Conjured up from memory, his blond father appeared to tower over him, a red cross on the shoulder of his white mantle. A warm hand gripped Daoud's, and his mother, her red-gold hair bound with pearls, smiled down at him. Her dress was blue, like the dress she had died in.

What memories torment Rachel, he wondered.

* * *

Just ahead of him, the narrow street opened into the broader one that ran past Cardinal Ugolini's mansion. He had just passed an inn called Vesuvio, after the burning mountain near Napoli, when a door opened softly behind him. Very softly, but it did not escape his trained ear. He glanced back and saw the upper half of a divided door mate with its lower half.

Watching for me? That was unlikely, because a spy watching for him would have had no idea when to expect him and would have had to stand by that door all night. He looked back again at the doorway and then at the cardinal's residence. The street was wide enough to allow a person standing in the doorway of the inn a good view of the front of the mansion.

He walked out into the square and turned to the right so that he could no longer be seen from the inn. Behind a filmy curtain on the third story of the mansion shone a yellow glow. Sophia's room. Was that Simon de Gobignon in the inn doorway?

No, it was not, because now he saw de Gobignon. The unmistakable tall figure was standing in the candlelit window behind the curtain. A thin arm pushed the curtain back, and though the light was behind de Gobignon, Daoud could see the Frenchman plainly, looking down into the square. Even though he was sure de Gobignon could not see him, Daoud stepped farther back into the shadows.

De Gobignon in Sophia's room. Daoud clenched his fists, and his lips drew back in a snarl.

The Scorpion would not carry that far. No, but he could stride closer in an instant, aim at that spidery figure silhouetted against Sophia's lighted window, and bring down his enemy with a single bolt.

Why am I thinking such a thing?

Was he going mad? Sophia would let Simon make love to her, and in his passion he would tell her much. Perhaps Daoud could find out more about why Simon had sent Sordello into his camp. Perhaps Simon would give Sophia some hint about the countermove he must be planning. Meanwhile Sophia would trick Simon into thinking that Fra Tomasso had turned against the alliance.

Killing Simon would be foolishness. Until now the mishaps that had befallen the French and the Tartars had seemed accidental. Murder Simon, and his enemies would have proof that there were plotters in Orvieto, and they would seek them out. And the first place they would look would be the place where Simon was killed,

the establishment of Cardinal Ugolini, the chief opponent of the
Tartar-Christian alliance.

Still, Daoud felt his blood seethe. He remembered a summer
night over ten years before, when he had bribed a slave and slipped
through an unlocked gate into the arms of Ayesha, the young wife
of Emir Tughril al-Din, then his commanding officer. They had lain
together all that night on the roof of the mansion of Tughril al-Din,
bathed in sweat, and the sweet terror of the blades that would hew
his naked body to pieces if they were discovered goaded him into
plunging into her again and again. Only the moon and stars bore
witness that he was enjoying the wife of his commander, the man
who ordered him about and punished him when he made an error,
the man who had the power of life and death over him. Toward
dawn, the delight of it bubbled up in his throat and he laughed so
loudly that the small Circassian girl put her hand over his mouth.

And now he does to me that which I did to Tughril al-Din.

Daoud shook his head. Nonsense. Sophia was not his wife, and
it was for this very purpose, to seduce, corrupt, and spy upon the
enemy, that he had brought her here.

*To use her, as I used Rachel and the women at Tilia's. First the
Tartar took Rachel, and now de Gobignon takes Sophia. And I am
nothing but a slave and a panderer.*

A second silhouetted figure appeared beside Simon, much
shorter, with unbound hair falling in waves and a narrow waist.
Daoud saw Sophia rest her hand on his shoulder. A moment later
she took the Frenchman's hand, and they both turned away from
the window. The curtain fell back in place behind them.

She leads him to bed!

Daoud was shaking with rage. Every muscle in his body ached
to kill de Gobignon.

Oh, God, give me the chance to destroy him!

He heard another sound to his left, the scrape of a boot on cobblestones. His hand darting to his sword, he glanced toward the
street he had just passed through. Nothing.

De Gobignon had brought a friend or servant with him. The
friend was waiting at that inn, where he could watch the front of
Ugolini's mansion, and, perhaps, signal to de Gobignon as dawn
approached.

De Gobignon's friend had been watching Daoud. He must be all
in a sweat, knowing that Daoud had seen the young count in Sophia's window. He would expect Daoud to raise an alarm. And if

Daoud did not, then de Gobignon would guess that David of Trebizond *approved* Simon's making love to the cardinal's niece. And from that it would only be a step to realizing that David and Sophia must be plotting together.

It would extinguish any suspicion of Sophia the count might have if Daoud were to rush into the mansion, raise an alarm, and pursue Simon. But if de Gobignon were caught, it would mean a scandal. His French compatriots would certainly do all they could to stop him from seeing Sophia again.

Again Daoud heard the scrape of a boot sole on the stone of the street. He drew farther back under the overhanging upper story of a house facing the mansion. Now de Gobignon's man could not see him without showing himself.

There was only one thing to do. And it gave Daoud grim satisfaction to realize it.

I cannot kill Simon de Gobignon, but I have to kill his man.

He drew the Scorpion from its pocket in the hem of his cloak. Quickly and silently he unfolded it. A leather case held a sting for the Scorpion, a steel dart half again as long as his finger, coated with the same paste he had used to render Sordello unconscious. He pulled the string of twisted rawhide back with his fist, slipped the dart into place.

The Frank took a step out of hiding. Daoud saw him as a big shadow at the corner of the building. He imagined the Frank's thoughts. He must be trying desperately to think of some way to warn his master before the cardinal's guards were roused.

Daoud raised the Scorpion, but the darkness made the shot difficult. De Gobignon's man was too hard to see.

"Pardonnez-moi, messire," he said in the language he had not used since he was ten. "I have a message for Monseigneur the Count de Gobignon." He spoke in as casual and friendly a tone as he could muster.

Daoud was close enough now to see that the man's hand was on his sword hilt.

"Why do you speak of the count to me?" The voice was young.

"Because you are his man," said Daoud, and he thumbed the notched wheel that held the bowstring in place. The string thrummed, the dowels sprang forward, and the dart buried itself in the Frenchman's body.

To avoid hitting breastbone or rib, Daoud had aimed for the

stomach. The Frank uttered a cry of pain and anger, and his left hand clutched at his middle as his right hand drew his sword.

"You Greek bastard!" he groaned, and fell first to his knees, then on his face. So he had recognized him as David of Trebizond. He must surely die.

Daoud rolled the unconscious man over on his back. His fingers quickly found the dart. Just a bit of it protruded from the Frank's stomach; his fall had driven it deeper. Daoud pulled the dart out, keeping his finger on the wound. He laid the dart on the ground and drew his dagger. He drove it upward just below the breastbone, striking the heart. The man's torso jerked violently, the body trying to save itself even though the mind was asleep. As Daoud pulled the blade out, blood flowed out after it, warm on his hand. He whispered a curse and wiped his hand and his blade on the man's tunic.

This must look like a street stabbing, a man murdered for his purse. Daoud thrust his dagger into the body again, this time in the place where the dart had gone in.

He felt for a heartbeat and found none. He sheathed his dagger, felt for the dart on the street beside the Frank, and put it back in its case. Case and Scorpion went back in the hidden pocket in his cloak.

The Frank's dead body was heavy as he dragged it into the deeper darkness under the overhang of the nearest house. He fumbled about the dead man until he found his purse, a small one and not very heavy, and tucked it into his own belt. The pottery maker would be shocked in the morning to find a robbed and murdered man on his doorstep.

Had anyone seen? The houses around the square were dark and silent as so many stone tombs. There was only that one light in the third-floor window of Ugolini's mansion.

He could not enter the mansion now, with blood on him. Whoever unlocked the gate for him would be sure to connect him with the murdered man who would be found in the morning. Orvieto's authorities would be questioning everyone, and Ugolini could not control what his servants might say.

Back to Tilia's, then.

He chose another street leading out of the square so as not to pass the inn where de Gobignon's man had been on watch. As he walked, he cast his mind back over what he had done. The killing left him troubled.

Saadi had taught him never to waste human life. *To wage war is a holy obligation. But have a care that you kill, not with a small soul, but with a great soul.*

This had been a necessary murder, Daoud thought. This young Frank had to die that Islam might be saved from infidel hordes of East and West. But, looking into his heart, Daoud knew that he had, indeed, killed with a small soul. He had been forced to kill de Gobignon's man, but he had also wanted to, and he had felt unworthy triumph over Simon de Gobignon. It had not even been an honorable fight. The Frank had no chance.

Purify my heart, oh, God, he prayed as he walked back to Tilia Caballo's brothel.

XXXII

SIMON REMEMBERED THOSE KISSES IN THE GARDEN OF THE PALazzo Monaldeschi as he looked again at Sophia, and his arms ached to hold her. But he must keep himself in check. He was still not sure he could trust her. And even if he were certain of her honesty, courtly love commanded him not to touch her until months, perhaps years, of worshipful wooing had passed.

Sophia said, "I must tell my uncle that his mansion is not as well protected as he thinks it is. His guards must have been asleep tonight."

Her oval face reflected the warm glow of the five or six small candles she had placed around her room. Her dark brown hair was unbound and fell in waves to her shoulders. He felt his heartbeat quicken as he looked at her.

"You did invite me here, Madonna." Simon felt rather proud of the way he had scaled the wall by the courtyard gate, waited till the cardinal's guards were out of sight, then climbed to the roof of the central wing.

"Yes, but I did nothing to help you, and I truly do not see how you got here." She stood facing him, her hands at her sides. He was not sure whether the gown she wore was for bed, or for him, or both. It was a translucent white tunic, sleeveless and cut deep in front, revealing the swelling of her breasts, pulled in at the waist by a cloth-of-gold belt. A large gold medallion stamped with a horse's head hung from a gold chain around her neck. His eyes kept traveling from her shoulders to her bosom to her narrow waist. The effort of holding himself back from touching her was agony. Sweet agony.

"I am trained in the art of stealing into castles."

"I thought the French were more given to marching up to a castello in broad daylight, banners flying, and taking it by storm," she said. Her teeth flashed in the candlelight. He wished she would invite him to sit down. But then he saw in what she said an opportunity to raise the subject of trust.

"True, Madonna. We French excel at open warfare, whereas you Italians seem more adept at intrigue."

"Intrigue? What do you mean?"

He tried to sound lighthearted. "Oh, for instance the clever way you diverted my attention at the Palazzo Mondaldeschi while David of Trebizond had the Tartar ambassadors making fools of themselves."

For a moment she did not speak.

Then she said abruptly, "I bid you good night, Your Signory."

He drew back, shocked. "Madonna!"

"The same way you came will see you out."

"I but meant to praise your skill at diplomacy. I hope I have not given offense."

"A gentleman always *knows* when he is giving offense."

"I—I merely wish to clear—to set my mind at rest," Simon stammered. He cursed himself for his heavy-handed attempt to test her. It was true, the French were no good at intrigue.

"Rest your mind somewhere else." She went to the door and stood there, back to him. Was she going to call for help? How embarrassing it would be if he were caught here.

The beautiful curve of her back distracted and confused him still more.

"If you do not leave, I will," said Sophia, grasping the black iron door handle. "You may stay in this room forever if you wish."

What a brouillement I have made of this rendezvous. Casting about frantically in his mind, Simon wondered what his troubadour father, Roland, would have done.

Or Sire Tristan or Sire Gawain, what would they do now?

There was no more time to think. He must act. He threw himself to his knees, arms outstretched, and waited. A long, silent moment passed. Finally Sophia turned her head. Her lips—those tender, rose-colored lips—parted and her eyes widened. She turned all the way around.

She started to laugh.

"Laugh at me if you will, but do not cast me out." The sound of her laughter was like the chiming of a bell. After a moment she stopped laughing and smiled. A lovely smile, he thought, a kindly smile. He could happily kneel here for as long as she went on smiling.

"I have never had a man kneel to me before." A faint vexation flickered across her face. "First you accuse me of kissing you only to further my uncle's plots against the Tartars. Then you kneel to me. What am I to make of you?"

Relief swept over him as he realized she was no longer angry.

"Make me your slave."

"My slave? You are toying with me, Your Signory."

"Toying with you? Never. Call me Simon if it please you."

"You would be my friend?"

"I would be more than your friend, Madonna."

She came to him and held out her hands. Her smile was dazzling.

"Well then, Simon, you may call me Sophia. And you may rise."

Simon grasped her hands, feeling joy in his very fingertips. He vaulted to his feet and thought of taking her in his arms, but she freed her hands with a quick, unexpected motion and took a step backward.

With just a movement of her hands she can lift me up or cast me down.

"For a man to kneel to a woman is not the custom in Sicily, Simon," she said softly.

It was as he suspected. She was not familiar with the ways of courtly love.

"If I do anything that seems strange to you, Sophia"—he used her name for the first time, and it thrilled him—"know that my actions are ruled by what we call l'amour courtois, which means that we know how to value women, whose value is beyond price."

"I have heard of courtly love. It sounds blasphemous to me, almost as if the man worships the woman. I do not think your patron saint would approve."

"My patron saint?"

"Him." She pointed to the small painting in a gilt wooden case that stood open on a large black chest. Candles in heavy enamel sticks stood on either side of the painting.

Sophia took his hand. At the touch of her cool fingers the muscles of his arms tensed. She led him across the room. Still holding his hand, she spread the wings of the case wider apart so he could see the image.

That it was a saint was apparent at once from the aureole of gold paint encircling the black hair. Simon saw a narrow face with huge, staring blue eyes painted with such bright paint they looked like sapphires. Compared with the saint's eyes the sky behind his head seemed pale. There were purplish shadows under the eyes, and the cheeks curved inward like those of a starving man. The beard and mustache hung straight but were ragged at the ends, and what little could be seen of the saint's robe was gray. To the left of the halo, in the background, stood a fluted ivory pillar with a square base and a flaring top. The pillar connected the azure sky and ochre ground. Simon felt admiration for the face; in that desolate scene the saint must have endured great privation and come through with holy wisdom.

"A wonderful face," he said, turning to Sophia with a smile. "And you say this is my patron saint?"

"Simon of the Desert," she said. "Simon Stylites."

"Stylites? What does that mean? I do not know Greek."

"Neither do I," she said, "but a priest told me that his name means 'he of the pillar.' Saint Simon was a hermit who lived ages ago, when the Church was young. He dwelt and prayed for thirty years on top of a pillar that was all that was left of an ancient pagan temple. That is the pillar behind him."

Live on top of a pillar for thirty years? Questions crowded into Simon's mind. How did he keep from falling off when he slept? Would not the burning desert sun have killed him? How did he get food and water? After thirty years the pillar ought to be surrounded by quite a pile of—

No, he put that thought firmly out of his mind. After all, the whole point about saints was that they were not subject to natural laws.

He asked only one question. "How high was the pillar?"

She shook her head. "I do not know. So high that he had to climb a ladder to get to the top. Then his disciples took the ladder away." She pointed at the pillar in the painting. "I tried to paint it so that it could be any height you might imagine."

"*You* painted this?"

"You find that hard to believe," she said with amused resignation. "That is why I hardly ever tell anyone. Many people would be sure I was lying. Others would think that a woman who paints is some kind of freak. Or that it is somehow dishonorable for a lady to paint, as if you, for instance, were to engage in trade. What do you think?"

"I think God has given you a very great gift," said Simon solemnly.

She squeezed his hand, giving him exquisite pleasure, and then, to his sorrow, let it go. "I hoped you would understand." She put the candlestick down, and Saint Simon Stylites receded into the shadows.

"I knew that you were going to be someone very important in my life when I found out your name is Simon," she said. "I think my saint wished us to meet."

How sweetly innocent she was, Simon mused. He was ashamed of the thoughts he had been entertaining about her ever since they had kissed in the Contessa di Monaldeschi's garden. Over the days and nights he had gradually grown more and more familiar with her—in his fancy.

He had thought about holding her breasts through her gown, then putting his hand on the warm, soft flesh, had thought about lying beside her in her bed, both of them nude. He had even, one cool night, allowed himself to imagine entering her body and lying very still, clasped inside her.

The ultimate act of l'amour courtois, this had been quite beyond his power of self-restraint with the women who played at courtly love with him in Paris. The way Sophia excited him, it was even less likely that he could hold himself back while remaining inside her for hours, as a true courtly lover was expected to do.

And now Sophia went over to the very bed he had imagined, and perched on it. The frame of the canopied bed was high above the floor, and when Sophia sat on it her feet dangled prettily, reminding Simon how much shorter than he she was. The sight of her on the bed made him tremble, frightened by his own passion. There was no one here to protect this innocent girl from him, except himself.

"Sit with me," she said, patting the coverlet beside her. He knew that the best way to protect her was to go nowhere near her. But he wanted desperately to sit beside her, to feel her hand in his again, to put his arms around her.

But if I take her in my arms, on her very bed, how can I stop myself?

Still, she had invited him to sit with her, and an invitation from his lady was a command.

He had intended to sing a love song to her. He had not the skill at making poetry to be a troubadour, but he had a good tenor voice, and he had learned dozens of troubadour songs early in life from Roland. He had sung them before he understood what they meant, because he liked the sound of them.

He bowed and went to the bed. He sat as far from her as possible. "Will you let me sing for you?"

When she smiled, he noticed, dimples appeared in her cheeks. "Oh, that would be a pleasure. But softly, please. We do not want to rouse my uncle's servants."

Softly, then, he sang.

> My love is the flower that opens at morning,
> That greets with her petals the radiant sun,
> Yet methinks 'tis not she who lives by the sun,
> But the sun gives its light so my lady may shine.

Sophia's smile was itself sunny as he finished the first verse. She leaned back, putting her hands out behind her on the bed, and closed her eyes as he sang the second and third. When he began the fourth verse, she drew closer to him till their legs were touching. Making himself concentrate on his music, he went on to the fifth verse. He resolved that at the end of it he would stand up and move away.

> At sunset my love will close up her petals
> Till with the dawn she awakens again,
> And her beauty will blaze out to dazzle the day.
> To see her the sun will be eager to rise.

By the end of that verse she was leaning against him and had reached around behind him to stroke his neck. Without his consciously willing it, his arm stole around her waist and pulled her to him.

His song, he realized, was insidious in its power. He had thought only to entertain her with his music, but he was seducing her. Her head rested on his shoulder, her eyes closed. Her fingers crept slowly, delicately, across the back of his neck under his hair, sending thrills down his spine. He could not move away from her.

"Stop," he whispered. "Please stop."

"Are you afraid of me?" she asked softly.

"I am afraid for both of us. You do not know what a raging fire a lovely woman like you can kindle in a man like me."

She withdrew her hand from his neck and let it rest on his thigh. That, he thought, made it even more difficult for him.

"I must tell you something," she said. "I am not—wholly innocent."

His heart felt a sudden chill. How could this dear creature be anything but innocent?

Now her hands were in her lap and her eyes were cast down. "As you surely know, most women past twenty, unless they are nuns, have been married for years. You must have wondered what I am doing in Orvieto, unmarried, living with my uncle."

"I never thought about it."

"Then *you* are very innocent."

Simon felt himself wilt inwardly. How could he have been so blind as not to wonder why Sophia was not married? She had seemed timeless to him and attached to no one. Even her relation to the cardinal, except that it put her in the enemy camp, seemed unimportant.

"You have a husband?" His voice was heavy with sorrow. Foolish as it was, he had dreamed that she might be virginal. But that made no sense, now that he considered it. The rule in courtly love was to fall in love with a lady who was married to someone else. His Parisian courtly lovers had been married women. If Sophia were already married, that should make it better.

Then why did he feel so disappointed?

"I was married at fourteen. His name was Alessandro. He died two years later of the damned fever that takes so many of our good Sicilian people. He was very kind to me, and I was inconsolable."

"Ah. You are still in mourning for him?"

She turned her hands over, showing empty palms. "I loved him so much that I could not think of marrying another man in Siracusa. At length my mother and father decided to send me to live with my uncle in the hope that I could forget Alessandro enough to consider marrying again."

"Do you wish to marry again?"

"I have met no one I am drawn to but you, Simon, and marriage between you and me would be unthinkable. My family's station is so far beneath yours."

His heart leapt happily. She was free, yet, as she said, not wholly innocent. He need not feel quite so guilty about the passionate thoughts he had been having about her. And as for marriage between them being unthinkable, she did not know that none of the great houses of France would consider a daughter of theirs taking the name de Gobignon. Her nonclerical family might be of low station, just as the pope's father had been a shoemaker, but Sophia was the niece of a cardinal, a prince of the Church.

It was love, not thoughts of marriage, that had brought him here tonight. Still, he must respect her honorable widowhood. Since she had loved her husband, she might be more susceptible to him, and he must guard her virtue all the more steadfastly. Perhaps she thought that he respected her less as a widow. He must reassure her.

She was not holding him any longer. He could stand up without tearing himself away from her. He sprang to his feet and strode to the center of the room.

"Believe me, I think you just as pure as if you had never been married at all."

She looked up at him, surprised, her hands still folded in her lap, her dark eyes wide.

"I am delighted to hear that. But"—she cast her eyes down and smiled faintly—"does that mean there is to be nothing at all between us?"

"I love you!" Simon declared. "I will always love you. I think of you night and day. I beg you to love me in return."

"Oh, Simon. How beautiful." She held out her arms to him. But he stayed where he was and raised his hands warningly.

"I mean to love you according to the commandments of l'amour courtois. With every fiber of my being I yearn to be altogether yours, but you must restrain me."

"I must?"

"You must be what the poets of old Languedoc called 'mi dons'— my lord. You must rule me. One day we will join together in body, but only after I have been tested and found worthy."

"Is that what courtly love means?"

"Yes, and that is why it is more beautiful than marriage. Husband and wife may embrace carnally the moment the priest says the words over them. No, they are *required* to. Courtly lovers know each other only when love has fully prepared the way, so that their coming together may be a moment of perfect beauty."

Sophia looked at him silently. Her face was suddenly unreadable.

"Do you understand?" he asked after he had stood awhile gazing into her lustrous brown eyes. "These ideas are perhaps new to you."

"The woman is ruler of the man?"

"Yes."

The corners of her mouth quirked. "Then what if I were to command you to get into this bed with me?"

He was certain from her sly smile that she was joking. But he could think of no clever answer. He considered what he had read, what he had been told, what he had done with other women. None of it helped. The women who fell into bed with him on the first tryst had not been serious about love, nor had he been. In all the lore of l'amour courtois the woman made the man wait—sometimes for years, sometimes for his entire life—and the man was happy to wait, and that was all there was to it.

Then he remembered something his mother had said, a secret so precious he would never tell anyone, not even Sophia. Not even Friar Mathieu needed to know it. But it guided Simon now.

The first time your father and I were alone together I wanted him then and there. But he was strong enough for both of us. It was a whole year before we possessed each other in body. And you came of that union.

"You will not command me so," he said with cheerful confidence.

Her eyebrows rose—they were strong and dark, like a raven's wings. "Indeed?"

"Because you know how much better it would be to wait. We both want each other now. But if we restrain that hunger, it will grow. It will be not just a desire of the flesh, but a longing of the spirit. It is said that the souls in paradise know no greater happiness than two lovers do, who are united in soul as well as body."

"Prodigioso," she said. "But I am just a Sicilian girl, and I do not perhaps have the refined spiritual appetite of a French nobleman. What if I cannot wait?"

"It is natural," Simon said, thinking again of what his mother had confided to him. "Then I must be strong enough for both of us."

The thought of her powerful passions, which she restrained with such difficulty, excited him. Holding himself back from her was going to be painful, but delightfully so. And think of the ecstasy when at last they were united.

Sophia released a long sigh and brought the palms of her hands down on her knees with a slap of finality. "So be it, Simon. You will teach me the ways of courtly love, and I will do my best to be your—what did you call it?"

"Mi dons. My lord."

Her teeth flashed white in the candlelight, and her lips glistened. Simon's own lips burned to taste hers.

"How strange. As if I were the man. Ah, but you are very much a man, Simon, and you make me feel very much a maiden."

Simon turned and went to the window. The night air blew through the gauze curtains, and he felt a wonderful aliveness all over his body. He wondered whether Alain, out there in the dark somewhere, could see him here in the window. He pushed the curtain aside so Alain, if he was there, could get a good look and know that his seigneur was safe and happy.

Dawn must still be hours away. What would he tell Alain about what transpired this night? The truth, assuredly. But would Alain believe him? And if he did, would he mock Simon for not bedding Sophia?

No, Alain would understand. He respected the good in men and women as much as Simon did. Which was why they were friends as well as lord and vassal.

Sophia stood beside him and put her hand on his shoulder.

"You cannot stand there all night, Simon. Come back and sit down."

He bowed. "As mi dons commands." He let her take his hand and draw him away from the window.

There was one chair in the room, and he took it. Foolish to expose himself to temptation by sitting beside her on the bed again. The chair was straight, with a tall back and no arms. The only touch of comfort in its rectilinear shape was a cushion laid upon its seat. Sophia smiled and shrugged and sat again on her bed.

Would she let him spend the night? Whenever he had been all night with a woman, they had made love. Should he sing to her again? Would she want to sleep? He pictured himself watching over her while she slept, perhaps kneeling by her bedside, and the beauty of it thrilled him.

Now he remembered something she had said earlier, that he had accused her of kissing him *only to further my uncle's plots against the Tartars*. She was aware, then, of what Ugolini was doing.

She has no idea how much she revealed to me.

He sang another troubadour song, "White Hands." She let him draw off her red silk slippers, and he almost cast away all his promises to himself as she curled her toes against the palm of his hand. He forced himself to stand up and pace the room while she lounged back on her bed, her head propped up on her elbow, watching him with that delicious smile of hers.

She questioned him about his life, and he offered her a simple version of it, telling her nothing about his secret illegitimacy and the dishonor of the man whose name he bore. It struck him while talking to her that perhaps these two sins that had shaped his life—Amalric de Gobignon's treason and Nicolette de Gobignon's adultery—had given him the strength to resist the temptation to assail Sophia's virtue. He told her how he had spent much of his youth in the household of the King of France and how this had led to Count Charles d'Anjou's giving him the task of protecting the Tartar ambassadors.

And thus, inevitably, their talk got around to the Tartars.

"Why did you accept this task from the Count of Anjou?" she asked. "You have a lofty title, huge estates, everything you could want. Why trouble yourself with all this intrigue?"

Having decided not to tell her the truth about his past, Simon now could not answer her question both honestly and fully. He could not say that he had committed himself to this mission to clear the stain of treason from the name of de Gobignon and to prove that he had a right to the title.

So he told her of another reason, equally true.

"I am in part an orphan, and the king was like a second father to me. It is his wish that Christians and Tartars join together to liberate the Holy Land. And I would do anything for him."

Sophia frowned. "I find that hard to understand. As for me, I hate the Tartars."

Simon's mind pounced on that. Could she be more involved in Ugolini's scheming than she had admitted?

"Why do you hate the Tartars? You know so little about them."

"I know that they almost made enemies of us because you thought I was kissing you just to help my uncle."

Walk carefully, Simon.

Again she was hinting at her uncle's involvement in all that had gone wrong for the alliance. But if he asked her about it outright, she might think—as he had thought of her—that he was courting her only to further his cause.

"Well, I am sure your uncle is following his conscience, as we all are," said Simon. Actually, he believed nothing of the kind. But he did not want to offend Sophia, and perhaps l'amour courtois would permit a small lapse in one bound to be truthful to his lady.

"And your conscience tells you to guard those savages?"

"I want to see Jerusalem liberated and the Saracens conquered," Simon said. "Every good Christian does."

She sat up in bed, looking at him earnestly. "Do you not fear that the Tartars are worse than the Saracens? That is what my uncle says."

Step by step, as if he were defending a philosophical proposition at the University of Paris, Simon explained to her what he believed. Yes, the Tartars were barbarians and had committed unspeakable atrocities. But the Saracens, united under the Mameluke Sultan of Egypt, were more powerful now than they had been in hundreds of years. If not stopped now, they would sweep all the crusaders out of Outremer, the land beyond the sea.

And a wave of Mohammedan conquests might well not end there. To this day the Moors were a power in Spain, and it was not that long ago that there were Saracens in France and here in Italy. Surely she remembered that her own island of Sicily had been conquered for a time by the Saracens. Indeed, King Manfred von Hohenstaufen's army was made up partly of Saracens, and he himself was an infidel.

With their belief in spreading their religion by the sword, the Saracens were a far greater danger to Christendom than the Tartars. The Tartars were simple pagans, easily converted to Christianity. Friar Mathieu had personally baptized over a dozen high-ranking Tartars.

She listened intently, her golden-brown eyes so fixed on his that he feared more than once to lose his train of thought. But he persevered to the end. When he finished, she nodded thoughtfully.

Now, he thought, he could turn the conversation to her uncle.

"All this is so obvious," he said, "it is hard to understand why your uncle should have formed a party to oppose the alliance."

She touched her fingertips to her mouth in surprise. That mouth—it was like a blooming rose.

"You mean my uncle is the *leader* of those who are against the alliance?"

This reminded him of mornings he had tiptoed through his forest at Gobignon, longbow drawn, catching a glimpse of a stag's brown coat and then losing sight of it again in the thick broussailles, trying to stay downwind and draw close enough for a good shot without frightening the deer into headlong flight.

"But I thought you already knew that," he said. If she denied that she knew any such thing, then his quarry had escaped him.

"So, he put David of Trebizond up to baiting the Tartars while you and I were so delightfully engaged? Wicked uncle! To think I almost lost you on his account." She clenched a pretty fist that looked as if it had been chiseled in marble. On one finger her small garnet ring glittered in the candlelight.

"I believe he brought David of Trebizond and his servant Giancarlo here to Orvieto, as well as that Hungarian knight, Sire Cosmas, who spoke at the pope's council, to discredit the Tartars." Simon wondered whether he should tell Sophia about the bravos Giancarlo was recruiting. No, if he told her what he knew about them, he would have to require her to keep it a secret, and that might make her feel disloyal to Ugolini.

She nodded. "Now I understand why he spends so much time closeted with that silk merchant, talking about—who is Fra Tomasso di—di—?"

God's robe!

"Fra Tomasso d'Aquino?"

She nodded. "That was the name. He sent David to see this Fra Tomasso, and when David came back I overheard my uncle joyfully shouting, 'Fra Tomasso is with us!' over and over again. Is he an important man, this Fra Tomasso?"

Simon tried to keep his face calm, but he was horrified. Simon recalled now that the d'Aquino family were from southern Italy, the kingdom of Manfred the unbeliever, as was Ugolini. And were not the d'Aquinos even related to the Hohenstaufens? Something must be done about this at once. How far had the plotters—that was what they were, plotters—gotten with d'Aquino?

How much further dare he pursue this subject before Sophia grew suspicious of him? And how much further before he began to feel that he was degrading their love?

Our love? But she has not said she loves me.

The realization was like a thunderclap in his mind.

What he really wanted to know was whether she loved him or not. To come right out and ask her was not the way of courtly love. He must wait for her to say. But she would never speak of love as long as they went on about the Tartars and Ugolini.

To the devil with Ugolini and David of Trebizond and Fra Tomasso and the Tartars!

He had learned enough anyway, he decided. She had confirmed his suspicion that Ugolini was the ringleader of the forces in Orvieto arrayed against the Tartars. She had let him know that they had drawn Fra Tomasso d'Aquino into their conspiracy.

Of one thing he felt certain. If she were working with her uncle to block the alliance, she would not have let him learn so much.

XXXIII

A HAND SHOOK SIMON'S SHOULDER. HIS WHOLE RIGHT SIDE ACHED. He fought wakefulness, trying to plunge deeper into sleep. He was in a cool blue lake surrounded by dark masses of spruce. He had just seen a wolf with a silver-white coat drinking from the lake on the opposite shore and he was trying to swim to it.

"Simon. You must wake up."

He opened his eyes. Right before his face was a twisting streak of orange against a royal blue background, and he realized he was lying on his side on the Persian carpet in Sophia's bedchamber. He rolled over on his back and rubbed his aching side. He saw Sophia's face just above him.

He could not help himself. He reached up with both arms and pulled her down to him and kissed her. Her lips felt cool and dry, and he had a sudden fear that his breath must be sour from sleep. She pushed herself away from him and he did not try to hold her.

"There is light coming through the window, and I hear birds singing," she said. "You must go now. Many of my uncle's servants get up at dawn."

He sat up. She was kneeling beside him, still wearing the same cream-colored gown. He remembered now that they had talked of courtly love, and a little about her childhood in Sicily. To his disappointment, she had not said that she loved him.

The necessities of nature had forced on them an intimacy of one sort—while each had pretended not to notice, the other had used the chamber pot discreetly placed behind the red and green diamonds of a screen.

She had been the first to fall asleep. Sleep had overtaken him, too, but each time he dozed off he started to topple off the small straight chair he was sitting on. The fourth or fifth time this had happened he gave up sitting and stretched out on the carpet.

"Quickly, Simon, please. If my uncle ever finds out you were here, he will send me back to Siracusa."

God forfend! The habits of his knightly training took over, and he strode quickly to the corner, where he had left his sword and belt leaning against the wall, and buckled them on.

He remembered that Alain was supposed to sing an aubade, a dawn song, in the street below to warn and rouse him. An old troubadour custom. Perhaps he had sung, and Simon, sleeping so soundly, had not heard.

"Did you hear anyone singing out in the street?" he asked.

Sophia smiled and shook her head.

Blast Alain. He must have overslept, too.

Sophia said, "But how will you get out of here? It is not as easy to climb up to the roof as it is to climb down from it."

Simon went to the window and pushed the curtain aside. The rope he had climbed down on was still dangling from above. He gave it a hard pull, and it held firm. He looked up at the sky. It was a deep violet with only a few faint stars and one brightly shining planet.

The morning star might be Venus, a good omen for a lover.

His heart was light, even though he was leaving Sophia. It had been a beautiful night.

A half-filled cup of wine stood on the table by her bed. He swigged it to rinse his mouth, swallowed, then wiped his lips with the back of his hand. He tried to think of some parting word worthy of a troubadour, but none occurred to him.

She stood by the bed, her eyes warm. He held out his arms and she slipped into them with as much ease as if they had been lovers for years. She was so much shorter than he that he had to lean down to kiss her, and as he did she arched her body against him.

"I love you," he whispered, embarrassed by its prosaic simplicity. But it was simple truth.

"And I love you." She kissed him quickly on the lips and turned away.

Her words stunned him. He felt for a moment as if he were going to fall dead on the spot. And that if he did, it would be a perfect moment to die.

The candles were almost burned to the bottom. He looked over at the painting of Saint Simon Stylites, whose blue eyes seemed to gleam out at him from the shadows.

He wrapped the rope around both arms, gave it another yank to be sure it was tied tightly above, and stepped up on the windowsill. He swung around so that he was facing the wall of the mansion and began to climb, his joy at her parting words making him feel stronger and more agile. His hands gripped the rough rope; his feet in calfskin boots pressed against the wall, pointed toes seeking out cracks. He did not look at the stone-paved street three stories below.

He heard voices in the street—and froze. There were men gathered down there. If they looked up, they would see him climbing up the front of the cardinal's mansion.

Move quickly, he told himself. He scrambled up to the square Guelfo merlon around which his rope was tied, pulled himself over the parapet, and dropped with relief to the flagstones of the flat roof.

He untied the rope. Curiosity made him want to look at the men whose raised voices he heard coming from across the street. Something had disturbed them. But he had the feeling that if he did not look at them, they would not see him.

Hurry. Holding the loosely coiled rope in one gloved hand, he ran as lightly as he could so as not to disturb anyone in the rooms below him.

He came to the back of the building, where, two stories below him, a crenelated lower wall protecting the courtyard joined the main building. He uncoiled the rope, found its center, and doubled the line around an angled merlon at the corner of the roof battlements so that both halves dangled down just above the courtyard wall. Then, gripping the doubled rope, he swung himself out and began to climb down.

A thunderous roar battered at his ears. He saw in the courtyard a big gray hound racing over the paving stones twice as fast as any man could run. It kept up a furious, enraged barking in a deep, bone-chilling voice. In an instant the dog was below him. Its bellowing was sure to rouse the cardinal's guards. Its huge, pointed white teeth glistened; its tail lashed from side to side.

If I fell, that damned dog would eat me alive.

He remembered seeing the dog before with Giancarlo, David of Trebizond's servant. It had been friendly enough that day. But now it saw him as an intruder.

Giancarlo called it by name. What the devil was it? If I could speak its name, maybe I could get it to shut up.

Simon stood on the courtyard wall, thankful that it was too high for the dog to reach him. The hound sprang at the top of the wall, at the same time emitting a bark so loud it almost knocked Simon off his perch.

Simon pulled on one end of the rope, and it snaked around the merlon and came rippling down to him. To his horror, one end fell past him into the courtyard.

In an instant those great ivory fangs had sunk into the braided hemp. Simon yanked on the rope, but there was no tearing it loose. Hoping to catch the dog by surprise, Simon gave the rope some slack and then jerked with all his might, but succeeded only in dragging the beast a foot or so, claws scraping on cobblestones. At least the animal could not bite the rope and bark at the same time. Enraged, muffled growls issued around its clenched teeth. It snapped its head from side to side, trying to tear the rope out of Simon's hands.

He cut part of the rope away with his dagger, letting the end the dog held fall into the courtyard. Even as he was coiling up the rest of the rope, the beast gave a howl of fury and with a tremendous leap was halfway up the wall.

The remaining rope tied to his belt, Simon hung by his hands on the outside of the wall and let himself drop, hitting the stone street with a thud that sent jolts of pain through his shinbones. He heard shouts on the other side of the wall mingling with the roars of the hound.

Limping a little at first from the force of the drop, he staggered into the nearest side street. He would have to circle back to the avenue that ran in front of the cardinal's palace, approaching it from another direction.

It seemed to take hours for him to find his way through the snake's nest of byways. But he felt not the least bit disturbed. It did not matter. Nothing mattered, because Sophia's parting words to him had been *And I love you*. He felt like dancing through the crooked streets.

By the time he emerged near the east side of the cardinal's palace, he could see quite clearly. There was no sun, though. The morning was damp and gray. He would have to cross the avenue and walk back past the cardinal's mansion to find the inn he and Alain had picked for their rendezvous. It must be near where that crowd of men had formed a circle around something.

"Are you the watch, Messere?" a man said, coming up to him as he approached the crowd.

"I am not," said Simon with a slight haughtiness, and the man fell back, eyeing Simon's rich clothing, sword and dagger.

"Scusi, Signore."

I really should not let myself be seen around here.

With deference to Simon's dress and manner, the crowd parted for him when he joined them to see what they were looking at.

It was the body of a dead man.

It was Alain.

Simon staggered back, feeling as if he had been struck in the heart by a mailed fist.

"No!" he cried.

"Do you know this man, Signore?" someone asked him.

Simon did not answer. He fell to his knees beside Alain, horrified by the face so white it seemed carved from marble. He saw now the great bloodstain down the front of Alain's pale green tunic. Flies with gleaming blue-green bodies were humming above the bloodstain, settling down again after Simon's arrival disturbed them.

He raised his head, and through the tears that clouded his vision he recognized a face. Last night's innkeeper. A short, balding man with large eyes and a generous nose.

"We have sent for the watch, Your Signory," said the man.

"Did anyone see or hear anything?"

"My wife heard your friend go out before dawn. He never came back."

Jesus, have mercy one me, thought Simon. *This is my fault. He went out to await the dawn so he could warn me. And someone killed him.* Tears were pouring from his eyes. He was sobbing convulsively.

"Poverello," he heard someone mutter sympathetically. Here he was a knight, a count, kneeling in the street weeping in front of a crowd of strangers. He did not care.

Guilt crushed him. He wanted to lie beside his friend's body and be dead with him. But how could he? No, he had to find and kill Alain's murderer.

Still kneeling beside Alain, he wiped his face with the edge of his cape and surveyed the crowd. To keep his identity a secret seemed unimportant now.

"I am the Count de Gobignon of France. I will pay handsomely anyone who helps me find the man who did this. If anyone can name the murderer, I will pay"—he thought a moment—"a thousand florins."

A murmuring ran through the crowd. A fortune! Foolish, perhaps, Simon thought, to offer such a reward. A man would accuse his own brother to get that much money.

I may hear many names. I will have to be sure.

He looked down at poor Alain. The flies were crawling on his face, and he brushed them away. Alain's lips had turned blue. He looked for Alain's purse and saw none on his belt.

Stabbed to death for the few coins he carried. Dead at twenty years of age. Tears overflowed his eyes again.

Oddly, Alain still wore his sword and dagger.

Alain's weapons were still both sheathed. Whoever had stabbed him had not given him time to defend himself. Yet, there were no recessed doorways or alley openings where an armed robber might hide himself.

The spot was unpleasantly familiar. This was where Simon's archers, at de Verceuil's orders, had shot two Orvietans.

Had Alain been tricked by someone pretending to be a friend? Was the killer someone Alain knew?

Ah, my poor friend, what a shame it is when a young knight dies without sword in hand. Simon clenched his fist, the tears falling unceasingly. *By the wounds in Christ's body I swear I will avenge the wounds that killed you, Alain.*

Simon remembered now that the watch was on the way. When they got here they would ask him questions about what he and Alain were doing here, questions he did not want to answer until he had time to think.

A scandal would give de Verceuil a chance to eat me alive. And I must get Friar Mathieu to help me.

"Send someone to the Palazzo Monaldeschi for my horse," he said to the innkeeper, standing suddenly.

"As you wish, Your Signory." The innkeeper hurried off.

Simon swept the crowd with his gaze. "Remember, all of you.
Anyone who saw anything, heard anything. You will be paid. Come
to the Palazzo Monaldeschi."

Simon sat down on the stone street to wait for the horse. Silently
the crowd that had gathered waited with him.

When the innkeeper's servant brought the horse, Simon lifted
Alain's body with the help of two other men and lashed it securely
facedown over his horse's back with the rope he had used to climb
to Sophia's room.

Sophia. He had been so happy just moments ago because she
said she loved him as they parted. Was she looking down now,
seeing this pitiful sight?

Fresh sobs forced their way into his throat, and he leaned against
his horse, covering his face with his arms.

I have to get away from here quickly.

He forced himself to stop crying and took hold of the reins. The
Orvietans fell back as he led the horse up the street leading northward to the Monaldeschi palace. He felt warmth on his neck and
looked up to see the sun through a break in the clouds.

Alain would never see the sun again.

*Whoever did this to you, Alain, I will not rest until I have killed
him with my own hands.*

XXXIV

SORDELLO'S FACE, LOOKING AS IF HEWN FROM GRANITE BY AN
indifferent sculptor, was gray with fatigue. His arms bound behind
his back, he knelt before Daoud, wearing a tattered brown frieze
robe Tilia had somewhere found for him.

Daoud sat once again on the former papal throne. Dressed in
black cassocks and hoods that covered their faces, Lorenzo and five
of Tilia's black servants stood along the walls of the room. Every
so often Sordello's eyes flickered to the implements of torture around
the room and quickly away again.

Yet the night's assault on his mind had not altogether broken his spirit. "If you think to frighten me with this clowning, think again, Messer David. I have stood undaunted before the Inquisition in my day, and they are a good deal more fearsome than you and your henchmen."

Leave him his shred of dignity, Daoud thought. *A man who has lost that is too dangerous.*

"We are beyond fear now, Sordello, are we not?"

Sordello's eyes glowed in the torchlight like a trapped animal's. "What kind of devil are you?"

Daoud tried to smile kindly. "You call me a devil after I have sent you to paradise?"

The old bravo sighed, and his eyes closed. "I did not know that my body was capable of feeling so much pleasure. Even when I was twenty and at my best, I never knew such delight. It shook me to the very root of my soul."

"I know," said Daoud. He was thinking back to his own initiation. Given sanctuary in Egypt, the Hashishiyya had built a tent-palace of wood and silk west of El Kahira, at the foot of the pyramids. Over a series of moonlit nights, Daoud had drunk the Old Man of the Mountain's brew. He had entered hell in the bowels of the Great Pyramid and then had ascended into paradise, where the houris promised by the Prophet had ministered to him for what seemed an eternity. Yes, he knew very well what spirit-freezing delights Sordello had experienced.

"What are you, then?" Sordello growled, his eyes flashing open. "Some kind of stregone? What was that witches' potion you made me drink?"

"Do you wish to return to paradise?"

"You *are* a devil, Maestro. You want my soul."

The man was quick, Daoud thought. For all that he was a flawed man, he had a strong mind. He remembered being made to drink the preparation of wine and hashish. And he already realized why Daoud had done this to him.

So delicate, this part.

Now the bond must be forged. As a succession of Old Men of the Mountain had forged it between themselves and their disciples in Alamut, in Masyaf, in all those mountain strongholds across Persia and Syria from which terror had gone forth for more than a hundred and fifty years.

"I am but a man like you, Sordello. I do not want your soul. I want your loyalty."

"You want my treachery, you mean. You want me to betray my master, the Count de Gobignon."

There was more than quickness here, Daoud thought. There was that foolhardiness he had seen in Sordello before. A man of sense, knowing that he was in the power of a force beyond his control, even beyond his understanding, would do nothing to antagonize that force. Yet Sordello persisted in challenging Daoud.

At the mention of Simon de Gobignon's name, Daoud's concentration wavered. When de Gobignon found his knight dead outside Ugolini's mansion, what would he do? There would be trouble over this, surely there would be trouble. Daoud cursed himself for leaving Tilia's house and going back to the cardinal's mansion.

He forced his mind back to Sordello. How to work with this provoking spirit?

"To send you into the enemy camp as he did, Count Simon must have great confidence in your ability."

Sordello laughed angrily. "Confidence? That high and mighty French fop? He was probably hoping you would catch me. Sia maledetto!"

He curses de Gobignon. Excellent. Or is this merely for my benefit? Daoud peered at Sordello, wishing the room were lit by more than a few torches burning in cressets. The flickering light was impressive, like this gilded throne, but if Daoud could get closer to Sordello and see better, he could be more sure of what the man was really feeling.

Daoud said, "He who is loyal to me is never cast out, no matter how foolishly he behaves."

"Does he who is loyal to you get to go to paradise often, Maestro?" Sordello's voice was thick with yearning.

It was time for the final step. Daoud beckoned. The nearest hooded figure on his right, who was actually Lorenzo, came forward with a green earthenware cup. He bent and held it before the kneeling Sordello.

"More of your stregoneria? Or have you finally decided to poison me?"

"Would I have showered you with wonders, as I have tonight, only to kill you? No, I have one final wonder to show you. Drink, Sordello."

This wonder probably will be the death of you, but not for a while.

After a long hesitation, the old bravo lifted his head and swallowed the liquid Lorenzo poured down his throat. He made a sour face. "Paugh! It tastes bad!"

Daoud said nothing and waited. After a few moments of silence Sordello sat back on his heels. His gray head began to nod. His eyes closed.

Daoud arose from the throne and went down to him, holding a candle in one hand.

"Look at me, Sordello." The prisoner's head lifted, and his brown eyes stared fixedly into Daoud's. Daoud bent and passed the candle flame before Sordello's face, but his eyes remained motionless.

"Do you love Simon de Gobignon, or do you hate him?"

"Hate. I hate him," Sordello said in a dull voice. "I have suffered much on his account."

"Would you kill him if you had the chance?"

Even in his trance Sordello's eyes seemed to glow, and his face flushed. "Yes. Oh, yes, Maestro. Gladly."

That was good. The will must already be there. Then it remained only to shape the deed. Daoud reached inside the collar of his tunic and pulled out the silver locket Blossoming Reed had given him. It was, he had decided, better than a word or combination of words. It was something Sordello would never see again unless Daoud wished him to see it.

He dangled the locket by its chain before Sordello's face, letting it swing from side to side. He held the candle so its flame reflected from the silver disk.

"Watch the locket, Sordello. Look closely at it. The design on its face is like no other in the world. Make certain that you would know it if you saw it again."

For a time he let the locket swing, and Sordello's head turned from side to side, following it.

"Do you know this locket now, Sordello? Truly know it?"

"Yes, Maestro."

"Could you mistake it for another?"

"No, Maestro."

"Good. Now I command you. When you see this locket again, it will be a sign. It will mean that you are to kill Simon de Gobignon at once. As soon as you see the locket, you will take up the first weapon that comes to hand, and you will await your first good chance, and you will strike him down. Do you understand?''

"Yes, Maestro."

"Will you do it?"

"Yes, Maestro. With much joy."

"Say what you will do, Sordello."

"When I see that locket, I will kill Simon de Gobignon at once."

"That is good. Now, in a little while you will wake up. And you will not remember anything I have said to you about the locket and about killing Simon de Gobignon. You will forget all about it until you see the locket again. And then you will strike."

"Yes, Maestro."

Daoud went back to the throne and sat down. He slipped the locket's chain over his head and dropped the silver disk back inside his tunic. Sordello slumped in his kneeling posture like a figure of wax that had been placed too close to a fire.

Daoud waited patiently, and in a few moments Sordello raised his head, his eyes bloodshot but alert.

"Will you let me visit paradise again soon?" His memory had gone back to the moment before he drank the drug.

"Not *very* soon," said Daoud. "But serve me well, and it will happen again." He could not make Sordello wait a year, as the Hashishiyya usually did with their initiates. But it must be a wait of some months, or the experience would lose its magic. And in months his work in Orvieto might be done.

And then again, I might still be here ten years from now.

"Tell me what I have to do, Maestro."

"Serve me faithfully, and from time to time, when it pleases me, you will visit paradise. Disobey me or betray me—we will know instantly if you do—and when you least expect it you will find yourself in hell. Not the one we created for you last night. The real one."

"You don't need to threaten me," said Sordello with a flash of his old rebelliousness. "Just tell me what you want."

"Simply go on doing what you have been doing. You will give the Count de Gobignon information about us—but from now on we will tell you what to tell him. And you will keep me informed about the young count. Hardly any work at all, you see."

Sordello grunted. "I doubt it will be that easy. But as long as you offer a reward so great, I am your man."

My slave, thought Daoud, hoping that his pity for this creature did not show in his face.

But he must remember that there were hidden places in this man's soul. And he had never before tried to enslave a man as the Hashishiyya did it. He could not be sure that he had succeeded fully, and so he had made a creature potentially as dangerous to himself as to anyone else. The flesh on the back of his neck crawled.

She was sitting by the window, staring out at the spot on the street where the young man's body had lain. She heard the door open behind her. She turned, and there was David. Golden-haired, lean, tall, with those light-filled eyes. She forgot herself and felt a leap of love, and then her heart clenched like a fist with anger.

Wait, let him tell it before I judge him.

He closed the door slowly, a strange expression on his face. She looked from him to the image of the saint. Yes. The look around the eyes was the same. They had accepted pain and sorrow, did not struggle against it as ordinary people did, and they knew *something.*

Except that David's eyes were not the bright blue of the saint's. David's eyes seemed to reflect whatever color was about him.

How could it be that the icon she had painted could remind her of two such different men as Simon de Gobignon and David of Trebizond?

He stood there looking at her, and she realized that he was waiting for her to speak. He wanted to know what she and Simon had done in this room, and he did not want to ask. And she knew at that instant, watching his face, that he was expecting to be hurt by what she would tell him about herself and Simon.

But what about that young Frenchman in the street? I saw Simon kneel by him, weep for him, bear him away.

"Something terrible has happened," she said.

His eyes narrowed. "You did not succeed with de Gobignon?"

"No, someone killed his friend, who was waiting for him, down there in the street. Everything is ruined. Simon will not want to see me again. He will be certain to blame me for that young man's death."

"Why should he?" David walked over to the chest, where the enameled candlesticks on either side of the painting of the saint still held burnt-out stumps of candles. He sat cross-legged on the floor in front of the chest. He rested his forearms on his knees and his gaze on the flame and azure carpet. There were deep lines in his face. He looked as if he had not slept all last night.

His face in front of the saint's face. Looking from one to the other, Sophia saw the resemblance more plainly than ever.

She sighed and spoke with elaborate patience. "What else can Simon think but that his friend was killed by some overzealous protector of mine?"

"Why would a protector kill a man standing in the street when there is another man up in the bedroom with the woman he is supposed to protect?" There was something in the harshness of his gaze, a flatness in his steel-colored eyes, that told her beyond the possibility of doubt that it was he who had killed Simon's young companion.

But had he not been at Tilia's house all night?

She nodded her head slowly. "Simon will probably think that way, too."

From his seat on the floor, David looked up at her with a hard smile. "And, since I am certain you gave him incomparable pleasure in bed, he will overcome any objections he has to seeing you again."

She felt as if he had stamped on her heart. To him she was nothing but a harlot to be used to ensnare his enemies.

And if that was all *he* thought she was, how could she find it possible to think any better of herself?

If I am not a whore, what am I?

But she would tell him the truth whether or not he chose to believe it.

"Nothing happened between us," she said tonelessly.

He stared at the carpet. She saw hope struggling with doubt in his face.

Doubt won. His smile was cynical.

"You failed to seduce him? I cannot believe that."

"Whatever you may believe, that was how it was."

"Why do you bother to lie to me?" Anger smoldered in his face. His cheeks were reddening.

"Why *would* I lie to you? It would make no difference to you if I went to bed with Simon."

"If, as you say, nothing happened, then explain to my why it did not." He folded his arms and sat hunched forward.

"When a man like Simon is in love—" she said, and stopped. "You *do* understand what I mean by love?" How did a man brought up in Egypt as a slave to Turks feel about women? Saracens, she knew, kept their many wives locked up most of the time.

Daoud shrugged. "I can only guess at what *you* mean by love."

"A man like Simon shows his love by holding back his ardor. He does not realize that I know this. I have let him think he is teaching me about courtly love."

"And what did you learn by letting him woo you in this courtly way?" He looked pleased. He was beginning to believe her.

"He tried to find out things from me. He is such an innocent. He had no idea that I was telling him what you told me to tell him."

David sighed, stood up, and walked to the window. She could see the tension in his back. How broad his shoulders were. Not huge, like those of some knights, but graceful and powerful. His posture was not just erect; it was perfect, straight yet flexible, like a blade of the finest steel. She imagined him with his shirt off. The palms of her hands tingled at the thought of stroking his shoulders.

"Did you not want to take him into your bed?" His voice was cold.

She thought back to her night with Simon. During those hours when she had been Sophia Orfali, she had been disappointed when Simon insisted that he would not touch her. But Sophia Orfali had to accept his judgment.

Earlier, she had wanted to take Simon to bed as a kind of revenge on David for letting Rachel be used by the Tartar. But last night she had let Simon decide what they would do. When she was with Simon, she was what Simon wanted her to be.

Is that what I am, a woman who becomes whatever the man she is with wishes?

She expelled her breath in a short, sharp sigh.

"I wanted to do whatever was necessary. If it had been necessary to make love to him, I would have done it."

She shut her eyes momentarily. Her head spun. Now, with David here, she wanted David, not Simon. And she hated herself for wanting him, when he saw her as no more than a useful object, as Manfred had.

If only Alexis had lived. These loves I feel for men, for Manfred, for Simon, for David. I cannot help myself, and it betrays me. It divides me against myself. And they do not return my love.

And yet, she was sure David did care for her, perhaps even loved her, though he would never admit it. Why else this jealous questioning?

That might even have been why he killed Simon's friend!

The thought made her heart stop beating for an instant and her body turn cold. Killing Simon would have upset David's plans, but he might have taken out his jealous rage on Simon's friend.

"But what did you *want* to do with de Gobignon?" he demanded, turning from the window.

He would not let it alone. She slid off the bed and got to her feet. She went to the chest and stood with her back to David, staring at the picture of the saint. Anger clouded over her vision so that she could not see the painting. She clasped her hands together to control their trembling.

"I do not have to tell you that," she said in a choked voice. "It does not matter. I do what is necessary."

"As I do!" There was a snarl in his voice.

What did he mean by that, she wondered. She turned and the look she saw on his face made her stomach knot itself. His teeth were bared and his eyes were narrowed to glowing slits.

Now she had to hear him say it. "Did you kill that boy?"

She watched him slowly regain command of himself. Calm returned to the hard, tan features. His eyes held hers, and their color seemed to change from white-hot to the cold gray of iron.

"Of course."

She felt something break inside her. Grief overwhelmed her. She mourned for the young Frenchman. She did not know the man David had killed, but she imagined him to be just like Simon. She wept for him and for Simon. And for David. She did not want to cry, but she could not help herself. She walked slowly to her bed and sat down heavily. She could feel the tears running down her cheeks.

"Why did you kill him?"

"I had to leave Tilia's. I made the mistake of coming back here. From across the street I saw de Gobignon in this window." His voice was tight, his words clipped, as if he were trying to hold something in. "At the same time, the Frank, who was on watch, saw me. If I had allowed him to live, de Gobignon would have known that I approved of his being with you. And he was no boy, but a knight, strong and trained."

"He could have been no match for you."

"I gave him no chance to match himself against me. This is not some tournament. Your life is in as much danger as mine is."

"I never forget that," she said.

David had killed Simon's friend. She wished that she had gone to bed with Simon.

"Do you think de Gobignon will now be afraid to try to see you again?" There was a sneer in David's voice, and she felt the heated blood rising to her face.

"He is no coward."

He looked at her with weary eyes and a tight little smile. "Well, then. He will want to see you again. Send a message to him. Have him meet you someplace other than here. Someplace where he will feel safe. A church, perhaps."

"A church. Yes, that is a good suggestion. Then you will not have to wonder what we are doing."

"From what I have heard of Christian churches, that is not necessarily true."

She wished she had the skull to throw at him again. That was all that poor young knight would soon be—a skull, buried in the earth.

"How dare you insult the religion you were born into?" she shouted. "Have you forgotten that I am a Christian?"

He glared at her, turned on his heel, and slammed the door behind him.

Feeling alone, unloved, and desolate, not even sure who she was, Sophia sat heavily on her bed. Sobs racked her chest, one after the other. Not willing to admit how much Daoud had hurt her, she struggled with her tears for a time, then gave in and threw herself full length on the bed, pain spreading through her body.

XXXV

"Is it not a sin, Father, to explore a man's body like that?"

"It is considered a crime in many places. But it is not a sin when it is done with reverence, to discover the truth."

Watching Friar Mathieu, Simon felt his stomach rebel. The old priest bent over the long naked form of Alain de Pirenne, stretched out on Simon's bed, wielding a freshly sharpened carving knife borrowed from the Monaldeschi kitchen. The knife flashed in the light of the many candles set around the bed as Friar Mathieu enlarged the wound in Alain's belly. Simon kept looking away and then staring back, fascinated.

"It hurts me to see you treat Alain so," said Simon. "Though I know you mean to do good."

"My brother Franciscan, Friar Roger of Oxford, says that if you want to know God, you must look as closely as possible at His works. He says that to read the book of God's creation is better than reading philosophy, and is a form of prayer."

"Philosophy. Yes," said Simon. "I learned last night that Fra Tomasso d'Aquino is an enemy."

"One moment." Friar Mathieu had tripled the width of the lower wound and was now pulling the lips of the gash apart, peering intently into it. If Alain had been alive, Simon knew, blood would have been pouring out of that incision.

Sickened, Simon turned away. He wondered if he could sleep again in this bed, knowing that Alain's poor naked body had been stretched out there, to be tormented in death by this old Franciscan physician-priest.

If he abandoned the bed, he would have to give up the room, though, and it was one of the few private rooms in the Monaldeschi palace. It was a warlike room, as befitted a young knight, decorated with battered Monaldeschi arms. Crossed halberds, spotted with rust, were hung on the stone chimney that ran up from the kitchen on the first floor. Shields, dented and scratched, each almost as tall as a man, faced each other from opposite walls. They were probably quite old, since they bore simple blazons. The one on Simon's right was ocher, with a black chevron dividing it across the middle. The other bore an azure cross against a white background.

This being the top floor of the palace, the mullioned window was spacious, and Friar Mathieu had drawn back the curtains and pulled the twin window frames inward on their hinges to get more light. Simon went to the window and looked through the protective iron grill down into the square. Two men and three horses were gathered by the steps leading to the front door. They wore yellow and blue livery, the colors of the city of Orvieto.

"I think I have found something," said Friar Mathieu. Just as he finished speaking, Simon's door shook under a heavy knock.

"Say nothing," said the Franciscan. "I will tell you later."

The knock sounded again. Simon went to the door and opened

it. A stocky man whose bald head came up to the middle of Simon's chest stood there. Simon observed that the man carried more muscle than fat on his sturdy, barrel-shaped frame. He wore a yellow silk tunic trimmed with blue, and a short sky-blue cape. A bright gold medallion on a gold chain hung from his neck. Two daggers, on long and stout, the other short and slender, hung from the right side of his belt. The sword on his left side reached from his waist to his ankle. Simon knew he had seen him before, but he could not remember where.

"Your Signory, Count de Gobignon, it is my honor to address you," the stout man said. His words were polite, but his tone was perfunctory. He had to tilt his head back to look at Simon, but his voice and expression made Simon feel very young and small. Even so, Simon held his silence and did not step aside to let the man in. Let him introduce himself first.

After a pause, the man said, "Your Signory, I am Frescobaldo d'Ucello, podesta of Orvieto." He stopped, eyeing Simon. He had sparkling black eyes, and his black mustache was trimmed so that it was no more than a thin line above his mouth. Simon remembered now having seen this man, the governor of the city, at the execution of that poor heretic a month ago.

"Signore Podesta," Simon bowed. "The honor is mine."

"Not at all, Your Signory." Now the stout man looked past Simon into the room, and his eyebrows flew up. Simon turned and saw Friar Mathieu anointing Alain's brow with his oil-dipped thumb, forming a cross on the white forehead. Most of Alain's body was under an embroidered coverlet, and the kitchen knife had disappeared.

D'Ucello blessed himself and said in a low voice, "I will examine the body after the good father is finished with the last rites. Would you be so kind as to step out of the room, Count, so that we can talk?"

Closing the door behind him, Simon followed d'Ucello through the corridor out to the colonnaded galleria overlooking the lemon trees where he and Sophia had kissed on the night of the contessa's reception for the Tartars.

So long ago that seemed now, though it was little more than a month, and so much tragedy had come of it.

Simon told d'Ucello the story he had worked out, that he and Alain had gone to that inn searching for women and had gotten separated.

There were large bags under the podesta's eyes, dark as bruises. They contracted as he listened to Simon.

"Forgive me, Your Signory, but I must be clear. Are you telling me that you slept with a woman last night?"

Simon tried to look abashed and reluctant to speak. "Yes."

"And where did this take place, Your Signory?"

"In my private room at the inn."

"Who was she?"

Simon had prepared his answer. "I do not know. A pleasant lady whom I met in the common room."

The bags under d'Ucello's eyes twitched. "There are no whores in that part of town, Signore. It is one of my duties to see that the prostitutes are limited to a quarter of the city where they will not offend the holy or the well-born. A cardinal has his residence across the street from where your friend's body was found." D'Ucello's mouth stretched, but neither his eyes nor the dark bulges under them joined in the smile. "The woman who entertained you must have been an ordinarily respectable person who chose to go astray that evening." He paused and looked grimly up at Simon.

Simon felt as if a clammy hand had taken him by the back of the neck. He should have realized this vaguely imagined woman would not satisfy any determined questioner. He struck his fist against his leg. D'Ucello's eyes flickered, and Simon knew he had caught the gesture. He felt as if a net were slowly being drawn around him, and he resented it. Back home no mere city governor would dare trouble the Count de Gobignon any more than he would disturb the king or one of his brothers.

As d'Ucello continued to stare silently at him, Simon studied the podesta. This was a man who was jealous of his power, Simon decided. A man who, despite his politeness, would enjoy embarrassing a young nobleman.

"What was the woman's name?" d'Ucello pressed him.

"I have no idea."

The thick black eyebrows rose again, wrinkling the balding scalp. "You spent the entire night with this woman and never called her by name?"

Simon had been intending to claim that honor forbade him to tell the woman's name. He felt certain the governor would reject that argument as trivial under the circumstances.

"We spoke very little. I addressed her with various foolish endearments."

"Could you describe her?"

"Most of the time we were in the dark." Simon felt d'Ucello had pressed him enough. It was time to fight back. "Signore Podesta, my good friend and vassal was murdered in the street, a street supposedly under the protection of your watch. I fail to see how it helps you to do your duty of finding his killer by questioning me as if I were a criminal."

The podesta's brows drew together, and he took a few steps backward, diminishing the importance of the difference in height between him and Simon.

"Your Signory, I have questioned everyone who lives in that neighborhood, and everyone I could find who was passing through it last night," he said. "I learned from the innkeeper at the Vesuvio that your friend slept alone last night. I know that you did not meet anyone in the inn, woman or man. You stopped there briefly, left your friend, and went somewhere else. You did not engage a private room for yourself. The innkeeper and several other people agree to that. Will Your Signory be good enough to tell me where you did go?"

Simon heard with dismay the weakness in his tone and was appalled at how easily d'Ucello had exposed his lies. "Those you spoke to about what I did must have been mistaken," he said. "Perhaps they did not notice my return to the inn." An inspiration struck him. "They may be trying to protect the woman I was with."

D'Ucello smiled thinly. "I see. Then you are telling me that you had carnal relations with this woman while your good friend and vassal looked on."

Simon was momentarily at a loss for words. It would have delighted him to reply by running d'Ucello through.

They stood bristling at each other like two hostile hounds when Simon heard a door open. A moment later, to his enormous relief, Friar Mathieu joined them by the marble railing overlooking the atrium.

"If you wish to examine young Sire de Pirenne's body, he lies in Count Simon's room waiting for you, Signore," said Friar Mathieu. "This is a very sad day for us."

With a black look at Simon, d'Ucello bowed to the old priest and left the galleria.

When they were alone, Friar Mathieu grunted. "A good thing I merely extended the wounds Sire Alain had already suffered. The podesta might well bring charges against me for desecrating a corpse if he saw I had made incisions in the body.''

"Did you learn anything?" Simon asked.

"I am convinced that Sire Alain was not merely stabbed to death.''

"What do you mean?" Simon was eager to get Friar Mathieu's advice on how to handle the podesta, but this was more important.

"When I looked closely at the wound in his stomach, I discovered that it was two wounds," said Friar Mathieu. "He was punctured there by a thin, round object, like a large needle. Then he was stabbed through the heart, and blood poured out of him. And then the killer stabbed him in the belly to try to mask the dart wound.''

"How do you know that?"

"The belly wound did not bleed much, so the heart wound must have preceded it. When the killer drove his knife into the puncture in the belly, it did not go in exactly the same direction. The smaller wound goes upward at a slight angle, as if the needle were driven in from the level of the killer's waist. The knife wound goes straight in. I had to dig below the skin and ribs to discover the needle wound.''

"A needle could not have killed Alain."

"It could have been a poisoned dart. Alain's lips are blue. That is sometimes a sign of poison.''

Simon heard a clumping of boots in the corridor. He hurried in from the galleria to find Cardinal Paulus de Verceuil, accompanied by two black-robed priests, striding toward the room where Alain lay.

"Now one of your knights has been killed!" de Verceuil boomed. He was dressed in a dark cerise tunic with particolored hose and forest-green boots with pointed toes. The only indications of his ecclesiastical office were the absence of a sword and the presence of the large jeweled cross hanging from his neck. A purple velvet cap adorned with a black feather was draped over his glossy black hair.

Simon told the cardinal he and Alain had been out late and had decided to stay at an inn rather than cross town during the dangerous night hours. Friar Mathieu came and stood beside him, greeting the two priests who had accompanied de Verceuil. They loftily eyed the old Franciscan's brown robe and responded with curt nods.

When Simon finished his recital, de Verceuil leaned forward, his small lower lip outthrust. "If you cannot protect your own knights, how can you protect the emissaries from Tartary?"

That was not a question but an assault, Simon decided, and required no answer. "We are doing everything we can to find his killer, Your Eminence."

"By God's footprints, I wish this were my bishopric!" de Verceuil exclaimed. "I would take a dozen men from that neighborhood and I would hang one man a day until the killer was found. I would have the man."

The door to the room where Alain lay swung open, and the stout podesta emerged. He stood silently glowering up at de Verceuil. Simon wondered whether d'Ucello had learned anything from looking at poor Alain's corpse.

"And what, Your Eminence, if the people of that neighborhood truly do not know who killed the Sire de Pirenne?" said Friar Mathieu.

Until that moment Simon had assumed Alain had met his death at the hands of some Orvietan cutthroat. If not such a one, then who? He remembered Giancarlo and the bravos he had met on the road. Alain's money had been taken, but not his weapons. And Giancarlo served David of Trebizond, and David served Ugolini. Was this Ugolini's way of protecting his niece's honor?

If Giancarlo had anything to do with it, Sordello ought to be able to find out.

"If we arrested all the men who live on the street where he was killed," said de Verceuil, "more than likely among them would be the man who did it. These Italians—shopkeepers by day and robbers by night."

The faces of the two priests with him tightened. Simon glanced at d'Ucello, and saw a flush darkening his brown cheeks.

"The people of that street are among the most respectable in Orvieto, Signore," the podesta growled. How delightful, Simon thought, if the odious de Verceuil and the odious d'Ucello were to tear into each other.

De Verceuil stared at the podesta in amazement and wrath, while the two priests turned their heads from one to the other in embarrassment. After a moment, one priest murmured de Verceuil's identity to d'Ucello, while the other softly told the cardinal who the podesta was.

"Forgive me, Your Eminence, if my tone was less respectful

than you deserve," said d'Ucello, bowing to kiss de Verceuil's haughtily extended sapphire ring.

"I have encountered nothing but disrespect from Orvietans since I came here," said the cardinal, and Simon remembered that vile smear of dung on his cheek the day they arrived. "I had actually thought Orvieto had no governor."

"Forgive me again that I did not pay my respects to you before," said d'Ucello. He did not rise to the bait, Simon noticed. An intelligent man.

"A French knight has been murdered in your city, Podesta," de Verceuil said. "Regardless of your high opinion of the people of the quarter where it happened, I expect you to press them hard until you find the killer. A thing like this cannot happen without someone seeing something or hearing something."

That reminded Simon that no one had come forward to claim the reward he had offered. If someone had heard or seen something, that person was doubtless too frightened to speak of it.

"Your Eminence gives me most valuable advice," said d'Ucello. "I promise you, we shall not rest until the killer is found." His round body bobbed forward in a bow, and he turned on his heel, sword and daggers swinging, and marched away.

"Pompous little man," said de Verceuil. "And doubtless incompetent and treacherous."

The cardinal turned to Simon now. "Do not leave it to that watch commander to find the killer. The knight—what was his name?" Simon told him. "De Pirenne was your man, and you are responsible for his death. Put all the men under you to work hunting down the murderer. Do whatever has to be done. We must not let the death of a French knight go unavenged."

"As Your Eminence wills, so I will," said Simon.

De Verceuil raised a finger. "And we will have a splendid funeral. The pope himself will be present. Let the grandeur of the ceremony show that we French do not take the death of one of our number lightly. Let these sneaking Italians tremble before our wrath."

Again the two priests looked at each other, and one of them shrugged resignedly.

What barbarians we must seem to them. Simon's face grew hot with embarrassment.

XXXVI

"CANAGLIA! GIVE WAY OR I WILL HAVE YOUR HEART ON A PLATTER!"

Hearing the shout, Simon stifled a curse and turned to see arms waving, a man in helmet and leather chest armor fall back, pushed by another. The man shouting and pushing was Peppino, one of Simon's Venetian crossbowmen. The man Peppino had knocked down was Grigor, one of the Tartars' bodyguards.

No, dear God, not today!

Sunk in grief though he was, he would have to do something. For Alain. That today of all days, the day of Alain's funeral, might not be marred by brawling.

From his seat atop a black-caparisoned stallion in the gateway of the Monaldeschi courtyard, he looked down on a boiling mass of bright conical helmets, all of them now moving toward the action in the center of the yard. He kicked his horse's flanks and drove into the crowd. He had to break up the fight before it started.

The Armenian was on his feet and reaching for his dagger. And Peppino had his hand on the hilt of his own blade. Before Simon could reach them, Teodoro, whom Simon had appointed capitano of the crossbowmen after dismissing Sordello, forced his way between the two men. He turned his back on the Armenian and gave Peppino a violent shove with both hands.

"Stupido! Back in line!"

"What devil's work is this?" Simon demanded.

Teodoro turned and saluted Simon smartly. "Your Signory, Peppino is a fool. But the Armenians provoked him. They insist on marching before us in the cortege. Are we not to march behind the French knights?"

Idiots! What difference did it make? They had forgotten that this parade was for Alain; they thought it was for them. He felt a dull hatred for both the Venetians and the Armenians.

Simon sent for Ana, the multilingual Bulgarian woman, who translated for the Armenians Simon's explanation that the French knights must ride as an honor guard directly behind Alain's bier, and that since the Venetians were directly under the command of the French, they must come next. Also, no one must come between the Tartar ambassadors and their Armenian bodyguards; therefore the Venetians must precede the Armenians.

"Sergentes, get your men back into line!" Simon shouted at the leaders of the hundred Monaldeschi men-at-arms milling about in the courtyard along with the Venetians and the Armenians.

Simon spurred his horse back to the head of the procession, where he took his position just behind Alain's bier, which was already in the street.

The Sire de Pirenne lay upon a huge square of red samite edged with gold, draped over the flat bed of a four-wheeled cart. Red ribbons were woven into the spokes of the wheels. The two farm horses that drew the cart, chosen for their docility, also wore red surcoats. Red, for martyrdom. Red for the blood poor Alain had shed. Simon sighed inwardly and hoped that God considered Alain a martyr and had taken him up to heaven. Had he not died while in the service of the Church? Was this not a crusade in all but name?

Alain was dressed in a white linen surcoat and a white silk mantle. Simon, Henri de Puys and the other four knights had dressed him themselves. What agony! The struggle to get poor dead Alain's big frame into his garments had taken nearly an hour.

Thank heaven de Puys had stopped Simon from trying to dress Alain in his mail shirt and hose, as Simon had originally intended. De Puys pointed out that Alain's family were poor, and that Alain's younger brother would have need of the expensive armor. So the armor would be sent back to the Gobignon domain along with the news that Alain was dead.

Oh, the woe Alain's widowed mother and younger brother would feel when Simon's letter reached them! Friar Mathieu had helped him compose the impossible lines, but Simon still felt they were not gentle enough, not comforting enough. He hated himself for feeling relieved that Alain's family was too far away for him to deliver the news in person. He had done the best he could, sending the letter and Alain's armor to his chaplain at Château Gobignon with instructions to take it personally to the de Pirennes and read it to them, offering them all possible consolation, they being almost certainly unlettered.

Around Alain's waist was clasped his jeweled belt of knighthood, and to his leather boots were fastened his knight's silver spurs. His velvet-gloved hands, resting on his chest, grasped the hilt of his naked longsword. Simon would buy another sword for his brother. His helmet, polished to mirror brightness by his sobbing equerry, rested beside his blond head. His shield, square at the top and pointed at the bottom, blazoned with five black eaglets on a gold ground, lay crosswise at his feet. Those things Alain must take to his final rest.

Simon's stomach was a hollow of anguish. Those splendid arms, and Alain had never had a chance to use any of them.

A breeze stirred the curly yellow locks of the pale head that lay on a red silk pillow. The air of Orvieto had grown chilly in the three days since Alain's murder. The city had enjoyed almost summer weather until late in the fall, but now November had fallen upon it with icy talons. The sky this morning was a heavy purple-gray, and a dampness in the air foretold chill rain.

At the very head of the procession walked Henri de Puys, bareheaded but in full armor, leading Alain's riderless great horse. The cart bearing the body, driven by a servant in orange and green Monaldeschi livery, followed. Then came Simon and the other French knights.

Please, God, let nothing else unseemly happen today. Let us bury your servant the Sire Alain de Pirenne with honor.

He looked back and saw that the two Tartars, wearing their cylindrical caps adorned with red stones and their red and blue silk jackets, had mounted their horses. Because Alain was a warrior and they were warriors, they rode horses to honor him today.

The sight of them was a reproach to Simon. If he had thought only of the Tartars and not become involved with Sophia, Alain would be alive today.

After the Tartars, rows of spear points and bowl-shaped helmets glittered, the Monaldeschi retainers and men-at-arms. Behind the Monaldeschi banner, two green chevrons on an orange background, rose a curtained sedan chair draped with black mourning streamers. In it, Simon knew, were the contessa and her grand-nephew.

Simon had been waiting for the contessa to appear. He raised his arm in a signal to de Puys, who began to walk southward, toward the Corso, pulling the reins of Alain's horse. The wheels of the cart creaked into motion.

As the procession wound its way through the larger streets of Orvieto, the thought occurred to Simon that Alain's killer might be among the onlookers, one of the faces that watched, with little emotion, from the sidelines or looked out of a second-story window.

Sordello had sent word through Ana that among Giancarlo's hired bravos, none had any idea who might have stabbed Alain.

Simon knew what the Orvietans, most of them, must be saying. *A French knight goes whoring and gets himself stabbed, and they give him the greatest funeral since Julius Casear's.*

A stab of guilt shot through him. To protect Sophia, he had told de Verceuil and d'Ucello that he and Alain had gone wenching. He had besmirched Alain's reputation.

The cortege stopped at every church in Orvieto, and before each Alain's body was blessed by two or three cardinals, who then with their entourages joined the long line of mourners. Looking back over his shoulder, Simon could no longer see the end of the procession. It disappeared around a distant turning in the street.

Not all Orvietans were without feeling. Many girls and young women wept, waved their handkerchiefs, and threw flowers from balconies to the handsome Frenchman, murdered in his prime. Alain would have welcomed more attention from them when he was alive, Simon thought bitterly.

At the convent of the Dominicans, a collection of brown stone buildings behind a high wall, the rotund Fra Tomasso d'Aquino emerged, followed by two dozen or more of his Dominican brothers, all in white wool tunics with black mantles. Three of the leading members of the preaching friars, the superior general, the father visitor for northern Italy, and the prior of the convent blessed the body. Fra Tomasso was to deliver the funeral sermon, a great honor for Alain. It must be downright painful for the fat friar to walk from his convent to the cathedral; that was an honor in itself.

But the sight of Fra Tomasso made Simon cold with anxiety, remembering how Sophia had told him that the stout Dominican had turned against the Tartars.

The one thing that might, even if only in a small way, make up for the infinite tragedy of Alain's death, was that important piece of information Sophia had unwittingly given Simon. And when Simon had told it to Friar Mathieu, the old Franciscan, feeling he had no choice, had taken the news to de Verceuil. Simon hated to see him do that, but he had to agree that de Verceuil was the only one in their party whose position was exalted enough to permit him to make demands on Fra Tomasso.

De Verceuil had paid a call on the superior general of the Dominicans, but what went on behind the walls of the preaching friars' convent Simon and Friar Mathieu had never learned. In his usual infuriating way, de Verceuil had refused to talk about it.

At the gateway to his palace, Pope Urban, all in gold and white, met the procession. As Simon dismounted and knelt on the stone street to receive the pope's blessing, he noted that the old man's face was as pale as his vestments, and that his hands were trembling. Had Alain's murder affected him so, or was he ill? Urban was flanked by six cardinals in broad-brimmed red hats and brilliant red robes. On his right were three French cardinals, including de Verceuil. Beside him was Guy le Gros, whom Simon had met at the pope's council.

Le Gros looked angry. Simon hoped he was angry about Alain's murder; every Frenchman in Orvieto should be. But what a shame that Alain had to die in order that all these people care about him.

On Urban's left were three Italians, the diminutive Ugolini standing right beside the pope. The sight of him was a blow to Simon's heart. Simon had been in his mansion wooing Sophia when Alain was murdered. Alain's bleeding body had lain across the street from Ugolini's mansion, for how many hours?

And where was Sophia? Anxiously Simon scanned the crowd for a sight of her. Would she not come? Had Alain's death frightened her? Would he ever see her again?

He despised himself for still wanting to see Sophia, when his tryst with her had caused Alain's death. He should give her up.

I cannot give her up.

After the blessing, Pope Urban took his place, with his escort of cardinals, at the head of the procession. They moved to the piazza before the cathedral, as packed with people as it had been the day the heretic was executed there. Death, death, here they were again, to celebrate death.

When Alain's body reached the cathedral, Pope Urban blessed it once more. Simon and the other French knights raised a pallet that was hidden under the red samite cloth and carried Alain into the cathedral.

The cathedral was a festival of light, and the sight of it made

Simon feel a little better. Simon and de Verceuil had agreed to share the expenses of the funeral, which included the rows of candles lighting the altar, all of the purest beeswax, and the double line of fat candles in tall brass sticks running down the middle of the church. Benches had been cleared from the nave of the cathedral to make room for the funeral procession.

The shadows where the massed candle flames did not reach were illuminated by a dim, underwater glow—faint because the sky was overcast—that seeped in through the narrow stained glass windows, touching a mourner here or there with a spot of red light, or blue or green.

The French knights carried Alain to the front of the cathedral and set his body down on a red-draped platform. Simon took a position to the right of the body. From here he could see rows of cardinals and bishops on either side of him. The cardinals in their red hats sat in the first row, and Simon recognized de Verceuil by his height and by the shining waves of black hair that tumbled from under the wide brim of his tasseled hat.

The Contessa di Monaldeschi walked slowly up the aisle, leaning on the arm of her plump grandnephew. As she neared the altar, Cardinal Ugolini suddenly broke away from his position beside Pope Urban and bustled down to take her other arm. With these two escorts, both the same height, the contessa tottered to a high-backed, cushioned seat on the right side of the altar. Ugolini stroked her hand, whispered to her, kissed her cheek, and went back up the altar steps to stand beside the pope.

I wish he were not so friendly with the contessa. It is a danger to the alliance.

It occurred to Simon suddenly that Alain's death would go for nothing if the pact between Tartars and Christians were not sealed. Now Simon had another reason, beside the restoration of his family honor, beside his love for King Louis, to strive for the alliance.

On the side of the altar opposite the contessa, also in a high-backed armchair, sat a dark young man about Simon's age in a surcoat of blue velvet with a heavy gold chain around his neck. He sat very erect, and his dark eyes burned with hatred as he stared across the altar at the contessa and her grandnephew. He had been pointed out before to Simon as Marco di Filippeschi, capo della famiglia of the Monaldeschi's archenemies.

The contessa herself had suggested that a Filippeschi might have murdered Alain just because he was a guest of the Monaldeschi family. Simon supposed the Filippeschi chieftain was paying public respect to Alain to demonstrate his family's innocence. The Filippeschi, Simon had heard, were opposed to a French presence in Italy—perhaps simply because the Monaldeschi were friendly to the French.

So opposed that they would murder an innocent young man? Simon burned to seize Marco di Filippeschi and throttle the truth from him.

By turning his head slightly, Simon could see Friar Mathieu on the left side of the church, sitting in the midst of the Franciscan congregation.

Beyond the Franciscans, in the shadow of a pillar, stood a stout man in dark cape and tunic. D'Ucello, the podesta, observing the funeral—thinking perhaps that Alain's killer might attend. He prayed that the podesta would stop wasting his time pursuing the nonexistent women Simon and Alain had been with.

Find Alain's killer, damn you! Simon thought, clenching his teeth.

Simon turned briefly to survey the crowd that filled the nave all the way to the doors. Halfway back, a spot of red light from a window fell on a man's blond hair. Simon was almost certain that was David of Trebizond. He still saw no sign of Sophia, and his heart fell.

As Simon watched the pope celebrate the mass, assisted by the two cardinals, the Italian Ugolini and the French le Gros, he wondered whether Alain was watching from heaven. He must be in heaven. Was he not a martyr?

But did Alain care about what was happening on this earth? Surely a man would want to see his own funeral. For a moment Simon imagined he could speak to Alain, reach out and touch him.

How do you like this, my friend? The pope himself says mass for you.

Simon choked on a sob and had to wipe tears from his face.

The pope sang the Gospel in a quavering voice, and a chorus of stout young priests boomed back the responses. The voices, rising and falling in the chant devised by Pope Gregory the Great, unaccompanied by any instrument, rebounded from the heavy stones of the vaulted ceiling.

Simon swore to himself he would write about this to Alain's mother.

When it came time for the sermon, Fra Tomasso d'Aquino rose from the bench that had been set for him at the front of the cathedral. He turned and bowed to the pope, who sat in a throne on the right side of the altar. Pope Urban's hand twitched in a small gesture of blessing.

Standing at the head of Alain's bier, Simon was close enough to Fra Tomasso to hear the breath whistling through his nostrils as he exerted himself to move his bulk from bench to altar steps. The black rosary around his middle rattled with his steps and creaked with his heavy breathing.

A hush, heavy with the odor of incense, fell over the crowd assembled in the nave. For a sermon by a bishop or even a cardinal, this crowd of high-ranking prelates would probably go on whispering to each other. But all were interested in hearing the philosopher-friar who was famous throughout Christendom, whom some revered as a living saint and a few others considered a subtle heretic.

Fra Tomasso spoke Latin, as was customary before any assemblage of churchmen. His tenor voice sent high-pitched reverberations through the nave of the great church. It is a sad moment, he said, when God chooses to cut off a young man in his prime, yet it happens all too often. I share the sorrow of the family and friends of this excellent young knight, he said, and Simon felt comforted. Indeed, all Christendom must mourn the loss of such a fine young man, killed while performing his duty, far from home, guarding an embassy to His Holiness from the other side of the earth.

And accompanying a friend making a secret visit to a lady.

The stout friar waxed philosophic, as was expected of him, discoursing on the Fifth Commandment, "Thou shalt not kill," using Alain as an example. The Sire de Pirenne's death was murder, ambush out of the dark, he said.

Loud coughing interrupted the sermon. Simon looked and saw that it was Pope Urban, bent double, Cardinal le Gros holding his arm and resting a hand on his shoulder, while Cardinal Ugolini looked alarmed. The coughing had a burbling sound to it, as if the old pope's lungs were full of fluid. A cough like that in November was an ominous thing, thought Simon.

Fra Tomasso resumed when His Holiness had quieted. To kill is not always a sin, he said, but to kill the innocent is. It is not a sin, therefore, to wage war on the Saracens, as pope after pope has called upon good Christian warriors to do, because the Saracens are not innocent. They hold in their clutches the most sacred places of Christendom, the lands where Our Lord Jesus Christ was born and died; they rob and murder pilgrims seeking to visit those holy places; and they seek to spread the false religion of Mohammed-anism which denies the central mystery of our faith—Christ cruci-fied, dead, and risen again. For all these reason the Saracens should be fought.

Fra Tomasso paused and looked about him. Simon felt that the pause was intended to be significant, that the great Dominican was about to say something very important. But the silence was dis-turbed by a whispering. It came from behind Simon and to his right. He glanced in that direction and saw that the Bulgarian woman, Ana, was sitting with the two Tartars and was whispering her trans-lation of Fra Tomasso's sermon to John, the older one, who was immediately on her left.

"We may ask ourselves, why does God permit an innocent young man like this to die?" Fra Tomasso went on. "The answer is, of course, that He permits it to make possible a greater good, the exercise of human free will. I say to you that Our Lord, Jesus Christ, crucified at the age of thirty-three, is the type of all innocent young men done to death by evil. And evil is a necessary conse-quence of human freedom."

Fra Tomasso looked out over his audience for another silent mo-ment, then said, "God must value freedom very highly if He allows so much evil to occur, just so freedom can exist."

I never thought of that.

But there was very little freedom in the world, Simon thought, apart from the power to sin. Everybody from kings down to the meanest serfs was bound in a net of obligations, duties, laws, loy-alties, obedience. Simon remembered what Friar Mathieu had said about using Fra Tomasso's vow of obedience, through de Verceuil's speaking to his Dominican superior, to force him to give up his opposition to the alliance.

And now Simon noticed that Fra Tomasso was looking at de Verceuil.

"Often, all too often, one man will seek to rob another of the freedom to do what is right," Fra Tomasso said. "If a superior commands another to do wrong, and the inferior obeys, the one who gives the wrongful order bears the greater burden of guilt. But some guilt also falls upon the one who obeys. It is only with the greatest reluctance and after the greatest deliberation that one should disobey any order from one of higher rank. But there are times when it must be done."

Again he looked at de Verceuil.

"Thus when we see a mighty nation that again and again does harm to the innocent," said Fra Tomasso, "we are bound in conscience to denounce it."

Simon felt as if he had been struck on the head with a rock. Now he was sure of what was coming. And so, evidently, were others, because a murmuring was arising in the church.

Fra Tomasso blinked slowly, as if to show his calm acceptance of the stir he was causing. "We are obliged to denounce unjust war even when the evildoer offers us the hand of fellowship. When a puissant nation takes up arms against the world, when it makes war its chief occupation, when it attacks peoples that have not harmed it, when it threatens all humanity, we are not permitted to condone such wrongs. When this nation carries war to innocent, unarmed men, women, and children, slaughtering these noncombatants by the tens and hundreds of thousands, we are obliged to condemn it."

Oh, my God! If this is the Church's verdict, all is lost.

Simon looked at the pope on his throne to the right of the altar. He sat slumped, his white mitre tilted forward, his eyes half shut as if in thought. Simon saw no sign that Urban objected to what Fra Tomasso was saying.

The murmur was louder now. Despairing, Simon turned to look back at the Tartars. Little points of candlelight were reflected in their black eyes, and their brown faces were tight. Simon could imagine what would happen to anyone, holy man or not, who spoke out against them so in their own camp.

The stout Dominican stretched an arm in a flowing white sleeve toward the still, mail-clad body on the red bier. "It may be asked, why do I speak of such things on this sad day, when we mourn a young man cruelly struck down in youth? I answer that this young man came here and died here because Christendom is now faced with this great moral dilemma. What we owe this young man, what we owe any man who dies in the performance of his duty, is to do our own duty."

"Enough! Sit down!" came a hoarse whisper from Simon's left, and he turned to see de Verceuil half out of his chair, fists clenched. It had been de Verceuil who had wanted Fra Tomasso, as the most distinguished speaker in Orvieto, to deliver the funeral sermon. And doubtless it was the cardinal's heavy-handed dealing with Fra Tomasso that had provoked this particular sermon. And now de

Verceuil was trying publicly to silence Fra Tomasso, making more enemies for their cause.

Fra Tomasso turned in the cardinal's direction, then once again slowly shut his eyes and slowly opened them as he turned away. He went on speaking.

"And perhaps God has taken this young man from us to remind us how many other innocent lives may be lost if we wage war unwisely."

Simon and the other five French knights turned the red-draped wooden pallet so that Alain's head was toward the altar and his feet toward the church door. The weight had not bothered Simon carrying Alain into the church, but now the burden seemed twice as heavy. He was afraid, as he descended the stairs in front of the cathedral, one worn stone step at a time, that his knees might buckle and he might spill Alain to the ground. He would be anxious until he got Alain back on the cart that would carry him to his final resting place in the cemetery on a hill to the north of Orvieto's great rock.

And where will I go?

Trying to get de Verceuil to change Fra Tomasso's mind had been a serious error in judgment. Every important churchman and official in Orvieto had heard the greatest thinker in Christendom attack the plan of Christians and Tartars waging war together on the Saracens. What would happen now?

Nothing.

Nothing would happen, and that was all that was needed for the alliance to fail. The Tartars would go home. They would continue their war against the Saracens, the war they had been losing lately, without Christian help. And eventually the Mameluke waves would roll over Palestine and Syria and the Christian strongholds in Outremer would crumble like sand castles.

And the escutcheon of Gobignon is a little more tarnished. And I have led my dearest vassal to useless death. Whenever the Tartars leave Italy, and it will probably be soon, I will return to Château Gobignon a failure.

He thought back to his meeting with Charles d'Anjou on the wall of the Louvre last July. It had seemed then that helping the Tartars to ally themselves with the Christians was a way to change his whole life for the better. He would take his rightful place in the kingdom as a great baron. He would end the shame and suffering he had always lived with. He would hold his head up among the nobility, and King Louis and Count Charles would love and respect him.

Now he would accomplish none of those things. He had been knocked from his horse and was rolling in the dust. He would go back to the living death of being afraid to show his face beyond the bounds of Gobignon, the only place in the world where he was known and respected.

Go back to Gobignon and never see Sophia again? She, at least, would not think less of him because the grand alliance had failed. She probably felt sorry for Alain. Perhaps even felt responsible for his death. Simon should go and reassure her.

And then what? Bid her farewell?

He and de Puys on the other side, two knights behind each of them, slid Alain's body with a dry, rasping sound along the un-painted gray wood of the cart bed. The red ribbons on the four tall cartwheels fluttered in the slight breeze.

A thought that had fleetingly occurred to Simon before now formed itself solidly in his mind.

What if he were to take Sophia back to Gobignon as his bride?

Many there were who would rail against him for doing it. His grandmother in particular, herself the daughter of a king, would be beside herself with fury. King Louis and Uncle Charles might even try to stop him. But he was the Count de Gobignon, a Peer of the Realm, almost a king in his own right, and he had tried to do what his elders expected of him, and he had failed.

Twice he had loved women whose lands and high birth made them proper matches for him in the eyes of the world, and twice he had been prevented from marrying the woman of his choice be-cause of Count Amalric's legacy of wickedness.

Well, the devil take all of them. If they would not accept him as a member of the noblesse, then he was not obliged to behave as one.

Surely his mother and father, considering the way their own mar-riage had come about, would understand and approve his choice.

And somehow he doubted that Cardinal Ugolini would raise any objection to his marrying his niece, Sophia.

XXXVII

An open letter from Fra Tomasso d'Aquino of the Order of Preaching Friars to the Christian sovereigns of Europe, from Orvieto, 7th day of November A.D. 1263

> Let us leave these wild beasts, Tartars and Muslims alike, to devour each other, that they may all be consumed and perish; and we, when we proceed against the enemies of Christ who remain, will slay them and cleanse the face of the earth, so that all the world will be subject to the one Catholic Church and there be one Shepherd and one fold.

When Simon and Friar Mathieu climbed the stone steps into Fra Tomasso's cell, pushing up a trapdoor to enter, he was bent over a scroll. He held the two rolled-up ends apart with his fingertips, and as he read he very gently pushed down the bottom part of the roll, allowing the part he had read to roll up. The scroll looked very old, and the Dominican friar handled it as if it might fall apart in his hands.

He did not look up at his two visitors. His large head moved ever so slightly from side to side as he scanned the lines of writing, and Simon could hear his loud breathing just as he had a week ago in the cathedral. Simon and Friar Mathieu stood quietly and waited for Fra Tomasso to stop reading and notice them.

It had taken Friar Mathieu's Franciscan superiors a week of delicate negotiations after Alain's funeral to arrange an audience with the Dominican philosopher for Friar Mathieu and Simon. Simon prayed, feeling the sweat break out on his forehead, that their intrusion would not annoy Fra Tomasso. He desperately hoped that they could persuade him to change his mind about the alliance.

It was really up to Friar Mathieu, he thought. That Simon could have any effect on such a brilliant philosopher was unthinkable.

Simon noticed a single deep crease between the great Dominican's eyebrows. His forehead bulged on either side of the crease, as if the muscles that made him frown had grown from much exercise. The brows themselves were so fair and sparse as to seem almost invisible.

Fra Tomasso laid a broad right hand on the scroll to hold it open, picked up a feather pen with his left hand, dipped the sharpened tip into a tiny ink jar, and began making small, rapid marks on a piece of parchment. Simon watched with interest. Since his university days, he rarely saw people reading and writing, and could not remember ever seeing anyone write with his left hand. When the pen ran dry, Fra Tomasso happened to glance up as he dipped it again.

"Dear Lord, forgive me," he said, his eyes round with surprise. "Friends, I did not hear you enter. Please pardon my rudeness." Simon was gratified to hear him speak French and impressed by his fluency.

"It is we who are guilty of rudeness, Fra Tomasso," said Friar Mathieu, "for interrupting your work."

"My brothers in Christ are more important than books," said the stout Dominican, gesturing to them to take seats on his bed.

His cell was a circular room occupying the top floor of a tower in the compound that housed his order in Orvieto. The curved walls of the room were painted as white as Fra Tomasso's robe. A black wooden cross surmounted by a white ivory figure of Jesus hung over the bed. Fra Tomasso sat, his chair hidden by his great bulk, with his back to a window, at a large trestle table with stacks of books and boxes of scrolls on either side of him. His bed was a wide, sturdy wooden platform covered with a straw-filled mattress and a blanket the size of a galley's sail. A giant could lie on that bed, Simon thought.

"I must admit this scroll is a great treasure, and I am reluctant to tear my eyes from it," he said. "A hitherto lost treatise of Aristotle on the composition and movements of the heavenly bodies. This copy might be over six hundred years old. In Greek. You are familiar with *the* philosopher?" He looked from Friar Mathieu to Simon eagerly.

"I did study for a year at Père Sorbonne's college in Paris, Your Reverence," said Simon. "We read the works of several philosophers."

Fra Tomasso smiled indulgently. "I always refer to Aristotle as *the* philosopher because I can learn more from him than from any other ancient or modern thinker. Do you not agree, Reverend Father?'' He turned to Friar Mathieu. "Or are you, like so many of your fellow Franciscans, uninterested in philosophy?"

Oh, God, he scorns Franciscans, thought Simon with dread. *We're sure to fail.*

"I truly would like to find the time for it," said Friar Mathieu, unruffled. "But I seem to be always traveling."

Fra Tomasso nodded. "You and that merchant from Trebizond are the only two Christians in Orvieto who have traveled among the Tartars. I found your testimony at His Holiness's council quite fascinating."

"But not persuasive?" Friar Mathieu leaned forward intently.

Simon caught his breath. Fra Tomasso had given them an opening.

"I presumed that was why you had come to see me," said Fra Tomasso with a self-satisfied smile. "Let me assure you, good friar and noble count, that until a little over a week ago I had tried to keep to a strict neutrality, feeling that in that way I could be more useful to His Holiness. Even after hearing the Tartars condemn themselves out of their own mouths at the Contessa di Monaldeschi's reception. But then I changed my mind."

"Let me ask you a rather delicate question, Your Reverence," said Friar Mathieu.

Fra Tomasso leaned back and rested his hands, fingers laced, on his huge belly. "Any question at all."

"Did Cardinal de Verceuil's behavior toward you have anything to do with your change of mind?"

The crease in the Dominican philosopher's forehead deepened. Simon winced inwardly. What if, now, they had truly offended Fra Tomasso?

"Surely you do not suggest that I would let personal pique determine my position on a matter so important to the future of Christendom?"

"I am not surprised, knowing Your Reverence's reputation, that you grasp just how important the matter is," Friar Mathieu said.

Neatly sidestepping Fra Tomasso's question, Simon thought.

"Exactly. Thus it was that when Cardinal de Verceuil went to Fra Augustino da Varda, my Superior General, demanding that he order me to change my position on the Tartars, I realized it was time for me to come to a conclusion."

"I made a terrible mistake," said Friar Mathieu as much to himself and Simon as to Fra Tomasso. "May God forgive me."

"What mistake was that?" asked Fra Tomasso.

"Not trying to discuss this with Your Reverence myself, as I am doing now. To be honest, I feared you would not care to meet with a poor Franciscan."

"Again you do me an injustice," said Fra Tomasso. "*The* philosopher tells us that we acquire knowledge first of all through the senses. Therefore, if you would know about something, ask of those who have seen it firsthand."

"Then perhaps you have new questions," said Friar Mathieu.

Simon felt despair pressing on him like a mail shirt that was too heavy. Fra Tomasso was a man whose whole life was argument. How could Friar Mathieu hope to persuade him to change his mind about anything?

His chair creaking loudly, Fra Tomasso leaned forward and rested his elbows on the table in front of him. "I am so sure of my conclusions that I have written to Emperor Sigismund in German, King Boleslav in Poland, and King Wenceslas in Hungary—all lands that have suffered from the depredations of the Tartars, urging them to beg His Holiness to repudiate this scheme that will bring the frontier of Tartary so much closer to us. I have written to King Louis of France, your liege lord, too, young Count de Gobignon, even though he is said to be eager for a pact with the Tartars. Furthermore, Father da Varda is considering my proposal that the Dominican order all over Christendom preach against an alliance with the Tartars."

Hearing in Fra Tomasso's words the ruin of all his hopes, Simon could not contain himself. He burst out. *"Why?"*

Fra Tomasso looked surprised, even a bit affronted. "For all the reasons you heard in church last Friday. They are not simple savages, my young friend. They are diabolical."

It was hopeless. Simon's heart sand lower and lower. The great preacher's mind was made up.

"Yes, but, Your Reverence"—Simon felt driven by desperation to debate with a man whom he knew was invincible in argument—"we all know of many times when Christians and Saracens have been just as cruel."

Friar Mathieu gave a little grunt of agreement.

Fra Tomasso looked down at his thumbs, the tips pressed together as they rested on his wide belly. There was a moment of silence. He was thinking, Simon realized. Hardly ever had Simon seen a man stop to think before speaking in an argument. He began to tremble inwardly, expecting to be crushed.

Fra Tomasso raised a fat finger. "Yes, I know that Christian knights have also committed barbarities. But they did so in mindless rage, and afterward they were ashamed. Even the Mohammedan faith teaches the Saracens to wage only just wars, to be compassionate, to spare the innocent and helpless. I stipulate that neither Christians nor Mohammedans live up to these laws. But they *profess* them. The Tartars have no such laws. In their bottomless ignorance they think that it is *good* to commit deeds of unimaginable horror, and they do it with calculation. Exemplum: As David of Trebizond has told me, when they wipe out the population of a city, they know there will be a few survivors. So, weeks later, they return to the ruins when the remaining few people have emerged from hiding, and they slaughter them all. That is the worst sort of evil—evil done with utter deliberation."

David of Trebizond, may he roast in hell! thought Simon.

"With respect, Your Reverence," said Friar Mathieu, "the Tartars have lived isolated in their prairie homeland since the beginning of time. But I beg of you to believe that they can be won to the mercy of Christ. I have seen it. I have *done* it."

We are gaining ground, Simon thought. If Fra Tomasso really could be swayed by the testimony of a person who had seen with his own eyes, they had a chance.

A hammering from beneath the floor made Simon start. Someone was knocking on the trapdoor. Friar Mathieu nibbled at his mustache in vexation while Fra Tomasso smiled broadly and called, "Come up."

The heavy door creaked upward, pushed by a hand in a white sleeve. A shiny, tonsured scalp reflected the light from the tower window.

The young Dominican who emerged was almost too breathless to speak. "Reverend Father! News from Bolsena! Un miracolo!"

Fra Tomasso's eyes widened. "Bolsena? Is that near here?"

"So near, Reverend Father, that the miracle happened yesterday and the news reached us this afternoon."

"What miracle?"

"A foreign priest—from some eastern country—was saying mass. And when he got to the consecration and raised the Sacred Host"— the young friar's eyes glowed—"the Host dripped blood!"

Simon's head spun in confusion. Frustrated rage at being interrupted when they were so close to victory struggled with amazement at this tale of a bleeding Communion wafer. He looked at Fra Tomasso, and all hope ebbed away. The philosopher's face fairly glowed with relief. Sadness swelled in Simon. They did not have a chance. Perhaps they had never had one.

Before they knew it, it seemed, Friar Mathieu and Simon were walking together out the gate of the Dominican convent. Behind them there were shouts and white-robed friars bustling to and fro like a flock of startled doves. The whole convent, it seemed, was in an uproar over the miracle at Bolsena.

Fra Tomasso had courteously but firmly dismissed Mathieu and Simon, saying that he must question the one who brought the news. He might, he said, be called upon to look further into the event at Bolsena, and he must be fully prepared.

Simon had wanted to protest. If Fra Tomasso would only give them a little more time, he would surely have to change his mind about the Tartars. But Simon sensed that Fra Tomasso did not want to change his mind.

The sky was cold and gray as chain mail. Carters, horsemen, and laborers on foot bustled along, their cloaks pulled tight around them against the chill north wind.

All is lost, Simon thought, as he had after Alain's funeral. Just when they were gaining ground with Fra Tomasso, news of a miracle. Was God Himself against them?

Skulking back to Gobignon. Forever to be known, not as the count who helped liberate Jerusalem, but as the son of the traitor Amalric.

Maybe I should give it all up and become a Franciscan, like Friar Mathieu.

"Where did he get that scroll?" Friar Mathieu wondered.

"What can we do now?" said Simon. He was not really asking; it was only a way of saying he thought nothing could be done. He was in despair over the failure of their mission.

Then he thought of Sophia.

In an instant a light bloomed within him. Skulking back to Gobignon? No, riding back in triumph, with the most beautiful woman in the world beside him as his bride.

He had not yet nerved himself to propose to Sophia, but now that they had failed with Fra Tomasso, he could not wait to see her again.

Friar Mathieu scratched his white beard thoughtfully. "It was de Verceuil who tipped the scales against the Tartars. And it was we who sent de Verceuil. I thought this might be the one time he could be useful to us."

"Fra Tomasso had already sided with Ugolini's faction," Simon said. "That is why we sent de Verceuil."

"He told us today that he had been trying to be neutral," said Friar Mathieu. "But Sophia told you that Fra Tomasso had already sided with Ugolini's party. Do you suppose the great Dominican was not being candid with us? Or was it Sophia who was not being candid?"

Simon gasped at the sudden pain of a blow that was worse than their failure with Fra Tomasso. Sophia not honest? No, he could not live with that.

He stiffened so suddenly that his horse stopped walking. He stared at Friar Mathieu in dismay.

Friar Mathieu reached over and put his hand on Simon's arm. His touch was light but firm.

"Know where you are going, Simon. Do not travel blindly."

Simon nodded. There was a way to find out the truth about Sophia.

He must put Sordello to work. The mere thought of that blackguard spying on Sophia twisted his heart with anguish. But he had to know the truth.

XXXVIII

A letter from Emir Daoud ibn Abdallah to El Malik Baibars al-Bunduqdari, from Orvieto, 13th day of Muharram, 663 A.H.:

O Pillar of the Faith, the gift of the ancient scroll to the Christian scholar Tomasso d'Aquino has served our purposes beyond my expectations. At the same time that I delivered the scroll to him, I arranged for the allies of the Tartars to be deceived into thinking that the priest Tomasso was already in our camp. They chose the arrogant Cardinal de Verceuil, of whom I have told you, to bring his influence to bear on the priest Tomasso. The cardinal's treatment of Tomasso so offended him that he was driven to take the side we wished of him.

This Tomasso has turned the clouds Ugolini and I stirred up into a veritable thunderstorm. The pope cannot proclaim a crusade unless he has the support of the Christian kingdoms and peoples. Otherwise, they will support him only halfheartedly or not at all. I confess I am surprised at how often the Christians of Europe choose to neglect or even refuse to do what the pope demands of them.

As we know, the Christians of today have not the zeal to make war on us that their forefathers had. Let time pass, and Hulagu Khan will lose patience and recall his ambassadors. The Christians will fight among themselves here in Europe. And, if God wills it, Islam will know peace. Such is my deepest desire.

Time, O Malik Dahir, is our ally.

Daoud stood at his writing desk, smiling at the tiny Arabic characters with which he had covered the thin square of parchment.

El Malik Dahir—the victorious king. How well Daoud remembered the day Baibars had, with his help, assumed that title.

Riding back from the victory at the Well of Goliath, the Mameluke army was camped outside Bilbeis, two days ride northeast of El Kahira. Tomorrow Sultan Qutuz would hold audience at Bilbeis, and soon after he would ride into El Kahira in triumph, a triumph Baibars had earned for him.

Baibars was alone in his tent when Daoud answered his summons. His blue eye glittered out of deep shadows cast on his face by a small oil lamp that hung in the center of the tent. With his own hand Baibars served Daoud kaviyeh from a pot on a brazier, and the two men sat side by side, turned toward each other.

"Again he refused me," Baibars said. "I have given him every chance, Daoud."

Baibars's face was calm, but Daoud knew that the fury of a Tartar was boiling within him.

A reddish haze obscured the tent for Daoud as he fought back his own rage at the injustice to Baibars.

"He thinks I want to be governor of Aleppo merely out of ambition," Baibars said.

"The sultan is a fool," said Daoud.

The single sighted eye transfixed him. "No, not a fool. He played the game of power well enough when he made himself sultan. No one could blame him for the murders of Ai Beg and Spray of Pearls.

He restored order to El Kahira. His mistake now is in not trusting me. And that is an understandable mistake.'' Baibars stretched his thin lips in a sudden grin.

"Understandable how?" Daoud experienced that unsettling sense he often had that the one-eyed emir was always two or three jumps ahead of him.

"It comes of too much cleverness," said Baibars. "He does not believe me when I say I want to be governor of Aleppo because it is the first city Hulagu Khan will attack. He suspects me of a hidden motive. He thinks that if he gives me Aleppo I will break with El Kahira and claim all of Syria for my own, because that is what *he* would do. But Hulagu Khan, seeking vengeance for the Well of Goliath, is coming from Persia with all his power. May God send to the eternal fire a commander wicked enough to divide the kingdom at such a time.''

The kaviyeh Daoud held had cooled. He drained the glazed earthenware cup and put it down beside him.

"The sultan himself divides the kingdom," said Daoud, "by dishonoring you.''

"It is more than dishonor. It is war. If he thinks me too dangerous to be ruler of Aleppo, it means that he thinks me too dangerous to live.''

Daoud felt as if his heart had dropped into the cold, black bottom of a well. If Qutuz destroyed Baibars, he would destroy Islam and El Kahira and all of them. Daoud's whole world.

"What will you do?" said Daoud.

"I do not know what I will do," said Baibars, fixing his one eye on Daoud. "But you know that if he kills me, he will kill all close to me. What will *you* do?''

Daoud felt the edge of the headsman's blade on the back of his neck as he had not felt it since that day Qutuz demanded his death. The thought of being executed at Qutuz's command outraged him. It was one thing to die as a mujahid, a martyr in holy war for Islam, destined to be taken at once into paradise. But what a shameful fate, to be murdered because your own sovereign lord did not trust you.

"I am your slave, Effendi.''

"Not slave, Daoud. You are as near a son to me as a Mameluke can be. Are you not the husband of my favorite daughter? I speak now with you because I must speak, and in all this camp you are the only one I can rely on absolutely.''

Daoud felt tears coming to his eyes. He was embarrassed, even though he knew it was a manly thing to weep easily. For him crying was rare.

Baibars rested a large, strong hand on Daoud's arm.

"Never to know any brothers but our khushdashiya, our barracks mates, never to know any father but the emir who trained and freed us, it makes us the hardest, the finest warriors in the world. But we long for the loving families we never had."

Daoud wiped his face with the sleeve of his robe.

They sat in silence for a long time, while Daoud, stroking his thick blond beard, grappled with what Baibars was asking of him. Asking, not in words, but in the spaces between the words.

Baibars spoke. "Remember what the Tartar general, Ket Bogha, called Qutuz? The murderer of his master. The world belittles us because each sultan has climbed to the throne over the murdered body of the last sultan. Turan Shah, murdered."

He held up his left hand, his sword hand.

"I myself killed Turan Shah because he betrayed the Mamelukes. Next, Ai Beg, murdered. The Sultana Spray of Pearls, murdered. Ali, son of Ai Beg, murdered. Each murder weakens the throne itself."

"The throne is as strong as the man who holds it," said Daoud.

Baibars continued to look at his left hand, his head turned to the side in his one-eyed way. "Even so, Ai Beg did not himself kill Turan Shah and Qutuz did not himself kill Ali. If I kill Qutuz and take the throne with his blood on my hand, I am inviting every other Mameluke emir to kill me when my back is turned. The title of El Malik, the sultan, chief sovereign of Islam, will be like a ball in a game of mall, flying this way and that."

Daoud felt as if he were standing at the mouth of an enormous black cave. It was one thing to know that Qutuz was not fit to rule. It was another thing to think of striking down the sultan, the anointed of God. If Daoud entered this cave, he might never come out again. He might leave it only to fall into the flames of hell. He seemed to see stars in the depths of the cave, as if he were looking into the world beyond the world. Somewhere among those stars, God dwelt in His paradise with those He loved around Him, the Archangel Gabriel, and the Prophet, and Abraham and Jesus, and the saints and martyrs of Islam.

Is it God's will that I kill the sultan? How can I know?

He could not know. But he did know that second only to his

submission to God, the most important thing in his life was devotion to his emir. As Baibars said, his khushdashiya and his emir were all a Mameluke had.

He leaned closer to Baibars.

"Whoever dishonors my lord Baibars deserves instant death at the hands of my lord's servant."

Baibars closed both eyes with a look of satisfaction.

"Have I asked you to kill—anyone?" he said.

"No, Effendi."

They sat in silence again. The desert wind hummed in the ropes of Baibars's tent, and the poles shifted and creaked.

"If someone wished to kill Qutuz," said Baibars, "he should recall that we are now very close to El Kahira. Once Qutuz rides on streets festooned with silks and carpeted with flowers, once people see him as the victor of the Well of Goliath, they will love him too much. They would never accept his being taken from them. We could not control their fury."

Daoud said, "Tomorrow, when he holds audience at the palace of the governor of Bilbeis, men from all over the district with requests for favors, with claims, with grievances, will surround him, clamoring. Anyone could easily approach him."

Baibars nodded. "Let him be struck down before the eyes of many. Let it be like a public sacrifice. I would rather see it done so than by poison or ambush." His thin lips curved in a smile. "I seem to recall that you, too, have a preference for taking vengeance in public."

"If the other emirs demand that he who killed the sultan be punished," said Daoud, "you will have to sacrifice your servant."

Baibars's face tightened. "They will not. They will accept what you and I do."

"Nevertheless, if it seems needful to secure your place on the throne, you must give the killer up. You will not have to explain that to me. And you will still be my lord. My father."

"Ah, Daoud," Baibars said. Daoud saw a wetness in both Baibars's eyes now, the sighted and the blind.

Daoud stood beside a spiral pillar near the front of the audience hall of the governor of Bilbeis. It was a small chamber, but an elegant one. The floor was of mottled green marble, and pink columns lined the approach from the front door to the massive gilded throne on its dais.

Merchants and small landholders, officials in red fezzes, Bedouin sheikhs in black robes and burnooses, crowded the hall. Each man held a petition scroll for the sultan.

Daoud carried no petition, but the sleeve of his left arm hid, strapped to his wrist, a scabbard holding a twisting dagger—a flame dagger, the weapon of the Hashishiyya.

He longed for Qutuz to come into the hall, for the dance of death he had rehearsed a thousand times in his mind, to begin.

He had prayed this morning longer and with greater fervor than he had for many years.

When would Qutuz come?

At the doorways and around the edges of the room stood warriors of the halkha, the sultan's bodyguard, their steel helmets and breastplates inlaid with gold, their tunics bright yellow. What would they do when they saw him strike at Qutuz? They were Mamelukes. They had seen Qutuz's fear at the Well of Goliath and his pretensions afterward. But it was their duty to protect him. Daoud could not guess what feelings would move them.

Here and there around the room rose the spherical white turbans of the Mameluke emirs who had been at the Well of Goliath. There was Kalawun, called al-Elfi, the Thousander, because his first master had bought him for the incredible price of a thousand gold dinars, there Bektout, beside a blue-white pillar, another Kipchaq like Baibars. Six or so others talked quietly under the pointed arch of the public entrance to the audience chamber. None of the emirs paid attention to the petitioners who streamed past them into the room.

In the corner of the room farthest from the dais, Baibars stood alone. A head taller than anyone around him, he swung his white-turbaned head from side to side so that he could survey the room with his one good eye. His glance seemed to pass over Daoud without seeing him.

A side door to the throne room from the governor's private apartments swung open, and two officers of the halkha strode through.

One of the officers drew himself up and shouted, "The Beloved of God, the Victor of the Well of Goliath, El Malik al-Mudhaffar Qutuz!"

The buss of conversation in the room at once stilled, and Daoud's heartbeat filled his ears.

Then a roar arose as Qutuz entered briskly, arrayed in a bejeweled green turban and a black and silver robe of honor. His chamberlain, a stout man carrying a basket, followed him.

The petitioners rushed forward, clamoring and waving their scrolls. The men of the halkha made no attempt to hold them back. A merchant in a blue robe was the first to reach Qutuz, and he hugged the sultan, weeping. He first thrust a small silk bag into Qutuz's hand, which disappeared quickly under the sultan's black robe, then pressed a scroll upon him.

Qutuz handed the scroll to his chamberlain, who put it into the basket.

The petitioners were the people of Islam, and it was their right, as it had been since the days of the Prophet, to clamor for their ruler's attention. And though they might shout and beg and even manhandle the sultan, he must endure it, because these were the richest men of the district, the men of highest rank, those on whom the sultan's power in this place depended.

Qutuz enjoyed, Daoud knew, playing father to his people. And though one might think the Sultan of El Kahira had wealth enough, he was not averse to increasing it with the gifts of gold and jewels offered him on occasions like this.

Qutuz moved slowly through the petitioners, head high, his oiled beard pointed like the prow of a majestic ship. A small, indulgent smile played about his lips. He allowed them to impede his progress to the throne. The petitioners crowded around him, some plucking at his sleeve, some falling at his feet, some pulling at the hem of his robe, even kissing it in their urgency.

Another man, this one a sheikh in desert robes, seized the sultan in an embrace, bellowing his entreaty. This time when Qutuz stopped he disappeared behind a forest of upraised arms.

The babble of voices, each one trying to outshout the other, made Daoud's head ache. Men elbowed those beside them and pushed their hands into one another's faces. Daoud even saw one man claw his way up the backs of two who stood in front of him and climb over their shoulders to get closer to Qutuz.

From his position near the front of the hall Daoud could catch only glimpses of the sultan's green turban from time to time and follow his progress by watching where the turmoil was fiercest. The melee was like one of those towering dust storms that whirl across the desert, and Qutuz was at the center.

When Daoud judged that Qutuz was halfway to the throne, he began to move.

He plunged now into that black cave where God dwelt somewhere in infinite spaces. Doubt and fear he left at the mouth of that cave. He must give all his strength and will to what he was about to do.

He charged into the storm around Qutuz. Though these magistrates and merchants were feeble compared to him, their frenzy and the mere weight of their struggling bodies formed a wall that took all his strength to break through. Each man was so intent upon his own desperate need to reach the sultan that none of them seemed to feel Daoud forcing his way past them.

Qutuz saw him coming. The dark brown eyes met Daoud's, questioning, frowning. A Mameluke emir of Daoud's rank did not usually join a crowd of petitioners. The sultan's arms and hands were full of scrolls. His chamberlain had long since been carried away from him in the crush.

"Oh, Sultan, grant my prayer!" Daoud shouted in a loud voice. *For your death.*

Qutuz's jaw clenched, and his eyes widened in the beginning of fear as Daoud bore down on him.

Daoud had reached the center of the storm. Color and movement whirled about him. Shouts deafened him. He forced his mind to blot out the chaos all around and to focus totally on Qutuz. He made himself as oblivious to the shrieking men around him as they were to him.

He threw his arms around the sultan, crushing the satin of his kaftan and his armload of scrolls against his body.

When Daoud's arms came together behind Qutuz's back, his right hand reached into his left sleeve and pulled the dagger from its sheath.

Qutuz's hands pushed against Daoud's chest. So tight was Daoud's embrace that he felt the sultan take a deep breath, to cry for help. They were locked together like lovers.

Daoud stretched out his right arm, and then with all the strength in that arm drove the dagger into the sultan's back. He struck for the center of the back, between two ribs, so that the point would reach and stop Qutuz's heart.

His thrust went true. The strong, lean body jerked violently, then went limp in his arms. Qutuz was a weight against him, sliding downward. Daoud was sure he was already dead, because he did not move or cry out.

Triumph blazed up within him. He had done it. He had killed the sultan.

Daoud let go of the dagger, hilt-deep in Qutuz's back. He stepped backward quickly, pressing himself into the crowd around them. His heartbeat was thundering in his ears and his knees were quivering.

Qutuz toppled toward him as he moved back.

"The sultan falls!" a man next to him screamed.

Hands reached out to catch Qutuz as he fell. Cried of "The sultan has fainted!" "God help us!" "The sultan is hurt!" went up all around Daoud.

He continued to back away through the crowd. If attacked, he had decided, he would draw his saif and fight. If he must die, he desperately wanted to die fighting, not on the headsman's block.

He had not truly believed he could strike Qutuz down without being seen, but no one was yet pointing at him.

"Blood!" someone shrieked. "A dagger!" The shrieks and prayers were deafening.

All the men who had clustered around the fallen sultan backed away. Daoud was carried farther from the dead Qutuz by the crowd. Craning his neck over the heads around him, he could see the body lying sprawled face down on the green marble floor, a spreading bright red stain in the black and silver robes around the dagger's hilt.

The babble of voices was so confused that Daoud could no longer tell what anyone was saying. Mansur ibn Ziri, commander of the halkha, and Anis, master of the hunt, pushed their way through to Qutuz's body, while some men still clutching scrolls ran from the chamber. They must fear even being in the room where the sultan was murdered.

I have killed the sultan.

Though his whole body shook with reaction and his limbs felt weak, his heart was full of joy.

His hand on his sword hilt, Daoud surveyed the large chamber. The Mameluke emirs were looking, not at Qutuz's body, but at one another. And they kept glancing at Daoud.

They had seen Daoud throw his arms around Qutuz. They knew who had killed Qutuz. And they knew why he had done it.

Baibars still stood apart in a far corner. His good eye met Daoud's, but his face was a mask.

As the last of the local men fled the place of death, a silence fell over the room. The Mamelukes were alone with the body of their sultan. The men of the halkha, the sultan they were sworn to protect now dead, looked at the emirs. The only voices now were the murmured words of Mansur and Anis as they bent over Qutuz's body.

With an effort Mansur pulled the dagger from Qutuz's back. Anis grunted when he saw the twisting blade.

Heart hammering, Daoud tensed himself. Would Mansur turn and accuse him? He glanced over his shoulder to make sure no one was behind him and took gliding steps backward until his shoulders were pressed against a pillar.

Mansur said in a voice that carried through the room, "The flame dagger. Our lord has been struck down by the Hashishiyya."

Daoud almost laughed aloud with relief. With an immense effort he held himself rigid, his fists clenched so tightly at his side they hurt. Mansur was telling everyone who knew what had happened what they were to tell everyone who did not know.

Would anyone contradict Mansur? No one did. Relief spread through him.

Carefully, almost delicately, Mansur laid the dagger on the floor beside Qutuz. He stood up, wiping his hands on his mantle.

With rapid strides the commander of the halkha crossed the chamber toward Baibars. To arrest him? What choice had Mansur made?

To bow deeply before Baibars. He made a graceful, sweeping gesture toward the vacant throne.

"My Lord, the power is yours."

Praise to God!

Baibars's single-eyed gaze paused for an instant, Daoud saw, as it fell upon each of the emirs. In the look he fixed upon each there was both question and challenge.

Some of the emirs bowed their turbaned heads slightly. Others, like Kalawun al-Elfi, simply looked back at him in silence, and that was assent enough.

Baibars raised his right hand toward the vaulted ceiling, the wide sleeve of his robe falling away from his powerful arm.

"With Your help, O God." He did not shout, but his deep voice carried through the room.

Slowly but with a terrible firmness he walked across the room. So quiet was the audience chamber that Daoud at the other end of the room could hear the scrape of Baibars's boots on the three

. marble steps to the throne. Baibars turned and sat on the throne, resting his hands on its arms. He leaned back a little, and his eye seemed to rest on some spot above and beyond the heads of those who watched him.

Mansur ibn Ziri turned to an officer of the halkha. "Let runners be sent to El Kahira. Let them tell the people, 'Pray for God's mercy on El Malik al-Mudhaffar Qutuz. Pray for the long life of your Sultan Baibars.' "

Let me hail him first, thought Daoud. *And if he wants to kill me for what I did, let it be now.*

Trembling with exhilaration, he strode through the crowd and up the center of the room toward the throne. "Lord Sultan!" he said in a loud voice, "El Malik Dahir! Victorious King!"

He dropped to his knees and prostrated himself, striking his forehead on the hard, cold floor.

Hearing a knock at his chamber door, Daoud rolled up the slip of thin parchment and dropped it into the purse at his belt.

Sordello entered at his command, greeting and saluting him.

"I see you are one of us, Messer David."

"One of who?"

Sordello pointed to the writing desk where Daoud had been standing and the sheaf of quill pens. "One who had his letters. I write down all my songs."

Daoud had no wish to feel kinship with Sordello. The bravo had not bothered to clean the whiskers from his face for several days, and there was untidy-looking gray stubble, like fur, under his nose and on his cheeks and chin. A man should grow a beard, Daoud thought, or keep his cheeks smooth.

"What brings you to me?" Daoud asked curtly.

"The Count de Gobignon sent a message to me by way of Ana, the Bulgarian woman. Would you care to read it?"

De Gobignon's note read: "The lady Sophia, Cardinal Ugolini's niece, has represented herself to me as an honest woman who knows nothing of politics and takes sides neither for nor against the Tartar alliance. Find out if she is telling the truth. Report to me in three days time."

Daoud felt pleased with himself. Turning Sordello into a spy for himself was yielding useful results. It was not surprising that the Frenchman was suspicious of Sophia. She was so close to the party opposing the alliance; how could he think otherwise? But now,

Daoud thought happily, they had the means to put his suspicions to rest.

Daoud handed the note back to Sordello, saying, "That is short and to the point, but he does not tell you how you are to learn whether Madonna Sophia is telling him the truth or not."

"I could tell him that I have sung at dinner for the cardinal's household," said Sordello. "I could report a conversation at table which shows Madonna Sophia to be the innocent he would like to think she is."

"You keep talking about your songs and your singing," Daoud said. "Answer me truly—are you any good at those things?"

Sordello shrugged. "I could claim to be one of the finest trovatores in all Italy, but if I did, you would rightfully ask why I have to make my living as a hired man-at-arms. So I will say only that I am good enough that I wish I could spend all my time making poetry and singing."

A worthy wish, Daoud thought. Hearing his careful self-estimate, Daoud's respect for the man increased a bit.

"Then you *will* sing at the cardinal's table. Your suggestion is a good one. I will also arrange for you to be with Madonna Sophia at other times as well, so that you can honestly claim to know something about her."

"Very good, Messer David." Sordello turned to go, then turned back again. "Messere?"

"Yes?"

"Do you think you might send me on another trip to paradise sometime soon?" The eager light in his eyes sickened Daoud.

"Do your work well, and I will see that you are properly rewarded."

Sordello left, and Daoud brooded over his shame at what he had done to the man—turned him into something less than human, less than animal, a kind of demon with a single appetite.

After a moment he forced himself to put that out of his mind. A fighter in jihad, holy war, must do many an ugly thing, but all was for the greater glory of God.

XXXIX

THE HYMN "O SALUTARIS HOSTIA," SUNG BY OVER A THOUSAND strong voices abetted by several thousand more uncertain ones, echoed from the hillsides. The entire clergy of Orvieto, from the pope down to the lowliest subdeacon, had come out of the city, and so had most of the lay population. But Daoud's attention was drawn, not by the great procession coming down the cliffside road, or by the crowd in the meadow around him, but by the astonishing change that had come over the landscape.

It was as if some devastating disease had struck all the growing things of the region, from the tallest trees to the very blades of grass. The leafless groves raised black, skeletal arms up to the bright blue sky, like men praying. The vineyards on the slopes were gray clumps of shrubbery. The meadow grass on which he stood was yellow and brittle; it broke to bits underfoot.

He had known, of course, that such changes came over the European landscape each winter. But to see such desolation with his own eyes was more amazing, even frightening, than he realized it would be. Soon the Christians would be celebrating the birth of Jesus the Messiah, whom they believed was God. Seeing death in the landscape all around him, Daoud found it easier to understand why these idolators might feel driven to worship a God who rose from the dead.

He hoped it would help his mission that the wave of enthusiasm for the miracle at Bolsena had swept everyone in Orvieto from the pope on down. He hoped they would have neither time to think about the Tartars nor interest in dealing with them.

But this miracle and all the talk about it made him uneasy. The frenzy in the Christian faces around him might be turned, he thought, in any direction. It must be the same frenzy that had driven generations of crusaders to hurl themselves against the Dar al-Islam.

Fra Tomasso was at the very center of the furor. It was he who had sent word from Bolsena that in his judgment the miracle was indeed authentic. Might this new preoccupation distract him from his efforts to prevent the alliance?

And there was something else, something that revived a terror buried deep in Daoud's soul. Jesus, the crucified God of the Christians, stirred in this miracle. As a boy growing up among Muslims, Daoud had renounced belief in the crucifixion and resurrection of Jesus. Now he felt again his father's ghostly hand on his shoulder, and the hairs lifted on the back of his neck.

"Look at the sick people and the cripples lining the road," said Lorenzo. "I would not have thought there could be that many infirm people in Orvieto." He and Daoud stood side by side, at a spot where the road between Bolsena and Orvieto passed through a wide valley, their horses tethered in a nearby grove of poplar trees. They had moved back a few paces from the edge of the road to make room for a dozen men and women on stretchers, wrapped in blankets, who had been carried here by Franciscan friars from their hospital.

All around Lorenzo and Daoud stood Cardinal Ugolini's men-at-arms, servants, and maids. Ugolini's entire household was here except for the few of highest rank who would march with the cardinal, who marched behind the pope.

Fearing that Scipio would go uncared for, Lorenzo had brought him along, holding him on a thick leather leash. The gray boarhound paced nervously and growled from time to time.

In the meadow across the road the pope's servants had erected a pavilion without walls—just a roof of silk, gold and white, the papal colors, coming to three points held up by a dozen or more stout poles. There Pope Urban would say mass after receiving the sanctified cloth.

Daoud glanced down the road to where Sophia stood. They had agreed that in public it would be best for them to appear far apart from each other. She was dressed as any well-to-do Italian woman might be, her hair covered with a round, flat linen cap bound under her chin, a midnight-blue chemise with long, tight sleeves, and a sleeveless gown of light blue silk over it. Beside Sophia stood a slighter figure in gray veil and gown. They had their heads close together, talking.

"Who is that with Sophia?" Daoud asked Lorenzo.

"Oh, Rachel, I think." Lorenzo studiously examined Scipio's head for fleas.

"She appears in public with Rachel?" Daoud said angrily.

Lorenzo shrugged. "No one knows who Rachel is." He slapped Scipio's rump. "Sit."

"I did not like Sophia visiting Rachel," Daoud said. "Even less do I like their being seen together in public."

Trumpets shrilled and drums sounded as the hymn came to an end. Daoud looked toward Orvieto. The road that wound down past the gray-yellow folds of tufa was filled with people.

At the head of the procession walked the pope in gold and white, and the cardinals of the Sacred College in bright red. The middle of the long line was bright with the purples of archbishops and bishops and the variegated raiment of the nobility. The rear was dark with the grays and browns of common folk.

From this distance Daoud could not see Pope Urban's face, but there was no mistaking the beehive-shaped mitre with its glittering triple crown.

Lucky for the pope the weather was cold, thought Daoud. Wearing those heavy vestments on a hot day would surely kill the old man. That today he chose to go on foot showed how much this miracle meant to him.

Daoud turned and looked to the west. The marchers from Bolsena were close, and people were falling to their knees all over the meadow.

I will have to kneel, too, and seem to worship their idols. Forgive me, God.

Daoud saw Sophia and Rachel drop to their knees.

Surely they think as little of this as I do.

Coming toward Daoud from the west was a great banner that offended his every religious feeling. Painted on the red cloth were the head and shoulders of a bearded man, Jesus the Messiah, with huge, staring eyes. On his head was a plaited wreath of thorns, and behind it a disk of gold. From the nail holes that pierced his upraised palms fell painted drops of blood.

An idol, such as the Koran forbade and the Prophet had come into this world to destroy.

And then he thought of the great crucifix that hung in the chapel of Château Langmuir outside Ascalon, and his mother taking him by the hand to pray before it.

"Because *He* lived and died here," he remembered her sweet voice saying, "that is why we are here in this Holy Land."

He felt momentarily dizzy. They, his mother and father and all these people here, thought that the bearded man, with the wounds of crucifixion in his hands, was God. And he had believed it once, too.

No, God was One. He could not be a Father who reigned in heaven and a Son who came down to earth. God was glorious and all-powerful; He could not be crucified. God was the Creator; He could not be part of His creation.

And yet—the cold hand still lay upon his shoulder. A gentle hand, but it frightened him.

All around Daoud the infidels were throwing themselves on their knees, even on their faces, in the road before the advancing banner. A man in a black robe was walking before the banner bearer. Despite his long gray beard there was something about his staring eyes and wide, downturned mouth that reminded Daoud of a fish.

The bearded priest, Father Kyril, was holding up by its corners a white square of linen. That, thought Daoud, must be the altar cloth on which the drops of blood had fallen from the wafer of bread. As he walked he slowly, solemnly, turned from side to side to allow people on both sides of the road to see the cloth.

"*Kneel*, David, for God's sake!" Lorenzo ground out beside him.

His curiosity had made him forget himself. He dropped to his knees, feeling dry grass prick his skin through his silk hose. Lorenzo knelt beside him, gripping the dog's collar. The sick and crippled people lying beside the road were wailing and holding up their arms in supplication.

Again Daoud asked God's forgiveness for his seeming idolatry.

Father Kyril and the altar cloth were only a dozen paces away, and now Daoud could see the brown bloodstains on the white cloth. Amazingly they appeared to form the profile of a bearded man.

As a cold wind against his spine, he felt his long-buried fear of the wrath of the Christian God.

The big hound, right beside him, let out a thunderous bark. Daoud started with surprise. His heart pounded in his chest.

Scipio barked and barked, so loudly Daoud put his hands over his ears. Father Kyril took a step backward. People who had been venerating the bloodstained cloth turned with angry shouts. The hands of the men-at-arms escorting Father Kyril twitched, groping for the weapons they were not carrying.

"Scipio!" Lorenzo gave the hound a sharp slap on the side of the head. The dog kept up its barking. Father Kyril had stopped walking and looked frightened. He clutched the stained cloth to his breast. At a word from him, Daoud thought, the crowd would tear to pieces the dog, Lorenzo, and perhaps Daoud himself.

Lorenzo grabbed Scipio's muzzle with both hands, forcing it shut. Scipio kept up a growling through his teeth. Lorenzo growled back, "Be still!" He wrestled the dog down until the lean gray head was pressed into the grass.

"Barking is the only way he knows to greet the Savior," said Lorenzo with an ingratiating grin, looking up at the people glaring at him.

"There could be a devil in that dog," a brown-robed friar said ominously. But Scipio relaxed under Lorenzo's hands, and those around Daoud and Lorenzo turned back to the procession.

Daoud was furious. Lorenzo's damned dog had been like a stone in his shoe ever since they set out from Lucera. Lorenzo was a valuable man, but he insisted on attaching others to him who caused endless trouble. Like the dog. Like Rachel.

A scream rose above the music, so shrill Daoud put his hands over his ears again.

"My God! I can see!" A woman was standing, clasping her hands together and flinging them wide again and again. One of the Franciscans threw his arms around her, whether to rejoice with her or restrain her, Daoud could not tell. But she pushed him away and went stumbling after Father Kyril. From the way her hands pawed the air, Daoud suspected she could not see very well, but she shouted with joy all the same.

She joined a crowd of people, many of them waving walking sticks and crutches, others with bloodstained bandages trailing from their hands. One man, Daoud saw to his horror, was missing a foot and was limping along in the dirt road, without the aid of crutch or cane, on one whole leg and one stump bound with a dirty cloth that ended at the ankle. His face was red, sweat-slick, and blindly ecstatic.

Behind the rejoicing invalids walked rows of clergymen from Bolsena. Daoud recognized a familiar figure in the foreground, Fra Tomasso d'Aquino, his cheeks crimson with cold and exertion, his black mantle blowing in the wind. He had spent the last two weeks,

Daoud knew, in Bolsena investigating the miracle and overseeing preparations for the altar cloth to be brought to Pope Urban.

What did he think now, Daoud ached to know. Would he still work as hard to defeat the Tartar alliance? Did this miracle mean Daoud had gained ground or lost ground?

A sudden silence fell over the meadow. Pope Urban, with trembling hands upraised, approached Father Kyril, whose back was to Daoud.

Father Kyril went down on his knees before the pope, holding up the white cloth over his head like a banner. Then the pope also knelt, somewhat shakily, with the assistance of two young priests in white surplices and black cassocks. Urban reached up for the cloth and pulled it down to his face and kissed it.

He is seeing that cloth for the first time, and yet he seems to have no doubt that he is looking at the blood of his God that died.

Daoud felt a chill that was colder than the December air.

Daoud pushed his way to the edge of the open pavilion, where the pope, assisted by Father Kyril and Fra Tomasso, was saying high mass. A band of musicians blew on hautboys and clarions, sawed at vielles, stroked harps, and thumped on drums.

The white cloth with its strange rust-colored stain was stretched on a gilded frame above the altar. Daoud felt uneasy whenever he looked at it. Just when it seemed he had found the key to wrecking the union of Tartars and crusaders—a miracle. What did it portend?

Memory showed him his mother and father celebrating Easter, standing hand in hand before the altar at Château Langmuir, receiving Holy Communion—the Sacred Host—from their chaplain. When he was old enough, his mother had told him he, too, would be allowed to take Jesus into his heart by swallowing the Communion wafer. What a strange belief! But at the time it had seemed beautiful.

I bear witness that God is One, that Muhammad is the Messenger of God. . . .

He glanced around the pavilion, and saw many faces he had come to know in the last few months. There was Cardinal de Verceuil with his big nose and small mouth. There was Ugolini, the size of a child, dressed up as a cardinal, blinking rapidly, looking rather bored. In the front row of standing worshippers were John and Philip, the Tartars, in silk robes. Beside them, Friar Mathieu, the

Franciscan, cleverest of Daoud's opponents. Daoud gauged him to be a genuinely holy man, if an infidel could be called holy.

And next to him was the pale young face of the Count de Gobignon.

As Daoud looked at him, de Gobignon looked back, and his eyes widened slightly.

One day, Count, you will die by my hand.

The mass began, and even though there must have been five thousand people in the valley, there was complete silence. The quiet was eerie. At a Muslim religious celebration this large, the crowd would be chanting in unison, there would be music, dervishes singing and dancing; impromptu sermons would be delivered in various parts of the crowd by mullahs or by ordinary men moved to speak. Here all was focused on the center.

Pope Urban rose to speak. He had removed his mitre to say mass. His white hair, his long beard, and his trailing mustache seemed much more sparse than they had been when Daoud had first seen the pope, last summer. His face was as pale as his hair, and his hands trembled.

A few months ago Daoud had heard Urban's voice rise robustly from the center of his body. Today his voice was high and thin and seemed to come from his throat. He told the story of the miracle of Bolsena, and explained that Father Kyril was a priest from Bohemia who had developed doubts about whether Christ was really present in each and every consecrated Communion wafer. Could a small piece of bread really become the body of Jesus when a priest said a few words over it?

Where is the illness? Daoud's Sufi-trained eye told him it was deep within Pope Urban; it had sunk its claws into his chest.

I do not think this pope has long to live.

Ugolini had told Daoud that Urban wanted desperately, before he himself died, to strike a death blow against the Hohenstaufen family. He wanted Count Charles d'Anjou, brother of the King of France, to wrest the crown of Sicily from Manfred, but King Louis had thus far forbidden his brother to make war on Manfred.

King Louis wanted a different war, a joint war of Christians and Tartars against Islam. Thus far, the pope had withheld his approval of any Christian monarch's allying himself with the Tartars.

As Urban heard the approaching wings of the Angel of Death, might he be more inclined to grant Louis what he wanted?

The crowd was no longer silent. Daoud heard waves of murmuring run through it as people relayed the pope's words to those who were too far away to hear him. He noticed now the hawklike profile of the Contessa di Monaldeschi. She was seated in a chair in front of the worshipers on the side of the pavilion opposite Daoud. A plump young boy in red velvet stood beside her.

Seeing her, Daoud looked for Marco di Filippseschi. He could not be sure, but the back of a dark head on this side of the pavilion looked like that of the Filippeschi chieftain. Those organizing this ceremony would, of course, be careful to separate the leaders of the two feuding families.

Pope Urban continued: Father Kyril, realizing that he was doomed to eternal damnation if he did not overcome his doubts, had set out on a pilgrimage to Rome. But Rome had fallen on evil days, its streets turned into battlefields by the Ghibellini followers of the vile Hohenstaufens, and Father Kyril found no peace there. He decided to ask the prayers of the pope himself at Orvieto. That decision was rewarded before he even reached here. Two months ago, while saying mass at Bolsena, on his way to Orvieto, and praying that his doubts be resolved, Father Kyril raised the Sacred Host over his head after the Consecration, and hundreds of witnesses saw drops of blood fall from it to the cloth spread on the altar.

And now—Pope Urban gestured to the cloth spread above the altar—we can behold with our own eyes the blood of Christ Himself and see this proof—which, having faith, we should not need to see—that Jesus lives in the Blessed Sacrament.

"We propose to offer triple thanks to God for His generosity in granting us this miracle," said Pope Urban. "First, let the day on which Father Kyril saw the Host bleed be celebrated henceforward as the feast of the Body of Christ, Corpus Christi. Let this be proclaimed throughout Christendom.

"Second, to house and display this most sacred relic, the blood of Our Savior Himself, let a great and beautiful new cathedral be built here at Orvieto, which will forever be the center for the veneration of the body of Christ."

Daoud sighed inwardly at the thought of still another great building dedicated to idolatry.

Yet the chapel at Château Langmuir had been such a lovely and quiet place.

As the pontiff's words were repeated, the murmuring grew louder.

Someone near Daoud said, "But the miracle happened in Bolsena." Someone else hushed the person who protested.

I should not wonder if these cities went to war with each other over such a relic, thought Daoud.

"Finally," said Pope Urban, oblivious of the discontent his previous proclamation had caused among the citizens of Bolsena, "we command that all priests of Holy Church shall read a special office on the feast of Corpus Christi of each year, commemorating this miracle. God has willed that there should be dwelling with us here at Orvieto the most gifted scholar and writer of this age, Fra Tomasso d'Aquino."

Daoud saw that Fra Tomasso's face was almost as bright a red as a cardinal's hat.

"And we charge our beloved and most gloriously gifted son, Fra Tomasso, with the duty of writing this office."

D'Aquino rose heavily from a bench on the right side of the altar. Puffing, sweating despite the chill of the day, he bowed to the pope with hands clasped before him.

A great honor, that must be, Daoud thought. Fra Tomasso was silent for the moment, but he would write words that would be repeated by thousands of priests all over the world as long as Christians celebrated this feast. D'Aquino was more than ever indebted to the pope. If the pope were to want d'Aquino's help in persuading the French to go to war against Manfred, he would collect that debt.

Looking at Fra Tomasso as he sat listening to Pope Urban talk on about his plans for the feast, for the cathedral, for the office, Daoud saw a glow on those rounded features that made him uneasy. Daoud had felt that with Cardinal Ugolini and Fra Tomasso stirring up opposition to the alliance throughout Christendom, he had but to wait for the plan to die of old age.

He could no longer be sure of that. Fra Tomasso's opposition to the alliance had a fragile basis at best, and this miracle might have shattered it.

The blood of the Messiah had power to change the course of events. Daoud felt himself trembling.

XL

DAOUD'S HANDS WERE COLD AND HIS HEART WAS RACING. HE HAD been waiting all morning for Ugolini to come back from the Dominican convent.

He sat at Ugolini's worktable, trying to read. He had found an old book in Arabic in Ugolini's library, the *Aphorisms* of ibn Zaina, a book Saadi had often praised. At another time he would have devoured it, but his mind refused to follow the words. Sending Ugolini to Fra Tomasso was his final effort to learn what had gone wrong and to see what might be saved.

What would Fra Tomasso say to Ugolini? At least Ugolini could be trusted not to make things worse, as de Verceuil had for their opponents.

This was the Christian month of February, and the chill that pervaded Daoud's body came from the air around him as well as from his troubled spirit. The small wood fire that burned on the hearth beside the table did little to dispel the cold in the room.

In the two months that followed the coming of the bloodstained altar cloth to Orvieto, Tomasso d'Aquino had gradually, but completely, reversed himself. According to a Dominican in Ugolini's pay, the philosopher had sent new letters to the European kings confessing that his opposition to an alliance between Christians and Tartars had been an error. At least three Italian cardinals had told Ugolini that Fra Tomasso had come to them personally with the same message. Cardinal Gratiano Marchetti whispered that Pope Urban, who did not expect to live through the winter, had promised the stout friar a voice in the election of the next pope. Where Urban had been neutral toward the alliance, perhaps even opposed, something now caused him to favor it. Just as the tumbling of a single grain of sand could bring a whole dune crashing down to bury a caravan, so those drops of blood at Bolsena had been the start of an avalanche of reversals.

Daoud awaited Ugolini's coming, and the message he bore, as a man accused of a capital crime awaits the verdict of his judge.

And if it was true that Fra Tomasso had irrevocably turned against them? Daoud must begin all over again with a new plan to stop the alliance.

The fire gave off the sour odor of strange substances Ugolini had previously burned on the hearth. Daoud pushed himself out of the cardinal's chair and went to get a breath of fresh air. He opened the casement window and saw Ugolini's sedan chair, borne by four servants, turning in toward the door of the mansion.

The cardinal's chair passed the shop across the street, where rows of large and small pots, brightly painted with floral designs, were laid out on a large blanket. The potter and his wife, bundled up in heavy cloaks, were calling out for the cardinal's blessing. Daoud saw a tiny hand emerge from the curtains of the sedan chair, closed against the February cold. The hand shaped the sign of the cross in the air as the shopkeepers fell to their knees.

Daoud wondered whether the potter and his wife felt they had an unlucky spot to offer their wares. That was where, last August, de Verceuil's archers had shot down two men in the crowd when the Tartars were entering the city. And it was in front of that shop, shuttered then for the night, that Alain de Pirenne's body had been found. Had the shopkeeper or his wife seen anything, and were they keeping silent only out of fear? Months had gone by, but the podesta, d'Ucello, was still investigating the killing, questioning and requestioning everyone who might know something about it.

Daoud paced the room anxiously until Ugolini came in, throwing his fur-trimmed cape and his wide-brimmed red hat to a servant. He sat down in the chair Daoud had been using. Daoud closed the door.

As a man dying of thirst begs for water, Daoud prayed for good news.

But Ugolini's pale face, haggard eyes, and downturned mouth told a different tale. Daoud's heart plunged into despair.

"Has he turned against us?" He hated the note of pleading he heard in his voice.

Ugolini went to his worktable, sighed, and sat down heavily. His eyes seemed to be crossed, staring down his pointed nose at the painted skull that grinned back at him. His restless fingers found the dioptra lying on the table, and he started to roll the brass tube in his hand.

"I used every argument I could think of," he said. "I even repeated back to him the arguments he used in the letters and sermons he wrote against the Tartars."

"Arguing with Fra Tomasso is like trying wrestle a djinn," Daoud said. "I admire your courage in even trying."

Ugolini raised a finger. "I thought I was getting somewhere with him. He kept trying to change the subject. He kept asking me, if the earth moves while the sun stands still—he seems to be convinced that is what happens—then what path does the earth follow? I told him that the Greeks"—he stopped and stared at Daoud— "Oh, never mind the Greeks. The point is, he was mocking me."

"Mocking you?"

"Yes, talking about the heavenly bodies. He was referring to that scroll you gave me to present to him, that work of Aristotle. What a waste, giving that to him. What would I not give to have it myself."

"Why did he keep changing the subject? Did he never tell you where he stands on the alliance?"

Ugolini closed his eyes and nodded. "Yes, finally. He said he made a grave mistake opposing the alliance. He said that if Christians do not seize this chance, the Tartars may be converted to the religion of Mohammed, as those in Russia already have been, which would be the worst of all possible disasters." He opened his eyes and looked at Daoud. "We have lost him."

"Is there nothing we can do to change his mind?"

"I truly believe it is hopeless."

Hearing those words, Daoud felt drained. He sagged against the wall of Ugolini's cabinet, wanting to sit on the floor but unable to do so because then he could not see the cardinal.

"It is Urban who has done this to us," said Ugolini. "He must have decided that supporting the alliance is the only way he can get French help against King Manfred. He tempted Fra Tomasso with something far more valuable to him than an old scroll. He offered him greater glory and power in the Church."

The Angel of Death, thought Daoud, had done it. Feeling himself mortally ill, the pope had realized he could no longer bargain with the King of France on an equal basis. He would have to offer Louis what he wanted, permission to ally himself with the Tartars.

"Will the pope now support the alliance openly?" If Daoud chose to fight, he thought, he would have to strike hard and fast. He would have to strike at the Tartars.

Despite the downward turn of his fortunes, Daoud felt a strange lightness of heart as he considered the prospect. He had tried every other way of preventing Tartars and Christians from forming an alliance—persuasion, bribery, the spreading of lies.

Now he could turn to the way he was best at. War.

"Urban will not come out for the alliance at once," said Ugolini. "Before Bolsena, Fra Tomasso and my Italian colleagues in the Sacred College stirred up so much feeling against the Tartars that Urban would lose support all over Europe if he were to call now for a pact between Christians and Tartars. So he must move slowly, with Fra Tomasso now working with him, winning approval for the alliance."

"What if the French sent an army to him now?" Daoud asked.

Ugolini laughed. "Do you think King Louis of France can sow dragon's teeth and have an army spring up in his fields overnight? He would have to summon the great barons of France. They would have to decide whether they support his cause, then assemble the lesser barons and knights. Supplies must be gathered, money found to pay the knights and men-at-arms. It can take years to raise an army big enough to wage a war."

The Mamelukes would be ready to ride in a day.

How had the crusaders managed to make any inroads at all in the Dar al-Islam?

"If the pope is not ready to declare for the alliance, there is time," said Daoud. "Nothing is settled yet."

"Time for what? What will you do now?"

He pushed himself away from the wall, went to a mullioned window, and pulled open one of the casements. To the northwest a tower of orange brick with square battlements looked arrogantly down upon the huddled masses of peaked red roofs. From the tower fluttered the orange and green banner of the Monaldeschi. There the Tartars were.

He turned from the window and moved slowly toward Ugolini's table.

"I am sorry," he said as gently as he could. "This is not ended."

Ugolini had been playing with the dioptra. He dropped it with a clank.

"What do you mean?" Fear made his voice shrill and quavering.

"I mean, I must attack the Palazzo Monaldeschi."

"Attack the Monaldeschi!" It was almost a scream.

Daoud spread his hands. "I have no choice."

Ugolini sprang to his feet. "Pazzia! You are mad!"

It is you who are almost mad, with terror, Daoud thought. He was going to have trouble with Ugolini, no question.

Aloud he said only, "We will discuss it. You can help us plan. Pardon me, Your Eminince, while I send for Lorenzo."

"It will have to be late at night, of course," said Lorenzo. "And I would think a Friday evening would be best, when the men-at-arms will be off their guard and many of them out carousing. But it finally depends on when Marco di Filippeschi says his family's men can be ready. They need to buy weapons."

Daoud and Lorenzo stood by the cardinal's table while Ugolini paced with many short steps between the windows and the hearth. He muttered to himself, and his hands trembled as he ran them through his tufts of white hair.

"What of our men?" said Daoud.

"We have over two hundred now, scattered throughout the city," said Lorenzo.

If I could be in the palazzo before the fighting begins . . .

Ugolini stopped his pacing and faced them. "You talk like moon-struck men! You would unleash a civil war right here in Orvieto?"

"Not us, Your Eminence," said Lorenzo. "Have not these two families been fighting for generations?"

"What is your objection?" said Daoud gently.

Ugolini fixed them with a ferocious glare. "For six months, half a year, I have lain awake imagining arrest, disgrace, torture, execution. Through miracles you have managed to carry out your plans without being caught. Now you want to launch still wilder plans—incredible, fantastic things. I have had enough. God has kept me alive this long. I will not tempt Him further."

"My dear Cardinal," Daoud said, "once the Tartars are dead, this will all be over. I will go back to Egypt. Lorenzo and Sophia will return to Manfred's kingdom. You will have nothing further to fear."

"You could have tried to kill the Tartars at any time since they came here," said Ugolini. "Why now?"

"I needed to create as much ill will as possible between Christians and Tartars," said Daoud. "If I had killed the Tartars at once, I could not have had them discredit themselves out of their own mouths. Fra Tomasso and your colleagues among the Italian cardinals could not have stirred up so much fear and hatred toward them. Now, though, I have done all I can along those lines, and Fra Tomasso is already undoing what together we have accomplished."

"And why involve the Monaldeschi and the Filippeschi?" Ugolini pressed him.

"To make it seem that the Tartars have been killed by feuding Italians. Then Hulagu Khan will think again about whether he wants such people as his allies."

Ugolini shook his head. "I do not have to tell you, of all people, what war is like. And I think Messer Lorenzo, by the way he carries himself, has known battle more than once. You both know that chance rules every moment in war."

"True," said Daoud.

And if chance decided against them? For a moment he saw Sophia naked, being torn apart by the torturers' pincers. He almost shuddered, and had to hold himself rigid.

"I take it you intend to be part of this attack on the Monaldeschi," Ugolini went on.

"I do," said Daoud.

Ugolini threw up his hands as if Daoud had already proved his case for him. "Well then, what if someone recognizes you attacking the palace?"

"I will not openly lead. I will enter the palace and kill the Tartars."

"So," said Ugolini. "You will not just be somewhere in the street outside the Palazzo Monaldeschi. You will be *in the palace*. In the midst of all your enemies. Alone. Attempting to assassinate the Tartars. Tell me, does that sound like the plan of a reasonable, cautious man to you?"

Daoud thought it sounded as if he were, to put it as Ugolini had, tempting God. But Ugolini did not understand that Daoud had not only the skills of Mameluke, but had also received the secret training of the Hashishiyya fighters, the fedawi, whose powers many in the lands of Islam thought magical.

"I will be masked. I will be dressed in garments that will make it almost impossible to see me. I will not expose myself. I will move in darkness. I have been trained to find my way in darkness as surely as if it were sunlight."

Ugolini shook his head. "Understand me. I would not go on arguing with you like this did I not feel I am arguing for my life. And Tilia's, and the lives of those who depend on you. You must admit that you might be captured or killed. My house guest, found trying to murder the Tartar ambassadors.''

Daoud spread his hands. ''You would then denounce me. You say you never knew what a demon you had taken into your home.''

Ugolini laughed loudly and bitterly. ''Are our opponents fools? Do you really think they would believe me, even for a moment? After perhaps hundreds of people have been killed, after a civil war in Orvieto, anyone who is even suspect will die. The Monaldeschi, the French, the Church authorities, all will take their revenge. Surely you understand that.''

Daoud's heart grew cold as he looked along the road Ugolini was describing and saw defeat, massacre, the hideous deaths of his comrades, and beyond that iron waves of crusaders and endless columns of Tartar horsemen sweeping over the Dar al-Islam. And he could not look into Ugolini's eyes and declare that all would turn out well.

But what would happen if he did nothing? He looked down that path and saw the same masses of crusaders and Tartars, saw the burning mosques, the emptied cities, the heaps of corpses. He saw the Gray Mosque in El Kahira ruined, his teacher Saadi hacked to pieces by crusader swords.

Then he heard words Saadi had spoken: *We are God's instruments, by which He brings about that which He wills. The fool does nothing and leaves the outcome to God. The ordinary man acts and prays that God will grant a good result. The wise man acts and leaves the outcome to God.*

He would act.

He turned to Lorenzo, standing near him by the cardinal's table. ''Your life is at stake in this. What do you think?''

Lorenzo's face was as grave as Daoud had ever seen it. ''If the Filippeschi attack the Palazzo Monaldeschi, they will be driven off. But with more than five hundred men attacking the palace, it will be impossible for the French to guard the Tartars adequately. If you get in, kill them, and get out safely, I think we can hide our part in the fighting. If you are caught or killed, I think it is as the cardinal says. We are all doomed.''

''Exactly!'' cried Ugolini from where he stood behind his table. ''Then why risk it?''

''Because we must,'' Lorenzo said to him. ''If we do not stop the alliance by force, the pope will strike a bargain with the King of France. There will be a French army marching against my King

Manfred, and after that crusaders and Tartars will fall upon Messer David's people.''

Ugolini uttered a deep groan and sank into his chair.

Relief swept over Daoud. He had already decided to make the attempt on the Palazzo Monaldeschi even if Lorenzo opposed it, but to have Lorenzo side with him gave him more confidence that he could carry it off.

Lorenzo turned those somber eyes to him again. ''It all depends on you. I am gambling that you can do it.''

Daoud felt a powerful warmth toward the Sicilian. There were times when he had wished Lorenzo were not with him, times when he distrusted him. The foolishness of involving them with Rachel and her husband. The fact that Lorenzo was a Jew who had abandoned his religion. Even his dog was a nuisance. But at this moment to have Lorenzo's support made him feel as strong and confident as if the Mameluke orta he commanded had suddenly appeared in Orvieto.

He grinned at Lorenzo. ''You proved how good a gambler you are by losing to de Verceuil.''

Lorenzo chuckled. ''What must we do first?''

Daoud said, ''Arrange for me to meet secretly with Marco di Filippeschi. And send word to King Manfred that the pope and the French are about to reach agreement on the Tartar alliance, and when they do the French will come pouring into Italy. Tell him now is the time for his Ghibellino allies in the north to march on Orvieto.''

Lorenzo nodded. ''I will send one of my men to Lucera.'' He shook his head. ''My God, how I wish I could go myself!''

''Once the Tartars are dead,'' Daoud said, ''we will all go home. Now, find Sordello and send him to my room.''

As Daoud left Ugolini's cabinet, he glanced back to see the little cardinal slumped over the table, knotting his fingers in his fuzzy white hair. He would have to spend more time with him, to build up his courage.

Sophia was standing in the hallway when Daoud emerged from his room that night, on his way to meet with the Filippeschi chieftain. He was not surprised to see her. Someone, Ugolini or Lorenzo, would have told her about his new plan. He beckoned her into his room and closed the door.

Each time the thought of defeat arose in his mind, he had felt the greatest anguish over what it would mean for Sophia. That forced him to admit to himself how much he cared for her. Now that he looked into her amber eyes and told her what he intended to do, the pain he felt was sharper than ever. He wanted to persuade her that she had nothing to fear. But he knew that would be a lie.

He tried to keep what he said simple, practical. "You, like Sordello, will bear witness that Lorenzo and I had gone to Perugia while the Monaldeschi palazzo was under siege. Lorenzo has allies in Perugia who will confirm that."

Sophia stared at him with wide, solemn eyes. "You are risking everything." She reached out and seized his hand, gripping it urgently. "If they find out who you are while you are in the Monaldeschi palace, it will be the end for all of us."

He felt the strength in her fingers, the softness of her palm, and wanted to take her in his arms, but he held himself in check. There could be nothing between them as long as de Gobignon was alive.

"I know a hundred ways to get into a castle and out again," he said, wishing there had been time to share with her more of his life. "Once I am inside, I will search out and kill the two Tartars while all the armed men are occupied with the fighting outside. And then I will leave." He spread his hands to show how easy it would be.

Inwardly he was ashamed. He was preparing to sacrifice this woman's life, knowing that she might die a terrible death—rape, torture, mutilation, public execution. How could he face her at all? That he had made his decision in order to save hundreds of thousands of his people from slaughter, his faith from destruction, was no comfort at this moment alone with Sophia.

"Will you fight Simon?"

He felt his blood go hot. That she should think at all of de Gobignon at this moment rather than of herself—or of him—made him so angry he forgot for a moment his own guilt and fear for her life.

"The young count will probably be leading the fight on the battlements." Daoud tasted the venom in what he was about to say, but he could not help himself. "It will be quite a shock when he finds the Tartars dead and realizes how he has failed."

Sophia stood breathing hard, her eyes glistening with tears. "If only you were not—"

Daoud was already wishing he had not spoken so to her. "Not what?"

"Not blind!" she cried.

She turned swiftly and reached for the door handle. But Daoud could not let her go. He was there before her, and he faced her and seized her hand.

"I am not blind," he rasped. "I see that pretending to be what you are not is tearing you apart. I wish we could be our true selves with each other—"

"We cannot," she said bitterly. "And to speak of it only makes it hurt more. Let me go."

He relaxed his grip on her hand, and she was gone.

Some day, he thought. *Some day, Sophia.*

Looking at the closed door, Daoud felt an almost unbearable inner pain. He had thrust her at Simon. He had lashed out at her, hurt her unjustly. Having done that to her, he was about to put her in far worse danger.

How could he claim, even in the secrecy of his own heart, that he loved her?

Daoud could barely see Marco di Filippeschi in the darkness. Moonlight touched the gold medallion that hung from Marco's neck and on the silver badge in his cap. For the rest he was a figure carved out of shadow. Despite the full moon, this narrow alleyway between a stone house and the city wall was almost as black as the bottom of a well.

Daoud's Hashishiyya-trained senses needed no light to see by. He had learned to see with his ears as well as with his sense of smell. He could sense what weapons Marco di Filippeschi was wearing—a shortsword and two daggers at his belt, and, from the difference in footfalls, a third dagger in a sheath in his right boot. He knew the position of Marco's hands, and he knew that Marco had told the truth when he said he had come to this rendezvous alone.

Lorenzo had assured him that Marco would leap like a hungry wolf at any chance to avenge himself on the Monaldeschi. But Daoud wondered, would the volatile young clan chieftain really be willing to undertake an attack on the Monaldeschi that had more chance of failing than succeeding?

"I can offer you over two hundred lusty bravos collected by one who is known to you," Daoud said. Hoping to make Marco a little less certain about who his ultimate benefactor was, he avoided naming Giancarlo. Marco could destroy Daoud and all his comrades by revealing the identity of the man who had incited his attack on the

Monaldeschi. If he were captured and tortured, strong and fierce though he might be, it was likely he would tell everything.

Daoud reached into the purse at his belt, where he had earlier put two emeralds. He held them out in his open palm so that the moonlight glistened on their polished surfaces.

"Please accept these as a gift," he said. "If you decide to assault the Palazzo Monaldeschi, your preparations will be costly."

The jewels must be called a gift. The capo della famiglia Filippeschi was not a man you paid to do your work for you.

Marco's hand closed around the emeralds, and his other hand seized Daoud's forearm.

"I shall spend this on weapons," he said. "Crossbows to kill more Monaldeschi. Stone guns to batter down their walls. I care not what price I must pay."

That is good, thought Daoud, *because the price may be very high.*

"I will need until spring," Marco continued. "It will take that long to buy the weapons. I must work slowly and quietly so the old vulture does not get wind of what I am doing."

"The Monaldeschi are collaborating with this French pope and his French cardinals," Daoud said to spur Marco on. "And the French party is about to invite an army under Charles of Anjou into Italy."

"Damn the French!" said Marco. "And damn that putana and her family for working with them."

"Also, as everyone knows," Daoud said, "the pope has not long to live. Strike a blow now for Italy, and you will frighten the cardinals at a time when they will soon be choosing the next pope. So your attack had better come no later than spring."

"We Filippeschi are as loyal to the papacy as the Monaldeschi. Perhaps more."

"My master, whom I prefer not to name," said Daoud, knowing that Marco would think he meant King Manfred, "does not wish to see the pope in league with the French."

"This war of Guelfi and Ghibellini leaves us prey to every French and German ladrone who wants to come down and loot our country," said Marco. Obviously he had no great love for the Hohenstaufens, either.

"How will you start the fighting?" Daoud asked him.

"Two or three of my cousins will take a walk in the piazza before the Palazzo Monaldeschi on a Friday evening, when everybody strolls," Marco said. "If their mere presence in that part of the city does not cause an incident, they will step on a few toes."

"It will take some courage to go into the lion's den," Daoud remarked.

The young Filippeschi chieftain laughed ruefully. "We possess more of courage than we do of anything else."

If they did not also possess some prudence and the ability to keep a secret, Daoud thought, everything was lost.

XLI

THE STAINED GLASS IN THE CATHEDRAL'S DEEPLY RECESSED REAR windows broke the sunlight of the April morning into blue, yellow, and red beams. Walking slowly through the nave, Simon wondered why Sordello had insisted this time on meeting him in person in the cathedral rather than sending his news through Ana. The departure from their routine gave Simon an uneasy feeling that some disaster was about to befall him.

The miraculous altar cloth with the dark spots in its center was mounted in a gilded frame above the altar. On each side of it a tall white candle burned. At the foot of the altar two priests in black cassocks and white surplices knelt on benches, their heads resting on their folded arms so that it was impossible to tell whether they were sleeping or praying. In the four months since the cloth had been brought to Orvieto, it had never been left unattended. The pope had decreed that priests in hourly shifts would watch day and night before the blood of the Savior.

Simon suspected reverence was not the only motive for this vigil. He knew several tales of famous relics being stolen, not only from pious zeal, but because relics attracted pilgrims and their money. And the people of Bolsena might still be jealous.

Hearing footsteps behind him, Simon approached the altar, genuflected, and walked into the shadows on the left side of the cathedral. He paused by a fluted pillar that rose like a tree trunk.

Approaching him was a beggar in a tattered gray cloak that hung to his ankles. A deep hood hid his face. The man gripped Simon's arm. The face of Sordello looked out of the shadows under the hood. Simon pulled his arm free.

"I have something important to tell Your Signory, but it is not about Cardinal Ugolini and his circle." Sordello spoke in a hoarse whisper. "The Filippeschi are going to make a surprise attack on the Palazzo Monaldeschi."

The news hit Simon like a kick in the belly.

The Tartars—and he and his men—would be caught in the middle. He thought back to Alain's murder. Even since then he had felt that Orvieto could be a death trap for him and all his men.

Simon leaned forward to peer into Sordello's pinkish eyes. "When will the attack come?"

"Tonight, after vespers."

Tonight! Now Simon's blood froze. *No time! No time!* a voice shrieked inside him. He wanted to run back to the palace shouting warnings all the way. It took all his strength to keep him standing with Sordello, to force his mind, galloping like a runaway horse, to slow down and frame questions.

"How did you find out?"

"Tavern talk. Some of Giancarlo's hired bravos were drinking with Filippeschi men."

Sweat that felt like a cold rain broke out all over Simon's body. The Tartars—he must get them out of the Monaldeschi palace. But the contessa had been his hostess for many months. He himself had no quarrel with the Filippeschi, but he had an obligation to defend the contessa.

"How long have you known this?"

"I just learned it last night, but they must have been preparing for months."

"Why *now*?"

Sordello's eyes met his. "The Filippeschi think the Monaldeschi are betraying Italy to you French."

If the Filippeschi were attacking now because he was at the Palazzo Monaldeschi, then indeed he had a quarrel with them, whether or not he wanted one. And it was his fault, in a sense, that the contessa was in danger.

"Betraying Italy to the French? What does that mean?"

Sordello ticked off points on his fingers. "The pope is French. He asks the contessa to take the Tartars into her house. Then you and Cardinal de Verceuil come with the Tartars. And now everyone has heard that the pope wants Charles d'Anjou to come in and take Sicily and southern Italy from King Manfred. The Filippeschi want to turn the tide now, they say, before the French own all of Italy.''

The face of Uncle Charles flashed vividly before Simon's mind, the big nose, the staring eyes. When they had talked of this mission over a year ago at the Louvre, he had said nothing of Sicily, had spoken only of the liberation of Jerusalem and the destruction of Islam. Was Sicily what he really wanted—or perhaps even all of Italy?

What should he do? It struck Simon with frightening force that there was no one but he to take the responsibility. He was in command. He must make the plans and the decisions. His heart thudded frantically, and he prayed that Sordello could not see the consternation that filled him.

"What forces do they have, what weapons?"

Sordello shook his head. "As to that, Your Signory, I know very little. I have been at Cardinal Ugolini's mansion, not among the Filippeschi. I would guess they must have at least five hundred men and siege weapons. They would be mad to start this thing with less."

"Five hundred men and siege weapons!"

Simon pictured the Monaldeschi palace with its great tower crumbling under a bombardment of boulders. He saw men swarming over it like ants. He saw the defenders lying dead in the ruins— de Puys, Thierry, the Armenians, the Venetians—himself. He saw the Tartars with their throats cut.

Again he felt the urge to run back to the palace to prepare at once. Again he suppressed the urge so he could ask more questions.

"Where did they get such forces?"

Sordello shrugged. "They are a big family. They have relatives in the outlying towns."

Simon bent down to look deep into Sordello's bloodshot eyes. "Are you sure Ugolini and David of Trebizond and the rest are not involved? If we French and the Tartars are the provocation, Ugolini must be behind this."

Sordello tapped his cheek just under his right eye. "Your Signory, I watch them as closely as those priests watch the miraculous altar cloth. Ugolini has been in despair all winter, since Fra Tomasso changed sides. He buries himself in his cabinet with his magical instruments. David has lost interest in the Tartars and thinks only about trade. He talks to Giancarlo of making up a caravan to go back to Trebizond. The two of them left for Perugia on business yesterday."

"What about Giancarlo's bravos?"

"Altogether, Giancarlo has hired only a dozen such men, including myself. We guard David's goods and escort his caravans." Sordello waved a hand in dismissal.

"And what of the cardinal's niece?" said Simon, trying not to sound especially interested.

Sordello shrugged. "That lovely lady stays apart. She goes to church, she reads, she paints."

Worried though he was about the impending Filippeschi attack, Simon's heart felt lightened by joy. Sophia was innocent. His love for her was vindicated. After this was over he would come to her and broach marriage.

"You must watch Madonna Sophia for me," Simon said. "Stay close to her. Do not let her go out tonight."

"Stay close to her." Sordello grinned. "That will not be hard, Your Signory."

Simon seized the front of Sordello's tunic. "Never speak that way of her."

Sordello jerked away from Simon and brushed his tunic. "I am a man, Your Signory. Do not treat me like a slave." The coarse face was pale with outraged pride.

He forgets his place so easily. But there is no one else to guard Sophia for me.

"I want you to be thinking about her safety, and that alone," he said in a calmer voice.

Sordello bowed. "I understand, Your Signory." But resentment still burned in his narrowed eyes.

In the midst of his fear, like a single candle glowing in a pitch-black cathedral, Simon felt a tingle of anticipation. There was something in him, deeply buried but powerful, that keenly looked forward to taking command in battle.

"If you learn any more, try to get word to me," he told Sordello.

He turned and hurried through the nave of the cathedral to the front doors, still holding in check the urge to run.

"For them to attack is pazzia," said the contessa. "We have twice the men-at-arms they do. Yet I pray God this rumor is true.

By tomorrow morning Marco di Filippeschi will be hanging from our battlements.'' The cords in her neck stood out, her nose was thrust forward like a falcon's beak, and her eyes glittered.

Simon said, ''With respect, Contessa, they must have more men than you do. I was told they might have five hundred. And siege machines.''

They were seated in the small council room of the Monaldeschi palace—Simon, the contessa, de Verceuil, Sire Henri de Puys, and Friar Mathieu—around a circular table of warm brown wood.

''But surely we have better men,'' said Henri de Puys in French. ''What sort of fighters could these Philippe-whatever-they-are muster? Routiers, highwaymen?''

Friar Mathieu turned to de Verceuil. ''Might I suggest that Your Eminence use your influence with Pope Urban. Perhaps his holiness can stop this battle.''

''Yes,'' said de Verceuil. ''I will try to speak to him. But he is sick, and pays little attention to anything.''

Probably de Verceuil is annoyed because he did not think first of going to the pope.

''I should think it would endanger his health even more if a war broke out in Orvieto,'' said Friar Mathieu.

''I will *see* him,'' said de Verceuil. ''But I will also arm myself and my men to help defend this place.''

Simon expected de Verceuil to next propose himself as commander of the defense, but, to his delight, the cardinal had nothing more to say. Then the suspicion crossed his mind that de Verceuil did not want to have to take the blame in case of defeat.

''Grazie, Your Eminence,'' said the contessa.

Simon said, ''I must go to Signore d'Ucello. Surely the podesta will not let civil war break out in the city he governs.''

The contessa laughed, a knowing cackle. ''Go to him if you like, but you waste your time. He cannot—will not—stop the Filippeschi. He has Filippeschi relatives, you know. But he could not stop me, either, if I chose to attack them.''

Friar Mathieu said, ''Perhaps we should take the ambassadors to the papal palace. That would get them out of harm's way until this is over.''

Simon's body went rigid. The Tartars were his responsibility. He would never give them up to the pope's men-at-arms.

''No!'' he said. ''The duty of guarding them is mine, and I will surrender it to no one.''

De Puys struck the table with his open palm. "Bravely spoken, Monseigneur."

Friar Mathieu sighed.

De Verceuil pointed a finger at Simon. "Count, you have no right to risk the ambassadors' lives just for your own glory."

Simon looked around the table. He was the youngest person here, and they were treating him like a child. He remembered the Doge Zeno's threat to have him thrown into the water of Venice's San Marco Canal. He remembered the many times de Verceuil had been overbearing with him. To think *that* man would accuse anyone else of being too concerned with his own glory.

He was about to shout defiance when he thought of royal councils he had attended as a page to King Louis. Those close to the king often disagreed with him, but they usually ended up doing what he wanted. Louis was perhaps the strongest man, in his gentle way, Simon had ever met, but he had never heard him raise his voice.

Instead of defying de Verceuil and the others, he tried to speak with dignity, even humility, as King Louis himself might.

"His Majesty's brother, Count Charles, entrusted this task to me. Shall I give it up at the first threat? Shall I turn over the ambassadors' protection to men unknown to me, some of whom may be moved by the same hatred of us French that moves the Filippeschi? I have a duty not to let the ambassadors go beyond the walls I guard."

When he finished there was silence.

Friar Mathieu said, "Count Simon makes an excellent point. John and Philip may well be safer guarded by our men, even under attack."

Now that they had agreed, Simon's heart sank. If the Tartars were killed in the coming battle because he had insisted on keeping them in the palace, he would bear the guilt. Instead of restoring his name, he would end by plunging it deeper into the mire.

De Puys looked from Simon to the cardinal and said, "Perhaps our knights and crossbowmen could go with the Tartars to the Pope's palace."

"No!" cried the contessa. "Now, when I am attacked because I opened my home to the Tartars and the French, will you all abandon me? All the men of my family are dead but the boy Vittorio." She turned to Simon and seized his wrist with her clawlike hand. "You must stay and defend me. You must be my cavaliere."

Simon pressed her hand in both of his and saw tears running down her withered cheeks.

"I would not think of leaving you, Contessa."

"But, Contessa," said Friar Mathieu, "if the Tartars were to leave your palace, the Filippeschi might not attack you."

"No, no." The contessa shook her head. "If they think they are strong enough to attack me, they will. They have long sought to kill me and Vittorio. Canaglia! May God send that little bastard Marco and all the Filippeschi straight to hell!"

Friar Mathieu winced and made the sign of the cross.

Inwardly Simon winced, too, as he always did at the word bastard. But, bastard or not, he was about to command a palace under siege. He felt his chest swelling at the thought.

The candlelit audience chamber of the podesta was hung with somber maroon drapes drawn against the night air. On the wall behind d'Ucello, a tapestry depicted Jesus and Barabbas being offered to the crowd in Jerusalem while Pilate washed his hands. Simon had never seen such a large scene with such finely embroidered figures, and he admired it aloud.

"I keep it here as a reminder that a judge who heeds the popular clamor may make a grave error," said the small man behind the large table. "How may I serve you, Count?"

As Simon told the podesta what he knew of the planned Filippeschi assault on the contessa's palace, d'Ucello leaned back in a tall chair that seemed too big for him, his eyes distant, the corners of his mouth turned down under his thin mustache.

When Simon finished, d'Ucello asked, "Are Cardinal Ugolini or any of his guests involved in this?"

The very question I asked Sordello. Interesting that the podesta shares my suspicions.

"The person who warned me said they were not."

D'Ucello peered at him. "And who warned you?"

"I would rather not say. I have an informant in Cardinal Ugolini's household."

"Really? Good for you." The podesta gave him a look of amused respect that kindled a warm glow of pride in him. "Well, Your Signory, if there is a battle between the Monaldeschi and the Filippeschi, I can do nothing about it."

Simon was swept by strange mixed feelings. He was ready to do almost anything to prevent the coming battle. But in the midst of his despair at d'Ucello's refusal to help, he kept seeing himself in armor rallying his men on the Monaldeschi battlements.

But he had to try to persuade d'Ucello to help. He could not leave without having done his best.

"Is it not your duty to keep the peace in Orvieto?"

"All my watchmen together are not a tenth of the number of armed men the Monaldeschi and the Filippeschi can put into the streets. I assure you that if the watch did try to stop the fight, the Monaldeschi and the Filippeschi would join forces and annihilate my men before they went on to tear each other to pieces. Look, Your Signory, mine is a lifetime appointment, which means that how long I live depends on how well I please those who appointed me. The families wish me to prevent or punish fraud, theft, rape, and murder. But when the families have quarrels that can be settled only by bloodshed, they want no interference. Did the contessa send you here to appeal for my help?"

"No, she told me you could not stop the Filippeschi," said Simon, appalled at this glimpse of the chaos that lay under the pretty surface of this town.

D'Ucello nodded with a look of satisfaction. "Of course. No doubt she sees this as her chance to kill off Marco di Filippeschi, something she has longed to do for years. I cannot do what you ask. I know the limits of my power."

Power, thought Simon. Brute strength. That was what would decide this clash, and all he could do was make sure his side was stronger. He felt a resolve, at once grim and gleeful, growing inside him.

He stood up and inclined his head. The stout little man rose and bowed back.

"Then I cannot rely on you?" Simon said.

D'Ucello shrugged. "I am still trying to discover the murderer of your companion. I have learned that neither David of Trebizond nor his servant, Giancarlo, were in Cardinal Ugolini's palace when your friend was killed. I think tonight while the Monaldeschi and the Filippeschi are at each other's throats, the best place for me would be at Ugolini's, asking those two worthies where they were that night. If I cannot find out, perhaps your informant in that household could help. Why not ask her?"

He thinks I was talking about Sophia.

Simon wished he could go to Sophia. What if he were killed

tonight and never saw her again? He wished there was at least time to send her a poem.

D'Ucello had probably guessed that Simon was visiting Sophia when Alain was murdered. Simon felt his face grow hot with chagrin. He had failed to keep his secret—his and Sophia's.

He remembered Sordello telling him that David and Giancarlo had gone to Perugia. Simon could save d'Ucello from a waste of time by telling him that.

But why bother? He's been no help to me.

Angry with the podesta and with himself, and unwilling to yield any more information to the little man, Simon took his leave.

With two of his knights, the Sires de Borione and de Vilbiz, flanking him, Simon hurried back from the podesta's palace to the Palazzo Monaldeschi. They looked over their shoulders so often as they strode through the darkening street that Simon began to feel they were looking backward as much as forward. But no bravos sprang at them from ambush, no arrows flew from housetops. Indeed, the streets were unusually quiet and empty for late Saturday afternoon, with the clink of the knights' spurs and the tramp of their heels on the cobbles the loudest sounds of all.

Windows were shuttered, doors closed tight. The whole neighborhood, thought Simon, must be aware of what was about to happen.

They turned a corner into the square before the Monaldeschi palace and heard the sound of hammers. Simon had ordered de Puys to supervise the building of slanting wooden screens above the battlements to be covered with wet blankets to protect the roof from fire arrows. The job was almost done, and Simon reminded himself to compliment de Puys when he saw him.

His first task here at the palace was to insure the safety of the Tartars. He had already decided that the safest place in the palace was the spice pantry in the cellar.

And what if the palace were overwhelmed and the Tartars were trapped and killed in the spice pantry? Simon made up his mind that he himself would not surrender. The Filippeschi would have to kill him to get to the Tartars.

Friar Mathieu answered Simon's knock. Simon had never seen the Tartars' chambers before, and he was shocked. Mattresses covered with blankets lay along the walls. Rugs and cushions were scattered about, but there was no bed, table, or chair to be seen.

An overpowering smell of burnt meat filled the first room Simon entered. In the center of the wooden floor an area about three feet across was covered with blackened flagstones, and atop the stones was a heap of charred wood. Beside this crude hearth was a pile of broken animal bones, melon rinds, and other refuse. An open wine barrel added its sweetish smell to the general odor of smoke and decay.

Simon wondered whether the contessa had seen this squalor. She had shown the Tartars special favor, giving them three rooms in the northwest corner of the third floor. In most palaces a single room was the most even a very distinguished visitor could expect. If she thought they were savages after David of Trebizond had baited them at her reception, what would she think after seeing this pigsty?

John and Philip rose at Simon's entrance and bowed, smiling broadly. They seemed not the least embarrassed by the foul condition of their chambers. Simon bowed back, trying also to smile.

"If Cardinal Ugolini were to show these rooms to the Sacred College, many of the cardinals would join him in detesting the Tartars," Simon said to Friar Mathieu. "A wonder the smoke has not smothered them."

With a wry smile Friar Mathieu pointed at the ceiling. An irregular hole had been broken through above the Tartars' hearth.

"Fortunately for everyone, they are on the top floor of the palace," the Franciscan said. "All they have tried to do is reproduce the kind of home they are used to living in, even to the smoke hole in the roof."

The white-bearded John said something in the Tartar tongue to Friar Mathieu.

"They have heard of the coming fight," the Franciscan said. "They want weapons and a place on the battlements. They say it is their duty as guests to defend their hostess, the contessa."

Simon tensed himself for trouble. He had feared this. He chose his words carefully.

"I am sure the contessa will be overwhelmed with gratitude when I tell her of such a gracious offer. But we would not want to have to answer to the mighty Hulagu Khan if something happened to them or to their noble mission. Tell them that, and that it is *our* duty to keep *them* safe. There is a stone storeroom underneath the kitchen, a spice pantry. I have explored the palace, and that is the securest place. They must go there the moment the Filippeschi attack. They should take the Armenians with them."

The Tartars looked angry and shouted vigorous staccato protests when Friar Mathieu translated this. Philip, the younger, black-haired one, especially addressed himself to Simon. Philip seized the oblong gold tablet of office that hung around his neck and shook it at Simon.

"He reminds you that his title is Baghadur, which means Valiant. He says you insult him by asking him to hide in the cellar. Among his people nobody hides. Even the women and children fight."

Simon felt his assurance collapsing. What if the Tartars simply refused to seek safety? He could not put them in chains.

Earnestly he said, "Tell them it is their duty to their khan to stay alive and continue negotiations. Be as courteous as you have the power to be in their language."

"Oh, I am being very polite. One always is, with them."

After another exchange Friar Mathieu said, "They say Hulagu Khan would expect them to fight."

Simon had a sudden inspiration. "Tell them that if they were to fight and if anything happened to them, even the slightest injury, the King of France would cut my head off."

There was a particle of truth in that, Simon thought as Friar Mathieu translated. Kindly as King Louis was, decapitation would be preferable to facing his reproach if Simon's weakness caused the Tartars' death.

John shrugged and answered Friar Mathieu quietly. Simon held his breath, praying that this last effort would work.

Friar Mathieu said, "John says that you are a brave young warrior, and it would be a shame to have your head cut off when you have a lifetime of battles ahead of you. For your sake they will forgo the pleasure of this fight. But they insist on taking only two guards with them. They insist that the rest of their men fight beside yours."

Relief washed over Simon. He hoped he would be able to think as quickly in the coming battle as he had just then.

"I can use their other men. Have whatever the ambassadors need for their comfort carried to the spice pantry." He looked again at the pile of garbage. "Tell them they will be next to the kitchen. They should like that."

XLII

"COUNT SIMON!" SIMON RECOGNIZED THE CRACKLING VOICE OF the contessa.

She was wearing a floor-length gown of deep purple velvet. She held up a disk-shaped bronze medallion on a silver chain.

"Please take this, my young paladino. Wear it into battle for me."

Simon went to her, his steel-shod feet echoing in the hallway. All his movements felt slow and clumsy in the mail shirt that hung to his thighs and the mail breeches that protected him from waist to ankle.

Embossed on the medallion was a mounted knight driving his lance into a coiling bat-winged dragon baring huge fangs in rage. Where the lance pierced the scales was set a tiny, teardrop-shaped ruby.

"Thank you, Donna Elvira," he breathed, full of admiration for the workmanship. "It is most beautiful."

She reached up and put it around his neck. He could feel its weight through his mail shirt.

"San Giorgio. It was my husband's, and I have kept it locked away in my jewel casket since the day the puzzolenti Filippeschi murdered him. It is yours now. San Giorgio will give you victory." She raised her thin body on tiptoe and he felt her dry lips press against his cheek.

"I will never forget this moment, Madonna." He touched her yellow cheeks with his fingertips to brush away her tears.

He did not want her to know that this was his first—his very first—battle.

Climbing the spiral stairs to the tower, his legs ached as he pushed his mailed weight upward, and his neck felt strained under his mail hood and steel helmet. It had been weeks since he had worn his mail, days since he had practiced his sword drill. He swore at himself.

He emerged through a trapdoor onto a square platform paved with flagstone. Three helmeted heads turned to him: De Puys, his head covered with tight-laced mail leaving only a circle for his eyes, nose, and mustached mouth; Teodoro, capitano of Simon's Venetian crossbowmen, wearing a bowl-shaped helmet; and De Verceuil, whose tall helmet was painted bright red and shaped like a cardinal's mitre covering his entire face with the stem of a gold cross running up the center and the arms of the cross spread over the eyeholes.

Dressed for war, de Verceuil looked more like a cardinal than he usually did, Simon thought ironically.

Of the four men on the tower platform, de Verceuil wore the most elaborate armor with steel plates over his mail at his shoulders, knees, and shins. Hanging from a broad belt at his side was a mace, an iron ball on the end of a steel handle a foot long. This was, Simon knew, the proper weapon for a clergyman, who was not supposed to shed blood.

Over his mail shirt de Verceuil wore a long crimson surcoat sewn with cloth-of-gold Maltese crosses. De Puys, like Simon, wore a purple surcoat on which the three gold crowns of Gobignon were embroidered over and over again. Teodoro's simple breastplate of hardened leather was reinforced with steel plates.

Leaning into a crenel between two square merlons, Simon took a deep breath of the mild spring air. It would be a pleasant evening, did he not know that many men were going to die.

He watched the last wagons bringing in casks of water and wine, loads of hay and sacks of grain and beans—supplies in case the fighting dragged on—over the drawbridge through the rear gate. Water, especially, was in short supply in the city on the rock. The palace had its own spring, but it did not produce enough water to supply the whole establishment. Simon remembered Sophia drinking from his hands in the garden.

He stopped short at the thought of her to whisper a little prayer for her safety. But she was in no danger. No one was threatening Cardinal Ugolini.

Simon had ordered that every cask of water available in Orvieto be bought and every vessel filled. The attackers would surely use fire as a weapon. He had also sent for a supply of rocks from a quarry outside the city, extra ammunition for the stone casters mounted on the roof.

He recalled that Sordello had said the Filippeschi intended a surprise attack. They were certain to learn of these preparations and realize that the Monaldeschi had discovered their plan. What if they did not come at all?

If the fact that the Monaldeschi were ready was enough to prevent the attack, that would be the best possible outcome. But Simon realized with a pang that if the Filippeschi did not come, he would be terribly disappointed.

He shook his head at his own madness.

Sunset reddened the tile roofs surrounding the Monaldeschi palace. From up there Simon could see the tall campaniles of Orvieto's five churches and the towers of the other palaces—all battlements square, because this was a Guelfo city. A green flag, too small from this distance to make out the device on it, flew over a tower on the southwest side of the city, the palace of the Filippeschi.

He went to the other side of the tower to look at the city wall. Orange and green Monaldeschi banners flew there. He had assigned twenty Monaldeschi archers, all he dared subtract from the defenders of the palace, to secure the nearest section of the wall. He had wanted to station men in the houses near the palace as well, but de Puys persuaded him that such outposts would surely be overrun and the men speedily lost. Better to concentrate his forces in the palace itself.

He could not make out Cardinal Ugolini's house, somewhere to the southeast of him. It had no tower to distinguish it. But he thought again of Sophia. How lovely it would be to be with her sitting and chatting instead of up in this tower awaiting a deadly onslaught. How wonderful if his only worry were whether or not she would accept his marriage proposal.

He stared out over the city and thought, somewhere out there was another enemy. Even if, as Sordello reported, Cardinal Ugolini were not behind this attack, there might be someone behind both the Filippeschi and Cardinal Ugolini. Ever since he had come to Orvieto, Simon had sensed the presence in this city of a hidden enemy. An enemy who knew him and watched him, but whom he did not know. The one—Simon was sure of it—who had killed Alain.

I am waiting for you, he said, gripping the red bricks of the battlements.

* * *

Every old soldier Simon had ever talked to had said that war consisted more of waiting than of fighting. Simon found the combination of boredom and fear well nigh unbearable.

De Puys sat with his back against the battlements and dozed like a large cat. De Verceuil also sat, his helmet on the tower floor beside him, reading from a small leather-bound book, whispering the Latin words. Simon supposed it must be his office, the prayers every priest was required to say every day. The cardinal would have to get today's office read quickly; the light was fading fast.

Capitano Teodoro preferred to be busy. He kept shuttling back and forth between the tower and rooftop two stories below, where his men were deployed. Teodoro would make a circuit of the tower battlements, frowning down at his company of archers. Then he would go down and order six or so men to change position. He would inspect everyone's weapons. He inspected the bows of even the eight Armenians, in their bright red surcoats, who would fight beside the Venetians. The friction between the Armenians and the Venetians, Simon had noticed, had lessened considerably after he promoted Teodoro. He was a good leader. At the contessa's request Teodoro inspected the Monaldeschi men-at-arms, who were mostly stationed at the two gates and in the hallways and apartment windows.

After each inspection tour, Teodoro would come back up, study the situation, then go down and rearrange the men, likely as not returning them to their earlier positions.

But staying busy made sense. It kept everyone alert.

Simon left the tower once to visit his four knights on the rooftop, each one stationed, with six men-at-arms, by a stone caster at a corner of the roof. So that their missiles would clear the screening he had built over the battlements, the long-armed machines were set well back from the edge of the roof. The knights did not like supervising the stone casters. They wanted, they told him, a chance to charge the enemy during the attack. Simon tried to be good-humored about insisting that they remain within the palace, but it was hard giving orders to men who were older than himself and combat veterans. He missed Alain, realizing only now how much he had relied on his young friend as a go-between for himself and the other knights.

Returning to the tower roof, Simon kept pacing from one corner to the other. He fingered the jeweled hilt of his scimitar. He tried to divert himself by thinking of Sophia, by imagining how he would phrase his marriage proposal to her. He dreaded the fighting, but wished it would start.

Like a rising tide the shadows spread and deepened, swallowing up the hills beyond the city, then the city walls, then the towers. The four men stood in darkness, no torchlight up here to make them an easy target. The only light on the roof below was the shimmer of charcoals burning in four braziers for fire arrows.

An orange glow appeared over the hills to the east, the moon starting to rise.

Simon heard distant shouting. Battle cries.

"Filippeschi!" It was Teodoro's voice.

Simon saw flickering red light dancing on house walls coming toward them, converging from front, sides, and rear. The streets were too narrow to permit sight of the advancing bravos and their torches.

So, even though they know we are ready for them, they have come.

From the street directly opposite the main entrance to the palace a long, dark shape emerged, like a gigantic tortoise. Similar shapes issued from other streets opening on the piazza. The tortoises were big enough to shelter at least a dozen men. There were six of them, crawling across the open space.

"Use the fire arrows!" Simon shouted. Teodoro repeated the order to his men. On the roof below, men raced from the battlements to the braziers and back again, and streaks of light arced from the rooftop at the tortoise shapes.

Simon could hear the burning arrows sizzle on the wet wooden frameworks and wet hides. The hides did not burn, but the light from the arrows made it easier for the crossbowmen shooting from the battlements to see their targets. Teodoro was down on the roof directing their fire. The archers volleyed at the closest tortoise. The steel bolts tore right through the skins, piercing the men beneath. Simon heard the thump of thirty bolts striking a tortoise at once, then screams. The framework stopped moving, and Simon saw men crawling from under it. Some ran frantically back to the shelter of the side streets; others crept a few paces and collapsed.

Something whizzed past Simon's head and struck the brick merlon beside him. A shower of chips clattered on his mail. One stung his cheek.

"Shooting back," said Teodoro. "From the sides."

Torchlight flickered from behind wooden mantlets at the mouths of the streets approaching the palace from the north and south. The rectangles of wood filled the street from side to side. From this height Simon could see the crowds of men behind each mantlet.

Fire arrows from mantlets and tortoises hissed overhead and fell, trailing sparks, into the atrium of the palace. Simon heard splashes as servants threw water on the trees.

"Put more of your men on the sides," he said to Teodoro, who hurried down the stairs inside the tower.

The moon was now a red oval low in the eastern sky. The light would help the Filippeschi target the defenders on the rooftop, but it would not expose them in the streets.

A loud crash startled Simon, and he felt the tower floor shake. Another crash and another. Stone casters. The stones were coming from all directions, and Simon could hear screams.

He turned to de Puys. "Fire our stone casters."

With de Puys gone, only Simon and the cardinal were left in the tower. They had nothing to say to each other. The cardinal had donned his miter-shaped helmet at the first sign of the Filippeschi, and Simon could not see his face. Simon longed for Teodoro to come back.

It was Simon's equerry, Thierry, who pushed open the trapdoor. "Capitano Teodoro is hit."

"Blood of God!" Simon pushed past de Puys to hurry down the tower's inner staircase.

Teodoro lay near the entrance to the tower, surrounded by a crowd of men-at-arms. His breathing came in hoarse gasps, alternating with grunts of pain. It was too dark for Simon to see him well. He knelt beside Teodoro, and a vile smell of excrement choked him. Someone beside Simon was sobbing. Teodoro had been much liked among the Venetians.

Carefully Simon felt down the capitano's body. The hard leather cuirass he wore was cracked down the center. Just below his chest Simon's hand met the huge rock. It was wet, probably with Teodoro's blood.

"It caught him right in the middle," said an archer standing over Simon. "Broke him in two. Crushed his belly and his spine. Only the part of him above the stone is alive."

A gurgling sound rose in Teodoro's throat. He was vomiting, and warm liquid gushed over Simon's hand. His own stomach writhed, and bile burned his throat. He stood up suddenly, and instantly regretted it, because he had wanted to comfort Teodoro in his dying. But the gasping had stopped.

Teodoro had probably never known he was there.

Simon's hands and knees were trembling.

So this is what it is like to be killed in battle.

He wiped his hand on his surcoat. Careful to make his voice firm, he ordered the archers back to their positions. The weight of his mail almost unbearable, he stumbled back to the doorway to the tower.

He felt his arm gripped and heard Friar Mathieu's voice. "Simon, I heard you lost your capitano of archers."

"This is much worse than I ever thought it would be, Father," he whispered, almost as if confessing.

The hand on his arm squeezed through his mail. "Trust yourself, Simon. You will do what you must do."

By the light of a fire arrow burning itself out in the overhead screen, Simon saw the contessa, her purple gown tied up to her knees so she could move more quickly. She called Friar Mathieu to see to a wounded man, then greeted Simon.

She thinks I am a hero. If only she knew the horror I feel.

Who was Teodoro's second-in-command? Yes, Peppino. Peppino was the one who had fought with the Armenians at Alain's funeral, but a new capitano must be appointed immediately. There was no time to balance considerations.

He managed to find Peppino and appointed him to lead the Venetians. Then on shaking legs he pushed himself back up to the roof of the tower.

"They are bombarding the rear gatehouse with mangonels," de Puys said. Simon heard rocks thudding against the drawbridge at the rear of the palace, the entrance for horses and wagons. By moonlight he was able to make out, across the street from the rear of the palace, four mangonels, stone guns shaped like giant crossbows.

"Where did the Filippeschi get so many men and machines?" Simon wondered aloud.

"One would suppose you could answer that," said de Verceuil, his voice muffled by his helmet. "Are you not our military expert?"

Simon was still too gripped by horror to be angry. But a part of his mind somehow kept trying to think about what the Filippeschi intended.

He became lost in thought as he gnawed at the problem, and all but forgot the battle raging around him. Numerous as they seemed, the Filippeschi had just a chance, no more than that, of overwhelming the Monaldeschi palace, especially having lost the advantage of surprise. Was their hatred of the Monaldeschi so deep that such an uncertain chance was reason enough for them to make this effort?

If I could but capture Marco di Filippeschi and force him to tell me why he is doing this . . .

What if this attack were a diversion, a cover for the real blow, to be struck by stealth?

Simon's body went cold.

"I must see to the Tartar ambassadors," he said. He turned toward the trapdoor in the tower roof.

"Monseigneur—look—the Filippeschi are attacking again," de Puys protested. Simon turned back, looked over the edge, and saw the tortoise shapes moving forward again over the piazza while stones from mangonels slammed into the second-story gatehouse.

No, he thought. *Even if they break down the door, they could never get up the stairs. This attack is a feint.*

"I believe the ambassadors are in danger," he said.

"By God's robe!" de Verceuil boomed from under his helmet. "You are quitting the battle?"

"The battle is where the ambassadors are," Simon said. "The whole purpose of this attack is to get at them."

"The whole purpose of your saying that is to get out of danger," de Verceuil retorted.

Simon quivered with rage. De Verceuil's eyes glittered coldly at him in the moonlight through holes cut in the bloodred helmet. Simon wished he could draw his sword and swing it at the damned cardinal's head. But he felt as if he were suddenly wrapped in chains. With de Verceuil accusing him of cowardice, how could he leave the tower?

De Puys put a steadying hand on his arm. "Monseigneur, no one can get at the ambassadors. Not as long as we hold fast here."

In the florid face with its drooping mustaches Simon saw pity, but also a trace of contempt. The old warrior, too, thought his young seigneur wanted to run away. If Simon left the tower now, he would have to bear his vassal's scorn. Nor was it likely that de Puys would keep silent about this. The tale would spread throughout the Gobignon domain.

But I know I am not a coward.

Searching his heart, he knew that though he was afraid of the flying crossbow bolts and stones, he could direct the battle from the tower all night if need be. Even after Teodoro's death, and the blood still sticky on the mailed glove that hung from his right wrist, he felt strong enough to go on fighting.

If he went to the ambassadors and no one struck at them, he would have been mistaken, but his leaving here would not affect the outcome of the battle. What was happening out here was a simple matter of force against force. If he remained here and the Tartars were attacked and murdered, all would be lost.

If I do not do what I believe I should because I am afraid of what these men think, then truly I am a coward.

He tried to make the other two understand. "The safety of the ambassadors is my first obligation. Enemies could be in the palace now."

De Verceuil brought his steel-masked face close to Simon's. "It is known that there is tainted blood in your family."

Simon's face went as hot as if a torch had suddenly been thrust at him. It was a moment before he could speak.

"If you were not a man of the church, I would kill you for saying that." His voice trembled.

"Really? I doubt you would dare." De Verceuil turned away.

"Monseigneur!" de Puys cried, his face redder than ever. "Do not make me ashamed to wear the purple and gold."

That hurt even more than what de Verceuil had said. It hurt so much Simon wanted to weep with anger and frustration.

Instead, he bent forward and lifted the trapdoor and hurried down the steps. He heard de Verceuil say something to de Puys, but he could not hear what it was. Fortunately.

He stopped on the roof to look for Friar Mathieu. Groups of crossbowmen were running from one side to the other. Friar Mathieu was making the sign of the cross over a fallen man.

"I think the Tartars may be in danger, Friar Mathieu," Simon said. "I want you to come with me so that I can talk to them."

To Simon's relief the old Franciscan did not object. "Let us take two of the Armenians with us," he said. "If there is danger, you should not go alone."

Now that he was away from de Verceuil and de Puys, Simon could reflect that he might, indeed, be mistaken. But he had to act, even though he doubted himself.

Simon, Friar Mathieu, and two Armenian warriors named Stefan and Grigor hurried down the tower's inner staircase to the ground floor. Single candles, burning low, lit the corridor at long intervals. Here were storerooms and cubbyholes where servants worked and lived. The relentless pounding of rocks reverberated in the stone walls, punctuated by occasional screams penetrating through the arrow slits.

Monaldeschi men-at-arms standing at the embrasures with crossbows kept their backs turned to Simon as he hurried past. An odor of damp stone pervaded the still air. Simon noted that as he had ordered, buckets of water had been placed along the corridor to douse fires.

The kitchen was on the north side of the building. It was dark as a cave. The cooking fire in the great fireplace, big enough for a man to walk into it, had been put out. They passed empty cauldrons, piles of full sacks, rows of barrels, all barely visible in the light of a half-consumed taper in a candlestick on a table. A large water cask surrounded by buckets and pots stood in the center of the kitchen.

Attackers could be hiding here. But Simon knew he did not have enough men to search. He must get to the Tartars and stay with them.

The pantry where the contessa kept her costly stock of spices imported from the East was below ground. Stefan lifted a heavy trapdoor, and one by one they climbed down a narrow flight of wooden steps without a banister. Grigor, bringing up the rear, held a candle to light their way.

A door of rough oaken planks bound together with iron straps stood before him. He felt his stomach knot as he walked up to it. What if he were too late?

Simon had ordered that the square black iron lock set in the door be left unlocked in the case the Tartars should have to escape. He pulled on the handle. The door was bolted from the inside, of course, with a bolt he had only that afternoon ordered the Monaldeschi carpenter to install. From the other side a voice asked a half-audible question.

"It is Count Simon," he said. "Let us in." Friar Mathieu added a few words in the Tartar tongue.

The bolt slid back and the door opened inward. Simon stepped forward to see how his charges had fared.

The storeroom was dimly lit by a small oil lantern. The two Armenians within had risen from chairs. They had their bows in their hands, arrows nocked. They stood in front of the Tartars. John, the white-haired Tartar, and Philip, the black-haired one, sat on cushions on the floor, leaning back against the shelves of spice jars that covered three walls of the room. Their bows were on the table and their curving swords, in scabbards, lay in their laps.

Simon was pleased to see that they looked alert. It must be maddening to sit down here in semidarkness and do nothing while a battle raged above.

He reminded himself that if no one attacked the Tartars while the Filippeschi besieged the palace, his reputation would be ruined. He felt a momentary pang of anguish, and found himself actually hoping that the enemy would come here. Quickly he stifled the feeling.

Do not call on the devil. He may hear you and come.

XLIII

HIDDEN IN THE CELLAR BEHIND A RACK OF WINE BARRELS, DAOUD watched the Frankish count, the old priest, and the two Armenians as they paused before the door of the spice pantry.

He thought: *Man can plan and plan, but God will surprise and surprise.*

He had been just about to try to trick the Tartars into letting him into the spice pantry when de Gobignon and the others came down the stairs. He suppressed his fury and forced himself to stay calm.

The spice pantry door opened for de Gobignon and those with him. From his hiding place Daoud caught just a glimpse of the Tartars, both sitting with sheathed swords in their laps, their two guards standing in front of them. Their refuge appeared to be lit by a single lantern.

Daoud was perhaps only twelve paces from the doorway, but the cellar was mostly in darkness, and he was dressed entirely in black, his head covered with a tight black hood, his face masked. For ease and silence of movement he wore no mail. The garb of a fedawi, a Hashishiyya fighter.

With gestures de Gobignon ordered his two Armenians to stand guard outside the door. One set a candle in a sconce high in the cellar wall. Then they unslung their bows and nocked arrows and stood on either side of the door, which closed behind Gobignon and the old priest. Daoud heard a bolt slide shut with a clank.

Baffled, he bit his lower lip. What demon had inspired de Gobignon to come down from the battlements and join the Tartars just at this moment? Now he could not get to the pantry door without being seen and having to fight the two Armenians outside. That would alert those inside, and the door was bolted from within. He took deep breaths to clear his head of frustration.

He would have to change his plan of attack.

To get into the Monaldeschi palace he had used a peasant's cloak and high boots like those he had worn last summer when he'd landed at Manfredonia. It had been an easy matter paying a few silver denari to a farmer and then helping with the loading and unloading of sacks of rice being delivered to the Monaldeschi. Once inside the palace courtyard it had been the work of a moment to slip away from the carts and hide himself in the maze of dark rooms on the ground floor of the palace. There he had shed the peasant costume, leaving his black Hashishiyya garb, and he'd pulled the hood and mask over his head.

But the very thing that made it easy for him to get into the palace with that cartload of rice left him shocked and uneasy. The Monaldeschi were preparing for a siege. He had seen screens against fire arrows being set up on the roof and householders in the neighborhood locking their doors and fleeing.

Someone had warned the Monaldeschi. When the Filippeschi came tonight, their hereditary enemies would be ready for them.

Heart pounding, he pondered. What if the Filippeschi called off the attack? He tried to tell himself that it would not matter. Even the expectation of a siege would so distract the Tartars' protectors that he would be able to get at them.

And, he promised himself, if he came out alive, he would search out and repay whoever had betrayed him.

He had rechecked his weapons—the strangling cord, the Scorpion, the tiny vessel of Greek fire in its padded pouch, the disk of Hindustan and a dagger, its blade painted black. After nightfall he would seek out the Tartars' apartment, which he knew was on the third floor of the palace, where the best rooms were. In the meantime, he had hidden in a corner of the kitchen behind a large water cask. He had squatted there and waited, taut as a bowstring, to find out whether the Filippeschi would attack.

When he heard the first battle shouts through the narrow embrasures on the ground floor, he let out a little sigh of relief. Of course Marco di Filippeschi would go through with the attack. Even without surprise, he was doubtless better prepared tonight to fight the Monaldeschi than ever before in his life. And Marco was not the sort of man who, once committed to a course, would turn back.

Even as these thoughts passed through his mind, Daoud had been surprised to see the two Tartars with two of their Armenian guards stride past him.

Of course, he thought, de Gobignon must have realized that the Tartars might be a target, and he was moving them to a safer place.

For a moment the Tartars had been abreast of him. Two poisoned darts from the Scorpion would do it.

But, just then, a dozen or so Monaldeschi archers, crossbows loaded and cranked back, had trotted into the kitchen and nearby rooms and taken up stations by the embrasures. Daoud, his body aquiver with excitement, the little crossbow already in his hands, had sunk back into hiding. If he shot the Tartars, he might have been able to escape the two Armenians, but so many men-at-arms would certainly kill or, worse, capture him. And once they discovered who he was, Sophia, Ugolini, all those working with him, would swiftly be in the hands of the Franks.

Seething with frustration, he had watched an Armenian open a cellar trapdoor. The two Tartars and the two Armenian guards descended out of sight.

Daoud, still crouched behind the water cask, then decided that God had been kind to him. Even if he had been denied this opportunity to kill them, at least he had seen where the Tartars were.

He had sat in his hiding place, relaxed but alert, listening to the Monaldeschi bowmen shout encouragement to one another as they fired on the Filippeschi trying to cross the piazza. The arrow slits were cut through the thick walls in angled pairs so that two archers side by side would have a full field of fire. After a while Daoud began to despair of ever getting into the cellar.

Several times servants came running to fill buckets from the cask to put out fires in the atrium. Crouched in the darkness behind the cask, Daoud saw, grouped around it, buckets, pots, and kettles, all sorts of vessels, already filled with water for immediate use.

Long after the battle began, a pageboy came running down the stairs to the ground floor with an order for the archers to come up to the roof.

They left only one man to watch through the arrow slots. His back, sheathed in a shiny brown leather cuirass, was turned toward Daoud. The noise of fighting from outside was loud enough, Daoud thought, to mask any sound he might make.

He slipped from behind the cask and picked up a wooden bucket full of water. Carrying the bucket he stepped, silent on his soft-soled boots, to the cellar trapdoor. Keeping his eyes on the cross-bowman, he put the bucket down and, holding his breath, grasped the handle of the trapdoor and lifted it. The archer moved as Daoud crouched by the open trapdoor. Daoud froze. But the man's back remained turned. He was only shifting from one arrow slot to the one beside it, it get a view of the piazza from a different angle.

When the archer was settled in his new position, Daoud crept down the cellar stairs, bucket in one hand, and lowered the door over his head. He watched the archer until the slab of wood cut off his view. He was in a pitch-black cellar smelling of wine.

He saw a crack of light from under a door and heard voices. He was about to go and knock, pretending to be a man-at-arms with a message. When the two Armenians within opened the door, he would douse their lantern with the water he was carrying, and then move in on the Tartars in the dark.

Just then the trapdoor above had opened. He hid behind the wine barrels as de Gobignon, the friar, and two more Armenians came down to join their Tartar charges.

Stones were slamming into the walls in such rapid succession that the building was continually shaking. This must be the climax of the Filippeschi attack. Next would come a rush of all the fighting men. They would storm the palace and either break through or be driven off. Probably, Daoud thought, the attack would fail. But even so, it would give him the opportunity he needed.

The two Armenian guards held their bows laxly, resting their backs against the wall by the door. The candle in the sconce was six paces away from the guards. Silently he lifted the bucket of water he had brought down with him and moved it out in front of the wine barrel rack so that later he could quickly reach it. Then he loaded the Scorpion, drawing back its string.

He stepped out from behind the barrels, aiming for the eye of the nearest guard, and fired. The steel dowels snapped forward, propelling the bolt through the eyeball and into the skull. The man collapsed without an outcry. His body, clad in leather and steel, hit the stone floor with a crash.

The other Armenian gave a shrill shout in his native tongue. He stared in horror at Daoud, and his heavy compound bow was up, the iron arrowhead pointing at Daoud's chest.

Daoud had already taken the disk of Hindustan out of the flat pouch on the left side of his belt. Dropping the Scorpion into its pocket, he transferred the disk to his right hand. The disk was heavy; by Frankish weight it would probably be half a pound. Its center was of strong, flexible steel; bonded to its edges was a more brittle steel that would take an edge sharp enough to slice a hair lengthwise.

Daoud scaled the disk at the candle that rested in the sconce at the door to the pantry. It sliced through the candle's tip, just below the wick. The flame went out, plunging the cellar into total darkness. The disk rang against the stone wall, then clanged to the floor. Daoud's trained hearing registered the place where it fell. The Armenian's bolt whistled past him and hit the wall with a sharp crack.

Voices from inside the spice pantry shouted questions. That must be the two Armenians who had first gone in there with the Tartars. The man outside answered, and Daoud could hear fear in his voice. De Gobignon would not want to open the door to help the Armenian, for fear of endangering the Tartars.

Somehow, he had to be made to open the door.

Daoud stood still, listening to the guard's rapid, heavy breathing, the scraping of his boot soles on the stone floor.

After a moment he tiptoed to the side of the chamber, retrieved his disk, and dropped it into its pouch in his tunic.

Silently picking up the water bucket in front of the wine barrel rack, he drifted closer to the guard, thinking of smoke, as the Hashishiyya had taught him, to make himself move even more quietly.

He heard the Armenian sling his bow over his shoulder, and the slithering of his sword coming out of his scabbard.

Daoud set the water down and crept close to the guard, utterly silent, listening for the many small noises that would tell him where the man was and how he was standing—breathing, swallowing and the licking of lips, the creak of leather armor, the rustle of cloth, the clink of steel. Slowly and very carefully Daoud reached out toward the guard's throat, then with a sudden movement seized it, his thumb and fingers gripping like a falcon's talons.

His action had the desired effect. The Armenian screamed, forcing air through his constricted throat again and again.

He tried to slash at Daoud's arm but missed.

With his free hand Daoud grabbed the guard's wrist and gave it a sharp turn. He let go of his opponent's throat and used both hands to force his sword arm down. He straightened the arm out and brought his knee down hard on the elbow, throwing all his weight on it.

The guard screamed with pain, and his sword clattered to the floor. Daoud kicked it off into the darkness, then danced away. The Armenian fell back against the spice pantry door, groaning in pain and fear.

Daoud heard muffled cries from the other side of the door. They demanded to know what was happening. They begged to know what was happening.

The Armenian's agonized voice cried out to them, also begging, to be let in, to be saved from the man who was killing him in the blackness.

Daoud readied himself, finding the water bucket again in the dark and picking it up. He held it with both hands, by the handle and by the base. He would have only a little time to use it, before they found some way to stop him.

He heard the men on the other side of the door slide back the iron bolt. It was the only thing they could do, Daoud thought. The other Armenians could not bear to keep the door shut and let their comrade die.

The wooden door swung inward. Light sprang out into the cellar from only one oil-fed lantern, but dazzled Daoud because he had been in complete darkness since he put out the candle. He now saw the man he had been fighting, a squat man with a thick black mustache, tears of pain running from his eyes, his right arm dangling limply.

In the fraction of an instant before his enemies saw him, Daoud took in everything in the spice pantry.

De Gobignon was standing just inside the door, holding his beautiful scimitar out before him in his right hand. With his left hand he reached for the wounded guard to pull him in. On either side of him were the other two Armenians, bows drawn, ready to fire. Beyond them Daoud glimpsed the Tartars, also with bows loaded and pulled, and the old priest.

But the most important thing in there was that small, weak flame flickering behind sheets of horn in a box-shaped lantern on the table in the center of the room.

Daoud stepped as close as he dared into the doorway and raised the bucket high, heaving the water in a stream at the table.

He heard a bow thrum and an arrow whistle past his shoulder. His eyes met de Gobignon's just as the light went out.

Like a stone fired from a catapult he hurled himself, crouching low, into the pantry.

Landing silently inside the room, he changed direction once, twice, a third time, ending up at the door. He slammed it shut and bolted it. They should all now be thoroughly confused.

In total darkness, seeing with his senses of hearing, smell, and touch, he began to stalk the Tartars.

XLIV

SIMON HEARD THE THICK DOOR SLAM AND THE IRON BOLT DRIVEN into place. He stood in a blackness darker than any night outdoors would have been, his scimitar heavy and invisible in his hand. It was all he had against an enemy who was also invisible. He felt death rushing upon him out of the darkness.

Except for the occasional vibrations of a rock hitting the palace wall, all sounds of battle were blocked out of the spice pantry. In the deep silence, Simon's heartbeat thundered in his ears like a kettledrum.

It was my stupidity that opened the door to him.

He had caught only a glimpse of the enemy. All in black from head to foot, eyes shining through oval holes in his mask. Truly like a devil.

The stalker had deliberately doused the light, which must mean he could find his victims in the dark.

Simon's body went from hot to cold. While he stood here helplessly, the men with him could be dying. He tried to force himself to think, but his mind was motionless as a stone.

All around Simon was confusion. He heard Grigor, the guard who had staggered into the room just before the light went out, moaning with pain. He heard men stumbling about. They kept bumping into him. He lowered his scimitar to avoid stabbing someone by accident.

A crash made Simon jump. That was the lantern, smashed probably, by the man in black, so that no one could relight it.

Next he would start killing them, one by one.

God, if only I had some light. Just a little.

The odors of the precious spices the Monaldeschi stored in this pantry pervaded the air—saffron, cardamom, pepper, cloves, ginger, nutmeg, cinnamon. When Simon had first entered the spice pantry a short time ago it had seemed a pleasant enough smell. Now it was making him sick.

Was there still a lighted candle in the cellar outside?

"The door!" he shouted. "Get the door open." Friar Mathieu repeated his command in the Armenian tongue.

He heard a scraping, as of someone pulling on the heavy bolt that held the door shut. Then a thud and a choking cry of pain. Then a sound like a heavy sack being dropped.

Simon groaned inwardly. He could picture what had happened. Now the door was held shut, not just by a bolt, but by a dead body.

He felt ice cold, but sweat trickled under his mail. The blackness was thick, a blanket, smothering him. The smells of the spices were cloying, dizzying. His stomach felt queasy.

"Flint and tinder!" Simon shouted, and Friar Mathieu repeated his words for the Armenians and Tartars. Everything he said had to be translated. The delay was maddening.

And, Simon realized, anyone who tried to strike a light would make himself the enemy's next target.

God's blood, even by answering Friar Mathieu the Tartars would give away their location to the stalker. The man in black must be able to find his victims by listening for them.

So, if sound would make them visible, then the only way to thwart this demon would be by silence. And even now men were starting to answer Simon's call for flint.

"Silence!" he shouted. His voice sounded shrill in his ears, like a frightened boy's.

For a moment there was no sound in the blackness.

"He finds us by the sounds we make," Simon said. "Everyone remain still, and we will hear him when he moves."

As Friar Mathieu translated, Simon realized that either he or Friar Mathieu could be the next victim. The stalker would want to kill the Franciscan so Simon could not communicate with the others.

And one Armenian was badly hurt, one was probably dead outside and one dead by the door. Left able to fight were only Simon, the Tartars, and one Armenian guard. They had swords and bows, but the bows would just be encumbrances in this total blackness.

In minutes the ambassadors could be dead. Simon felt terrified, drowning in darkness, almost overcome with helplessness.

I must make him come to me.

The thought frightened Simon even more. He did not know whether he would have the courage to act on it.

What weapons did the stalker have? In the glimpse Simon had of him before he put the candle out, the man in black had seemed to be empty-handed. His weapons must be small ones that could kill, but might not be quite so dangerous to a man in mail.

"Everyone remain still," Simon said loudly. "You will hear me moving steadily about. If you hear someone else as well, it is the enemy."

He racked his brain to remember the size and shape of the room. Holding his sword low, he put his hand up before his face and forced himself to take one step, then another. An attack might come from any direction. The trembling of his hands and knees made his mail jingle faintly.

The mailed glove dangling from his wrist rattled as his bare hand encountered a man's face. The man gasped and pulled away.

"C'est moi," said Simon, just to let the man hear his voice, knowing it did not matter what language he spoke. He was not afraid of calling attention to himself. He wanted the stalker to come for him. And he wanted those on his side to know where he was so they would not attack him by mistake.

The face he felt was hot, sweaty, with a bushy mustache—one of the Armenians. The killer had been masked. Simon patted the man on the shoulder and moved on. He doubted that he could find the man in black this way. If the stalker were as skilled at moving about in the dark as he seemed to be, he could easily evade Simon.

The Tartars seemed to have understood the peril they were in; they had been silent now for a long time.

The thought struck him like ice between his shoulder blades: What if the killer had already gotten to them, and they were silent because they were dead? He wanted to call out to them, or to Friar Mathieu, to be sure they were all right. He suppressed the urge and reached out for another face.

This time he felt a beard. It was long and full. Friar Mathieu.

"C'est moi," Simon said again, and a hand reached up and squeezed his reassuringly.

The next face was hard, bony. There was a mustache that his fingers followed long below the mouth. The beard was thin, sprouting from the chin only. One of the Tartars. Simon felt the face move under his touch. Thank God, the man was alive.

He reached beyond the Tartar and felt a shoulder. This must be the other Tartar. But no—the shoulder was high, as high as the Tartar's head.

Just as he was about to jump back he felt something brush over his hair.

A cord was around his neck.

It jerked tight with such force that Simon's breath was instantly cut off. Pain circled his neck like a band of fire.

His scream forced its way through his throat as a drawn-out grunt as the cord tightened still more. He could feel the blood in his head pressing out against his temples and eyeballs. He felt as if nails were being driven into his head.

He had his scimitar. He raised it and drove it back over his right shoulder. It went through empty air. The killer had felt it coming and ducked out of the way. But for a moment the cord cutting into Simon's throat let up just a bit.

He heard voices all around him. The others knew what was happening. They stumbled about, but they could not see to reach him. He felt himself being dragged backward, pulled away from his comrades. The cord was digging into his windpipe harder and harder. In a moment his mind would go black. He would not even know when he died. He fought his terror, knowing that if he yielded to it, he would surely die.

He *would* live. He *would* see Sophia again.

He tried to lean forward, to bend his knees, to find some purchase on the stone for his iron-shod feet. Still, the attacker pulled him. Simon felt he had only a child's strength compared to the man in black.

Dizzily Simon remembered tug-of-war games when he had been a page at the royal palace.

When one side lets go, everyone on the other side falls down.

With his last bit of consciousness, Simon squeezed his whole body into a crouch, then sprang up and backward, like a bow released.

His mail-clad weight and the attacker's momentum threw them both backward. They crashed together against shelving, and Simon heard porcelain shatter. Clouds of ground spices enveloped them, and they fell sideways to the floor, Simon on top of his attacker.

He heard a gasp as the man's breath was knocked out of him. And now *he* could breathe. He choked on air saturated with cinnamon and curry, but the cord was loose.

The fall had knocked his scimitar out of his hand. Anguished, he felt for it, but it was as if it had fallen into a well.

"Simon! Where are you?" Friar Mathieu shouted.

"Ah! Ah!" Simon let his breath out and sucked it in, gasping. He wanted to cry for help, but he could not use his voice. His body shook with terror.

And he felt the body under him moving with swift and terrible power. The cord snapped tight again.

But not before Simon got his right hand under it. The killer gave a vicious jerk on the thin cord, and it felt as if it might slice through his fingers. But Simon pushed against it with all the strength in his right arm, and loosened the cord enough to be able to pull air into his throat. He worked his other hand under it.

His shout burst from his throat. "M'aidez! Help me! Here! Here!"

Boots pounded toward him. He felt men around him. He heard them coughing and sneezing from the spices that filled the air. A sword poked him through his mail.

"Under me! Stab! Stab! You cannot hurt me!"

The cord went lax. The attacker had let go of it. Simon drew air frantically through his tortured windpipe.

Before he could get to his feet, an arm, hard as if clad in mail, whipped around his neck, clamping him to his enemy. He felt the edge of a dagger at his throat.

Simon could hear the devil's breathing right by his ear. Frantic, he jerked his head forward and drove it back, ramming the back of his head into his attacker's face, slamming the enemy's head against the stone floor. Simon felt stunned, but the other must have been stunned, too. He heard a whispered gasp.

How can the devil be so silent?

He heard men speaking above him and feet shuffling around him, but despite his command, no swords were jabbing downward. They were afraid of stabbing him, even though he was wearing mail.

He arched his body and brought all his mailed weight down hard. He felt the edge of the enemy's dagger scrape across the chain around his neck. A bolt of terror shot through him. If not for that medallion, he would be bleeding to death right now. Simon thrust his steel-encased elbows into his enemy's ribs. The gasp was louder this time, and with a violent heave he freed himself.

He twisted over, arms reaching to wrap around his enemy.

I have to pin him down. I cannot let him get loose in this room again.

But the knees below him drew up and the feet kicked against him, throwing him back.

"Right in front of me!" Simon cried. "Get him!" And then he realized despairingly that none of the armed men on his side could understand him.

And no one, it seemed, had flint and steel to strike a light. He knew he was carrying none. Such a simple thing, yet tonight its lack might be his death.

His foot kicked something that rang against the stone floor. His sword. He swooped down on it, seized it, and thrust blindly straight ahead. The point struck a stone wall, and he felt the blade bend. He checked his thrust just in time to keep the scimitar from breaking.

He heard a movement to his left and stabbed again. Again he struck blank stone.

The devil is somewhere in this part of the room.

"The door!" Simon shouted. "Mathieu, get the door open."

He heard the iron bolt shoved back, the creak of hinges, the scrape of a body being pushed aside.

But the blackness remained absolute.

He must have put out the candle in the cellar before he broke in here.

Simon heard running footsteps outside the spice pantry. Sandals slapping up wooden stairs. The creaking of the trapdoor at the top of the cellar steps. And then there was light. Gray, faint, but after what seemed like hours spent in utter darkness, it was as if the sun had suddenly risen.

God bless you, Mathieu.

Scimitar at the ready, Simon swept the room with his gaze.

A shadowy figure stood halfway along one of the side walls, holding something out before him in both hands. A miniature crossbow, a vicious-looking thing. Simon turned to see where it was pointed.

He saw John Chagan on the other side of the pantry facing the killer.

He heard a snap.

But Grigor, the Armenian who had been hurt outside the spice pantry, had stepped between John and the crossbow, and he took the bolt in his leather cuirass. Simon felt his mind moving much more slowly than things were happening, trying to grasp it all.

Grigor's eyes opened wide. Perhaps, Simon thought, he had expected that a bolt from such a little bow would merely bounce off his hardened leather armor. Or perhaps he knew that it would kill him.

In the semidarkness Simon could not see the hole in the cuirass, but Grigor's hand went to his chest, and then he toppled over.

The Tartar Philip had picked up a bow from the floor, and so had the other Armenian. Both raised their weapons toward the man in black.

Now we have him cornered and in a moment I will rip off his mask and know who he is.

The stalker's black-gloved hand flashed upward and he threw a tiny, round object into the pile of broken wooden shelves on the floor. A roar deafened Simon, and a blaze of white flame blinded him. The wooden shelves were afire, the flames feeding on the powdered spices that floated in the air. Heat seared Simon's face.

Death of God! He truly is a devil!

By the time Simon and the others had recovered from the burst of fire, the enemy was out the door and running for the cellar stairs. Simon cried out wordlessly in frustrated rage. He must not get away, not after all he had done to them.

As the man in black reached the foot of the stairs, Philip stepped into the doorway, drew his bow as calmly and carefully as if he were hunting, and loosed an arrow. The man in black jerked to a stop. Simon could see the shaft of the arrow protruding from his right thigh.

The man reached down and with a sudden movement snapped away the arrow shaft. He drew a dagger with a strange blade that did not gleam; it was dead black. He raced on up the stairs, limping, but with inhuman strength and speed. Two more arrows flew at him, but missed, clattering against the cellar walls.

Frair Mathieu stood at the top of the stairs. He held his arms out, a lit white candle in one hand, blocking the stalker's path. The man came at him with the dagger.

"No!" Simon screamed.

With a sweep of his arm the man in black threw Friar Mathieu down from the banisterless stairs. The old priest fell six feet to the cellar floor, struck with a loud, sickening thump, and lay there, still.

And the enemy was gone.

By the time Simon and the others had climbed up to the kitchen, the man in black had vanished into the maze of dark rooms on the first floor of the palace.

Simon, wild with rage and grief, forced himself to think. He was alive, God be thanked, and he had saved the Tartars, but just for this moment. The man in black, seemingly routed, might renew his attack at any time.

And Friar Mathieu. Dear God, don't let him be dead!

What was the creature Simon had fought in the darkness? Christian? Saracen? Or, as his most frightening imaginings hinted, a being from hell itself?

Clearly it was not some Filippeschi bravo who had somehow broken through the palace's defenses. Simon's inspiration on the battlements had been right; the Filippeschi attack had been only a diversion.

If a demon of this sort opposed the alliance, Simon felt more than ever determined that the alliance must succeed. This was the hidden enemy whose presence he had sensed since coming to Orvieto. The force determined to prevent the alliance of Christians and Tartars. The one who had incited Orvieto's people against the Tartars when they first came. Who had set that poor devil of a heretic to draw his dagger against them in the cathedral. Alain's murderer. Stalker. Enemy. Killer. Devil.

Hatred blazed up within Simon.

If only he could have killed the man in black or caught him before he escaped. Now he must guard against an enemy as evil as Satan. An enemy powerful enough to throw an army against a fortified palace, subtle enough to reach into an impregnable chamber and strike at his intended victims. A being whose strength and skills made him seem more than human. Cruel and pitiless, ready to murder anyone who stood in his way.

It was as certain as the judgment of God that they would fight again. This was war to the death.

To be concluded in
THE HOLY WAR
Book Two of THE SARACEN

The Gates of
Exquisite View
John Trenhaile

The new bestseller by the author of
The Mahjong Spies

'I WELCOME YOU THROUGH THE GATES OF EXQUISITE VIEW'
– a phrase carved above the entrance to the torture-
chamber of executioner Lai Chun-Ch'en.

To save his life Mat Young must tell his inquisitors the
secret of Apogee – a fifth generation supercomputer.
But it is a secret he does not possess.

Mat has been caught in Red China's deadly ambitions
to take back Taiwan by force. As has Simon Young his
tai-pan father, and Mat's lover, one of Taiwan's most
glamorous actresses . . .

FONTANA PAPERBACKS

The Cardinal of the Kremlin
Tom Clancy

The new superseller by the author of *Patriot Games*

'Clancy is the best there is . . . He is a master.'
San Francisco Chronicle

The superpower arms negotiations appear to be making progress. But a US spy-satellite reveals that the Soviets are building a massive laser-defence system controlled from an other-worldly array of pillars and domes near the border of war-torn Afghanistan.

The Americans need more information. The man to give it is Colonel Mikhail Filitov, codename Cardinal, America's highest-placed agent in the Kremlin. But Filitov's cover is about to be betrayed to the KGB and CIA adviser Jack Ryan must rescue Filitov and bring him to safety . . .

Tom Clancy's new bestseller looks to the skies and one of the most remarkable technological competitions of our time – the race to develop 'Star Wars'.

Tom Clancy's previous bestsellers *The Hunt for Red October*, *Red Storm Rising* and *Patriot Games* are all available in Fontana Paperbacks.

FONTANA PAPERBACKS

Fontana Paperbacks: Fiction

Fontana is a leading paperback publisher of fiction.
Below are some recent titles.

You can buy Fontana paperbacks at your local bookshop or
newsagent. Or you can order them from Fontana Paperbacks,
Cash Sales Department, Box 29, Douglas, Isle of Man. Please
send a cheque, postal or money order (not currency) worth the
purchase price plus 22p per book for postage (maximum postage
required is £3.00 for orders within the UK).

NAME (Block letters) _____

ADDRESS _____

_____

While every effort is made to keep prices low, it is sometimes necessary to increase them at short
notice. Fontana Paperbacks reserve the right to show new retail prices on covers which may differ
from those previously advertised in the text or elsewhere.